Willam W. Goodwin

Plutarch's Morals.

Volume V

Willam W. Goodwin

Plutarch's Morals.
Volume V

ISBN/EAN: 9783741123818

Manufactured in Europe, USA, Canada, Australia, Japa

Cover: Foto ©Lupo / pixelio.de

Manufactured and distributed by brebook publishing software (www.brebook.com)

Willam W. Goodwin

Plutarch's Morals.

PLUTARCH'S MORALS.

TRANSLATED FROM THE GREEK BY SEVERAL HANDS.

CORRECTED AND REVISED

BY

WILLIAM W. GOODWIN, Ph. D.,

PROFESSOR OF GREEK LITERATURE IN HARVARD UNIVERSITY.

WITH

AN INTRODUCTION BY RALPH WALDO EMERSON.

Vol. V.

BOSTON:
LITTLE, BROWN, AND COMPANY.
1883.

CONTENTS OF VOLUME FIFTH.

WITH THE TRANSLATORS' NAMES.

OF EATING OF FLESH.

By WILLIAM BAXTER, GENT.

The very idea of eating the carcasses of slain animals is repulsive, 3. Who could have begun the practice, but from the direst necessity? 4. Men must have been driven to the deed of slaying animals for food, because the supply of food from the vegetable world had utterly failed, 4, 5. We have no such necessity, 5. Man is not by nature a carnivorous animal, 7. Our conduct in slaying animals and then preparing them for food is wholly against nature, 8. Animal food is injurious: it clogs and confuses the mind and renders it stupid, 9. It operates unfavorably on character, 9, 10. If we must eat flesh, let it be with sorrow and pity; not tormenting and abusing the poor animal before taking its life, 11. Passing the bounds of nature in our feeding, intemperate appetites and shameful lusts are gratified, 12. Cruelty to mankind is induced, 12. Animals have senses; they have faculties for seeing, hearing, understanding: is it right to extinguish these faculties? 13. Who knows but the bodies of animals may contain the souls of deceased men; of a father, brother, son, or other friend? 14, 15.

LIVES OF THE TEN ORATORS.

By CHARLES BARCROFT, LECTURER OF ST. MILDRED'S, BREAD STREET.

1. Antiphon, 17-21. 2. Andocides, 21-23. 3. Lysias, 24-26. 4. Isocrates, 27-33. 5. Isaeus, 33. 6. Aeschines, 34-36. 7. Lycurgus, 36-42. 8. Demosthenes, 43-53. 9. Hyperides, 53-57. 10. Dinarchus, 57, 58. Decrees proposed to the Athenians for statues to be set up to Demosthenes, 58-63.

WHETHER AN AGED MAN OUGHT TO MEDDLE IN STATE AFFAIRS.

By F. FETHERSTON, D.D.

It is maintained by some, that after a certain time men should not employ themselves in public affairs, 64. The love of honor and zeal for the public good never grows old, 65. It is not well for a man who has never been accustomed to public business to commence such employment late in life, 66. An aged man may usefully conduct public affairs, as we see in the instances of Augustus Caesar, Pericles, and Agesilaus, 67, 68. Simonides and Sophocles, in old age, were good poets, 68. It is unworthy of a man who has served the public many years, to descend, in the decline of life, to mean employments, 69, 70. Political life has pleasures very great and honorable, 71. A man should not suffer his glory to wither in old age, 72. Reputation once acquired is easily maintained, and the people readily trust their old and faithful servants, 73. Envy and jealousy do not assail old age, 37, 74. It is not easy to terminate a long and faithful public service, 74. An old man staying at home, and spending his time in small matters is not honored, 75. Old men, full of experience and of wisdom, are often compelled by their fellow-citizens to conduct difficult negotiations, 76. Old age of itself is not a good reason for quitting the public service, 77, 78. Young men for war, but old men for counsel, 78. The Roman council of state is called the Senate, 79. The regal dignity has cares and toils, but who would advise the king to abdicate? 80. Old men in office may instruct and guide younger statesmen, 81, 82. Old men are often hale and vigorous, and so not disabled for the service of the state, 83. Examples of Phocion, Masinissa, and Cato, 83. Idleness enervates even great men, as Lucullus, while constant employment invigorates, 84. Our country has claims on our services, 85. Yet old age should have becoming employment, 86. An aged man should abstain from small and frivolous matters, 87. Offices of honor and dignity befit old men, 88. They should not eagerly seek office, 88. Old men should not be forward to speak in public: they should speak on grave occasions, 89. On other occasions, let them yield to younger men, 89, 90. Let them comfort and encourage deserving young men in their failures, 91. To be a statesman is not only to hold office and conduct negotiations, but also to guide, instruct, and assist those who conduct public affairs, when occasion requires, 93, 94. Even men in private stations may do this, and thus serve their country till death, 95, 96.

POLITICAL PRECEPTS.

By SAMUEL WHITE, M.D.

Counsels to a politician, 97. In the administration of public affairs, be guided by reason and judgment, 98. Act not from vain-glory, emulation, or want of other employment, 98, 99. Accommodate yourself to the temper and disposition of the citizens, 99, 100. Having obtained power among the people, endeavor to reform their disposition, 101. Do not give them an opportunity of finding fault with your own life or manners, 102. Beware of little faults, 102, 103. Cultivate the graces of speech, 104, 105. Orators sway the multitude, as in the case of Pericles, 106, 107. What the speech of a statesman should be, 107. How to use satire and invective, 108, 109. Think before you speak, and speak right on, 110. Speak in full, round tones, 110, 111. Two ways of entering on public life, 111. First, with a bold, vigorous hand, like Aratus, Alcibiades, Scipio, Pompey, &c., 112. Secondly, by procuring the assistance of some man of influence and authority, 114. Be careful in the choice of your man, lest your success inspire him with jealousy, 115. Pompey owed his success to Sylla, 115. Avoid flatterers and favorites, 116. Do not gratify friends in derogation of law and right, 117. Grant favors to friends when consistent with duty and public advantage, 120. Be generous and just towards your enemies, 121, 123. Let patriotism overshadow all private griefs, 122 How to meet invective, 124. Allow others to assist in public affairs, 128. Undertake nothing for which you lack qualification, 128, 129. Keep the helm in your own hand, but carry yourself with moderation; do not forget the limits of your power, 130, 131. As Greece is under the Roman sway, it is well to remember that fact, and to cultivate the favor of some powerful man at Rome, 132. Yet you should avoid, as much as possible, foreign interference, 133. Let the affairs of every city be settled by its own citizens, 133. When commotions arise, try to compose them, 134. One man's virtue has often saved a state, 135. Treat colleagues in office with honor and respect, 136. Plutarch relates an incident in his own life, 137. Honor the magistrates, even if you are personally their superior, 138. If a magistrate should be remiss in duty, do what you can to supply the defect, 139. Yield to the multitude in small things, that you may hinder their misdoings in greater, 140. When the people desire something which would be injurious to the state, use evasion and delay, 141. When about to undertake some difficult affair, secure the assistance of well-qualified persons, rather than of persons like yourself, 142. Divest yourself of the desire for riches, and of a mean, ignoble ambition, 143, 144. Decline not the honors which the people are disposed to bestow, 145, 146. The good-will of the people towards a public servant helps him greatly in the discharge of his duty, 147. If you are rich, and can give largesses to the people, bestow them, but with due care, 148. If you are poor, hesitate not to confess it, and incur no expense you cannot afford, 149, 150. In case of a sedition, try to compose it, 152. Especially try to prevent seditions and commotions, 153. In the present state of Greece, subject to the will of a Roman proconsul, no good can arise from public commotions, 154.

WHICH ARE THE MOST CRAFTY, WATER-ANIMALS OR THOSE CREATURES THAT BREED UPON THE LAND?

By John Philips, Gent.

Field sports, the slaughter of wild and at length of tame animals, prepared the way for men to kill one another, 158. Have brutes a soul? they certainly have sense and imagination, 160. They learn to desire some things and to avoid others, 161. They have expectation, memory, design, hope, fear, desire, and grief, 161. If they have sense, they have understanding, 161. They have what in men is called understanding, 162. Men punish dogs and horses for their faults, as if for the purpose of producing repentance, 162. Beasts are susceptible of pleasure, joy, anger, fear, 163. But are they capable of virtue? 163. They love their offspring, 164. They may have reason, and yet not have it perfectly, or in a high degree, 164. As sight and swiftness exist in different degrees, so may reason and mental force, 165. Animals differ widely in their faculties, as in their habits, 165. Many brute animals excel men in the faculties of sight and hearing, as well as in swiftness and strength; but we may not therefore say that men are blind, &c., 166. There are mad dogs and horses; what is this but a disturbance of the reason? 167. Mankind are chargeable with great injustice in dealing with beasts as they do, 169. There is a necessary and convenient use of the brute creation, 169, 170. Beyond this, we ought not to go, 170. In the exercise of what so nearly resembles reason, do land animals excel those that live in the water? 172 There is sufficient reason to believe that they do, 173. Observe the habits of bulls, lions, and elephants. 173. Of the ichneumon, of swallows, and spiders, 174. Of bees, crows, geese, and cranes, 175. The contrivances and labors of emmets, 176, 177. The sagacity of the elephant and the fox, 178, 179. The affection of the dog for his master; some striking instances related, 180, 181. Story of a mule at Athens, 182. Another dog story, 182, 183. The elephant that carried King Porus, 183. The horse Bucephalus, 183. Where there is one virtue in a brute, there are commonly others, 183, 184. Instances of subtlety and cunning, 184-186. Elephants and lions have a taste for society, 187. Amorous propensities of some brutes towards mankind; singular instances given, 188. Starlings, magpies, and parrots learn to talk, 188, 189. Swans and nightingales sing, 189. Story of a magpie at Rome imitating the music of trumpets exactly, 190. Wonderful docility of a dog, 191. Men have learned of the spider to weave; of the swallow to build; and have acquired from other animals skill in medicine, 191, 192. Some oxen have learned to count, 193. Soothsaying and divination is by means of birds, 194. What now can be said of the sagacity and intelligence of fishes and other water-animals? living in the sea, and remote from our observation, they are but little known to us, 195. Crocodiles come when called, 196. Fish are not easily caught, a proof of great cunning and wariness, 197, 198. Fish stand by and defend each other in danger, 199. Sagacity of the dolphin and the cuttle-fish, 200. Subtlety of the fish in taking their own prey, the torpedo, polypus, and others, 201, 202. Sagacity of the tunny, 203, 204. Mutual affection of the crocodile and the trochilus, 206. Sagacity of fish in depositing their spawn, 207, 208. Care of the tortoise and crocodile for their young, 209, 210. Intelligence and conjugal affection of the halcyon, 211, 212. Story of a dolphin which served as a guide to messengers of Ptolemy Soter, king of Egypt, 213, 214. The dolphin, a solitary instance among the brutes of disinterested love for man, 214. Stories of affectionate dolphins, 215, 216.

THAT BRUTE BEASTS MAKE USE OF REASON.

By Sir A. J.

A satire on the boasted wisdom, fortitude, magnanimity, and temperance of man, in the form of a dialogue between Ulysses in the island of Circe, and Gryllus, whom she had changed into a swine, and who now prefers his swinish condition to a return to the human form; Ulysses asks Circe for permission to restore his companions to the human shape, 218. Circe will grant the request if the men themselves desire it, 219. Gryllus, one of them, is brought forward to answer in behalf of the entire company, 219. He refuses, and gives his reasons, 220, *et seq.* He says that by making him and his companions beasts, Circe has done them a great favor, 220. Beasts have more fortitude than men; they fight in fair, open combat, without trick or artifice; they are no cowards, they never cry for mercy, 222. Beasts are courageous and daring, even the females; while the courage of men is artificial, and women are timid, 223, 224. Beasts are more temperate and chaste than men; they indulge their appetites only in a natural way, and at the proper season, 225, 226, 228. Beasts do not value silver or gold, 227. They have no adventitious desires, 227. Their senses are more accurate, 227. Men are incontinent: they indulge unnatural and excessive appetites; are never satisfied, 229, 230. Beasts are satisfied with one kind of food, and this procured without difficulty; they have nature for their teacher, and could teach men many useful lessons, 231, 232.

OF THE FACE APPEARING WITHIN THE ORB OF THE MOON.

By A. G., Gent.

In abstruse speculations, if we fail of satisfaction in one direction, we must inquire in another, 234. A face or form is seen in the moon; how is this to be explained? 234.

The appearance of a form in the moon is not the result of any acuteness or dulness of our vision, 234, 235. The appearance in question some think may be a reflection of the ocean from the moon's disc, 236. This opinion refuted, 236, 237. Some think the moon to be a compound of air and fire, a disturbance of which causes the appearance in question, 238. This notion disproved, 238, 239, 242. That the earth is a larger body than the moon, is shown by eclipses of the moon, 241. The moon must be a solid body, though much lighter than the earth, 241, 242. The spherical form of the earth, the antipodes, and all motion tending towards the earth's centre, are pronounced absurdities, 243, 244. The moon is not far from the earth, and feels its influence, though not of the same substance, 245, 246. Computation of the respective distances of the sun and moon from the earth, 246. The spherical form of the earth again denied, 247. If the earth is in the middle, of what is it the middle? not of the universe, surely, 247. Relations of bodies *above* and *beneath*, 248. We are not, in our philosophy, to reduce every thing to the place to which it naturally belongs, 249, 250. All things do not follow their natural course, 250. In the human body the heaviest parts are not placed lowermost, 251. So it may be in the structure of the world, 252. The moon, though placed in high heaven, may be a heavy body, 253. It is not therefore composed of fire and air, 253. But has the moon the nature of earth? 254. Does the moon reflect the light of the sun? 255. Reasons why this is probable, 256. When the moon appears only half-enlightened, ought not the light reflected to come at right angles? and is it so? 256–258. Aspect of the moon when gibbous or crescent, 258. Only solid bodies reflect light; the moon therefore must be a solid body, 259, 260. That the moon is a solid body is further proved by eclipses of the sun, 260–262. Size of the moon; as large as Peloponnesus, 261. Its proportionate size in relation to the earth, 261. Further arguments from eclipses, 263–265. Objections answered, 266–268. The moon is not a star, or a burning body, 266. Its nature is like that of the earth, 268. This need not impugn her divinity, 268. There may be cavities and other inequalities on the surface of the moon, and these may be immensely large, so as to be seen by us, 269. The shadow of Mount Athos falls on Lemnos, the shadow being immensely larger than the mountain, 270. An objection from this answered, 270–273. Is the moon inhabited? is it fit for the abode of animated beings? 274, 275. Answer, (1.) If it be not, it does not prove that the moon was made in vain, 276. (2.) The moon may be inhabited: we can see no reasons to the contrary, 277–279. Objections considered, 277, 278. That the moon is inhabited is not more incredible than that the ocean should be inhabited, 280. A description of the isle Ogygia, in the Western Ocean, the abode of Saturn; its inhabitants; the phenomena and customs of the place, 281–283. Man is compounded of three parts: the body, the soul, and the understanding, 286. The understanding is from the sun, the soul from the moon, that is from Proserpine, 286. Every soul, dismissed from the body, wanders for a time between the earth and the moon, 286. When they reach the moon, they behold its greatness and beauty, 288 The moon described as it appears to them, 289. The Elysian fields are there, 289. If any of the dwellers there commit a fault, they are thrust down to earth again, 289. After a long time, they come back to the moon, 291. This about the moon may be taken for what one pleases, 292

CONTENTS OF VOL. V.

OF FATE.

By the Same Hand.

Fate is either (1) an energy, a law, an act, 293; or (2) a substance, the soul of the world, 294. Though comprehending infinite, it is itself finite, for law is in its nature finite, 294, 295. Every thing moves in a circle; all beings and all actions that now exist will come around again : we shall again do what we are now doing, and in the same manner, 295. Fate, the Divine Law, the Law of Nature, determines all things, 296. It determines both conditionally and universally, 297. What relation has Fate to Divine Providence ? what to fortune ? what to human ability ? what to contingent events ? 298. As the civil law comprehends and relates to many things which are not lawful, so it is with Fate, 298. The words *possible* and *contingent* defined; also *power*, *necessity*, &c., 299, 300. Of causes : some are causes *per se*, others are causes by accident, 301. Fortune is a cause by accident, 302. Fortune is not the same thing as Chance, though Chance comprehends Fortune, 303. Fortune relates to men only; Chance includes things animate and inanimate, 303. Of Divine Providence. (1) the will of the Supreme Deity; (2) the will of the subordinate deities; (3) the will of the Daemons, 304. Of the Providence of the Supreme God, 305. Of the Providence of the inferior gods, 306. Of the Providence of the Daemons, 307, 308.

CONCERNING THE FIRST PRINCIPLE OF COLD.

By F. Fetherston, D.D.

Is cold the mere privation of heat? 309. This is denied, for cold seems to act on fluids and on solids: like heat or other actual substances, it has a productive power, 310. Further, a mere privation is not capable of degrees; but cold exists in different degrees, 310. A privation is nothing; cold is something, 311. A privation is not the object of any of our senses; but cold can be felt, 311. Privation is something single and simple; substances have differences, continually varying; and thus it is with cold, therefore cold must be a substance, 312. Cold acts as a substance; it resists heat, and overcomes it or is vanquished by it, 312. As there are four elements, of which all things are composed, so there should be four qualities, heat and cold, drought and moisture, 313. What sort of substance is cold? 314. The air, when it becomes dark, becomes also cold, 315. The freezing of water is caused by cold air, 316. Great rivers and lakes are not frozen to the bottom, because the air does not reach so far; the power of cold is therefore as many think, from the air, 317; but this is doubtful, 318. Water makes things black; air makes them white, 318. Oil is transparent because so much air is in it, 318. It does not easily freeze, 319. Cold things are always heavy, 319. Fire and water are opposites, 320. In winter, heat is driven inward by cold, 321. It is driven downward from the surfaces of great rivers, 321. Several considerations show that water, and not air, is the cause of cold, 322. Water is cold of itself, being the opposite of fire, 323. Opinion of Chrysippus combated, 324. The earth, because it is dark, might be considered the cause of cold, 324, 325. But many hot things are dark, 326. Cold makes things hard, heavy, rigid, and capable of resistance : the earth is therefore the source of cold, 326, 327. Several considerations which seem to prove that heat exists in every thing except the earth, and that cold proceeds as a substance from the earth; which, and the whole subject, in conclusion, is left in doubt, to be decided as the reader pleases. 827–330.

WHETHER WATER OR FIRE BE MOST USEFUL.

BY THE SAME HAND.

1. Arguments of the superior usefulness of Water: We need it at all times and in all places; it is not so with fire. Water was given to man at his first creation; fire was introduced by Prometheus. Some men and all brute animals can live without fire, but not without water. Fire is often pernicious; water never. Fire cannot be kept up without expense; water requires no expense. Water, or the sea, is the great civilizer of man, 331–334. 2. Arguments in behalf of Fire: Heat is the exciting cause of vegetation; water becomes putrid when fire leaves it; animals perish without heat; death is only the absence of heat; water is made more useful by fire; the arts cannot exist without fire, 334–337.

AGAINST COLOTES, THE DISCIPLE AND FAVORITE OF EPICURUS.

BY A. G., GENT.

Occasion of this tract; a book written by Colotes, 338. Plutarch undertakes to answer it, and why, 339, 340. Colotes wrongly represents Democritus, 341. Our senses give us true information, but it does not follow that the different qualities which are perceived in the same object by different persons prove that nothing is of one nature more than another, 341–343. This argument further applied, 344. Does color exist in the dark? 344, 345. Doctrine of Democritus concerning atoms, 346. Are atoms immutable and impassible? 347, 348. How then can any thing be generated? 348. Is generation the mere union of atoms? 348. According to Colotes life cannot exist, 349. His doctrines virtually abolish nature, 349. Is nature nothing distinct from bodies and their place? 350. Is death nothing but that which dies? 350. Empedocles defended from the misrepresentations of Colotes, 350, 351. Parmenides also defended, 352–354. A thing positively existing distinguished from its sensible qualities, 354. Aristotle and the Peripatetics differed from Plato, 355. Colotes misrepresents Plato, 355, 356. Difference between that which exists by itself, and that which participates of something else; or between essence and form, 356–359. Colotes falls at the feet of Epicurus, 360. Epicurus accepts the homage, 360. Disparagement of Socrates by Colotes, 361. Though our senses are not perfect, they may in general be safely relied on, 362. If self-knowledge is valuable, Colotes is blamable for scoffing at those who seek it, 363. Stilpo defended against Colotes, 365–367. That one thing cannot be predicated of another may not endanger life, 365. It is bad to withhold reverence and worship from the gods, as Colotes and the Epicureans do, 366. Colotes assaults the philosophers of his own time, 367. He condemns even the opinions of Epicurus, when he finds them held by others, 368, 369. The Cyrenaic philosophers ridiculed, 369. Arcesilaus unfairly treated by Colotes, 371. Three sorts of motions in the soul: what they are; their influence, 371, 372. Absurdity of Epicureanism, 373. The opinions of Epicurus tend to universal scepticism, 374. It is well and safe in some cases to withhold our assent, and to doubt in matters which do not appear credible, as did Arcesilaus and his followers, 371–376. Safety of believing and following the doctrines of Socrates, Plato, and the Academy, 377. Degradation and danger resulting from the doctrines of Epicurus, 377, 378. Those doctrines fatal to the state, 379. No people, no city, is found without some religion, but Epicureanism subverts all religion, 380. Great public spirit of Democritus, Parmenides, Socrates, Plato, and others, who are reviled by Colotes and other Epicureans, 381, 382. Men of the school of Epicurus do not contribute to the public welfare, 383–385.

PLUTARCH'S CONSOLATORY LETTER TO HIS WIFE.

By ROBERT MIDGLEY, M.D., AND COLL. MED. LOND. CAND.

He counsels patience, 386. The child was affectionate and interesting; her memory should be cherished, 387. The mother is commended for controlling her grief excessive grief is unreasonable, 388. The mother's admirable conduct on the previous death of her eldest son, 389. Women are frantic with joy at the birth of their children, and mourn excessively at their death, 389, 390. The body should not suffer through grief, 390. Women nourish and increase the grief of bereaved wives and mothers, by their tears and lamentations when visiting them; Plutarch does not fear this in the present case, 390. We should remember the pleasure our deceased child has afforded us, 391. True happiness arises from the mind itself, and not from external circumstances, 392. You have much left to comfort you, 392. State of the soul after death; the soul will return to earth in a new body; an early death is desirable, 393, 394.

OF THE THREE SORTS OF GOVERNMENT, — MONARCHY, DEMOCRACY, AND OLIGARCHY.

By R. SMITH, M.A.

Which of these three sorts is best? 395. The word *policy* or government defined, 396. The Persians had monarchy; Sparta had an oligarchy; Athens was a democracy: and all were powerful and prosperous, 397. The author prefers monarchy, 398.

WHETHER THE ATHENIANS WERE MORE RENOWNED FOR THEIR WARLIKE ACHIEVEMENTS OR THEIR LEARNING.

By THE SAME HAND.

Historians, even the most admired and popular, only relate the actions of other men, 399. Athens was the nurse of History, of Painting, and of Poetry; and has derived great reputation thereby, 400, 401. But what are historians, painters, and poets, compared with the generals, admirals, and statesmen, whom they commemorate? 402, 403. Athens not renowned for epic or lyric verse, 404. Tragedy flourished there, but what benefit did tragedy procure for the Athenians? 405. They lavished money on scenes and shows, to the neglect of more important interests, 406. True renown belongs to those commanders who have upheld the honor of their country, and they merit a lasting remembrance, 407, 408. But not so poets, rhetoricians, and orators, 408–411. Miltiades and other commanders, compared with Demosthenes and other orators, to the disadvantage of the latter, 408–411.

CONTENTS OF VOL. V. xl

AGAINST RUNNING IN DEBT, OR TAKING UP MONEY UPON USURY.

BY THE SAME HAND.

Running in debt should not be resorted to but in the last necessity, 412. To avoid it, practise the closest economy, 413. The borrower is slave to the lender, 414 415. Usurers are chargeable with oppression, fraud, and falsehood, 416, 417 They take a man's money without an equivalent, 417. It is shameful to be in the power of another, 418. We incur debt, not to procure necessaries, but to purchase ornaments and superfluities, 420. We must avoid the usurer or be ruined, 421-424.

PLATONIC QUESTIONS.

BY R. BROWN, M.L.

1. Why did Socrates act the midwife's part, rather than the parent's? in other words, why did he prefer to develop in the minds of others the germs of knowledge, rather than communicate knowledge to them? 425–427. 2. Why does Plato call the supreme God the Father and Maker of all things? 428, 429. 3. What does Plato, in his Republic, mean by dividing the universe into unequal parts? and of the sections, thus made, which is the greater, the Intelligible or the Sensible? 429–432. 4. Plato always says that the Soul is elder than the Body, and the cause and principle of its rise. Yet he also says that neither could the Soul exist without the Body, nor the Reason without the Soul, but the Soul in the Body, and the Reason in the soul. How can this be explained? 432. 5. Since geometrical figures and solids are contained, partly by Rectilinears and partly by Circles, why does Plato make Isosceles Triangles and Triangles of unequal sides the Principles of Rectilinears, &c.? 433–435. 6. Why does Plato say that the nature of a Wing participates most of the Body of God? 435. 7. In what sense does Plato say that the Antiperistasis, or Reaction, of Motion, is the cause of the effect, in using cupping-glasses, in swallowing, in throwing of weights, in the use of the loadstone, &c.? 435–438. 8. What does he mean in the Timaeus when he says that Souls are dispersed into the Earth, the Moon, and into other instruments of time? Is the Earth, is the Sun, an instrument of time? 438–441. 9. Did Plato, in his Republic, place the Rational or the Irascible Faculty in the middle chord of the human faculties? 441–444. 10. Why did he say that Speech is composed of Nouns and Verbs? 444–449. Because they are the principal elements, *ib.*

PARALLELS, OR A COMPARISON BETWEEN THE GREEK AND ROMAN HISTORIES.

BY JOHN OSWALD, M.A.

1. Invasion of Attica by Datis; the story of Cynaegirus, matched with the story of a Roman, 450, 451. 2. Invasion of Greece by Xerxes; war of Porsena against Rome; a story under each, 451, 452. 3. Combat of the Argives with the Lacedaemonians in Thyreatis; defeat of the Romans at the Caudine Forks, 452, 453 4. Leonidas at Thermopylae; Fabius Maximus in the Punic War, 453. 5 Chasms in the earth closed by men leaping into them, 454. 6. Amphiaraus, and Valerius

CONTENTS OF VOL. V.

Conatus, swallowed up alive by the earth, 455. 7. A king of Euboea, and a king of Alba, drawn in pieces by horses, 455. 8. Philip of Macedon and Aster the archer, Porsena of Clusium and Horatius Cocles, 456. 9. Saturn and his four children, 456, 457. 10. Pausanias, the Spartan traitor, and Cassius, a Roman traitor, both starved to death, 457. 11. Filial treachery in Persian and in Roman history, and its punishment, 458. 12. A son of Epaminondas, the Theban general, and a son of Manlius, the Roman consul, beheaded for disobeying the orders of their fathers, 458, 459. 13. Iole, the beloved of Hercules, threw herself from a wall without hurt; this story matched from Roman history, 459. 14. The sacrifice of Iphigenia at Aulis, matched among the Romans, 459, 460. 15. The story of Tarpeia, promising to betray the Roman capitol, matched at Ephesus, 460. 16. The combat of the Horatii and Curiatii in Roman history has a parallel in Tegea, 460, 461. 17. The Palladium in Ilinm and in Rome, 461. 18. Codrus of Athens, and Decius of Rome, 462. 19. A Syracusan and a Roman, each having refused worship to Bacchus, are intoxicated to commit incest, and are slain, 462, 463. 20. A daughter of Erechtheus, and a daughter of Marius, sacrificed by their fathers to procure victory, 463. 21. A Thessalian wife, and a Sybarite wife, torn in pieces by dogs of their husbands, 463, 464. 22. Two maidens, a Greek and a Roman, who had carnal knowledge of their fathers; their punishment, 464, 465. 23. Diomedes and Calpurnius Crassus liberated from captivity by women who loved them, 465. 24. Priam commits his son to the care of one who murdered him; the story matched in Roman history, 465, 466. 25. Aeacus and his two sons; Caius Maximus and his two sons, 466. 26. Mars, and his lascivious misdoings in Greece and Italy, 466, 467. 27. Telamon deflowers a virgin, whose father orders her to be thrown into the sea; a parallel at Rome, 467. 28. Six sons and six daughters in two different families; incest of a brother with a sister, 467, 468. 29. Two cases of men having carnal knowledge of brutes, and what followed, 468. 30. As the price of peace women are given up to the embraces of the enemy, 468, 469. 31. The allowance of soldiers shortened in war, and the fatal result to him who did it, 469. 32. Romulus murdered in the senate, and his body carried away in pieces; a parallel in the Peloponnesian war, 470. 33. Pelops and his two sons, Atreus and Thyestes, their story; a parallel in Italy, 470, 471. 34. Theseus and his son Hippolytus; the latter is killed by his horses running away: a parallel in Italy, 471, 472. 35. A noble virgin to be sacrificed to obtain relief from pestilence: an instance in Lacedaemon, another in Falerii, 472, 473. 36. The story of Romulus and Remus suckled by a she-wolf: a parallel in Arcadia, 473. 37. Orestes slays his mother, in revenge of his father's death: a similar story from Rome, 474. 38. Strangers murdered by Busiris in Egypt, and by Faunus in Italy, 474. 39. A brazen cow made for Phalaris of Agrigentum, a brazen horse for a tyrant of Egesta, 474, 475. 40. Ev enus cannot keep his daughter a virgin: neither can Anius, king of the Tuscans, 475.

OF THE NAMES OF RIVERS AND MOUNTAINS, AND OF SUCH THINGS AS ARE TO BE FOUND THEREIN.

By R. WHITE, M.A.

1 Hydaspes, a river in India, why it received the name, &c., 477, 478. 2. Ismenus, a river of Boeotia, Cadmus, mount Cithaeron, Tisiphone, &c., 478–480. 3. Hebrus, a river of Thrace; mount Pangaeus, 480, 481. 4. Ganges; the mountain Anatole,

CONTENTS OF VOL. V. xiii

481, 482. 5. Phasis, a river of Thrace; mount Caucasus, 482–484. 6. Arar, a river of Gaul; mount Lugdunum, 484, 485. 7. Pactolus, in Lydia; mount Tmolus 485–487. 8. Lycormas, in Aetolia, 487. 9. Maeander, in Asia; mount Sipylus, 488, 489. 10. Marsyas, in Phrygia, 490. 11. Strymon, in Thrace; the mountains Rhodope and Haemus, 491, 492. 12. Sagaris, in Phrygia, 492. 13. Scamander, in Troas; mount Ida, 493. 14. Tanais, in Scythia; mount Brixaba, 494. 15. Thermodon, in Scythia, 495. 16. Nile, formerly Melas and Aegyptus, 495–497. 17. Eurotas, in Laconia; mount Taygetus, 497, 498. 18. Inachus, in Argolis; mount Mycenae, &c., 498–501. 19. Alpheus, in Arcadia; mount Cronium, 501, 502. 20. Euphrates, 502. 21. Caicus, in Mysia; mount Teuthras, 503, 504. 22. Acheloüs, in Aetolia; mount Calydon, 504, 505. 23. Araxes, in Armenia; mount Diorphus, 506, 507. 24. Tigris; mount Gauran, 507, 508. 25. Indus; mount Lilaeus, 508, 509.

INDEX. 511

PLUTARCH'S MORALS.

PLUTARCH'S MORALS.

OF EATING OF FLESH.

TRACT I.

1. You ask of me then for what reason it was that Pythagoras abstained from eating of flesh. I for my part do much admire in what humor, with what soul or reason, the first man with his mouth touched slaughter, and reached to his lips the flesh of a dead animal, and having set before people courses of ghastly corpses and ghosts, could give those parts the names of meat and victuals, that but a little before lowed, cried, moved, and saw; how his sight could endure the blood of slaughtered, flayed, and mangled bodies; how his smell could bear their scent; and how the very nastiness happened not to offend the taste, while it chewed the sores of others, and participated of the saps and juices of deadly wounds.

> Crept the raw hides, and with a bellowing sound
> Roared the dead limbs; the burning entrails groaned.*

This indeed is but a fiction and fancy; but the fare itself is truly monstrous and prodigious, — that a man should have a stomach to creatures while they yet bellow, and that he should be giving directions which of things yet alive and speaking is fittest to make food of, and ordering the several manners of the seasoning and dressing them and serving them up to tables. You ought rather, in my opinion, to have enquired who first began this practice, than who of late times left it off.

* Odyss. XII. 395.

2. And truly, as for those people who first ventured upon eating of flesh, it is very probable that the whole reason of their so doing was scarcity and want of other food; for it is not likely that their living together in lawless and extravagant lusts, or their growing wanton and capricious through the excessive variety of provisions then among them, brought them to such unsociable pleasures as these, against Nature. Yea, had they at this instant but their sense and voice restored to them, I am persuaded they would express themselves to this purpose:

"Oh! happy you, and highly favored of the Gods, who now live! Into what an age of the world are you fallen, who share and enjoy among you a plentiful portion of good things! What abundance of things spring up for your use! What fruitful vineyards you enjoy! What wealth you gather from the fields! What delicacies from trees and plants, which you may gather! You may glut and fill yourselves without being polluted. As for us, we fell upon the most dismal and affrighting part of time, in which we were exposed by our first production to manifold and inextricable wants and necessities. As yet the thickened air concealed the heaven from our view, and the stars were as yet confused with a disorderly huddle of fire and moisture and violent fluxions of winds. As yet the sun was not fixed to an unwandering and certain course, so as to distinguish morning and evening, nor did he bring back the seasons in order crowned with wreaths from the fruitful harvest. The land was also spoiled by the inundations of disorderly rivers; and a great part of it was deformed with sloughs, and utterly wild by reason of deep quagmires, unfertile forests, and woods. There was then no production of tame fruits, nor any instruments of art or invention of wit. And hunger gave no time, nor did seed-time then stay for the yearly season. What wonder is it if we made use of the flesh of beasts contrary to Nature, when mud was eaten and the bark of wood, and when it was thought a happy thing to find either a sprouting grass or a root of any plant! But when they had by chance tasted of or eaten an acorn, they danced for very joy about some oak or esculus, calling it by the names of life-giver, mother, and nourisher. And this was the only festival that those times were acquainted with; upon all other occasions, all things were full of anguish and dismal sadness. But whence is it that a certain ravenousness and frenzy drives you in these happy days to pollute yourselves with blood, since you have such an abundance of things necessary for your subsistence? Why do you belie the earth as unable to maintain you? Why do you profane the lawgiver Ceres, and shame the mild and gentle Bacchus, as not furnishing you with sufficiency? Are you not ashamed to mix tame fruits with blood and slaughter? You are indeed wont to call serpents, leopards, and lions savage creatures; but yet yourselves are defiled with blood, and come nothing behind them in cruelty. What they kill is their ordinary nourishment, but what you kill is your better fare."

3. For we eat not lions and wolves by way of revenge; but we let those go, and catch the harmless and tame sort, and such as have neither stings nor teeth to bite with, and slay them; which, so may Jove help us, Nature seems to us to have produced for their beauty and comeliness only. *[Just as if one seeing the river Nilus overflowing its banks, and thereby filling the whole country with genial and fertile moisture, should not at all admire that secret power in it that produces plants and plenteousness of most sweet and useful fruits, but beholding somewhere a crocodile swimming in it, or an asp crawling along, or mice

---

* "I see not how this that is included within these marks [   ] agreeth with this place, or matter in hand: I suppose therefore it is inserted heere without judgement, and taken out of some other booke."—HOLLAND.

(savage and filthy creatures), should presently affirm these to be the occasion of all that is amiss, or of any want or defect that may happen. Or as if indeed one contemplating this land or ground, how full it is of tame fruits, and how heavy with ears of corn, should afterwards espy somewhere in these same cornfields an ear of darnel or a wild vetch, and thereupon neglect to reap and gather in the corn, and fall a complaining of these. Such another thing it would be, if one — hearing the harangue of some advocate at some bar or pleading, swelling and enlarging and hastening towards the relief of some impending danger, or else, by Jupiter, in the impeaching and charging of certain audacious villanies or indictments, flowing and rolling along, and that not in a simple and poor strain, but with many sorts of passions all at once, or rather indeed with all sorts, in one and the same manner, into the many and various and differing minds of either hearers or judges that he is either to turn and change, or else, by Jupiter, to soften, appease, and quiet — should overlook all this business, and never consider or reckon upon the labor or struggle he had undergone, but pick up certain loose expressions, which the rapid motion of the discourse had carried along with it, as by the current of its stream, and so had slipped and escaped the rest of the oration, and hereupon undervalue the orator.]

4. But we are nothing put out of countenance, either by the beauteous gayety of the colors, or by the charmingness of the musical voices, or by the rare sagacity of the intellects, or by the cleanliness and neatness of diet, or by the rare discretion and prudence of these poor unfortunate animals; but for the sake of some little mouthful of flesh, we deprive a soul of the sun and light, and of that proportion of life and time it had been born into the world to enjoy. And then we fancy that the voices it utters and screams forth to us are nothing else but certain inarticulate

sounds and noises, and not the several deprecations, entreaties, and pleadings of each of them, as it were saying thus to us: "I deprecate not thy necessity (if such there be), but thy wantonness. Kill me for thy feeding, but do not take me off for thy better feeding." O horrible cruelty! It is truly an affecting sight to see the very table of rich people laid before them, who keep them cooks and caterers to furnish them with dead corpses for their daily fare; but it is yet more affecting to see it taken away, for the mammocks left are more than that which was eaten. These therefore were slain to no purpose. Others there are, who are so sparing of what is set before them that they will not suffer it to be cut or sliced; thus abstaining from them when dead, while they would not spare them when alive.

5. Well then, we understand that that sort of men are used to say, that in eating of flesh they follow the conduct and direction of Nature. But that it is not natural to mankind to feed on flesh, we first of all demonstrate from the very shape and figure of the body. For a human body no ways resembles those that were born for ravenousness; it hath no hawk's bill, no sharp talon, no roughness of teeth, no such strength of stomach or heat of digestion, as can be sufficient to convert or alter such heavy and fleshy fare. But even from hence, that is, from the smoothness of the tongue, and the slowness of the stomach to digest, Nature seems to disclaim all pretence to fleshy victuals. But if you will contend that yourself was born to an inclination to such food as you have now a mind to eat, do you then yourself kill what you would eat. But do it yourself, without the help of a chopping-knife, mallet, or axe, — as wolves, bears, and lions do, who kill and eat at once. Rend an ox with thy teeth, worry a hog with thy mouth, tear a lamb or a hare in pieces, and fall on and eat it alive as they do. But if thou hadst rather stay until what thou eatest is become dead, and if thou art loath to force a soul

out of its body, why then dost thou against Nature eat an animate thing? Nay, there is nobody that is willing to eat even a lifeless and a dead thing as it is; but they boil it, and roast it, and alter it by fire and medicines, as it were, changing and quenching the slaughtered gore with thousands of sweet sauces, that the palate being thereby deceived may admit of such uncouth fare. It was indeed a witty expression of a Lacedaemonian, who, having purchased a small fish in a certain inn, delivered it to his landlord to be dressed; and as he demanded cheese, and vinegar, and oil to make sauce, he replied, if I had had those, I would not have bought the fish. But we are grown so wanton in our bloody luxury, that we have bestowed upon flesh the name of meat (ὄψον), and then require another seasoning (ὄψον), to this same flesh, mixing oil, wine, honey, pickle, and vinegar, with Syrian and Arabian spices, as though we really meant to embalm it after its disease. Indeed when things are dissolved and made thus tender and soft, and are as it were turned into a sort of a carrionly corruption, it must needs be a great difficulty for concoction to master them, and when it hath mastered them, they must needs cause grievous oppressions and qualmy indigestions.

6. Diogenes ventured once to eat a raw pourcontrel, that he might disuse himself from meat dressed by fire; and as several priests and other people stood round him, he wrapped his head in his cassock, and so putting the fish to his mouth, he thus said unto them: It is for your sake, sirs, that I undergo this danger, and run this risk. A noble and gallant risk, by Jupiter! For far otherwise than as Pelopidas ventured his life for the liberty of the Thebans, and Harmodius and Aristogiton for that of the Athenians, did this philosopher encounter with a raw pourcontrel, to the end he might make human life more brutish. Moreover, these same flesh-eatings not only are preter-

natural to men's bodies, but also by clogging and cloying them, they render their very minds and intellects gross. For it is well known to most, that wine and much flesh-eating make the body indeed strong and lusty, but the mind weak and feeble. And that I may not offend the wrestlers, I will make use of examples out of my own country. The Athenians are wont to call us Boeotians gross, senseless, and stupid fellows, for no other reason but our over-much eating; and Pindar calls us also hogs, for the same reason. Menander the comedian calls us "fellows with long jaws." It is observed also that, according to the saying of Heraclitus, "the wisest soul is like a dry light."* Earthen jars, if you strike them, will sound; but if they be full, they perceive not the strokes that are given them. Copper vessels also that are thin communicate the sound round about them, unless some one stop and dull the ambient stroke with his fingers. Moreover, the eye, when seized with an over-great plenitude of humors, grows dim and feeble for its ordinary work. When we behold the sun through a humid air and a great quantity of gross and indigested vapors, we see it not clear and bright, but obscure and cloudy, and with glimmering beams. Just so in a muddy and clogged body, that is swagged down with heavy and unnatural nourishments; it must needs happen that the gayety and splendor of the mind be confused and dulled, and that it ramble and roll after little and scarce discernible objects, since it wants clearness and vigor for higher things.

7. But to pass by these considerations, is not accustoming one's self to mildness and a human temper of mind an admirable thing? For who could wrong or injure a man that is so sweetly and humanly disposed with respect to the ills of strangers that are not of his kind? I remember that three days ago, as I was discoursing, I made mention

---

* See Mullach, Fragm. Philos. p. 325 (No. 73).

of a saying of Xenocrates, and how the Athenians gave judgment upon a certain person who had flayed a living ram. For my part I cannot think him a worse criminal that torments a poor creature while living, than a man that shall take away its life and murder it. But (as it seems) we are more sensible of what is done against custom than against Nature. There, however, I discoursed on these matters in a more popular style. But as for that grand and mysterious principle which (as Plato speaks) is incredible to base minds and to such as affect only mortal things, I as little care to move it in this discourse as a pilot doth a ship in a storm, or a comedian his machine while the scenes are moving; but perhaps it would not be amiss, by way of introduction and preface, to proclaim certain verses of Empedocles. . . . For in these, by way of allegory, he hints at men's souls, as that they are tied to mortal bodies, to be punished for murders, eating of flesh and of one another, although this doctrine seems much ancienter than his time. For the fables that are storied and related about the discerption of Bacchus, and the attempts of the Titans upon him, and of their tasting of his slain body, and of their several punishments and fulminations afterwards, are but a representation of the regeneration. For what in us is unreasonable, disorderly, and boisterous, being not divine but demoniac, the ancients termed Titans, that is *tormented* and *punished* (from τίνω). . . .

TRACT II.

1. REASON persuades us now to return with fresh cogitations and dispositions to what we left cold yesterday of our discourse about flesh-eating. It is indeed a hard and a difficult task to undertake (as Cato once said) to dispute with men's bellies, that have no ears; since most have

OF EATING OF FLESH. 11

already drunk that draught of custom, which is like that of Circe,

<blockquote>Of groans and frauds and sorcery replete.*</blockquote>

And it is no easy task to pull out the hook of flesh-eating from the jaws of such as have gorged themselves with luxury and are (as it were) nailed down with it. It would indeed be a good action, if as the Egyptians draw out the stomach of a dead body, and cut it open and expose it to the sun, as the only cause of all its evil actions, so we could, by cutting out our gluttony and blood-shedding, purify and cleanse the remainder of our lives. For the stomach itself is not guilty of bloodshed, but is involuntarily polluted by our intemperance. But if this may not be, and we are ashamed by reason of custom to live unblamably, let us at least sin with discretion. Let us eat flesh; but let it be for hunger and not for wantonness. Let us kill an animal; but let us do it with sorrow and pity, and not abusing and tormenting it, as many nowadays are used to do, while some run red-hot spits through the bodies of swine, that by the tincture of the quenched iron the blood may be to that degree mortified, that it may sweeten and soften the flesh in its circulation; others jump and stamp upon the udders of sows that are ready to pig, that so they may trample into one mass, (O Piacular Jupiter!) in the very pangs of delivery, blood, milk, and the corruption of the crushed and mangled young ones, and so eat the most inflamed part of the animal; others sew up the eyes of cranes and swans, and so shut them up in darkness to be fattened, and then souse up their flesh with certain monstrous mixtures and pickles.

2. By all which it is most manifest, that it is not for nourishment, or want, or any necessity, but for mere gluttony, wantonness, and expensiveness, that they make a

* Odyss. X. 234.

pleasure of villany. Just as it happens in persons who cannot satiate their intemperance upon women, and having made trial of every thing else and falling into vagaries, at last attempt things not to be mentioned; even so inordinateness in feeding, when it hath once passed the bounds of nature and necessity, studies at last to diversify the lusts of its intemperate appetite by cruelty and villany. For the senses, when they once quit their natural measures, sympathize with each other in their distempers, and are enticed by each other to the same consent and intemperance. Thus a distempered ear first debauched music, the soft and effeminate notes of which provoke immodest touches and lascivious tickling. These things first taught the eye not to delight in Pyrrhic dances, gesticulations of hands, or elegant pantomimes, nor in statues and fine paintings; but to reckon the slaughtering and death of mankind and wounds and duels the most sumptuous of shows and spectacles. Thus unlawful tables are accompanied with intemperate copulations, with unmusician-like balls, and theatres become monstrous through shameful songs and rehearsals; and barbarous and brutish shows are again accompanied with an unrelenting temper and savage cruelty towards mankind. Hence it was that the divine Lycurgus in his Three Books of Laws gave orders that the doors and ridges of men's houses should be made with a saw and an axe, and that no other instrument should so much as be brought to any house. Not that he did hereby intend to declare war against augers and planes and other instruments of finer work; but because he very well knew that with such tools as these you will never bring into your house a gilded couch, and that you will never attempt to bring into a slender cottage either silver tables, purple carpets, or costly stones; but that a plain supper and a homely dinner must accompany such a house, couch, table, and cup. The beginning of a vicious diet is presently followed by all sorts of luxury and expensiveness,

Ev'n as a mare is by her thirsty colt.

3. And what meal is not expensive? That for which no animal is put to death. Shall we reckon a soul to be a small expense. I will not say perhaps of a mother, or a father, or of some friend, or child, as Empedocles did; but one participating of feeling, of seeing, of hearing, of imagination, and of intellection; which each animal hath received from Nature for the acquiring of what is agreeable to it, and the avoiding what is disagreeable. Do but consider this with yourself now, which sort of philosophers render us most tame and civil, they who bid people to feed on their children, friends, fathers, and wives, when they are dead; or Pythagoras and Empedocles, that accustom men to be just towards even the other members of the creation. You laugh at a man that will not eat a sheep: but we (they will say again) — when we see you cutting off the parts of your dead father or mother, and sending it to your absent friends, and calling upon and inviting your present friends to eat the rest freely and heartily — shall we not smile? Nay, peradventure we offend at this instant time while we touch these books, without having first cleansed our hands, eyes, feet, and ears; if it be not (by Jupiter) a sufficient purgation of them to have discoursed of these matters in potable and fresh language (as Plato speaketh), thereby washing off the brackishness of hearing. Now if a man should set these books and discourses in opposition to each other, he will find that the philosophy of the one sort suits with the Scythians, Sogdians, and Melanchlaenians, of whom Herodotus's relation is scarce believed; but the sentiments of Pythagoras and Empedocles were the laws and customs of the ancient Grecians.

4. Who then were the first authors of this opinion, that we owe no justice to dumb animals?

> Who first beat out accursed steel,
> And made the lab'ring ox a knife to feel.

In the very same manner oppressors and tyrants begin first to shed blood. For example, the first man that the Athenians ever put to death was one of the basest of all knaves, whom all thought deserving of death; after him they put to death a second and a third. After this, being now accustomed to blood, they patiently saw Niceratus the son of Nicias, and their own general Theramenes, and Polemarchus the philosopher suffer death. Even so, in the beginning, some wild and mischievous beast was killed and eaten, and then some little bird or fish was entrapped. And the love of slaughter, being first experimented and exercised in these, at last passed even to the laboring ox, and the sheep that clothes us, and to the poor cock that keeps the house; until by little and little, unsatiableness being strengthened by use, men came to the slaughter of men, to bloodshed and wars. Now even if one cannot demonstrate and make out, that souls in their regenerations make a promiscuous use of all bodies, and that that which is now rational will at another time be irrational, and that again tame which is now wild, — for that Nature changes and transmutes every thing,

> With different fleshy coats new clothing all, —

this thing should be sufficient to change and reclaim men, that it is a savage and intemperate habit, that it brings sickness and heaviness upon the body, and that it inclines the mind the more brutishly to bloodshed and destruction, when we have once accustomed ourselves neither to entertain a guest nor keep a wedding nor to treat our friends without blood and slaughter.

5. And if what is argued about the return of souls into bodies is not of force enough to beget faith, yet methinks the very uncertainty of the thing should fill us with apprehension and fear. Suppose, for instance, one should in

some night-engagement run on with his drawn sword upon one that had fallen down and covered his body with his arms, and should in the mean time hear one say, that he was not very sure, but that he fancied and believed, that the party lying there was his own son, brother, father, or tent-companion; which were more advisable, think you, — to hearken to a false suggestion, and so to let go an enemy under the notion of a friend, or to slight an authority not sufficient to beget faith, and to slay a friend instead of a foe? This you will all say would be insupportable. Do but consider the famous Merope in the tragedy, who taking up a hatchet, and lifting it at her son's head, whom she took for her son's murderer, speaks thus as she was ready to give the fatal blow,

Villain, this pious blow shall cleave thy head;*

what a bustle she raises in the whole theatre while she raises herself to give the blow, and what a fear they are all in, lest she should prevent the old man that comes to stop her hand, and should wound the youth. Now if another old man should stand by her and say, "Strike, it is thy enemy," and this, "Hold, it is thy son;" which, think you, would be the greater injustice, to omit the punishing of an enemy for the sake of one's child, or to suffer one's self to be so transported with anger at an enemy as to kill one's child? Since then neither hatred nor wrath nor any revenge nor fear for ourselves carries us to the slaughter of a beast, but the poor sacrifice stands with an inclined neck, only to satisfy thy lust and pleasure, and then one philosopher stands by and tells thee, "Cut him down, it is but an unreasonable animal," and another cries, "Hold, what if there should be the soul of some kinsman or God inclosed in him"? — good Gods! is there the like danger if I refuse to eat flesh, as if I for want of faith murder my child or some other friend?

* Eurip. Cresphontes, Frag. 457.

6. The Stoics' way of reasoning upon this subject of flesh-eating is no way equal nor consonant with themselves. Who is this that hath so many mouths for his belly and the kitchen? Whence comes it to pass, that they so very much womanize and reproach pleasure, as a thing that they will not allow to be either good or preferable, or so much as agreeable, and yet all on a sudden become so zealous advocates for pleasures? It were indeed but a reasonable consequence of their doctrine, that, since they banish perfumes and cakes from their banquets, they should be much more averse to blood and to flesh. But now, just as if they would reduce their philosophy to their day-books, they lessen the expenses of their suppers in certain unnecessary and needless matters, but the untamed and murderous part of their expense they nothing boggle at. "Well! What then?" say they. "We have nothing to do with brute beasts." Nor have you any with perfumes, nor with foreign sauces, may some one answer; therefore expel these from your banquets, if you are driving out every thing that is both useless and needless.

7. Let us therefore in the next place consider, whether we owe any justice to the brute beasts. Neither shall we handle this point artificially, or like subtle sophisters, but by casting our eye into our own breasts, and conversing with ourselves as men, we will weigh and examine the whole matter. . . .

LIVES OF THE TEN ORATORS.

I. ANTIPHON.

ANTIPHON, the son of Sophilus, by descent a Rhamnusian, was his father's scholar; for Sophilus kept a rhetoric school, to which it is reported that Alcibiades himself had recourse in his youth. Having attained to competent measure of knowledge and eloquence, — and that, as some believe, from his own natural ingenuity, — he dedicated his study chiefly to affairs of state. And yet he was for some time conversant in the schools, and had a controversy with Socrates the philosopher about the art of disputing, — not so much for the sake of contention as for the profit of arguing, as Xenophon tells us in his Commentaries of Socrates. At the request of some citizens, he wrote orations by which they defended their suits at law. Some say that he was the first that ever did any thing of this nature. For it is certain there is not one juridical oration extant written by any orator that lived before him, nor by his contemporaries either, as Themistocles, Aristides, and Pericles; though the times gave them opportunity, and there was need enough of their labor in such business. Not that we are to impute it to their want of parts that they did nothing in this way, for we may inform ourselves of the contrary from what historians relate of each of them. Besides, if we inspect the most ancient of those known in history who had the same form and method in their pleadings, such as Alcibiades, Critias, Lysias, and Archinous, we shall find that they all followed Antiphon when he was old. For being a man of incomparable sagacity, he was the first that published institutions of oratory; and by reason of his profound learning, he was surnamed Nestor. Caecilius, in a tract which he wrote of him, supposes him to have been Thucydides's pupil, from what Antiphon delivered in praise of him. He is most accurate in his orations, in invention subtle; and he would frequently baffle his adversary at unawares, by a covert sort of pleading; in troublesome and intricate matters he was very judicious and sharp; and as he was a great admirer of ornamental speaking, he would always adapt his orations to both law and reason.

He lived about the time of the Persian war and of Gorgias the rhetorician, being somewhat younger than he. And he lived to see the subversion of the popular government in the commonwealth which was wrought by the four hundred conspirators, in which he himself is thought to have had the chiefest hand, being sometimes commander of two galleys, and sometimes general, and having by the many and great victories he obtained gained them many allies, he armed the young men, manned out sixty galleys, and on all their occasions went ambassador to Lacedaemon at the time when Eetionia was fortified. But when those Four Hundred were overcome and taken down, he with Archeptolemus, who was likewise one of the same number, was accused of the conspiracy, condemned, and sentenced to the punishment due to traitors, his body cast out unburied, and all his posterity infamous on record. But there are some who tell us, that he was put to death by the Thirty Tyrants; and among the rest, Lysias, in his oration for Antiphon's daughter, says the same; for he left a little daughter, whom Callaeschrus claimed for his wife by the law of propinquity. And Theopompus likewise, in his Fifteenth Book of Philippics, tells us the same thing. But this must have been another Antiphon, son of Lysidonides, whom Cratinus mentions in his Pytine as a rascal. But how could he be executed in the time of the Four Hundred, and afterward live to be put to death by the Thirty Tyrants? There is likewise another story of the manner of his death: that when he was old, he sailed to Syracuse, when the tyranny of Dionysius the First was most famous; and being at table, a question was put, what sort of brass was best. When others had answered as they thought most proper, he replied, That is the best brass, of which the statues of Harmodius and Aristogiton were made. The tyrant hearing this, and taking it as a tacit exhortation to his subjects to contrive his ruin, he commanded Antiphon to be put to death; and some say that he put him to death for deriding his tragedies.

This orator is reported to have written sixty orations; but Caecilius supposes twenty-five of them to be spurious and none of his. Plato, in his comedy called Pisander, traduces him as a covetous man. He is reported to have composed some of his tragedies alone, and others with Dionysius the tyrant. While he was poetically inclined, he invented an art of curing the distemper of the mind, as physicians are wont to provide cure of bodily diseases. And having at Corinth built him a little house, in or near the market, he set a postscript over the gate, to this effect: that he had a way to cure the distemper of men's minds by words; and let him but know the cause of their malady, he would immediately prescribe the remedy, to their comfort. But after some time, thinking that art not worth his while, he betook himself to the study and teaching of oratory. There are some who ascribe the book of Glaucus of Rhegium concerning Poets to him as author. His orations concerning Herodes, against Erasistratus concerning Peacocks,* are very much commended, and also that which, when he was accused, he penned for himself against a

---

* Concerning Ideas, according to the MSS. (G.)

public indictment, and that against Demosthenes the general for moving an illegal measure. He likewise had another against Hippocrates the general; who did not appear on the day appointed for his trial, and was condemned in his absence.

Caecilius has recorded the decree of the senate for the judicial trial of Antiphon, passed in the year* in which Theopompus was chief magistrate of Athens, the same in which the Four Hundred were overthrown, — in these words:

"Enacted by the senate on the twenty-first day of the prytany. Demonicus of Alopece was clerk; Philostratus of Pallene was president.

"Andron moved in regard to those men, — viz. Archeptolemus, Onomacles, and Antiphon, whom the generals had declared against, for that they went in an embassage to Lacedaemon, to the great damage of the city of Athens, and departed from the camp in an enemies' ship, and went through Decelea by land, — that they should be apprehended and brought before the court for a legal trial.

"Therefore let the generals, with others of the senate, to the number of ten, whom it shall please the generals to name and choose, look after these men to present them before the court, that they may be present during the proceedings. Then let the Thesmothetes summon the defendants to appear on the morrow, and let them open the proceedings in court at the time at which the summonses shall be returnable. Then let the chosen advocates, with the generals and any others who may have any thing to say, accuse the defendants of treason; and if any one of them shall be found guilty, let sentence be passed upon him as a traitor, according to the law in such case made and provided."

---

* Theopompus was Archon in B.C. 411. (G.)

At the bottom of this decree was subscribed the sentence: —

"Archeptolemus son of Hippodamus, the Agrylian, and Antiphon son of Sophilus, the Ramnusian, being both present in court, are condemned of treason. And this was to be their punishment: that they should be delivered to the eleven executioners, their goods confiscated, the tenth part of them being first consecrated to Minerva; their houses to be levelled with the ground, and in the places where they stood this subscription to be engraven on brass, '[The houses] of Archeptolemus and Antiphon, traitors.' . . .* That Archeptolemus and Antiphon should neither of them be buried in Athens, nor anywhere else under that government. And besides all this, that their posterity should be accounted infamous, bastards as well as their lawful progeny; and he too should be held infamous who should adopt any one of their progeny for his son. And that all this should be engrossed and engraven on a brass column, and that column should be placed where that stands on which is engraven the decree concerning Phrynichus."

II. ANDOCIDES.

ANDOCIDES, the son of Leogoras, [and grandson of that Andocides] who once made a peace between the Athenians and the Lacedaemonians, by descent a Cydathenian or Thorian, of a noble family, and, as Hellanicus tells us, the offspring of Mercury himself, for the race of Heralds belongs to him. On this account he was chosen by the people to go with Glaucon, with twenty sail of ships, to aid the Corcyraeans against the Corinthians. But in

---

* The corrupt clause indicated by . . . probably means, that the Demarchs were to make inventories (ἀποφῆναι) of the traitors' estates. (G.)

process of time he was accused of some notorious acts of impiety, as that he was of the number of those who defaced the statues of Mercury and divulged the sacred mysteries of Ceres. And withal, he had been before this time wild and intemperate, and had once been seen in the night in masquerade to break one of the statues of Mercury; and when on his trial he refused to bring his servant to examination whom his accusers named, he not only remained under this reproach, but was also on this account very much suspected to be guilty of the second crime too. This later action was laid to his charge soon after the expedition of the navy sent by the Athenians into Sicily. For, as Cratippus informs us, when the Corinthians sent the Leontines and Egestians to the Athenians, who hesitated to lend them assistance, they in the night defaced and brake all the statues of Mercury which were erected in the market. To which offence Andocides added another, that of divulging the mysteries of Ceres. He was brought to his trial, but was acquitted on condition he would discover who were companions with him in the crime. In which affair being very diligent, he found out who they were that had been guilty, and among the rest he discovered his own father. He proved all guilty, and caused them all to be put to death except his father, whom he saved, though in prison, by a promise of some eminent service he would do to the commonwealth. Nor did he fail of what he promised; for Leogoras accused many who had acted in several matters against the interest of the commonwealth, and for this was acquitted of his own crime.

Now, though Andocides was very much esteemed of for his skill in the management of the affairs of the commonwealth, yet his inclinations led him rather to traffic by sea; and by this means he contracted friendship with the kings of Cyprus and other great princes. At which time he privily stole a damsel of the city, the daughter of Aristides, and his own niece, and sent her as a present to the king of Cyprus. But suspecting he should be called in question for it, he again stole her from Cyprus, for which the king of Cyprus took him and clapped him up in prison; whence he brake loose, and returned to Athens, just at that time when the four hundred conspirators had usurped the government. By whom being confined, he again escaped when the oligarchical government was broken up. . . . . But when the Thirty Tyrants were uppermost, he withdrew to Elis, and there lived till Thrasybulus and his faction returned into the city, and then he also repaired thither. And after some time, being sent to Lacedaemon to conciliate a peace, he was again suspected to be faulty, and on that suspicion banished.

He himself has given an account of all these transactions, in his orations, which he has left behind him. For some of them contain his defence of himself in regard to the mysteries; others his petition for restoration from exile; there is one extant on *Endeixis* (or information laid against a criminal); also a defence against Phaeax, and one on the peace. He flourished at the same time with Socrates the philosopher. He was born in the seventy-eighth Olympiad, when Theogenides was chief magistrate of Athens, so that he should seem to be about ten years before Lysias. There is an image of Mercury, called from his name, being given by the tribe Acgeis; and it stood near the house where Andocides dwelt, and was therefore called by his name. This Andocides himself was at the charge of a cyclic chorus for the tribe Aegeis, at the performance of a dithyrambus. And having gained a victory, he erected a tripod on an ascent opposite to the tuffstone statue of Silenus. His style in his orations is plain and easy, without the least affectation or any thing of a figurative ornament.

III. LYSIAS.

Lysias was the son of Cephalus, grandson of Lysanias, and great-grandson of Cephalus. His father was by birth a Syracusan; but partly for the love he had to the city, and partly in condescension to the persuasions of Pericles the son of Xanthippus, who entertained him as his friend and guest, he went to live at Athens, being a man of great wealth. Some say that he was banished Syracuse when the city was under the tyranny of Gelo. Lysias was born at Athens when Philocles, the successor of Phrasicles, was chief magistrate, in the second year of the eightieth Olympiad.* At his first coming, he was educated among the most noble of the Athenians. But when the city sent a colony to Sybaris, which was afterwards called Thurii, he went thither with his other brother Polemarchus, his father being now dead (for he had two other brothers, Euthydemus and Brachyllus), that he might receive his portion of his father's estate. This was done in the fifteenth year of his age, when Praxiteles was chief magistrate.† There then he stayed, and was brought up under Nicias and Tisias, both Syracusans. And having purchased a house and received his estate, he lived as a citizen for thirty-three years, till the year of Cleocritus.‡ In the year following, in the time of Callias, viz. in the ninety-second Olympiad, when the Athenians had met with their disasters in Sicily, and when other of their allies revolted, and especially the Italians, he, being accused of favoring the Athenians, was banished with three other of his association; when coming to Athens, in the year wherein Callias succeeded Cleocritus, the city then laboring under the tyranny of the four hundred conspirators, he there sat down. But after the fight at Aegospotami, when the Thirty Tyrants had usurped the

---

* B.C. 459.   † B.C. 444.   ‡ B.C. 413.

government, he was banished thence, after he had remained in Athens seven years. His goods were confiscated ; and having likewise lost his brother Polemarchus, he himself escaped by a back door of the house in which he was kept for execution, fled to Megara and there lived. But when the citizens endeavored to return from Phyle, he also behaved himself very well, and appeared very active in the affair, having, to forward this great enterprise, deposited two thousand drachms of silver and two hundred targets, and being commissioned with Hermas, he maintained three hundred men in arms, and prevailed with Thrasylaeus the Elean, his old friend and host, to contribute two talents. Upon entering the city, Thrasybulus proposed that, for a consideration of his good service to the public, he should receive the rights of citizenship : this was during the so-called time of anarchy before Euclides. Which proposal being ratified by the people, Archinus objected that it was against the laws, and a decree without authority of the senate. The decree was thereupon declared void, and Lysias lost his citizenship. He led the remainder of his life in the rank of an *Isoteles* (or citizen who had no right to vote or hold office), and died at last at Athens, being fourscore and three years old, or as some would have it, seventy-six ; and others again say, that he lived above fourscore years, till after the birth of Demosthenes. It is supposed he was born in the year of Philocles.

There are four hundred and twenty-five orations which bear his name, of which Dionysius and Caecilius affirm only two hundred and thirty to be genuine, and he is said to have been overcome but twice in all. There is extant also the oration which he made in defence of the forementioned decree against Archinus, who indicted it and thereby prevented Lysias from receiving the citizenship, as also another against the Thirty Tyrants. He was very cogent in his persuasions, and was always very brief in what he delivered. He would commonly give orations to private persons. There are likewise his institutions of oratory, his public harangues, his epistles, his eulogies, funeral orations, discourses of love, and his defence of Socrates, accommodated to the minds of the judges. His style seems plain and easy, though hardly imitable. Demosthenes, in his oration against Neaera, says that he was in love with one Metanira, Neaera's serving-maid, but afterwards married his brother Brachyllus's daughter. Plato in his Phaedrus makes mention of him, as a most eloquent orator and ancienter than Isocrates. Philiscus, his companion, and Isocrates's votary, composed an epigram concerning him, whence the same that we have urged from Plato is deducible; and it sings to this effect:

> Calliope's witty daughter, Phrontis, show
> If aught of wit or eloquence thou hast;
> For 'tis decreed that thou shalt bear a son,
> Lysias by name, to spread the name of him
> Whose great and generous acts do fill the world,
> And are received for glorious above.
> Let him who sings those praises of the dead,
> Let him, my friend, too, praise our amity.

He likewise wrote two orations for Iphicrates, — one against Harmodius, and another accusing Timotheus of treason, — in both which he overcame. But when Iphicrates made himself responsible for Timotheus's actions, and would purge himself of the allegation of treason made also against him, Lysias wrote an oration for him to deliver in his defence; upon which he was acquitted, but Timotheus was fined in a considerable sum of money. He likewise delivered an oration at the Olympic games, in which he endeavored to convince the Greeks of how great advantage it would be to them, if they could but unanimously join to pull down the tyrant Dionysius.

IV. ISOCRATES.

ISOCRATES was the son of Theodorus, of Erchia, reckoned among the middle class of citizens, and a man who kept servants under him to make flutes, by which he got so much money as enabled him not only to bring up his children after the most genteel manner, but likewise to maintain a choir. For besides Isocrates, he had other sons, Telesippus and Diomnestus, and one daughter. And hence, we may suppose, those two comical poets, Aristophanes and Stratis, took occasion to bring him on the stage. He was born in the eighty-sixth Olympiad,* Lysimachus being archon, about two and twenty years after Lysias, and seven before Plato. When he was a boy, he was as well educated as any of the Athenian children, being under the tuition of Prodicus the Cean, Gorgias the Leontine, Tisias the Syracusan, and Theramenes the rhetorician. And when Theramenes was to be apprehended by the order of the Thirty Tyrants, and flying for succor to the altar of the senate, only Isocrates stood his friend, when all others were struck with terror. For a long time he stood silent; but after some time Theramenes advised him to desist, because, he told him, it would be an aggravation of his grief, if any of his friends should come into trouble through him. And it is said that he made use of certain institutions of rhetoric composed by Theramenes, when he was slandered in court; which institutions have since borne Boton's name.

When Isocrates was come to man's estate, he meddled with nothing of state affairs, both because he had a very weak voice and because he was something timorous; and besides these two impediments, his estate was much impaired by the loss of a great part of his patrimony in the

---
* B.C. 436.

war with the Lacedaemonians. It is evident that he composed orations for others to use, but delivered only one, that concerning Exchange of Property. Having set up a school, he gave himself much to writing and the study of philosophy, and then he wrote his Panegyrical oration, and others which were used for advice, some of which he delivered himself, and others he gave to others to pronounce for him; aiming thereby to persuade the Greeks to the study and practice of such things as were of most immediate concern to them. But his endeavors in that way proving to no purpose, he gave those things over, and opened a school in Chios first, as some will have it, having for a beginning nine scholars; and when they came to him to pay him for their schooling, he weeping said, "Now I see plainly that I am sold to my scholars." He admitted all into his acquaintance who desired it. He was the first that made a separation between wrangling pleas and political arguments, to which latter he rather addicted himself. He instituted a form of magistracy in Chios, much the same with that at Athens. No schoolmaster ever got so much; so that he maintained a galley at his own charge. He had more than a hundred scholars, and among others Timotheus the son of Conon was one, with whom he visited many cities, and composed the epistles which Timotheus sent to the Athenians; who for his pains gave him a talent out of that which he got at Samos. Theopompus likewise the Chian, Ephorus the Cumaean, Asclepiades who composed arguments for tragedies, and Theodectes of Phaselis, who afterwards wrote tragedies, were all Isocrates's scholars. The last of these had a monument in the way to the shrine of Cyamites, as we go to Eleusis by the Sacred Way, of which now remains only rubbish. There also he set up with his own the statues of other famous poets, of all which only Homer's is to be seen. Leodamas also the Athenian, and Lacritus who gave laws to the Athenians, were both his scholars; and some say, Hyperides and Isaeus too. They add likewise, that Demosthenes also was very desirous to learn of him, and because he could not give the full rate, which was a thousand drachms, he offered him two hundred, the fifth part, if he would teach him but the fifth part of his art proportionable: to whom Isocrates answered, We do not use, Demosthenes, to impart our skill by halves, but as men sell good fish whole, or altogether, so if thou hast a desire to learn, we will teach thee our full art, and not a piece of it. He died in the year when Charondas was chief magistrate,* when, being at Hippocrates's public exercise, he received the news of the slaughter at Chaeronea; for he was the cause of his own death by a four days' fast, which he then made, pronouncing just at his departure the three verses which begin three tragedies of Euripides·

> Danaus, father of the fifty sisters, —
> Pelops, son of Tantalus, in quest of Pisa, —
> Cadmus, in time past, going from Sidon.

He lived ninety-eight years, or, as some say, a hundred, not being able to behold Greece the fourth time brought into slavery. The year (or, as some say, four years) before he died, he wrote his Panathenaic oration. He labored upon his Panegyric oration ten years, or, as some tell us, fifteen, which he is supposed to have borrowed out of Gorgias the Leontine and Lysias. His oration concerning Exchange of Property he wrote when he was eighty-two years old, and those to Philip a little before his death. When he was old, he adopted Aphareus, the youngest of the three sons of Plathane, the daughter of Hippias the orator. He was very rich, both in respect of the great sums of money he exacted of his scholars, and besides that, having at one time twenty talents of Nicocles, king of Cyprus, for an oration which he dedicated to him. By

---

* B.C. 338.

reason of his riches he became obnoxious to the envy of others, and was three times named to maintain a galley; which he evaded twice by the assistance of his son and a counterfeit sickness, but the third time he undertook it, though the charge proved very great. A father telling him that he had allowed his son no other companion than one slave, Isocrates replied, Go thy way then, for one slave thou shalt have two. He strove for the prize which Artemisia dedicated to the honor and memory of her husband Mausolus; but that oration is lost. He wrote also another oration in praise of Helen, and one called Areopagiticus. Some say that he died when he had fasted nine days, — some again, at four days' end, — and his death took its date from the funeral solemnities of those that lost their lives at Chaeronea. His son Aphareus likewise wrote several orations.

He lies buried with all his family near Cynosarges, on the left hand of the hill. There are interred Isocrates and his father Theodorus, his mother and her sister Anaco, his adoptive son Aphareus, Socrates the son of Anaco, Theodorus his brother, bearing his father's name, his grandsons, the sons of his adopted Aphareus, and his wife Plathane, the mother of Aphareus. On these tombs were erected six tables, which are now demolished. And upon the tomb of Isocrates himself was placed a column thirty cubits high, and on that a mermaid of seven cubits, which was an emblem of his eloquence; there is nothing now extant. There was also near it a table, having poets and his schoolmasters on it; and among the rest, Gorgias inspecting a celestial globe, and Isocrates standing by him. There is likewise a statue of his of bronze in Eleusis, dedicated by Timothy the son of Conon, before the entry of the porch, with this inscription:

> To the fame and honor of Isocrates,
> This statue's sacred to the Goddesses;
> The gift of Timothy.

This statue was made by Leochares. There are threescore orations which bear his name; of which, if we credit Dionysius, only five and twenty are genuine; but according to Caecilius, twenty-eight; and the rest are accounted spurious. He was an utter stranger to ostentation, insomuch that, when there came at one time three persons to hear him declaim, he admitted but two of them, desiring the third to come the next day, for that two at once were to him as a full theatre. He used to tell his scholars that he taught his art for ten minas; but he would give any man ten thousand, that could teach him to be bold and give him a good utterance. And being once asked how he, who was not very eloquent himself, could make others so, he answered, Just as a whetstone cannot cut, yet it will sharpen knives for that purpose. Some say that he wrote institutions to the art of oratory; others are of opinion that he had no method of teaching, but only exercise. He would never ask any thing of a free-born citizen. He used to enjoin his scholars being present at public assemblies to repeat to him what was there delivered. He conceived no little sorrow for the death of Socrates, insomuch that the next day he put himself in mourning. Being asked what was the use and force of rhetoric, he answered, To make great matters small, and small great. At a feast with Nicoceon, the tyrant of Cyprus, being desired by some of the company to declaim upon some theme, he made answer, that that was not a season for him to speak what he knew, and he knew nothing that was then seasonable. Happening once to see Sophocles the tragedian amorously eying a comely boy, he said to him, It will become thee, Sophocles, to restrain not only thy hands, but thine eyes. When Ephorus of Cumae left his school before he had arrived at any good proficiency, his father Demophilus sent him again with a second sum of money in his hand; at which Isocrates jocosely called him Diphorus, that is, *twice bringing* his fee. However, he took a great deal of pains and care with him, and went so far as to put him in the way of writing history.

He was wantonly given; and used to lie upon a . . mat for his bed, and his bolster was commonly made moist with saffron. He never married while he was young; but in his old age he kept a miss, whose name was Lagisce, and by her he had a daughter, who died in the twelfth year of her age, before she was married. He afterwards married Plathane, the wife of Hippias the rhetorician, who had three sons, the youngest of which, Aphareus by name, he adopted for his own, as we said before. This Aphareus erected a bronze statue to him near the temple of Jupiter, as may be seen from the inscription:

> In veneration of the mighty Jove,
> His noble parents, and the Gods above,
> Aphareus this statue here has set,
> The statue of Isocrates his father.

He is said to have run a race on a swift horse, when he was but a boy; for he is to be seen in this posture in the Citadel, in the tennis court of the priestesses of Minerva, in a statue. There were but two suits commenced against him in his whole life. One whereof was with Megaclides, who provoked him to exchange of property; at the trial of which he could not be personally present, by reason of sickness; but sending Aphareus, he nevertheless overcame. The other suit was commenced against him by Lysimachus, who would have him come to an exchange or be at the charge of maintaining a galley for the commonwealth. In this case he was overthrown, and forced to perform the service. There was likewise a painting of him in the Pompeum.

Aphareus also wrote a few orations, both judicial and deliberative; as also tragedies to the number of thirty-seven, of which two are contested. He began to make his works public in the year of Lysistratus, and continued it to the year of Sosigenes, that is, eight and twenty years.* In these years he exhibited dramas six times at the city Dionysiac festivals, and twice went away with the prize through the actor Dionysius; he also gained two other victories at the Lenaean festival through other actors.

There were to be seen in the Citadel the statues of the mother of Isocrates, of Theodorus, and of Anaco his mother's sister. That of the mother is placed just by the image of Health, the inscription being changed; that of Anaco is no longer there. [Anaco] had two sons, Alexander by Coenes, and Lysicles by Lysias.

V. ISAEUS.

ISAEUS was born in Chalcis. When he came to Athens, he read Lysias's works, whom he imitated so well, both in his style and in his skill in managing causes, that he who was not very well acquainted with their manner of writing could not tell which of the two was author of many of their orations. He flourished after the Peloponnesian war, as we may conjecture from his orations, and was in repute till the reign of Philip. He taught Demosthenes — not at his school, but privately — who gave him ten thousand drachms, by which business he became very famous. Some say that he composed orations for Demosthenes, which he pronounced in opposition to his guardians. He left behind him sixty-four orations, of which fifty are his own; as likewise some peculiar institutions of rhetoric. He was the first that used to speak or write figuratively, and that addicted himself to civil matters; which Demosthenes chiefly followed. Theopompus the comedian makes mention of him in his Theseus.

* B.C. 869–842.

VI. AESCHINES.

He was the son of Atrometus — who, being banished by the Thirty Tyrants, was thereby a means of reducing the commonwealth to the government of the people — and of his wife Glaucothea; by birth a Cothocidian. He was neither nobly born nor rich; but in his youth, being strong and well set, he addicted himself to all sorts of bodily exercises; and afterwards, having a very clear voice, he took to playing of tragedies, and if we may credit Demosthenes, he was a petty clerk, and also served Aristodemus as a player of third parts at the Bacchanalian festivals, in his times of leisure rehearsing the ancient tragedies. When he was but a boy, he was assisting to his father in teaching little children their letters, and when he was grown up, he listed himself a private soldier. Some think he was brought up under Socrates and Plato; but Caecilius will have it that Leodamas was his master. Being concerned in the affairs of the commonwealth, he openly acted in opposition to Demosthenes and his faction; and was employed in several embassies, and especially in one to Philip, to treat about articles of peace. For which Demosthenes accused him for being the cause of the overthrow and ruin of the Phocians, and the inflamer of war; which part he would have him thought to have acted when the Amphictyons chose him one of their deputies to the Amphissians who were building up the harbor [of Crissa]. On which the Amphictyons put themselves under Philip's protection, who, being assisted by Aeschines, took the affair in hand, and soon conquered all Phocis.* But Aeschines, notwithstanding all that Demosthenes could do, being favored by Eubulus the son of Spintharus, a Probalisian, who plead-

---

* The Greek text is corrupt; but it is evident that the author confounds the Phocian war, which ended in 346 B.C., with the Amphissian war of 339 B.C. The next sentence shows the same mistake. (G.)

ed in his behalf, carried his cause by thirty voices, and so was cleared. Though some tell us, that there were orations prepared by the orators, but the news of the conquest of Chaeronea put a stop to the present proceedings, and so the suit fell.

Some time after this, Philip being dead, and his son Alexander marching into Asia, Aeschines impeached Ctesiphon for acting against the laws, in passing a decree in favor of Demosthenes. But he having not the fifth part of the voices of the judges on his side, was forced to go in exile to Rhodes, because he would not pay his mulct of a thousand drachms. Others say, that he incurred disfranchisement also, because he would not depart the city, and that he went to Alexander at Ephesus. But upon the death of Alexander, when a tumult had been excited, he went to Rhodes, and there opened a school and taught. And on a time pronouncing the oration which he had formerly made against Ctesiphon, to pleasure the Rhodians, he did it with that grace, that they wondered how he could fail of carrying his cause if he pleaded so well for himself. But ye would not wonder, said he, that I was overthrown, if ye had heard Demosthenes pleading against me. He left a school behind him at Rhodes, which was afterwards called the Rhodian school. Thence he sailed to Samos, and there in a short time died. He had a very good voice, as both Demosthenes and Demochares testified of him.

Four orations bear his name, one of which was against Timarchus, another concerning false embassage, and a third against Ctesiphon, which three are really his own; but the fourth, called Deliaca, is none of his; for though he was named to plead the cause of the temple at Delos, yet Demosthenes tells us that Hyperides was chosen in his stead.* He says himself, that he had two brothers,

* See Demosthenes on the Crown, p. 271, 27.

Aphobetus and Philochares. He was the first that brought the Athenians the news of the victory obtained at Tamynae, for which he was crowned for the second time. Some report that Aeschines was never any man's scholar, but having passed his time chiefly in courts of justice, he raised himself from the office of clerk to that of orator. His first public appearance was in a speech against Philip; with which the people being pleased, he was immediately chosen to go ambassador to the Arcadians; and being come thither, he excited the Ten Thousand against Philip. He indicted Timarchus for profligacy; who, fearing the issue, deserted his cause and hanged himself, as Demosthenes somewhere informs us. Being employed with Ctesiphon and Demosthenes in an embassage to Philip to treat of peace, he appeared the most accomplished of the three. Another time also he was one of ten men sent in embassage to conclude a peace; and being afterwards called to answer for it, he was acquitted, as we said.

VII. LYCURGUS.

Lycurgus was the son of Lycophron, and grandson of that Lycurgus whom the Thirty Tyrants put to death, by the procurement of Aristodemus the Batesian, who, also being treasurer of the Greeks, was banished in the time of the popular government. He was a Butadian by birth, and of the line or family of the Eteobutades. He received his first institutions of philosophy from Plato the philosopher. But afterward entering himself a scholar to Isocrates the orator, he employed his study about affairs of the commonwealth. And to his care was committed the disposal and management of the city stock, and so he executed the office of treasurer-general for the space of twelve years; in which time there went through his hands fourteen thousand talents, or (as some will have it) eighteen thousand six hundred and fifty. It was the orator Stratocles that procured him this preferment. At first he was chosen in his own name; but afterwards he nominated one of his friends to the office, while he himself performed the duties; for there was a law just passed, that no man should be chosen treasurer for above the term of four years. But Lycurgus plied his business closely, both summer and winter, in the administration of public affairs. And being entrusted to make provision of all necessaries for the wars, he reformed many abuses that were crept into the commonwealth. He built four hundred galleys for the use of the public, and prepared and fitted a place for public exercises in Lyceum, and planted trees before it; he likewise built a wrestling-court, and being made surveyor of the theatre of Bacchus, he finished this building. He was likewise of so great repute among all sorts, that he was entrusted with two hundred and fifty talents of private citizens. He adorned and beautified the city with gold and silver vessels of state, and golden images of victory. He likewise finished many things that were as yet imperfect, as the dockyards and the arsenal. He built a wall also about the spacious Panathenaic race-course, and made level a piece of uneven ground, given by one Dinias to Lycurgus for the use of the city. The keeping of the city was committed wholly to his care, and power to apprehend malefactors, of whom he cleared the city utterly; so that some sophisters were wont to say, that Lycurgus did not dip his pen in ink, but in blood. And therefore it was, that when Alexander demanded him of the people, they would not deliver him up. When Philip made the second war upon the Athenians, he was employed with Demosthenes and Polyeuctus in an embassy to Peloponnesus and other cities. He was always in great repute and esteem with the Athenians, and looked upon as a man of that justice and integrity, that in the courts of judicature his good word was at all times prevalent on the behalf of those persons for whom he undertook to speak. He was the author of several laws; one of which was, that there should be certain comedies played at the Chytrian solemnities, and whoever of the poets or players should come off victor, he should thereby be invested with the freedom of the city, which before was not lawful; and so he revived a solemnity which for want of encouragement had for some time before been out of request. Another of his laws was, that the city should erect statues to the memory of Aeschylus, Sophocles, and Euripides; and that their tragedies, being fairly engrossed, should be preserved in the public consistory, and that the public clerks should read these copies as the plays were acted, that nothing might be changed by the players; and that otherwise it should be unlawful to act them. A third law proposed by him was, that no Athenian, nor any person inhabiting in Athens, should be permitted to buy a captive, who was once free, to be a slave, without the consent of his former master. Further, that in the Piraeus there should be at least three circular dances played to Neptune; and that to the victor in the first should be given not less than ten minas; in the second, eight; in the third, six. Also, that no woman should go to Eleusis in a coach, lest the poor should appear more despicable than the rich, and so be dejected and cast down; and that whoever should ride in a coach contrary to this law should be fined six thousand drachms. And when even his own wife was taken in the violation of it, he paid to the discoverers of it a whole talent; for which being afterwards called in question by the people: See therefore, said he, I am called to answer for giving, and not for receiving money.

As he was walking one day in the streets, he saw an officer lay hand on Xenocrates the philosopher; and when nothing would serve his turn but the philosopher must to prison, because he had not deposited the tribute due from strangers, he with his staff struck the officer on the head for his unmannerly roughness toward a person of that character, and freeing Xenocrates, cast the other into prison in his stead. And not many days after, Xenocrates meeting with the children of Lycurgus said: I have returned thanks unto your father right speedily, my good children, for his friendship towards me, for I hear his kindness commended by all people where I go. He made likewise several decrees, in which he made use of the help of an Olynthian named Euclides, one very expert in such matters. Though he was rich enough, yet he was used to wear the same coat every day, both summer and winter; but he wore shoes only when he was compelled to do it. Because he was not ready to speak extempore, he used to practise and study day and night. And to the end he might not at any time oversleep himself and so lose time from his study, he used to cover himself on his bed only with a sheepskin with the wool on, and to lay a hard bolster under his head. When one reproached him for being in fee with rhetoricians when he studied his orations, he answered, that, if a man would promise to restore his sons better, he would give him not only a thousand drachms, but half what he was worth. He took the liberty of speaking boldly upon all occasions, by reason of his greatness; as when once the Athenians interrupted him in his speaking, he cried out, O thou Corcyraean whip, how many talents art thou worth? And another time, when some would rank Alexander among the Gods, What manner of God, said he, must he be, when all that go out of his temple had need to be dipped in water to purify themselves?

After his death Menesaechmus accusing and indicting them by virtue of an instrument drawn by Thracycles, his sons were delivered to the eleven executioners of Justice. But Demosthenes, being in exile, wrote to the Athenians, to let them know that they were wrongfully accused, and that therefore they did not well to hear their accusers; upon which they recanted what they had done, and set them at liberty again,—Democles, who was Theophrastus's scholar, likewise pleading in their defence. Lycurgus and some of his posterity were buried publicly, at or near the temple of Minerva Paeonia, where their monuments stand in the garden of Melanthius the philosopher, on which are inscriptions to Lycurgus and his children, which are yet extant. The greatest thing he did while he lived was his raising the revenue of the commons totally from sixty talents, as he found it, to twelve hundred. When he found he must die, he was by his own appointment carried into the temple of the Mother of the Gods, and into the senate-house, being willing before his death to give an account of his administration. And no man daring to accuse him of any thing except Menesaechmus, having purged himself from those calumnies which he cast upon him, he was carried home again, where in a short time he ended his life. He was always accounted honest; his orations were commended for the eloquence they carried in them; and though he was often accused, yet he never was overthrown in any suit.

He had three children by Callisto, the daughter of Abron, and sister of Callias, Abron's son, by descent a Batesian,—I mean, of him who, when Chaerondas was magistrate, was paymaster to the army. Of this affinity Dinarchus speaks in his oration against Pastius. He left behind him three sons, Abron, Lycurgus, and Lycophron; of which, Abron and Lycurgus died without issue, though the first, Abron, did for some time act very acceptably and worthily in affairs of the commonwealth. Lycophron marrying Callistomacha, the daughter of Philip of Aexone, begat Callisto, who married Cleombrotus the son of Dinocrates the Acharnian, to whom she bare Lycophron, who, being adopted by his grandfather, died without issue. He being dead, Socrates married Callisto, of whom he had his son Symmachus. To him was born Aristonymus; to Aristonymus, Charmides, who was the father of Philippe. Of her and Lysander came Medeius, who also was an interpreter, one of the Eumolpids. He begat two children of Timothea, the daughter of Glaucus, viz. Laodamia and Medius, who were priests of Neptune Erechtheus; also Philippe a daughter, who was afterward priestess of Minerva; for before, she was married to Diocles of Melite, to whom she bare a son named Diocles, who was a colonel of a regiment of foot. He married Hediste, the daughter of Abron, and of her begat Philippides and Nicostrata, whom Themistocles the torch-bearer, son of Theophrastus, married, and by her had Theophrastus and Diocles; and he likewise constituted the priesthood of Neptune Erechtheus.

It is said that he penned fifteen orations. He was often crowned by the people, and had statues dedicated to him. His image in brass was set up in Ceramicus by order of the public, in the year of Anaxicrates; in whose time also it was ordered that he and his eldest son should be provided for with diet in the Prytaneum; but he being dead, Lycophron his eldest son was forced to sue for that donation. This Lycurgus also was used frequently to plead on the account of sacred things; and accused Autolycus the Areopagite, Lysicles the general, Demades' the son of Demeas, Menesaechmus, and many others, all whom he caused to be condemned as guilty. Diphilus also was called in question by him, for impairing and diminishing the props of the metal mines, and unjustly making himself rich therefrom; and he caused him to be condemned to die, according to the provision made by the laws in that case.

He gave out of his own stock fifty drachms to every citizen, the sum total of which donation amounted to one hundred and sixty talents;* but some say he gave a mina of silver to each. He likewise accused Aristogiton, Leocrates, and Autolycus for cowardice. He was called the Ibis: ...

The ibis to Lycurgus, to Chaerephon the bat.†

His ancestors derived their pedigree from Erechtheus, the son of the Earth and of Vulcan; but he was nearest to Lycomedes and Lycurgus, whom the people honored with public solemnities. There is a succession of those of the race who were priests of Neptune, in a complete table placed in the Erechtheum, painted by Ismenias the Chalcidian; in the same place stood wooden images of Lycurgus, and of his sons, Abron, Lycurgus, and Lycophron; made by Timarchus and Cephisodotus, the sons of Praxiteles. His son Abron dedicated the table; and coming to the priesthood by right of succession, he resigned to his brother Lycophron, and hence he is painted as giving a trident. But Lycurgus had made a draught of all his actions, and hung it on a column before the wrestling-court built by himself, that all might read that would; and no man could accuse him of any peculation. He likewise proposed to the people to crown Neoptolemus, the son of Anticles, and to dedicate statues to him, because he had promised and undertaken to cover the altar of Apollo in the market with gold, according to the order of the oracle. He decreed honors likewise to Diotimus, the son of Diopithes of Euonymus, in the year when Ctesicles was magistrate.

---

* This is one of the statements which seem to fix the number of Athenian citizens in the age of the Orators at about 20,000. See Boeckh's Public Economy of the Athenians, I. Book 1, chap. 7. (G.)

† Aristoph. Birds, 1296.

VIII. DEMOSTHENES.

Demosthenes, the son of Demosthenes by Cleobule, the daughter of Gylon, was a Paeanian by descent. He was left an orphan by his father, when he was but seven years old, together with a sister of the age of five. Being kept by his mother during his nonage, he went to school to Isocrates, say some; but the generality are of opinion that he was pupil to Isaeus the Chalcidian, who lived in Athens and was Isocrates's scholar. He imitated Thucydides and Plato, and some affirm that he more especially attended the school of Plato. Hegesias the Magnesian writes, that he entreated his master's leave to go to hear Callistratus the son of Empaedus, an Amphidnean, a noble orator, and sometime commander of a troop of horse, who had dedicated an altar to Mercury Agoraeos, and was to make an oration to the people. And when he heard him, he became a lover of oratory, and so long as he continued at Athens, remained his disciple.

But Callistratus being soon banished to Thrace, and Demosthenes arrived at some years of maturity, he joined with Isocrates and Plato. After this, he took Isaeus into his house, and for the space of four years labored very hard in imitation of his orations. Though Ctesibius in his book of philosophy affirms that, by the help of Callias the Syracusan, he got the orations of Zoilus the Amphipolite, and by the assistance of Charicles the Carystian those also of Alcidamas, and devoted himself to the imitation of them. When he came to age, in the year of Timocrates[*] he called his tutors and guardians to account for their maladministration, in not allowing him what was fitting and requisite out of his estate. And these tutors or guardians were three, Aphobus, Therippides, and Demophon (or Demeas), the last of whom, being his uncle, he

[*] B.C. 364.

charged more severely than the other two. He arrested each of them in an action of ten talents, and cast them, but did not exact of them what the law had given him, releasing some for money and others for favor.

When Aristophon, by reason of his age, could not hold the office any longer, he was chosen choregus, or overseer of the dances. During the execution of which office, Midias the Anagyrasian striking him as he was ordering the dances in the theatre, he sued him upon it, but let fall his suit upon Midias's paying him three thousand drachms.

It is reported of him that, while he was a youth, he confined himself to a den or cave, and there studied his orations, and shaved half of his head that he might not be allured to divert himself from it; and that he lay upon a very narrow bed, that he might awake and rise the sooner. And for that he could not very well pronounce the letter R, he accustomed himself very much to that, that he might master it if possible; and using likewise an unseemly motion of his shoulder when he spake at any time, he remedied that by a spit (or, as some say, a sword) stuck in the ceiling just over his shoulder, that the fear of being pricked with it might break him of that indecent gesture. They report of him further that, when he could declaim pretty well, he had a sort of mirror made as big as himself, and used always in declaiming to look in that, to the end that he might see and correct what was amiss. He used likewise at some certain times to go down to the Phalerian shore, to the end that, being accustomed to the surges and noise of the waves, he might not be daunted by the clamors of the people, when he should at any time declaim in public. And being naturally short-winded, he gave Neoptolemus a player ten thousand drachms to teach him to pronounce long sentences in one breath.

Afterwards, betaking himself to the affairs of the commonwealth, and finding the people divided into two different factions, one in favor of Philip, and the other standing for the liberty and properties of the people, he took part with them that opposed Philip, and always persuaded the citizens to help those who were in danger and trouble by Philip's oppression; taking for his companions in council Hyperides, Nausicles, Polyeuctus, and Diotimus; and then he drew the Thebans, Euboeans, Corcyraeans, Corinthians, Bocotians, and many more into a league with the Athenians. Being in the assembly one day and his memory failing him, his oration was hissed; which made him return home very heavy and melancholy; and being met by Eunomus the Thriasian, an old man, by him he was comforted and encouraged. But he was chiefly animated by Andronicus the player, who told him that his orations were excellent, but that he wanted something of action, thereupon rehearsing certain places out of his oration which he had delivered in that same assembly. Unto which Demosthenes gave good ear and credit, and he then betook himself to Andronicus. And therefore, when he was afterwards asked what was the first part of oratory, he answered, "Action;" and which was the second, he replied, "Action;" and which was the third, he still answered, "Action." Another time, declaiming publicly, and using expressions too youthful for one of his years and gravity, he was laughed at, and ridiculed by the comedians, Antiphanes and Timocles, who in derision used to repeat such phrases as these, as uttered by him:

<blockquote>By the earth, by the fountains, by the rivers, by the floods!</blockquote>

For having sworn thus in presence of the people, he raised a tumult about him. He likewise used to swear by Asclepius, and accented the second syllable ('Ασκλήπιος)* through some mistake, and yet afterwards defended it; for

---

* This name was properly pronounced with the accent on the last syllable,'Ασκληπιός. (G.)

this Asclepius, he said, was called ἤπιος, that is a *mild* God. This also often caused him to be interrupted. But all these things he reformed in time, being sometime conversant with Eubulides, the Milesian philosopher. Being on a time present at the Olympic games, and hearing Lamachus the Myrrhinaean sound the praises of Philip and of Alexander the Great, his son, and decry the cowardice of the Thebans and Olynthians, he stood up in their defence against him, and from the ancient poets he proclaimed the great and noble achievements of the Thebans and Olynthians; and so elegantly he behaved himself in this affair, that he at once silenced Lamachus, and made him convey himself immediately out of the assembly. And even Philip himself, when he had heard what harangues he made against him, replied, that if he had heard him, he should have chosen him general in the war against himself. He was used to compare Demosthenes's orations to soldiers, for the force they carried along with them; but the orations of Isocrates to fencers, because of the theatrical delight that accompanied them.

Being about the age of seven and thirty, reckoning from Dexitheus to Callimachus,* — in whose time the Olynthians sent to beg aid of the Athenians against Philip, who then made war upon them, — he persuaded them to answer the Olynthians' request; but in the following year, in which Plato died,† Philip overthrew and destroyed the Olynthians. Xenophon also, the scholar of Socrates, had some knowledge of Demosthenes, either at his first rise, or at least when he was most famous and flourishing; for he wrote the Acts of the Greeks, as touching what passed at the battle of Mantinea, in the year of Chariclides; ‡ our Demosthenes having sometime before overthrown his guardians in a suit he had commenced against them, in the year of Timocrates. When Aeschines, being condemned,

* B. C. 385–384 to 349–348.   † B.C. 348–347.   ‡ B. C. 363–362.

fled from Athens, Demosthenes hearing of it took horse and rode after him; which Aeschines understanding, and fearing to be apprehended again, he came out to meet Demosthenes, and fell at his feet, covered his face, and begged his mercy; upon which Demosthenes bid him stand up, be assured of his favor, and as a pledge of it, gave him a talent of silver. He advised the people to maintain a company of mercenary soldiers in Thasos, and thither sailed himself as captain of the galleys. Another time, being entrusted to buy corn, he was accused of defrauding the city, but cleared himself of the accusation and was acquitted. When Philip had seized upon Elatea, Demosthenes with others went to the war of Chaeronea, where he is said to have deserted his colors; and flying away, a bramble caught hold of his vest behind, when turning about in haste, thinking an enemy had overtaken him, he cried out, Save my life, and say what shall be my ransom. On his buckler he had engraven for his motto, To Good Fortune. And it was he that made the oration at the funerals of such as died in that battle.

After these things, he bent his whole care and study for the reparation of the city and wall; and being chosen commissary for repairing the walls, besides what money he expended out the city stock, he laid out of his own at least a hundred minas. And besides this, he gave ten thousand drachms to the festival fund; and taking ship, he sailed from coast to coast to collect money of the allies; for which he was often by Demotelus, Aristonicus, and Hyperides crowned with golden crowns, and afterwards by Ctesiphon. Which last decree had like to have been retracted, Diodotus and Aeschines endeavoring to prove it to be contrary to the laws; but he defended himself so well against their allegations, that he overcame all difficulties, his enemies not having the fifth part of the votes of the judges.

After this, when Alexander the Great made his expedition into Asia, and Harpalus fled to Athens with a great sum of money, at first he would not let him be entertained, but afterwards, Harpalus being landed and having given him a thousand darics he was of another mind; and when the Athenians determined to deliver Harpalus up to Antipater, he opposed it, proposing to deposit the money in the Citadel, still without declaring the amount to the people. Thereupon Harpalus declared that he had brought with him from Asia seven hundred talents, and that this sum had been deposited in the Citadel; but only three hundred and fifty or a little more could be found, as Philochorus relates. But when Harpalus broke out of the prison wherein he was kept till some person should come from Alexander, and was escaped into Crete, — or, as some will have it, into Taenarum in Laconia, — Demosthenes was accused that he had received from him a sum of money, and that therefore he had not given a true account of the sum delivered to him, nor had impeached the negligence of the keepers. So he was judicially cited by Hyperides, Pytheus, Menesaechmus, Himeraeus, and Patrocles, who prosecuted him so severely as to cause him to be condemned in the court of Areopagus; and being condemned, he went into exile, not being able to pay fivefold; for he was accused of receiving thirty talents. Others say, that he would not run the risk of a trial, but went into banishment before the day came. After this tempest was over, when the Athenians sent Polyeuctus to the republic of Arcadia to draw them off from the alliance with the Macedonians, he not succeeding, Demosthenes appeared to second him, where he reasoned so effectually that he easily prevailed. Which procured him so much credit and esteem, that after some time a galley was dispatched to call him home again. And the Athenians decreed that, whereas he owed the state thirty talents, as a fine laid on him for the misdemeanor he was accused of, he should be excused for only building an altar to Jupiter Servator in the Piraeus; which decree was first proposed by Demon his near kinsman. This being agreed on, he returned to the administration of affairs in the commonwealth again.

But when Antipater was blocked up in Lamia, and the Athenians offered sacrifices for the happy news, he happened, being talking with Agesistratus, one of his intimate friends, to say, that his judgment concerning the state of affairs did not jump with other men's, for that he knew the Greeks were brisk and ready enough to run a short course but not to hold on a long race. When Antipater had taken Pharsalus, and threatened to besiege Athens itself if they refused to deliver up such orators as had declaimed against him, Demosthenes, suspecting himself to be one of the number, left the city, and fled first into Aegina, that he might take sanctuary in the temple of Aeacus; but being afraid to trust himself long there, he went over to Calauria; and when the Athenians had decreed to deliver up those orators, and him especially as one of them, he continued a suppliant in the temple of Neptune. When Archias came thither, — who, from his office of pursuing fugitives, was called Phygadotheres and was the scholar of Anaximines the orator, — when he, I say, came to him, and persuaded him to go with him, telling him that no doubt he should be received by Antipater as a friend, he replied: When you played a part in a tragedy, you could not persuade me to believe you the person you represented; no more shall you now persuade me by your counsel. And when Archias endeavored to force him thence, the townsmen would not suffer it. And Demosthenes told them, that he did not flee to Calauria to save his life, but that he might convince the Macedonians of their violence committed even against the Gods themselves. And with that he called for a writing-table; and if we may credit Demetrius the Maguesian, on that he wrote a distich, which afterwards the Athenians caused to be affixed to his statue ; and it was to this purpose :

> Hadst thou, Demosthenes, an outward force
> Great as thy inward magnanimity,
> Greece should not wear the Macedonian yoke.

This statue, made by Polyeuctus, is placed near the cloister where the altar of the twelve Gods is erected. Some say this writing was found: " Demosthenes to Antipater, Greeting." Philochorus tells us that he died by drinking of poison ; and Satyrus the historiographer will have it, that the pen was poisoned with which he wrote his epistle, and putting it into his mouth, soon after he tasted it he died. Eratosthenes is of another opinion, that being in continual fear of the Macedonians, he wore a poisoned bracelet on his arms. Others say again, that he died with holding his breath ; and others, lastly, say that he carried strong poison in his signet. He lived to the age of seventy, according to those who give the highest number, — of sixty-seven, according to other statements. And he was in public life two and twenty years.

When King Philip was dead, he appeared publicly in a glorious robe or mantle, as rejoicing for his death, though he but just before mourned for his daughter. He assisted the Thebans likewise against Alexander, and animated all the other Greeks. So that when Alexander had conquered Thebes, he demanded Demosthenes of the Athenians, threatening them if they refused to deliver him. When he went against Persia, demanding ships of the Athenians, Demosthenes opposed it, saying, who can assure us that he will not use those ships we should send him against ourselves?

He left behind him two sons by one wife, the daughter of one Heliodorus, a principal citizen. He had but one daughter, who died unmarried, being but a child. A sister too he had, who married with Laches of Leuconoe, his kinsman, and to him bore Demochares, who proved inferior to none in his time for eloquence, conduct, and courage. His statue is still standing in the Prytaneum, the first on the right as you approach the altar, clothed with a mantle and girt with a sword, because in this habit he delivered an oration to the people, when Antipater demanded of them their orators.

Afterwards, in process of time, the Athenians decreed nourishment to be given to the kindred of Demosthenes in the Prytaneum, and likewise set up a statue to his memory, when he was dead, in the market, in the year of Gorgias,* which honors were paid him at the request of Demochares his sister's son. And ten years after, Laches, the son of Demochares of Leuconoe, in the year of Pytharatus, required the same honor for himself, that his statue should be set up in the market, and that both he and the eldest of his line for the future should have their allowance in the Prytaneum, and the highest room at all public shows. These decrees concerning both of them are engrossed, and to be found among the statute laws. The statue of Demochares, of which we have spoken before, was afterwards removed out of the market into the Prytaneum.

There are extant sixty-five orations which are truly his. Some report of him, that he lived a very dissolute and vicious life, appearing often in women's apparel, and being frequently conversant at masks and revellings, whence he was surnamed Batalus; though others say, that this was a pet name given him by his nurse, and that from this he was called Batalus in derision. Diogenes the Cynic espying him one day in a victualling-house, he was very much ashamed, and to shun him, went to withdraw; but Diogenes called after him, and told him, The more you shrink inward, the more you will be in the tavern. The same Diogenes once upon the banter said of him, that in his

* B.C 280.

orations he was a Scythian, but in war a delicate nice citizen. He was one of them who received gold of Ephialtes, one of the popular orators, who, being sent in an embassy to the king of Persia, took money privily, and distributed it among the orators of Athens, that they might use their utmost endeavors to kindle and inflame the war against Philip; and it is said of Demosthenes, that he for his part had at once three thousand darics of the king. He apprehended one Anaxilas of Oreus, who had been his friend, and caused him to be tortured for a spy; and when he would confess nothing, he procured a decree that he should be delivered to the eleven executioners.

When once at a meeting of the Athenians they would not suffer him to speak, he told them he had but a short story to tell them. Upon which all being silent, thus he began: A certain youth, said he, hired an ass in summer time, to go from hence to Megara. About noon, when the sun was very hot, and both he that hired the ass and the owner were desirous of sitting in the shade of the ass, they each thrust the other away, — the owner arguing that he let him only his ass and not the shadow, and the other replying that, since he had hired the ass, all that belonged to him was at his dispose. Having said thus, he seemed to go his way. But the Athenians willing now to hear his story out, called him back, and desired him to proceed. To whom he replied: How comes it to pass that ye are so desirous of hearing a story of the shadow of an ass, and refuse to give ear to matters of greater moment? Polus the player boasting to him that he had gotten a whole talent by playing but two days, he answered, and I have gotten five talents by being silent but one day. One day his voice failing him when he was declaiming publicly, being hissed, he cried out to the people, saying, Ye are to judge of players, indeed, by their voice, but of orators by the gravity of their sentences.

Epicles upbraiding him for his premeditating what he was to say, he replied, I should be ashamed to speak what comes uppermost to so great an assembly. They say of him that he never put out his lamp — that is, never ceased polishing his orations — until he was fifty years old. He says of himself, that he drank always fair water. Lysias the orator was acquainted with him; and Isocrates knew him concerned in the management of public affairs till the battle of Chaeronea; as also some of the Socratical sect. [He delivered most of his orations extempore, Nature having well qualified him for it.]* The first that proposed the crowning him with a coronet of gold was Aristonicus, the son of Nicophanes, the Anagyrasian; though Diondas interposed with an indictment.

IX. HYPERIDES.

HYPERIDES was son of Glaucippus, and grandson of Dionysius, of the borough of Colyttus. He had a son, who bare the same name with his father Glaucippus, an orator, who wrote many orations, and begat a son named Alphinous. At the same time with Lycurgus, he had been a scholar of the philosopher Plato and of the orator Isocrates. In Athens his concern in the commonwealth was at that time when Alexander accosted Greece, whom he vigorously opposed in his demands made of the Athenians for the generals as well as for galleys. He advised the people not to discharge the garrison of Taenarum, and this he did for the sake of a friend of his, Chares, who was commander of it. At first he used to plead causes for a fee. He was suspected to have received part of the money which Ephialtes brought out of Persia, and was chosen to maintain a galley, and was sent to assist the Byzantines,

---

* This is supposed to have been added by some other hand, because a contrary sentence is given of him before.

when Philip was besieging their city. Nevertheless, in the same year he took the charge of defraying the expense of the solemn dances, whereas the rest of the captains were exempt from all such public burdens for that year. He obtained a decree for some honors to be paid to Demosthenes; and when that decree was indicted at the instance of Diondas, as being contrary to the laws, he, being called in question upon it, cleared himself. He did not continue his friendship with Demosthenes, Lysicles, and Lycurgus to the last; for, Lysicles and Lycurgus being dead, and Demosthenes being accused of having received money of Harpalus, he, among all the rest, was pitched upon, as the only person who was not corrupted with bribery, to draw up his indictment, which he accordingly did. Being once accused at the instance of Aristogiton of publishing acts contrary to the laws after the battle of Chaeronea, — that all foreign inhabitants of Athens should be accounted citizens, that slaves should be made free, that all sacred things, children, and women should be confined to the Piraeus, — he cleared himself of all and was acquitted. And being blamed by some, who wondered how he could be ignorant of the many laws that were directly repugnant to those decrees, he answered, that the arms of the Macedonians darkened his sight, and it was not he but the battle of Chaeronea that made that decree. But Philip, being affrighted at somewhat, gave leave to carry away their dead out of the field, which before he had denied to the heralds from Lebadea.

After this, at the overthrow at Crannon, being demanded by Antipater, and the people being resolved to deliver him up, he fled out of the city with others who were under the same condemnation to Aegina; where meeting with Demosthenes, he excused himself for the breach of friendship between them. Going from thence, he was apprehended by Archias, surnamed Phygadotheres, by country a

Thurian, formerly a player, but at that time in the service of Antipater; by this man, I say, he was apprehended, even in the very temple of Neptune, though he grasped the image of that God in his arms. He was brought before Antipater, who was then at Corinth; where being put upon the rack, he bit out his tongue, because he would not divulge the secrets of his country, and so died, on the ninth day of October. Hermippus tells us that, as he went into Macedonia, his tongue was cut out and his body cast forth unburied; but Alphinous his cousin-german (or, according to the opinion of others, his grandson, by his son Glaucippus) obtained leave, by means of one Philopithes a physician, to take up his body, which he burnt, and carried the ashes to Athens to his kinsfolk there, contrary to the edicts both of the Athenians and Macedonians, which not only banished them, but likewise forbade the burial of them anywhere in their own country. Others say, that he was carried to Cleonae with others, and there died, having his tongue cut out, as above; however, his relations and friends took his bones, when his body was burned, and buried them among his ancestors before the gate Hippades, as Heliodorus gives us the relation in his Third Book of Monuments. His monument is now altogether unknown and lost, being thrown down with age and long standing.

He is said to have excelled all others in his way of delivering himself in his orations to the people. And there are some who prefer him even to Demosthenes himself. There are seventy-seven orations which bear his name, of which only two and fifty are genuine and truly his. He was much given to venery, insomuch that he turned his son out of doors, to entertain that famous courtesan Myrrhina. In Piraeus he had another, whose name was Aristagora; and at Eleusis, where part of his estate lay, he kept another, one Philte a Theban, whom he ransomed for twenty minas. His usual walk was in the fish-market.

It is thought that he was accused of impiety with one Phryne, a courtesan likewise, and so was sought after to be apprehended, as he himself seems to intimate in the beginning of an oration; and it is said, that when sentence was just ready to be passed upon her, he produced her in court, opened her clothes before, and discovered her naked breasts, which were so very white, that for her beauty's sake the judges acquitted her. He at leisure times drew up several declamations against Demosthenes, which were thus discovered: Hyperides being sick, Demosthenes came one day to visit him, and caught him with a book in his hand written against him; at which seeming somewhat displeased, Hyperides told him: This book shall hurt no man that is my friend; but as a curb, it may serve to restrain my enemy from offering me any injury. He obtained a decree of some honors to be paid to Iolas, who gave the poisoned cup to Alexander. He joined with Leosthenes in the Lamian war, and made an admirable oration at the funerals of those who lost their lives therein.

When Philip was prepared to embark for Euboea, and the Athenians heard the news of it with no little consternation, Hyperides in a very short time, by the voluntary contributions of the citizens, fitted out forty sail, and was the first that set an example, by sending out two galleys, one for himself and another for his son, at his own charge.

When there was a controversy between the Delians and the Athenians, who should have the pre-eminence in the temple at Delos; Aeschines being chosen on the behalf of the Athenians for their advocate, the Areopagites refused to ratify the choice and elected Hyperides; and his oration is yet extant, and bears the name of the Deliac oration.*

He likewise went ambassador to Rhodes; where meet-

---

* See Demosthenes on the Crown, p. 221, 27.

ing other ambassadors from Antipater, who commended their master very highly for his goodness and virtue, We know, replied he, that Antipater is good, but we have no need of a good master at present.

It is said of him, that he never affected much action in his orations to the people, his chief aim being to lay down the matter plainly, and make the case as obvious to the judges as he could.

He was sent likewise to the Eleans, to plead the cause of Callippus the fencer, who was accused of carrying away the prize at the public games unfairly; in which cause he got the better. But when he opposed the sentence of paying honors to Phocion, obtained by Midias the son of Midias the Anagyrasian, he was in that cause overthrown. This cause was pleaded on the twenty-fourth day of May, in the year when Xenius was magistrate.

X. DINARCHUS.

DINARCHUS, the son of Socrates or Sostratus, — born, as some think, at Athens, but according to others, at Corinth, — came to Athens very young, and there took up his dwelling, at that time when Alexander made his expedition into Asia. He used to hear Theophrastus, who succeeded Aristotle in his school. He was frequently conversant with Demetrius the Phalerian too. He betook himself more especially to the affairs of the commonwealth after the death of Antipater, when some of the orators were killed and others banished. Having contracted friendship with Cassander, he became in a short time vastly rich, by exacting great rates for his orations of those for whom he wrote them. He opposed himself to the greatest and most noble orators of his time, not by being overforward to declaim publicly, — for his faculty did not lie that way, — but by composing orations for their adversaries. And when Harpalus had broken out of prison, he wrote several orations, which he gave to their accusers to pronounce against those that were suspected to have taken bribes of him.

Some time after, being accused of a conspiracy with Antipater and Cassander about the matter of Munychia, when it was surprised by Antigonus and Demetrius, who put a garrison into it, in the year of Anaxicrates,* he turned the greatest part of his estate into money, and fled to Chalcis, where he lived in exile about fifteen years, and increased his stock; but afterwards, by the mediation of Theophrastus, he and some other banished persons returned to Athens. Then he took up his abode in the house of one Proxenus, his intimate friend; where, being very aged and withal dim-sighted, he lost his gold. And because Proxenus refused to make inquiry after the thief, he apprehended him; and this was the first time that ever he appeared in court. That oration against Proxenus is extant; and there are sixty-four that bear his name, whereof some are believed to be Aristogiton's. He imitated Hyperides; or, as some incline to judge, rather Demosthenes, because of that vigor and force to move the affections, and the rhetorical ornaments that are evident in his style.

DECREES PROPOSED TO THE ATHENIANS.

I.

Demochares, the son of Laches of Leuconoe, requires that a statue of brass be set up for Demosthenes, the son of Demosthenes the Paeanian, in the market-place, as

* b.c. 307.

likewise that provision of diet be made in the Prytaneum for himself and the eldest of his progeny successively, and the chief seat in all public shows; for that he had done many good offices for the Athenians, had on most occasions been a good counsellor, and had spent his patrimony in the commonwealth ; had expended eight talents for the fitting out and maintenance of one galley, when they delivered Euboea, another, when Cephisodorus sailed into the Hellespont, and a third, when Chares and Phocion were commissioned by the people to go captains to Byzantium; that he at his own charge had redeemed many who had been taken prisoners by Philip at Pydna, Methone, and Olynthus; that himself had maintained a choir of men, when no provision had been made therefor through the neglect of the tribe Pandionis; that he had furnished many indigent citizens with arms; that being chosen by the people to oversee the city works, he had laid out three talents of his own stock towards the repairing of the walls, besides all that he gave for making two trenches about the Piraeus; that after the battle of Chaeronea he deposited one talent for the use of the public, and after that, another to buy corn in time of scarcity and want; that by his beneficence, wholesome counsels and effectual persuasions, he allured the Thebans, Euboeans, Corinthians, Megarians, Achaeans, Locrians, Byzantines, and Messenians to a league with the Athenians; that he raised an army of ten thousand foot and a thousand horse, and contracted plenty to the people and their allies; that being ambassador, he had persuaded the allies to the contribution of above five hundred talents; that in the same quality, by his influence and the free gift of money, he obtained of the Peloponnesians that they should not send aid to Alexander against the Thebans ; and in consideration of many other good offices performed by him, either as to his counsels, or his personal administra-

tion of affairs in the commonwealth, in which, and in
defending the rights and liberties of the people, no man in
his time had done more or deserved better; and in regard
of his sufferings when the commonwealth was ruined,
being banished by the insolence of the oligarchy, and at
last dying at Calauria for his good-will to the public, there
being soldiers sent from Antipater to apprehend him; and
that notwithstanding his being in the hands of his enemies,
in so great and imminent danger, his hearty affection to his
countrymen was still the same, insomuch that he never to
the last offered any unworthy thing to the injury of his
people.

II.

In the magistracy of Pytharatus,* Laches, the son of
Demochares of Leuconoe requires of the Athenian senate
that a statue of brass be set up for Demochares, the son
of Laches of Leuconoe, in the market-place, and table and
diet in the Prytaneum for himself and the eldest of his
progeny successively, and the first seat at all public shows;
for that he had always been a benefactor and good counsellor to the people, and had done these and the like good
offices to the public: he had gone in embassies in his own
person; had proposed and carried in bills relating to his
embassage; had been chief manager of public matters;
had repaired the walls, prepared arms and machines;
had fortified the city in the time of the four years' war, and
composed a peace, truce, and alliance with the Boeotians;
for which things he was banished by those who overturned
and usurped the government; — and being called home
again by a decree of the people, in the year of Diocles,
he had contracted the administration, sparing the public
funds; and going in embassage to Lysimachus, he had at

* B.C. 269.

one time gained thirty, and at another time a hundred talents of silver, for the use of the public; he had moved the people to send an embassage to Ptolemy, by which means the people got fifty talents; he went ambassador to Antipater, and by that got twenty talents, and brought it to Eleusis to the people, — all which measures he persuaded the people to adopt while he himself carried them out; furthermore, he was banished for his love for the commonwealth, and would never take part with usurpers against the popular government; neither did he, after the overthrow of that government, bear any public office in the state; he was the only man, of all that had to do in the public administration of affairs in his time, who never promoted or consented to any other form of government but the popular; by his prudence and conduct, all the judgments and decrees, the laws, courts, and all things else belonging to the Athenians, were preserved safe and inviolate; and, in a word, he never said or did any thing to the prejudice of the popular government.

III.

LYCOPHRON, the son of Lycurgus of Butadae, requires that he may have diet in the Prytaneum, according to a donation of the people to Lycurgus. In the year of Anaxicrates,* in the sixth prytany, — which was that of the tribe Antiochis, — Stratocles, the son of Euthydemus of Diomea, proposed; that, — since Lycurgus, the son of Lycophron of Butadae, had (as it were) an ingenerated good-will in him towards the people of Athens; and since his ancestors Diomedes and Lycurgus lived in honor and esteem of all people, and when they died were honored for their virtue so far as to be buried at the

* B.C. 307.

public charge in the Ceramicus; and since Lycurgus himself, while he had the management of public affairs, was the author of many good and wholesome laws, and was the city treasurer for twelve years together, during which time there passed through his own hands eighteen thousand and nine hundred talents, besides other great sums of money that he was entrusted with by private citizens for the public good, to the sum of six hundred and fifty talents; in all which concerns he behaved himself so justly, that he was often crowned by the city for his fidelity; besides, being chosen by the people to that purpose, he brought much money into the Citadel, and provided ornaments, golden images of victory, and vessels of gold and silver for the Goddess Minerva, and gold ornaments for a hundred Canephoroe;* since, being commissary-general, he brought into the stores a great number of arms and at least fifty thousand shot of darts, and set out four hundred galleys, some new built, and others only repaired; since, finding many buildings half finished, as the dock-yards, the arsenal, and the theatre of Bacchus, he completed them; and finished the Panathenaic race, and the court for public exercises at the Lyceum, and adorned the city with many fair new buildings; since, when Alexander, having conquered Asia, and assuming the empire of all Greece, demanded Lycurgus as the principal man that confronted and opposed him in his affairs, the people refused to deliver him up, notwithstanding the terror inspired by Alexander; and since, being often called to account for his management of affairs in so free a city, which was wholly governed by the people, he never was found faulty or corrupt in any particular; — that all people, therefore, may know, not only that the people do highly esteem all such as act in defence of their liberties and rights while they live, but likewise that they pay them

---

* Persons who carried baskets, or panniers, on their heads, of sacred things.

honors after death, in the name of Good Fortune it is decreed by the people, that such honors be paid to Lycurgus, the son of Lycophron of Butadae, for his justice and magnanimity, as that a statue of brass be erected in memory of him in any part of the market which the laws do not prohibit; as likewise that there be provision for diet in the Prytaneum for every eldest son of his progeny, successively for ever. Also, that all his decrees be ratified, and engrossed by the public notary, and engraven on pillars of stone, and set up in the Citadel just by the gifts consecrated to Minerva; and that the city treasurer shall deposit fifty drachms for the engraving of them, out of the money set apart for such uses.

WHETHER AN AGED MAN OUGHT TO MEDDLE IN STATE AFFAIRS.

---

1. WE are not ignorant, O Euphanes, that you, being an extoller of Pindar, have often in your mouth this saying of his, as a thing well and to the purpose spoken by him:

> When as the combat's once agreed,
> Who by pretence seeks to be freed
> Obscures his virtue quite.

But since sloth and effeminacy towards civil affairs, having many pretences, do for the last, as if it were drawn from the sacred line, tender to us old age, and thinking by this chiefly to abate and cool our honorable desire, allege that there is a certain decent dissolution, not only of the athletical, but also of the political period, or that there is in the revolution of our years a certain set and limited time, after which it is no more proper for us to employ ourselves in the conduct of the state than in the corporeal and robust exercises of youth; I esteem myself obliged to communicate also to you those sentiments of mine concerning old men's intermeddling with public matters, which I am ever and anon ruminating on by myself; so that neither of us may desert that long course we have to this day held together, nor rejecting the political life, which has been (as it were) an intimate friend of our own years, change it for another to which we are absolute strangers, and with which we have not time to become acquainted and familiar, but that we may persist in what we had chosen and have been inured to from the beginning, putting the same conclusion to our life and our living honorably; unless we would, by the short space of life we have remaining, disgrace that longer time we have already lived, as having been spent idly and in nothing that is commendable. For tyranny is not an honorable sepulchre, as one told Dionysius, whose monarchy, obtained by and administered with injustice, did by its long continuance bring on him but a more perfect calamity; as Diogenes afterwards let his son know, when, seeing him at Corinth, of a tyrant become a private person, he said to him: "How unworthy of thyself, Dionysius, thou actest! For thou oughtest not to live here at liberty and fearless with us, but to spend thy life, as thy father did, even to old age, immured within a tyrannical fortress." But the popular and legal government of a man accustomed to show himself no less profitable in obeying than in commanding is an honorable monument, which really adds to death the glory accruing from life. For this thing, as Simonides says, "goes last under the ground;" unless it be in those in whom humanity and the love of honor die first, and whose zeal for goodness sooner decays than their covetousness after temporal necessaries; as if the soul had its active and divine parts weaker than those that are passive and corporeal; which it were neither honest to say, nor yet to admit from those who affirm that only of gaining we are never weary. But we ought to turn to a better purpose the saying of Thucydides, and believe that it is not the desire of honor only that never grows old,[*] but much more also the inclinations to society and affection to the state, which continue even in ants and bees to the very last. For never did any one know a bee to become by age a drone, as some think it requisite of statesmen, of whom they expect that, when the vigor of their youth is past, they should retire and sit mouldy at home, suffering their active virtue to be consumed by idle-

---

[*] Thuc. II. 44.

ness, as iron is by rust. For Cato excellently well said, that we ought not willingly to add the shame proceeding from vice to those many afflictions which old age has of its own. For of the many vices everywhere abounding, there is none which more disgraces an old man than sloth, delicacy, and effeminateness, when, retiring from the court and council, he mews himself up at home like a woman, or getting into the country oversees his reapers and gleaners; for of such a one we may say,

Where's Oedipus, and all his famous riddles ?

But as for him who should in his old age, and not before, begin to meddle with public matters, — as they say of Epimenides, that having fallen asleep while he was a young man, he awakened fifty years after, — and shaking off so long and so close-sticking a repose, should thrust himself, being unaccustomed and unexercised, into difficult and laborious employs, without having been experienced in civil affairs, or inured to the conversations of men, such a man may perhaps give occasion to one that would reprehend him, to say with the prophetess Pythia:

Thou com'st too late,

seeking to govern in the state and rule the people, and at an unfit hour knocking at the palace gate, like an ill-bred guest coming late to a banquet, or a stranger, thou wouldst change, not thy place or region, but thy life for one of which thou hast made no trial. For that saying of Simonides,

The state instructs a man,

is true in those who apply themselves to the business of the commonweal whilst they have yet time to be taught, and to learn a science which is scarce attained with much labor through many strugglings and negotiations, even when it timely meets with a nature that can easily undergo toil and difficulty. These things seem not to be impertinently spoken against him who in his old age begins to act in the management of the state.

2. And yet, on the contrary, we see how young men and those of unripe years are by persons of judgment diverted from meddling in public matters; and the laws also testify the same, when by the crier in the assemblies they summon not first the men like Alcibiades and Pytheas to come to the desk, but those who have passed the age of fifty years, to make speeches and consult together for the good of the people. For the being unused to boldness and the want of experience are not so much to every soldier. . . .

[Here is a defect in the original.]

But Cato, when above eighty years of age he was to plead his own cause, said, that it was a difficult thing for a man to make his apology and justify his life before others than those with whom he had lived and been conversant.

All men indeed confess, that the actions of Augustus Caesar, when he had defeated Antony, were no less royal and useful to the public towards the end of his life, than any he had done before. And himself severely reprehending the dissoluteness of young men by establishing good customs and laws, when they raised an uproar, he only said to them: Young men, refuse not to hear an old man, to whom old men not unwillingly gave ear when he was young. The government also of Pericles exerted itself with most vigor in his old age, when he both persuaded the Athenians to make war, and at another time, when they were eagerly bent unseasonably to go forth and fight sixty thousand armed men withstood and hindered them, sealing up in a manner the arms of the people and the keys of the gates. Now as for what Xenophon has written of Agesilaus, it is fit it should be set down in his own words. "What youth," says he, " was ever so gallant but that his old age surpassed it? Who was ever so terrible to his enemies in the very flower of his virility, as Agesilaus in the declension of his days? At whose death were adversaries ever seen more joyful than at that of Agesilaus, though he departed not this life till he was stooping under the burden of his years? Who more emboldened his confederates than Agesilaus, though being at the utmost period of his life? What young man was ever missed more by his friends than Agesilaus, who died not till he was very old?"

3. Age then hindered not these men from performing such gallant actions; and yet we, forsooth, being at our ease in states which have neither tyranny, war, nor siege to molest them, are afraid of such bloodless debates and emulations, as are for the most part terminated with justice only by law and words; confessing ourselves by this not only worse than those ancient generals and statesmen, but even than poets, sophisters, and players. Since Simonides in his old age gained the victory by his choral songs, as the epigram testifies in these concluding verses:

> Fourscore years old was Leoprepes' son,
> Simonides, when he this glory won.

And it is said of Sophocles, that, to avoid being condemned of dotage at the instance of his children, he repeated the entrance song of the Chorus in his tragedy of Oedipus in Colonus, which begins thus:

> Welcome, stranger, come in time
> To the best place of this clime,
> White Colonus, which abounds
> With brave horses. In these grounds,
> Spread with Nature's choicest green,
> Philomel is often seen.
> Here she her hearers charms with sweetest lays,
> Whilst with shrill throat
> And warbling note
> She moans the sad misfortunes of her former days:*

and that, this song appearing admirable, he was dismissed

---

* Soph. Oed. Colon. 668.

from the court, as from the theatre, with the applause and acclamations of all that were present. And this short verse is acknowledged to be written of him:

> When Sophocles framed for Herodotus
> This ode, his years were fifty-five.

Philemon also the comedian and Alexis were snatched away by death, whilst they were acting on the stage and crowned with garlands. And as for Polus the tragedian, Eratosthenes and Philochorus related of him that, being seventy years of age, he a little before his death acted in four days eight tragedies.

4. Is it not then a shame, that those who have grown old in councils and courts of judicature should appear less generous than such as have spent their years on the stage, and forsaking those exercises which are really sacred, cast off the person of the statesman, to put on instead of it I know not what other? For to descend from the state of a prince to that of a ploughman is all over base and mean. For since Demosthenes says that the Paralus, being a sacred galley, was unworthily used in being employed to carry timber, pales, and cattle to Midias; would not a man who should, after his having quitted the office of superintendent at the public solemnities, governor of Boeotia, or president in the council of the Amphictyons, be seen measuring of corn, weighing of raisins, and bargaining about fleeces and wool-fells, — would not such a one, I say, wholly seem to have brought on himself, as the proverb has it, the old age of a horse, without any one's necessitating him to it? For to set one's self to mechanical employments and trafficking, after one has borne office in the state, is the same as if one should strip a well-bred virtuous gentlewoman out of her matron-like attire, and thrust her with an apron tied about her into a public victualling-house. For the dignity and greatness of political virtue is overthrown, when it is debased to such mean

administrations and traffics for gain. But if (which is the only thing remaining) they shall, by giving effeminacies and voluptuousness the name of living at quiet and enjoying one's self, exhort a statesman leisurely to waste away and grow old in them, I know not to which of the two shameful pictures his life will seem to have the greater resemblance, — whether to the mariners who, leaving their ship for the future not in the harbor but under sail, spend all their time in celebrating the feasts of Venus; or to Hercules, whom some painters merrily but yet ridiculously represent wearing in Omphale's palace a yellow petticoat, and giving himself up to be boxed and combed by the Lydian damsels. So shall we, stripping a statesman of his lion's-skin, and seating him at a luxurious table, there be always cloying his palate with delicacies, and filling his ears with effeminate songs and music; being not a whit put to the blush by the saying of Pompey the Great to Lucullus, who after his public services both in camp and council, addicted himself to bathing, feasting, conversing with women in the day, and much other dissoluteness, even to the raising and extravagantly furnishing of sumptuous buildings, and who, once upbraiding Pompey with an ambition and desire of rule unsuitable to his age, was by him answered, that it was more misbecoming an old man to live voluptuously than to govern? The same Pompey, when in his sickness his physican had prescribed him the eating of a thrush, which was then hard to be got, as being out of season, being told that Lucullus bred great store of such birds, would not send to him for one, but said: What! Cannot Pompey live, unless Lucullus be luxurious?

5. For though Nature seeks by all means to delight and rejoice herself, yet the bodies of old men are incapacitated for all pleasures, except a few that are absolutely necessary. For not only

> Venus to old men is averse,*

as Euripides has it; but their appetite also to their meat and drink is for the most part dull, and as one would say, toothless; so that they have but little gust and relish in them.

They ought therefore to furnish themselves with pleasures of the mind, not ungenerous or illiberal, like those of Simonides, who said to those who reproached him with covetousness, that being by his years deprived of other pleasures, he recreated his old age with the only delight which remained, that of heaping up riches. But political life has in it pleasures exceeding great, and no less honorable, being such as it is probable the very Gods do only or at least chiefly enjoy themselves in; and these are the delights which proceed from doing good and performing what is honest and laudable. For if Nicias the painter took such pleasure in the work of his hands, that he often was fain to ask his servants whether he had washed or dined; and if Archimedes was so intent upon the table in which he drew his geometrical figures, that his attendants were obliged by force to pluck him from it and strip him of his clothes that they might anoint him, whilst he in the mean time drew new schemes on his anointed body; and if Canus the piper, whom you also know, was wont to say that men knew not how much more he delighted himself with his playing than he did others, for that then his hearers would rather demand of him than give him a reward; do we not thence conceive how great pleasures the virtues afford to those who practise them, from their honest actions and public-spirited works tending to the benefit of human society? They do not tickle or weaken, as do such sweet and gentle motions as are made on the flesh; for these indeed have a furious and unconstant itching, mixed with a feverish inflammation; whereas those which accom-

* Eurip. Aeolus, Frag. 23.

pany such gallant actions as he who rightly administers the state is worker of, not like the golden plumes of Euripides, but like those celestial wings of Plato, elevate the soul which has received a greatness of courage and wisdom accompanied with joy.

6. Call to mind a little, I entreat you, those things you have so often heard. For Epaminondas indeed, being asked what was the most pleasant thing that ever befell him, answered, his having gained the victory at Leuctra whilst his father and mother were yet living. And Sylla, when, having freed Italy from civil wars, he came to Rome, could not the first night fetch the least wink of sleep, having his soul transported with excessive joy and content, as with a strong and mighty wind; and this he himself has written in his Commentaries. For be it indeed so, as Xenophon says, that there is no sound more pleasing than one's own praises; yet there is no sight, remembrance, or consideration which gives a man so much satisfaction as the contemplation of his own actions, performed by him in offices of magistracy, and management of the state, in eminent and public places.

It is moreover true, that the courteous thanks attending as a witness on such virtuous acts, and the emulous praise conferred on them, which is as a guide conducting us in the way of just benevolence, add a certain lustre and shining gloss to the joy of virtue. Neither ought a man negligently to suffer his glory to wither in his old age, like a wrestler's garland; but, by adding always something new and fresh, he should awaken, meliorate, and confirm the grace of his former actions. For as those workmen on whom was incumbent the charge of keeping in repair the Delian ship, by supplying and putting into the place of the decayed planks and timber others that were new and sound, seem to have preserved it from ancient times, as if it were eternal and incorruptible; so the preserving and upholding of one's glory is as the keeping in of a fire, a work of no difficulty, as requiring only to be supplied with a little fuel, but when either of them is wholly extinct and suppressed, one cannot without great labor rekindle it again. Lampis, the sea commander, being asked how he got his wealth, answered: "My greatest estate I gained easily enough, but the smaller slowly and with much labor." In like manner, it is not easy at the beginning to acquire reputation and power in the state; but to augment and conserve it, when it is grown great, is not at all hard for those who have obtained it. For neither does a friend, when he is once had, require many and great services that he may so continue, but assiduity does by small signs preserve his good-will; nor do the friendship and confidence of the people expect to have a man always bestowing largesses, defending their causes, or executing of magistracy, but they are maintained by a readiness, and by not failing or being weary of carefulness and solicitude for the public. For even wars themselves have not alway conflicts, fights, and sieges; but there sometimes intervene sacrifices and parleys, and abundance of leisure for sports and pastimes. Whence then comes it, that the administration of the commonwealth should be feared as inconsolable, laborious, and unsupportable, where theatres, processions, largesses, music, joy, and at every turn the service and festival of some God or other, unbending the brows of every council and senate, yield a manifold pleasure and delight?

7. As for envy, which is the greatest evil attending the management of public affairs, it least attacks old age. For dogs indeed, as Heraclitus has it, bark at a stranger whom they do not know; and envy opposes him who is a beginner on the very steps of the tribune, hindering his access, but she meekly bears an accustomed and familiar glory, and not churlishly or difficultly. Wherefore some resemble envy to smoke; for it arises thick at first, when the fire

begins to burn; but when the flame grows clear, it vanishes away. Now men usually quarrel and contend about other excellences, as virtue, nobility, and honor, as if they were of opinion that they took from themselves as much as they give to others; but the precedency of time, which is properly called by the Greeks Πρεσβεῖον (or the honor of old age), is free from jealousy, and willingly granted by men to their companions. For to no honor is it so incident to grace the honorer more than the honored, as to that which is given to persons in years. Moreover, all men do not expect to gain themselves authority from wealth, eloquence, or wisdom; but as for the reverence and glory to which old age brings men, there is not any one of those who act in the management of the state but hopes to attain it.

He therefore who, having a long time contended against envy, shall when it ceases and is appeased withdraw himself from the state, and together with public actions desert communities and societies, differs nothing from that pilot who, having kept his ship out at sea when in danger of being overwhelmed by contrary and tempestuous waves and winds, seeks to put into harbor as soon as ever the weather is grown calm and favorable. For the longer time there has been, the more friends and companions he has made; all which he cannot carry out with him, as a singing-master does his choir, nor is it just to leave them. But as it is not easy to root up old trees, so neither is it to extirpate a long-continued practice in the management of the state, which having many roots is involved in a tangled mass of affairs, which create more troubles and vexations to those who retire from them than to those who continue in them. And if there is any remainder of envy and emulation against old men from former contentions about civil affairs, they should rather extinguish it by authority, than turn their backs on it and go away naked and disarmed. For envious persons do not so much assail those who contend against them, as they do by contempt insult over such as retire.

8. And to this bears witness that saying of the great Epaminondas to the Thebans, when in the winter the Arcadians requested them to come into their city and dwell in their houses, — which he would not permit, but said to them: Now the Arcadians admire you, seeing you exercise yourselves, and wrestle in your armor; but if they shall behold you sitting by the fire and pounding of beans, they will think you to differ nothing from themselves. So an old man speaking to the people, acting in the state, and honored, is a venerable spectacle; but he who wastes away his days in his bed, or sits discoursing of trivial matters and wiping his nose in the corner of a gallery, easily renders himself an object of contempt. And this indeed Homer himself teaches those who hear him aright. For Nestor, who fought before Troy, was highly venerated and esteemed; whilst Peleus and Laertes, who stayed at home, were slighted and despised. For the habit of prudence does not continue the same in those who give themselves to their ease; but by little and little diminishes and is dissolved by sloth, as always requiring some exercise of the thought to rouse up and purify the rational, active faculty of the soul. For,

Like glittering brass, by being used it shines.*

For the infirmity of the body does not so much incommode the administrations of those who, almost spent with age, go to the tribune or to the council of war, as they are advantageous by the caution and prudence which attend their years, and keep them from thrusting themselves precipitately into affairs, abused partly by want of experience and partly by vain-glory, and hurrying the people along with them by violence, like a sea agitated by the winds;

* Sophocles, Frag. 779.

causing them mildly and moderately to manage those with whom they have to do.

Whence cities, when they are in adversity and fear, desire the government of grave and ancient personages; and often having drawn out of his field some old man who had not so much as the least thought of it, have compelled him, though unwilling, to put his hand to the helm, and conduct the ship of the state into the haven of security, rejecting generals and orators, who not only knew how to speak loud and make long harangues without drawing their breath, but were able also valiantly to march forth and fight their enemies. So when the orators one day at Athens, before Timotheus and Iphicrates uncovering Chares the son of Theochares, a vigorous and stout-bodied young man, said they were of opinion that the general of the Athenians ought to be such a one; Not so, by all the Gods, answered Timotheus, but such a one he should be that is to carry the general's bedding; but the general himself ought to be such a one as can at the same time see both forwards and backwards, and will suffer not his reasonings about things convenient to be disturbed by any passion.

Sophocles indeed said, he was glad that he was got free from the tyranny of wanton love, as being a furious and raging master; but in the administrations of state, we are not to avoid this one only master, the love of women or boys, but many who are madder than he, such as obstinacy in contending ambition, and a desire of being always the first and greatest, which is a disease most fruitful in bringing forth envy, jealousy, and conspiracies; some of which vices old age abates and dulls, while it wholly extinguishes and cools the others, not so much detracting from the practical impulse of the mind, as repressing its impetuous and over-hot passions, that it may apply a sober and settled reasoning to its considerations about the management of affairs.

9. Nevertheless let this speech of the poet,

Lie still at ease, poor wretch, in thy own bed,*

both be and seem to be spoken for the dissuading of him who shall, when he is now grown gray with age, begin to play the youth; and for the restraining an old man who, rising from a long administration of his domestic affairs, as from a lingering disease, shall set himself to lead an army to the field, or perform the office of secretary of state.

But altogether senseless, and nothing like to this, is he who will not suffer one that has spent his whole time in political administrations, and been thoroughly beaten to them, to go on to his funeral torch and the conclusion of his life, but shall call him back, and command him (as it were) to turn out of the long road he has been travelling in. He who, to draw off from his design an old fellow who is crowned and is perfuming himself to go a wooing, should say to him, as was heretofore said to Philoctetes,

What virgin will her blooming maidenhead
Bestow on such a wretch? Why would'st thou wed?

would not be at all absurd, since even old men break many such jests upon themselves, and say,

I, old fool, know, I for my neighbors wed;

but he who should think, that a man which has long cohabited and lived irreprehensibly with his wife ought, because he is grown old, to dismiss her and live alone, or take a concubine in her place, would have attained the utmost excess of perverseness. So he would not act altogether unreasonably, that should admonish an old man who is making his first approaches to the people, whether he be such a one as Chlidon the farmer, or Lampon the mariner, or some old dreaming philosopher of the garden, and

---

* Eurip. Orestes, 258.

advise him to continue in his accustomed unconcernedness for the public; but he who, taking hold of Phocion, Cato, or Pericles, should say to him, My Athenian or Roman friend, who art come to thy withered old age, make a divorce, and henceforth quit the state; and dismissing all conversations and cares about either council or camp, retire into the country, there with an old maid-servant looking after thy husbandry, or spending the remainder of thy time in managing thy domestic affairs and taking thy accounts, — would persuade a statesman to do things misbeseeming him and unacceptable.

10. What then! may some one say; do we not hear the soldier in the comedy affirming,

Henceforth my gray hairs exempt me from wars?

Yes indeed, my friend, it is altogether so; for it becomes the servants of Mars to be young and vigorous, as managing

War, and war's toilsome works;*

in which, though an helmet may also hide the old man's gray hairs,

Yet inwardly his limbs are all decayed,†

and his strength falls short of his good-will. But from the ministers of Jupiter, the counsellor, orator, and patron of cities, we expect not the works of feet and hands, but those of counsel, providence, and reason, — not such as raises a noise and shouting amongst the people, but such as has it in understanding, prudent solicitousness, and safety; by which the derided hoariness and wrinkles appear as witnesses of his experience, and add to him the help of persuasion, and the glory of ingenuity. For youth is made to follow and be persuaded, age to guide and direct; and that city is most secure, where the counsels of the old and the prowess of the young bear sway. And this of Homer, ‡

* Il. VIII. 453. † Il. XIX. 165. ‡ Il. II. 53.

> A council first of valiant old men
> He called in Nestor's ship,

is wonderfully commended. Wherefore the Pythian Apollo called the aristocracy or council of noblemen in Lacedaemon, joined as assistants to their kings, Πρεσβυγενεῖς (or the *ancients*), and Lycurgus named it plainly Γέροντες (or the *council of old men*); and even to this day the council of the Romans is called the senate (from *senium*, signifying *old age*). And as the law places the diadem and crown, so does Nature the hoariness of the head, as an honorable sign of princely dignity. And I am of opinion, that γέρας (signifying *an honorable reward*) and γεραίρειν (signifying *to honor*) continue still in use amongst the Greeks, being made venerable from the respect paid to old men, not because they wash in warm water and sleep on softer beds than others, but because they have as it were a king-like esteem in states for their prudence, from which, as from a late-bearing tree, Nature scarcely in old age brings forth its proper and perfect good. Therefore none of those martial and magnanimous Achaeans blamed that king of kings, Agamemnon, for praying thus to the Gods,

> O that among the Greeks I had but ten
> Such counsellors as Nestor; *

but they all granted, that not in policy only, but in war also, old age has great influence;

> For one discreet advice is much more worth
> Than many hands, †

and one rational and persuasive sentence effects the bravest and greatest of public exploits.

11. Moreover, the regal dignity, which is the perfectest and greatest of all political governments, has exceeding many cares, labors, and difficulties; insomuch that Seleucus is reported ever and anon to have said: If men knew how laborious are only the writing and reading of so many

---

* Il. II. 372.   † Eurip. Antiope, Frag. 220.

epistles, they would not so much as stoop to take up a diadem thrown on the ground. And Philip, when, being about to pitch his camp in a fair and commodious place, he was told that there was not there forage for his regiments, cried out: O Hercules, what a life is ours, if we must live for the conveniency of asses! It is then time to persuade a king, when he is now grown into years, to lay aside his diadem and purple, and putting on a coarse coat, with a crook in his hand, to betake himself to a country life, lest he should seem to act superfluously and unseasonably by reigning in his old age. But if the very mentioning such a thing to an Agesilaus, a Numa, or a Darius would be an indignity; let us not, because they are in years, either drive away Solon from the council of the Areopagus, or remove Cato out of the senate; nor yet let us advise Pericles to abandon the democracy. For it is besides altogether unreasonable and absurd, that he who has in his youth leaped into the tribunal should, after he has discharged all his furious ambitions and impetuous passions on the public, when he is come to that maturity of years which by experience brings prudence, desert and abandon the commonwealth, having abused it as if it were a woman.

12. Aesop's fox indeed would not permit the hedge-hog, who offered it, to take from him the ticks that fed upon his body. For, said he, if thou remov'st those that are full, other hungry ones will succeed them. So it is of necessity, that a commonwealth which is always casting off those who grow old must be replenished with young men, thirsting after glory and power, and void of understanding in state affairs. For whence, I pray, should they have it, if they shall have been neither disciples nor spectators of any ancient statesman? For if treatises of navigation cannot make those skilful pilots who have not often in the stern been spectators of the conflicts against the waves, winds, and pitchy darkness of the night,

> When the poor trembling seaman longs to see
> The safety-boding twins, Tyndaridae;

how should a raw young man take in hand the government of a city, and rightly advise both the senate and the people, having only read a book or written an exercise in the Lyceum concerning policy, though he has seldom or never stood by the reins or helm, when grave statesmen and old commanders have in debating alleged both their experiences and fortunes, whilst he was wavering on both sides, that so he might with dangers and transacting of affairs gain instruction? This is not to be said. But if it were for nothing else, yet ought an old man to manage in public affairs, that he may instruct and teach those who are young. For as those who teach children reading and music do, by pronouncing and by singing notes and tunes before them, lead and bring on their scholars; so an old statesman, not by speaking and dictating exteriorly, but by acting and administering public affairs, directs and breeds up a young one, who is by his deeds joined with his words interiorly formed and fashioned. For he who is exercised after this manner, not amongst the disputes of nimble tongued sophisters, as in the wrestling-schools and anointings, where there is not the least appearance of any danger, but really, and as it were in the Olympian and Pythian games, will tread in his teacher's steps,

> Like a young colt, which runs by th' horse's side, —

as Simonides has it. Thus Aristides followed Clisthenes, Cimon Aristides, Phocion Chabrias, Cato Fabius Maximus, Pompey Sylla, and Polybius Philopoemen; for these, when they were young, joining themselves with their elders, and afterwards as it were flourishing and growing up by their administrations and actions, gained experience, and were inured to the management of public affairs with reputation and power.

13 Aeschines therefore the Academic, being charged

by certain sophisters that he pretended himself a disciple of Carneades when he was not so, said: I was then a hearer of Carneades, when his discourse, having dismissed contention and noise by reason of his old age, contracted itself to what was useful and fit to be communicated. Now an aged man's government being not only in words but in deeds far remote from all ostentation and vain-glory, — as they say of the bird ibis, that when she is grown old, having exhaled all her venomous and stinking savor, she sends forth a most sweet and aromatical one, — so in men grown into years, there is no opinion or counsel disturbed, but all grave and settled. Wherefore, even for the young men's sake, as has been said, ought an old man to act in the government of the state; that, (as Plato said of wine allayed with water, that the furious God was made wise, being chastised by another who was sober) so the caution of old age, mixed among the people with the fervency of youth, transported by glory and ambition, may take off that which is furious and over-violent.

14. But besides all this, they are under a mistake who think that, as sailing and going to the wars, so also acting in the state is done for a certain end, and ceases when that is obtained. For the managing of state affairs is not a ministry which has profit for its end; but the life of gentle, civil, and sociable animals, framed by nature to live civilly, honestly, and for the benefit of mankind. Wherefore it is fit he should be such a one as that it may be said of him, he is employed in state affairs, and not he has been so employed; as also, that he is true, and not he has been true; he acts justly, and not he has acted justly; and that he loves his country and fellow-citizens, and not he has loved them. For to these things does Nature direct, and these voices does she sound to those who are not totally corrupted with sloth and effeminacy:

> Thy father has engendered thee a man,
> Worthy of much esteem with men:

and again,

> Let us not cease to benefit mankind.

15. Now as for those who pretend weakness and impotency, they accuse rather sickness and infirmity of body than old age; for there are many young men sickly, and many old ones lusty; so that we are not to remove from the administration of the state aged, but impotent persons; nor call to it such as are young, but such as are able. For Aridaeus was young, and Antigonus old; and yet the latter conquered in a manner all Asia, whereas the former, as if he had only been to make a dumb show with his guards upon a stage, was but the bare name of a king, a puppet always mocked by those who were in power. As therefore he would be a very fool that should think Prodicus the sophister and Philetas the poet — men indeed young, but withal weak, sickly, and almost always confined by their infirmity to their beds — fit to be concerned in the management of the state; so he would be no less absurd that should hinder such vigorous old men as were Phocion, Masinissa the Libyan, and Cato the Roman, from governing or leading forth of armies. For Phocion, when the Athenians were at an unseasonable time hurrying to war, made proclamation that all who were not above sixty years of age should take up arms and follow him; and when they were offended at it, he said, There is no hardship put upon you, for I, who am above fourscore years old, will be your general. And Polybius relates, that Masinissa, dying at the age of ninety years, left behind him a young son of his own begetting, not above four years old; and that, having a little before been in a great fight, he was the next day seen at the door of his tent eating a dirty piece of bread, and that he said to those who wondered at it, that he did this. . . .

> For brass by use and wear its gleam displays,
> But every house untenanted decays;*

as Sophocles has it; we all say the same of that light and lustre of the soul, by which we reason, remember, and think.

16. Wherefore also they say, that kings become better in wars and military expeditions than when they live at ease. Attalus therefore, the brother of Eumenes, being enervated with long idleness and peace, was with little skill managed by Philopoemen, one of his favorites, who fattened him like a hog in the sty; so that the Romans were wont in derision to ask those who came out of Asia, whether the king had any power with Philopoemen. Now one cannot find amongst the Romans many stouter generals than Lucullus, as long as he applied his mind to action; but when he gave himself up to an unactive life, to a continuing lazily at home, and an unconcernedness for the public, being dulled and mortified, like sponges in calm weather, and then delivering his old age to be dieted and ordered by Callisthenes one of his freedmen, he seemed bewitched by him with philters and other incantations; till such time as his brother Marcus, having driven away this fellow, did himself govern and conduct the remainder of his life, which was not very long. But Darius, father of Xerxes, said, that by difficulties he grew wiser than himself. And the Scythian Ateas affirmed, that he thought there was no difference between himself and his horse-keepers, when he was idle. And Dionysius the Elder, when one asked him whether he was at leisure, answered, May that never befall me. For a bow, they say, will break, if over-bent; and a soul, if too much slackened. For even musicians, if they over-long omit to hear accords, geometricians, if they leave off demonstrating their propositions, and arithmeticians, if they discontinue their casting

---

* Sophocles, Frag. 779.

up of accounts, do, together with the actions, impair by their progress in age the habits, though they are not practical but speculative arts; but the habit of statesmen — being wise counsel, discretion, and justice, and besides these, experience which seizes upon the right opportunities and words, the very faculty which works persuasion — is maintained by frequent speaking, acting, reasoning, and judging. And a hard thing it would be, if by avoiding to do these things it should suffer such and so great virtues to run out of the soul. For it is probable also that humanity, friendly society, and beneficence will then also decay, of which there ought to be no end or limit.

17. If then you had Tithonus to your father, who was indeed immortal, but yet by reason of his old age stood perpetually in need of much attendance, I do think you would shun or be weary of looking to him, discoursing with him, and helping him, as having a long time done him service. Now our fatherland (or, as the Cretans call it, our *motherland*), being older and having greater rights than our parents, is indeed long lasting, yet neither free from the inconveniences of old age nor self-sufficient; but standing always in need of a serious regard, succor, and vigilance, she pulls to her and takes hold of a statesman,

And with strong hand restrains him, who would go.*

And you indeed know that I have these many Pythiads served the Pythian Apollo; but yet you would not say to me: Thou hast sufficiently, O Plutarch, sacrificed, gone in procession, and led dances in honor of the Gods; it is now time that, being in years, thou shouldst in favor of thy old age lay aside the garland and leave the oracle. Therefore neither do you think that you, who are the chief priest and interpreter of religious ceremonies in the state, may

* Il. XVI. 9.

leave the service of Jupiter, the protector of cities and governor of assemblies, for the performance of which you were long since consecrated.

18. But leaving, if you please, this discourse about withdrawing old men from performing their duties to the state, let us make it a little the subject of our consideration and philosophy, how we may enjoin them no exercise unfitting or grievous to their years, the administration of a commonwealth having many parts beseeming and suitable for such persons. For as, if we were obliged to persevere in the practice of singing to the end of our days, it would behoove us, being now grown old, of the many tones and tensions there are of the voice, which the musicians call harmonics, not to aim at the highest and shrillest, but to make choice of that in which there is an easiness joined with a decent suitableness; so, since it is more natural for men to act and speak even to the end of their lives, than for swans to sing, we must not reject action, like a harp that is set too high, but rather let it a little down, accommodating it to such employs in the state as are easy, moderate, and fitting for men in years. For neither do we suffer our bodies to be altogether motionless and unexercised because we cannot any longer make use of spades and plummets, nor yet throw quoits or skirmish in armor, as we have formerly done; but some of us do by swinging and walking, others by playing gently at ball, and some again by discoursing, stir up our spirits and revive our natural heat. Therefore neither let us permit ourselves to be wholly chilled and frozen by idleness, nor yet on the contrary let us, by burthening ourselves with every office or intermeddling with every public business, force on old age, convinced of its disability, to break forth into these exclamations:

> The spear to brandish, thou, right hand, art bent;
> But weak old age opposes thy intent.

Since even that man is not commended who, in the vigor and strength of his years, imposing all public affairs in general on himself, and unwilling to leave any thing for another (as the Stoics say of Jupiter), thrusts himself into all employs, and intermeddles in every business, through an insatiable desire of glory, or through envy against those who are in some measure partakers of honor and authority in the state. But to an old man, though you should free him from the infamy, yet painful and miserable would be an ambition always laying wait at every election of magistrates, a curiosity attending for every opportunity of judicature or assembling in counsel, and a humor of vain-glory catching at every embassy and patronage. For the doing of these things, even with the favor and good liking of every one, is too heavy for that age. And yet the contrary to this happens; for they are hated by the young men, as leaving them no occasions of action, nor suffering them to put themselves forth; and their ambitious desire of primacy and rule is no less odious to others than the covetousness and voluptuousness of other old men.

19. Therefore, as Alexander, unwilling to tire his Bucephalus when he now began to grow old, did before the fight ride on other horses, to view his army and draw it up for battle, and then, after the signal was given, mounting this, marched forth and charged the enemy; so a statesman, if he is wise, moderating himself when he finds years coming on, will abstain from intermeddling in unnecessary affairs, and suffering the state to make use of younger persons in smaller matters, will readily exercise himself in such as are of great importance. For champions indeed keep their bodies untouched and unemployed in necessary matters, that they may be in a readiness for unprofitable engagements; but let us on the contrary, letting pass what is little and frivolous, carefully preserve ourselves for worthy and gallant actions. For all things perhaps, as

Homer says, equally become a young man;[*] all men now esteem and love him; so that for undertaking frequently little and many businesses, they say he is laborious and a good commonwealths-man; and for enterprising none but splendid and noble actions, they style him generous and magnanimous; nay, there are also some occurrences when even contention and rashness have a certain seasonableness and grace, becoming such men. But an old man's undertaking in a state such servile employs as the farming out of the customs, and the looking after the havens and market-place, or else his running on embassies and journeys to princes and potentates when there are no necessary or honorable affairs to be treated of, but only compliments and a maintaining of correspondence, — such management, dear friend, seems to me a thing miserable and not to be imitated, but to others, perhaps, odious and intolerable.

20. For it is not even seasonable for such men to be employed in magistracies, unless it be such as bear somewhat of grandeur and dignity; such is the presidency in the council of Areopagus, which you now exercise, and such also, by Jove, is the excellency of the Amphictyonic office, which your country has conferred on you for your life, having an easy labor and pleasant pains. And yet old men ought not ambitiously to affect even these honors, but accept them with refusal, not seeking but being sought; nor as taking government on themselves, but bestowing themselves on government. For it is not, as Tiberius Caesar said, a shame for those that are above threescore years old to reach forth their hands to the physician; but it far more misbeseems them to hold up their hands to the people, to beg their votes or suffrages for the obtaining offices; for this is ungenerous and mean, whereas the contrary has a certain majesty and comeliness, when, his country choosing, inviting, and expecting him, he comes

[*] Il. XXII. 71.

down with honor and courtesy to welcome and receive the present, truly befitting his old age and acceptance.

21. After the same manner also ought he that is grown old to use his speech in assemblies, not ever and anon climbing up to the desk to make harangues, nor always, like a cock, crowing against those that speak, nor letting go the reins of the young men's respect to him by contending against them and provoking them, nor breeding in them a desire and custom of disobedience and unwillingness to hear him; but he should sometimes pass them by, and let them strut and brave it against his opinion, neither being present nor concerning himself much at it, as long as there is no great danger to the public safety nor any offence against what is honest and decent. But in such cases, on the contrary, he ought, though nobody call him, to run beyond his strength, or to deliver himself to be led or carried in a chair, as historians report of Appius Claudius in Rome. For he having understood that the senate, after their army had been in a great fight worsted by Pyrrhus, were debating about receiving proposals of peace and alliance, could not bear it, but, although he had lost both his eyes, caused himself to be carried through the common place straight to the senate house, where entering among them and standing in the midst, he said, that he had formerly indeed been troubled at his being deprived of his sight, but that he now wished he had also lost his ears, rather than to have heard that the Roman senators were consulting and acting things so ungenerous and dishonorable. And then partly reprehending, and partly teaching and exalting them, he persuaded them to betake themselves presently to their arms, and fight with Pyrrhus for the dominion of Italy. And Solon, when the popularity of Pisistratus was discovered to be only a plot for the obtaining of a tyranny, none daring to oppose or impeach it, did himself bring forth his arms, and setting them before

the doors of his house, called out to the people to assist him; and when Pisistratus sent to ask him what gave him the confidence to act in that manner, "My old age," answered he.

22. For matters that are so necessary as these inflame and rouse up old men who are in a manner extinct, so that they have but any breath yet left them; but in other occurrences, an old man, as has been said, should be careful to avoid mean and servile offices, and such in which the trouble to those who manage them exceeds the advantage and profit for which they are done. Sometimes by expecting also till the citizens call and desire and fetch him out of house, he is thought more worthy of credit by those who request him. And even when he is present, let him for the most part silently permit the younger men to speak, as if he were an arbitrator, judging to whom the reward and honor of this their debate about public matters ought to be given; but if any thing should exceed a due mediocrity, let him mildly reprehend it, and with sweetness cut off all obstinate contentions, all injurious and choleric expressions, directing and teaching without reproof him that errs in his opinions, boldly praising him that is in the right, and often willingly suffering himself to be overcome, persuaded, and brought to their side, that he may hearten and encourage them; and sometimes with commendations supplying what has been omitted, not unlike to Nestor, whom Homer makes to speak in this manner:

> There is no Greek can contradict or mend
> What you have said; yet to no perfect end
> Is your speech brought. No wonder, for't appears
> You're young, and may my son be for your years.*

23. And it were yet more civil and politic, not only in reprehending them openly and in the face of the people, to forbear that sharpness of speech which exceedingly

---

* Il. IX. 55.

dashes a young man and puts him out of countenance, but rather, wholly abstaining from all such public reproofs, privately to instruct such as have a good genius for the managing of state affairs, drawing them on by setting gently before them useful counsels and political precepts, inciting them to commendable actions, enlightening their understanding, and showing them, as those do who teach to ride, how at their beginning to render the people tractable and mild, and if any young man chances to fall, not to suffer him to lie gasping and panting on the ground, but to help him up and comfort him, as Aristides dealt by Cimon, and Mnesiphilus by Themistocles; whom they raised up and encouraged, though at first they were harshly received and ill spoken of in the city, as audacious and intemperate. It is said also, that Demosthenes being rejected by the people and taking it to heart, there came to him a certain old man, who had in former years been an hearer of Pericles, and told him, that he naturally resembled that great man, and did unjustly cast down himself. In like manner Euripides exhorted Timotheus, when he was hissed at for introducing of novelty, and thought to transgress against the law of music, to be of good courage, for that he should in a short time have all the theatres subject to him.

24. In brief, as in Rome the Vestal virgins have their time divided into three parts, in one of which they are to learn what belong to the ceremonies of their religion, in the second to execute what they have learned, and in the third to teach the younger; and as in like manner they call every one of those who are consecrated to the service of Diana in Ephesus, first Mell-hiere (one that is to be a priestess), then Hiere (priestess), and thirdly Par-hiere (or one that has been a priestess), so he that is a perfect statesman is at first a learner in the management of public affairs, then a practitioner, and at last a teacher and instructor in

the mysteries of government. For indeed he who is to oversee others that are performing their exercise or fighting for prizes cannot judge at the same exercise and fight himself. Thus he who instructs a young man in public affairs and negotiations of the state, and prepares him

Both to speak well and act heroicly *

for the service of his country, is in no small or mean degree useful to the commonwealth, but in that at which Lycurgus chiefly and principally aimed himself, when he accustomed young men to persist in obedience to every one that was elder, as if he were a lawgiver. For to what, think you, had Lysander respect, when he said that in Lacedaemon men most honorably grew old? Was it because old men could most honorably grow old there enjoying idleness, putting out money to use, sitting together at tables, and after their game taking a cheerful cup? You will not, I believe, say any such thing. But it was because all such men, being after some sort in the place of magistrates, fatherly governors, or tutors of youth, inspected not only the public affairs, but also made inquiry — and that not slightly — into every action of the younger men, both as concerning their exercises, recreations, and diet, being terrible indeed to offenders, but venerable and desirable to the good. For young men indeed always venerate and follow those who increase and cherish the neatness and generosity of their disposition without any envy.

25. For this vice, though beseeming no age, is nevertheless in young men veiled with specious names, being styled emulation, zeal, and desire of honor; but in old men, it is altogether unseasonable, savage, and unmanly. Therefore a statesman that is in years must be very far from being envious, and not act like those old trees and stocks which, as with a certain charm, manifestly with-

* Il. IX. 443.

draw the nutritive juice from such young plants as grow near them or spring up under them, and hinder their growth; but he should kindly admit and even offer himself to those that apply themselves to him and seek to converse with him, directing, leading, and educating them, not only by good instructions and counsels, but also by affording them the means of administering such public affairs as may bring them honor and repute, and executing such unprejudicial commissions as will be pleasing and acceptable to the multitude. But for such things as, being untoward and difficult, do like medicines at first gripe and molest, but afterwards yield honor and profit, — upon these things he ought not to put young men, nor expose those who are inexperienced to the mutinous clamors of the rude and ill-natured multitude, but he should rather take the odium upon himself for such things as (though harsh and unpleasing) may yet prove beneficial to the commonwealth; for this will render the young men both more affectionate to him, and more cheerful in the undertaking other services.

26. But besides all this, we are to keep in mind, that to be a statesman is not only to bear offices, go on embassies, talk loud in public meetings, and thunder on the tribune, speaking and writing such things in which the vulgar think the art of government to consist; as they also think that those only philosophize who dispute from a chair and spend their leisure time in books, while the policy and philosophy which is continually exercised in works and conspicuous in actions is nowise known to them. For they say, as Dicaearchus affirmed, that they who fetch turns to and fro in galleries walk, but not they who go into the country or to visit a friend. But the being a statesman is like the being a philosopher. Wherefore Socrates did philosophize, not only when he neither placed benches nor seated himself in his chair, nor kept the hour of confer-

ence and walking appointed for his disciples, but also when, as it happened, he played, drank, went to war with some, bargained, finally, even when he was imprisoned and drank the poison ; having first shown that man's life does at all times, in every part, and universally in all passions and actions, admit of philosophy. The same also we are to understand of civil government, to wit, that fools do not administer the state, even when they lead forth armies, write dispatches and edicts, or make speeches to the people ; but that they either endeavor to insinuate themselves into the favor of the vulgar and become popular, seek applause by their harangues, raise seditions and disturbances, or at the best perform some service, as compelled by necessity. But he that seeks the public good, loves his country and fellow-citizens, has a serious regard to the welfare of the state, and is a true commonwealthsman, such a one, though he never puts on the military garment or senatorial robe, is yet always employed in the administration of the state, by inciting to action those who are able, guiding and instructing those that want it, assisting and advising those that ask counsel, deterring and reclaiming those that are ill-given, and confirming and encouraging those that are well-minded ; so that it is manifest, he does not for fashion's sake apply himself to the public affairs, nor go then to the theatre or council when there is any haste or when he is sent for by name, that he may have the first place there, being otherwise present only for his recreation, as when he goes to some show or a concert of music ; but on the contrary, though absent in body, yet is he present in mind, and being informed of what is done, approves some things and disapproves others.

27. For neither did Aristides amongst the Athenians, nor Cato amongst the Romans often execute the office of magistrate; and yet both the one and the other employed

their whole lives perpetually in the service of their country. And Epaminondas indeed, being general, performed many and great actions ; but yet there is related an exploit of his, not inferior to any of them, performed about Thessaly when he had neither command in the army nor office in the state. For, when the commanders, having through inadvertency drawn a squadron into a difficult and disadvantageous ground, were in amaze, for that the enemies pressed hard upon them, galling them with their arrows, he, being called up from amongst the heavy-armed foot, first by his encouraging them dissipated the trouble and fright of the army, and then, having ranged and brought into order that squadron whose ranks had been broken, he easily disengaged them out of those straits, and placed them in front against their enemies, who, thereupon changing their resolutions, marched off. Also when Agis, king of Sparta, was leading on his army, already put in good order for fight, against the enemies, a certain old Spartan called out aloud to him, and said, that he thought to cure one evil by another ; meaning that he was desirous the present unseasonable promptness to fight should salve the disgrace of their over-hasty departure from before Argos, as Thucydides says. Now Agis, hearing him, took his advice, and at that present retreated ; but afterwards got the victory. And there was every day a chair set for him before the doors of the government house, and the Ephori, often rising from their consistory and going to him, asked his advice and consulted him about the greatest and most important affairs ; for he was esteemed very prudent, and is recorded to have been a man of great sense. And therefore, having now wholly exhausted the strength of his body, and being for the most part tied to his bed, when the Ephori sent for him to the common hall of the city, he strove to get up and go to them ; but walking heavily and with great difficulty, and meeting by the way certain boys, he asked them whether they knew any thing stronger than the necessity of obeying their master; and they answering him that inability was of greater force, he, supposing that this ought to be the limit of his service, turned back again homewards. For a readiness and good will to serve the public ought not to fail, whilst ability lasts; but when that is once gone, it is no longer to be forced. And indeed Scipio, both in war and peace, always used Caius Laelius for a counsellor; insomuch that some said, Scipio was the actor of those noble exploits, and Caius the poet or author. And Cicero himself confessed, that the honorablest and greatest of his counsels, by the right performance of which he in his consulship preserved his country, were concerted with Publius Nigidius the philosopher.

28. Thus is there nothing that in any manner of government hinders old men from helping the public by the best things, to wit, by their reason, sentences, freedom of speech, and solicitous care, as the poets term it. For not only our hands, feet, and corporeal strength are the possession and share of the commonwealth; but chiefly our soul, and the beauties of our soul, justice, temperance, and prudence; which receiving their perfection late and slowly, it were absurd that men should remain in charge of house and land and other wealth, and yet not be beneficial to their common country and fellow-citizens by reason of their age, which does not so much detract from their ministerial abilities as it adds to their directive and political. And this is the reason why they portrayed the Mercuries of old without hands and feet, but having their natural parts stiff, enigmatically representing that there is no great need of old men's corporeal services, if they have but their reason (as is convenient) active and fruitful.

POLITICAL PRECEPTS.

1. IF ever, O Menemachus, that saying of Nestor's in Homer,

> There is no Greek can contradict or mend
> What you have said, yet to no perfect end
> Is your speech brought,*

might pertinently be made use of and applied, it is against those exhorting, but nothing teaching nor any way instructing, philosophers. For they do (in this respect) resemble those who are indeed careful in snuffing the lamps, but negligent in supplying them with oil. Seeing therefore that you, being by reason moved to engage yourself in the affairs of the state, desire, as becomes the nobility of your family,

> Both to speak and act heroicly †

in the service of your country, and that, not having attained to such maturity of age as to have observed the life of a wise and philosophical man openly spent in the transactions of the state and public debates, and to have been a spectator of worthy examples represented not in word but in deed, you request me to lay you down some political precepts and instructions; I think it no ways becoming me to give you a denial, but heartily wish that the work may be worthy both of your zeal and my forwardness. Now I have, according to your request, made use in this my discourse of sundry and various examples.

---

* Il. IX. 55. † Il. IX. 443.

2. First then for the administration of state affairs, let there be laid, as a firm and solid foundation, an intention and purpose, having for its principles judgment and reason, and not any impulse from vain-glory, emulation, or want of other employment. For as those who have nothing grateful to them at home frequently spend their time in the forum, though they have no occasion that requires it; so some men, because they have no business of their own worth employing themselves in, thrust themselves into public affairs, using policy as a divertisement. Many also, having been by chance engaged in the negotiations of the commonweal, and being cloyed with them, cannot yet easily quit them; in which they suffer the same with those who, going on board a ship that they may be there a little tossed, and being after carried away into the deep, send forth many a long look towards the shore, being sea-sick and giddy-headed, and yet necessitated to stay and accommodate themselves to their present fortune.

> Past is the lovely pleasure
> They took, when th' sea was calm and weather bright,
> In walking at their leisure
> On the ship's deck,
> Whilst her sharp beak
> With merry gale,
> And full blown sail,
> Did through the surging billows cut its course aright.

And these do most of all discredit the matter by their repenting and being discontented, when either hoping for glory they fall into disgrace, or expecting to become formidable to others by their power they are engaged in affairs full of dangers and troubles. But he who on a well grounded principle of reason undertakes to act in the public, as an employ very honorable and most beseeming him, is dismayed by none of these things; nor does he therefore change his opinion. For we must not come to the management of the commonweal on a design of gaining and growing rich by it, as Stratocles and Dromo clides exhorted one another to the golden harvest, — so in mirth terming the tribunal, or place of making harangues to the people, — nor yet as seized with some sudden fit of passion, as did heretofore Caius Gracchus, who having, whilst his brothers' misfortunes were hot, withdrawn himself to a retired life most remote from public affairs, did afterwards, inflamed by indignation at the injuries and affronts put on him by some persons, thrust himself into the state, where being soon filled with affairs and glory, when he sought to desist and desired change and repose, he could not (so great was it grown) find how to lay down his authority, but perished with it. And as for those who through emulation frame themselves for the public as actors for the stage, they must needs repent of their design, finding themselves under a necessity of either serving those whom they think themselves worthy to govern, or disobliging those whom they desire to please. Now I am of opinion, that those who by chance and without foresight stumble upon policy, falling as it were into a pit, connot but be troubled and repent; whereas they that go leisurely into it, with preparation and a good resolution, comfort themselves moderately in all occurrences, as having no other end of their actions but the discharging of their duty with honor.

3. Now they that have thus grounded their choice within themselves, and rendered it immovable and difficult to be changed, must set themselves to contemplate that disposition of the citizens which, being compounded (as it were) of all their natures, appears most prevalent among them. For the endeavoring presently to form the manners and change the nature of a people is neither easy nor safe, but a work requiring much time and great authority. But as wine in the beginning is overcome by the nature of the drinker, but afterwards, gently warming him and mixing itself in his veins, assimilates and changes him who drinks

it into its own likeness, so must a statesman, till he has by his reputation and credit obtained a leading power amongst the people, accommodate himself to the dispositions of the subjects, knowing how to consider and conjecture those things with which the people are naturally delighted and by which they are usually drawn. The Athenians, to wit, are easily moved to anger, and not difficultly changed to mercy, more willing to suspect quickly than to be informed by leisure; and as they are readier to help mean and inconsiderable persons, so do they embrace and esteem facetious and merry speeches; they are exceedingly delighted with those that praise them, and very little offended with such as jeer them; they are terrible even to their governors, and yet courteous to their very enemies. Far other is the disposition of the Carthaginians, severe, rigid, obsequious to their rulers, harsh to their subjects, most abject in their fear, most cruel in their anger, firm in their resolutions, untractable, and hard to be moved by sportive and pleasant discourse. Should Cleon have requested them to defer their assembly, because he had sacrificed to the Gods and was to feast certain strangers, they would not have risen up, laughing and clapping their hands for joy; nor, if Alcibiades, as he was making an harangue to them, had let slip a quail from under his cloak, would they have striven who should catch her and restore her to him again, but would rather have killed them both on the place, as contemning and deriding them; since they banished Hanno for making use of a lion to carry his baggage to the army, accusing him of affecting tyranny. Neither do I think, that the Thebans, if they had been made masters of their enemies' letters, would have foreborne looking into them, as did the Athenians, when, having taken the messengers of Philip who were carrying a letter superscribed to Olympias, they would not so much as open it, or discover the conjugal secrets of an absent husband, written to his wife.

Nor yet do I believe that the Athenians on the other side would have patiently suffered the haughtiness and disdain of Epaminondas, when, refusing to answer an accusation brought against him, he rose up from the theatre, and went away through the midst of the assembly to the place of public exercises. And much less am I of opinion that the Spartans would have endured the contumely and scurrility of Stratocles, who persuaded the people to offer sacrifices of thanksgiving to the Gods, as having obtained the victory, and afterwards, when, being truly informed of the loss they had received, they were angry with him, asked them what injury they had sustained in having through his means spent three days merrily.

Courtly flatterers indeed, like to quail-catchers, by imitating the voices and assimilating themselves to the manners of kings, chiefly insinuate into their favors and entrap them by deceit; but it is not convenient for a statesman to imitate the people's manners, but to know them, and make use of those things toward every person by which he is most likely to be taken. For the ignorance of men's humors brings no less disorders and obstacles in commonweals than in the friendships of kings.

4. When therefore you shall have already gotten power and authority amongst the people, then must you endeavor to reform their disposition, treating them gently, and by little and little drawing them to what is better. For the changing of a multitude is a difficult and laborious work. But as for your own manners and behavior, so compose and adorn them, as knowing that you are henceforth to lead your life on an open stage; and if it is no easy task for you wholly to extirpate vice out of your soul, at least take away and retrench those offences which are most notorious and apparent. For you cannot but have heard how Themistocles, when he designed to enter upon the management of public affairs, withdrew himself from drink-

ing and revelling, and fell to watching, fasting, and studying, saying to his intimate friends, that Miltiades's trophy suffered him not to sleep. And Pericles also so changed himself, both as to the comportment of his body and his manner of living, that he walked gravely, discoursed affably, always showed a staid and settled countenance, continually kept his hand under his robe, and went only that way which led to the assembly and the senate. For a multitude is not so tractable as that it should be easy for every one to take it with safety, but it is a service much to be valued, if, being like a suspicious and skittish beast, it can be so managed that, without being frighted either by sight or voice, it will submit to receive instruction.

These things therefore are not slightly to be observed; nor are we to neglect taking such care of our own life and manners that they may be clear from all stain and reprehension. For statesmen are not only liable to give an account of what they say or do in public; but there is a busy enquiry made into their very meals, beds, marriages, and every either sportive or serious action. For what need we speak of Alcibiades, who, being of all men the most active in public affairs, and withal an invincible commander, perished by his irregularity in living and his audaciousness, and who by his luxury and prodigality rendered the state unbenefited by all his other good qualities? — since the Athenians blamed Cimon's wine; the Romans, having nothing else to cavil at, found fault with Scipio's sleeping; and the enemies of Pompey the Great, having observed that he scratched his head with one finger, upbraided him with it. For as a freckle or wart in the face is more prejudicial than stains, maims, and scars in the rest of the body; so little faults, discerned in the lives of princes and statesmen, appear great, through an opinion most men have conceived of government and policy, which they look on as a great and excellent thing, and such as ought to be pure from all absurdity and imperfection. Therefore not unjustly is Livius Drusus commended, who, when several parts of his house lay open to the view of his neighbors, being told by a certain workman that he would for the expense only of five talents alter and remedy that fault, said: I will give thee indeed ten, to make my whole house so transparent that all the city may see how I live. For he was a temperate and modest man. And yet perhaps he had no need of this perspicuity; for many persons pry into those manners, counsels, actions, and lives of statesmen which seem to be most deeply concealed, no less loving and admiring one, and hating and despising another, for their private than for their public transactions. What then! perhaps you may say: Do not cities make use also of such men as live dissolutely and effeminately? True; for as women with child frequently long for stones and chalk, as those that are stomach-sick do for salt-fish and such other meats, which a little after they spit out again and reject; so also the people sometimes through wantonness and petulancy, and sometimes for want of better guides, make use of those that come first to hand, though at the same time detesting and contemning them, and after rejoice at such things spoken against them as the comedian Plato makes the people themselves to say:

> Quick, take me by the hand, and hold me fast,
> Or I'll Agyrrius captain choose in haste.

And again he brings them in, calling for a basin and feather that they may vomit, and saying,

> A chamber-pot by my tribunal stands.

And a little after,

> It feeds a stinking pest, foul Cephalus.

And the Roman people, when Carbo promised them something, and (to confirm it) added an oath and execration, unanimously swore on the contrary that they would not believe him. And in Lacedaemon, when a certain dissolute man named Demosthenes had delivered a very convenient opinion, the people rejected it; but the Ephori, who approved of his advice, having chosen by lot one of the ancient senators, commanded him to repeat the same discourse, pouring it (as it were) out of a filthy vessel into a clean one, that it might be acceptable to the multitude. Of so great moment either way in political affairs is the belief conceived of a person's disposition and manners.

5. Yet are we not therefore so to lay the whole stress on virtue, as utterly to neglect all gracefulness and efficacy of speech; but esteeming rhetoric, though not the worker, yet a coadjutor and forwarder of persuasion, we should correct that saying of Menander,

> The speaker's manners, not his speech, persuade.

For both manners and language ought to concur, unless any one forsooth shall say that — as it is the pilot who steers the ship, and not the rudder, and the rider that turns the horse, and not the bridle — so political virtue, using not eloquence but manners as an helm and bridle, persuades and guides a city, which is (to speak with Plato) an animal most easy to be turned, managing and directing it (as it were) from the poop. For since those great and (as Homer calls them) Jove-begotten kings, setting themselves out with their purple, sceptres, guards, and the very oracles of the Gods, and subjecting to them by their majesty the multitude, as if they were of a better nature and more excellent mould than other men, desired also to be eloquent orators, and neglected neither the gracefulness of speech,

> Nor public meeting, that more perfect they
> Might be for feats of war,*

---

* Il. IX. 441.

not only venerating Jupiter the counsellor, Mars the slaughterer, and Pallas the warrior, but invocating also Calliope,

>Who still attends on regal Majesty,*

by her persuasive oratory appeasing and moderating the fierceness and violence of the people; how is it possible that a private man in a plebeian garb and with a vulgar mien, undertaking to conduct a city, should ever be able to prevail over and govern the multitude, if he is not endowed with alluring and all-persuading eloquence? The captains indeed and pilots of ships make use of others to deliver their commands; but a statesman ought to have in himself not only a spirit of government, but also a commanding faculty of speech, that he may not stand in need of another's voice, nor be constrained to say, as did Iphicrates when he was run down by the eloquence of Aristophon, " My adversaries have the better actors, but mine is the more excellent play," nor yet be often obliged to make use of these words of Euripides,

> O that the race of miserable men
> Were speechless!

and again,

> Alas! Why have not men's affairs a tongue,
> That those fine pleaders who of right make wrong
> Might be no longer in request? †

For to these evasions perhaps might an Alcamenes, a Nesiotes, an Ictinus, and any such mechanical persons as get their bread by their hands, be permitted on their oath to have recourse. As it sometime happened in Athens, where, when two architects were examined about the erecting a certain public work, one of them, who was of a free and voluble speech and had his tongue (as we say) well hung, making a long and premeditated harangue concerning the method and order of raising such a fabric, greatly

* See Od. VII. 165. † Eurip. Frag. 977 and 442.

moved the people; but the other, who was indeed the better workman though the worse speaker, coming forth into the midst, only said, " Ye men of Athens, what this man has spoken, I will do." For those men venerate only Minerva surnamed Ergane (or the Artisan), who, as Sophocles says of them,

> Do on the massy anvil lay
> A lifeless iron bar, where they
> With blows of heavy hammer make
> It pliant to the work they undertake.

But the prophet or minister of Minerva Polias (that is, the protectress of cities) and of Themis (or Justice) the counsellor,

> Who both convenes assemblies, and again
> Dissolves them,*

making use of no other instrument but speech, does, by forming and fashioning some things and smoothing and polishing others that, like certain knots in timber or flaws in iron, are averse to his work, embellish and adorn a city. By this means the government of Pericles was in name (as Thucydides† says) a democracy, but in effect the rule of one principal man through the power of his eloquence. For there were living at the same time Cimon, and also Ephialtes and Thucydides,‡ all good men; now Thucydides, being asked by Archidamus, king of the Spartans, whether himself or Pericles were the better wrestler, thus answered: "That is not easily known; for when I in wrestling overthrow him, he, by his words persuading the spectators that he did not fall, gains the victory." And this did not only bring glory to himself, but safety also to the city; for being persuaded by him, it preserved the happiness it had gotten, and abstained from intermeddling with foreign affairs. But Nicias, though having the same design, yet falling short in the art of persuasion, when he

---

* Od. II. 69. † Thuc. II. 65.
‡ The son of Melesias, not the historian. (G.)

endeavored by his speech, as by a gentle curb, to restrain and turn the people, could not compass it or prevail with them, but was fain to depart, being violently hurried and dragged (as it were) by the neck and shoulders into Sicily. They say, that a wolf is not to be held by the ears; but a people and city are chiefly to be drawn by the ears, and not as some do who, being unpractised in eloquence, seek other absurd and unartificial ways of taking them, and either draw them by the belly, making them feasts and banquets, or by the purse, bestowing on them gifts and largesses, or by the eye, exhibiting to them masks and prizes or public shows of dancers and fencers, — by which they do not so much lead as cunningly catch the people. For to lead a people is to persuade them by reason and eloquence; but such allurements of the multitude nothing differ from the baits laid for the taking of irrational animals.

6. Let not yet the speech of a statesman be youthful and theatrical, as if he were making an harangue composed, like a garland, of curious and florid words; nor again — as Pytheas said of an oration made by Demosthenes, that it smelt of the lamp and sophistical curiosity — let it consist of over-subtle arguments and periods, exactly framed by rule and compass. But as musicians require that the strings of their instruments should be sweetly and gently touched, and not rudely thrummed or beaten; so in the speech of a statesman, both when he counsels and when he commands, there should not appear either violence or cunning, nor should he think himself worthy of commendation for having spoken formally, artificially, and with an exact observation of punctualities; but his whole discourse ought to be full of ingenuous simplicity, true magnanimity, fatherly freedom, and careful providence and understanding, joined with goodness and honesty, gracefulness and attraction, proceeding from grave expressions

and proper and persuasive sentences. Now a political oration does much more properly than a juridical one admit of sententious speeches, histories, fables, and metaphors, by which those who moderately and seasonably use them exceedingly move their hearers; as he did who said, Make not Greece one-eyed; and Demades, when he affirmed of himself, that he was to manage the wreck of the state; and Archilochus, when he said

> Nor let the stone of Tantalus
> Over this isle hang always thus;

and Pericles, when he commanded the eyesore* of the Piraeus to be taken away; and Phocion, when he pronounced of Leosthenes's victory, that the beginning or the short course of the war was good, but that he feared the long race that was to follow. But in general, majesty and greatness more benefit a political discourse, a pattern of which may be the Philippics, and (amongst the orations set down by Thucydides) that of Sthenelaidas the Ephor, that of Archidamus at Plataea, and that of Pericles after the plague. But as for those rhetorical flourishes and harangues of Ephorus, Theopompus, and Anaximenes, which they made after they had armed and set in order the battalions, it may be said of them,

> None talks thus foolishly so near the sword.†

7. Nevertheless, both taunts and raillery may sometimes be part of political discourse, so they proceed not to injury or scurrility, but are usefully spoken by him who either reprehends or scoffs. But these things seem most to be allowed in answers and replies. For in that manner to begin a discourse as if one had purposely prepared himself for it, is the part of a common jester, and carries with it an opinion of maliciousness; as was incident to the biting jests of Cicero, Cato the Elder, and Euxitheus, an intimate

---

* So he called the little island Aegina. † Eurip. Autolycus, Frag. 284, vs. 22.

acquaintance of Aristotle, — all of whom frequently began first to jeer; but in him, who does it only in revenge, the seasonableness of it renders it not only pardonable but also graceful. Such was the answer of Demosthenes, when one that was suspected of thievery derided him for writing by night: I know that the keeping my candle burning all night is offensive to you. So when Demades bawled out, Demosthenes forsooth would correct me: thus would the sow (as the proverb has it) teach Minerva;—That Minerva, replied Demosthenes, was not long since taken in adultery. Not ungraceful also was that of Xenaenetus to those citizens who upbraided him with flying when he was general, 'Twas with you, my dear hearts. But in raillery great care is to be taken for the avoiding of excess, and of any thing that may either by its unseasonableness offend the hearers or show the speaker to be of an ungenerous and sordid disposition; — such as were the sayings of Democrates. For he, going up into the assembly, said that, like the city, he had little force but much wind; and after the overthrow at Chaeronea, going forth to the people, he said: I would not have had the state to be in so ill a condition that you should be contented to hear me also giving you counsel. For this showed a mean-spirited person, as the other did a madman; but neither of them was becoming a statesman. Now the succinctness of Phocion's speech was admired; whence Polyeuctus affirmed, that Demosthenes was the greatest orator, but that Phocion spake most forcibly, for that his discourse did in very few words contain abundance of matter. And Demosthenes, who contemned others, was wont, when Phocion stood up, to say, The hatchet (or pruning-knife) of my orations arises.

8. Let your chief endeavor therefore be, to use to the multitude a premeditated and not empty speech, and that with safety, knowing that Pericles himself, before he made

any discourse to the people, was wont to pray that there might not a word pass from him foreign to the business he was to treat of. It is requisite also, that you have a voluble tongue, and be exercised in speaking on all occurrences; for occasions are quick, and bring many sudden things in political affairs. Wherefore also Demosthenes was, as they say, inferior to many, withdrawing and absconding himself when sudden occasion offered. And Theophrastus relates that Alcibiades, desirous to speak not only what he ought but as he ought, often hesitated and stood still in the midst of his speech, seeking and composing expressions fit for his purpose. But he who, as matters and occasions present themselves, rises up to speak, most of all moves, leads, and disposes of the multitude. Thus Leo Byzantius came to make an harangue to the Athenians, being then at dissension amongst themselves; by whom when he perceived himself to be laughed at for the littleness of his stature, What would you do, said he, if you saw my wife, who scarce reaches up to my knees? And the laughter thereupon increasing, Yet, went he on, as little as we are, when we fall out with one another, the city of Byzantium is not big enough to hold us. So Pytheas the orator, who declaimed against the honors decreed to Alexander, when one said to him, Dare you, being so young, discourse of so great matters? made this answer, And yet Alexander, whom you decree to be a God, is younger than I am.

9. It is requisite also for the champion of the commonweal to bring to this not slight but all-concerning contest a firm and solid speech, attended with a strong habit of voice and a long lasting breath, lest, being tired and spent with speaking, he chance to be overcome by

Some ravening crier, with a roaring voice,
Loud as Cycloborus.*

---

* A brook near Athens, the waters of which fell with an extraordinary noise. Aristoph. Eq. 137.

Cato, when he had no hopes of persuading the people or senate, whom he found prepossessed by the courtships and endeavors of the contrary party, was wont to rise up and hold them a whole day with an oration, by that means depriving his adversaries of their opportunity. And thus much concerning the preparation and use of speech may be sufficient for him who can of himself find out and add what necessarily follows from it.

10. There are, moreover, two avenues or ways of entering into the government of the state; the one short and expeditious to the lustre of glory, but not without danger; the other more obscure and slow, but having also greater security. For some there are who, beginning with some great and illustrious action which requires a courageous boldness, do, like to those that from a far extended promontory launch forth into the deep, steer directly into the very midst of public affairs, thinking Pindar to have been in the right when he said,

>If you a stately fabric do design,
>Be sure that your work's front with lustre shine.*

For the multitude do, through a certain satiety and loathing of those to whom they have been accustomed, more readily receive a beginner; as the beholders do a fresh combatant, and as those dignities and authorities which have a splendid and speedy increase dazzle and astonish envy. For neither does that fire, as Ariston says, make a smoke, nor that glory breed envy, which suddenly and quickly shines forth; but of those who grow up slowly and by degrees, some are attacked on this side, others on that; whence many have withered away about the tribunal, before ever they came to flourish. But when, as they say of Ladas,

>The sound o' th' rope † yet rattled in his ear,
>When Ladas having finished his career
>Was crowned,

* Pind. Olymp. VI. 4.   † From whence they set forth to run.

any one suddenly and gloriously performs an embassy, triumphs, or leads forth an army, neither the envious nor the disdainful have like power over him as over others. Thus did Aratus ascend to glory, making the overthrow of the tyrant Nicocles his first step to the management of the commonweal. Thus did Alcibiades, settling the alliance with the Mantineans against the Lacedaemonians. Pompey also required a triumph, being not yet admitted into the senate; and when Sylla opposed it, he said to him, More adore the rising than the setting sun; which when Sylla heard, he yielded to him. And the people of Rome on a sudden, contrary to the ordinary course of the law, declared Cornelius Scipio consul, when he stood candidate for the aedileship, not from any vulgar reason, but admiring the victory he had got, whilst he was but a youth, in a single combat fought in Spain, and his conquests a little after, performed at Carthage, when he was a tribune of foot: in respect of which Cato the Elder cried out with a loud voice,

He only's wise, the rest like shadows fly.*

Now then, since the affairs of the cities have neither wars to be managed, tyrannies to be overthrown, nor leagues and alliances to be treated, what can any one undertake for the beginning of an illustrious and splendid government? There are yet left public causes and embassies to the emperor, which require the courage and prudence of an acute and cautious person. There are also in the cities many good and laudable usages neglected, which may be restored, and many ill practices brought in by custom, to the disgrace or damage of the city, which may be redressed, to gain him the esteem of the people. Moreover, a great suit rightly determined, fidelity in defending a poor man's cause against a powerful adversary, and freedom of speech in behalf of justice to some unjust nobleman, have afforded

---

* See Odyss. X. 495.

some a glorious entrance into the administration of the state. Not a few also have been advanced by enmity and quarrels, having set themselves to attack such men whose dignity was either envied or terrible. For the power of him that is overthrown does with greater glory accrue to his overthrower. Indeed, through envy to contend against a good man, and one that has by virtue been advanced to the chiefest honor, — as Simmias did against Pericles, Alcmacon against Themistocles, Clodius against Pompey, and Meneclides the orator against Epaminondas, — is neither good for one's reputation nor otherwise advantageous. For when the multitude, having outraged some good man, soon after (as it frequently happens) repent of their indignation, they think that way of excusing this offence the easiest which is indeed the justest, to wit, the destroying of him who was the persuader and author of it. But the rising up to humble and pull down a wicked person, who has by his audaciousness and cunning subjected the city to himself (such as heretofore Cleon and Clitophon were in Athens), makes a glorious entrance to the management of public affairs, as it were to a play. I am not ignorant also that some, by opposing — as Ephialtes did at Athens, and Phormio amongst the Eleans — an imperious and oligarchical senate, have at the same time obtained both authority and honor; but in this there is great danger to him who is but entering upon the administration of state. Wherefore Solon took a better beginning; for the city of Athens being divided into three parts, the Diacrians (or inhabitants of the hill), the Pedieans (or dwellers on the plain), and the Paralians (or those whose abode was by the water side), he, joining himself with none of them, but acting for the common good of them all, and saying and doing all things for to bring them to concord, was chosen the lawgiver to take away their differences, and by that means settled the state.

Such then and so many beginnings has the more splendid way of entering upon state affairs.

11. But many gallant men have chosen the safe and slow method, as Aristides, Phocion, Pammenes the Theban, Lucullus in Rome, Cato, and Agesilaus the Lacedaemonian. For as ivy, twining about the strongest trees, rises up together with them; so every one of these, applying himself, whilst he was yet young and inglorious, to some elder and illustrious personage, and growing up and increasing by little and little under his authority, grounded and rooted himself in the commonweal. For Clisthenes advanced Aristides, Chabrias preferred Phocion, Sylla promoted Lucullus, Maximus raised Cato, Pammenes forwarded Epaminondas, and Lysander assisted Agesilaus. But this last, injuring his own reputation through an unseasonable ambition and jealousy, soon threw off the director of his actions; but the rest honestly, politically, and to the end, venerated and magnified the authors of their advancement, — like bodies which are opposed to the sun, — by reflecting back the light that shone upon them, augmented and rendered more illustrious. Certainly those who looked asquint upon Scipio called him the player, and his companion Laelius the poet or author of his actions; yet was not Laelius puffed up by any of these things, but continued to promote the virtue and glory of Scipio. And Afranius, the friend of Pompey, though he was very meanly descended, yet being at the very point to be chosen consul, when he understood that Pompey favored others, gave over his suit, saying that his obtaining the consulship would not be so honorable as grievous and troublesome to him, if it were against the good-will and without the assistance of Pompey. Having therefore delayed but one year, he enjoyed the dignity and preserved his friendship. Now those who are thus by others led, as it were, by the hand to glory do, in gratifying one, at the same time also

gratify the multitude, and incur less odium, if any inconvenience befalls them. Wherefore also Philip (king of Macedon) exhorted his son Alexander, whilst he had leisure during the reign of another, to get himself friends, winning their love by kind and affable behavior.

12. Now he that begins to enter upon the administration of state affairs should choose himself a guide, who is not only a man of credit and authority but is also such for his virtue. For as it is not every tree that will admit and bear the twining of a vine, there being some which utterly choke and spoil its growth; so in states, those who are no lovers of virtue and goodness, but only of honor and sovereignty, afford not young beginners any opportunities of performing worthy actions, but do through envy keep them down and let them languish whom they regard as depriving them of their glory, which is (as it were) their food. Thus Marius, having first in Afric and afterwards in Galatia done many gallant exploits by the assistance of Sylla, forbare any farther to employ him, and utterly cast him off, being really vexed at his growing into repute, but making his pretence the device engraven on his seal. For Sylla, being paymaster under Marius when he was general in Afric, and sent by him to Bocchus, brought with him Jugurtha prisoner; but as he was an ambitious young man, who had but just tasted the sweetness of glory, he received not his good fortune with moderation; but having caused the representation of the action to be engraven on his seal, wore about him Jugurtha delivered into his hands; and this did Marius lay to his charge, when he turned him off. But Sylla, passing over to Catulus and Metellus, who were good men and at difference with Marius, soon after in a civil war drove away and ruined Marius, who wanted but little of overthrowing Rome. Sylla indeed, on the contrary, advanced Pompey from a very youth, rising up to him and uncovering his head as he passed by, and not

only giving other young men occasions of doing captain-like actions, but even instigating some that were backward and unwilling. He filled the armies with emulation and desire of honor; and thus he had the superiority over them all, desiring not to be alone, but the first and greatest amongst many great ones. These therefore are the men to whom young statesmen ought to adhere, and with these they should be (as it were) incorporated, not stealing from them their glory, — like Aesop's wren, which, being carried up on the eagle's wings, suddenly flew away and got before her, — but receiving it of them with friendship and good-will, since they can never, as Plato says, be able to govern aright, if they have not been first well practised in obedience.

13. After this follows the judgment that is to be had in the choice of friends, in which neither the opinion of Themistocles nor that of Cleon is to be approved. For Cleon, when he first knew that he was to take on him the government, assembling his friends together, brake off friendship with them, as that which often disables the mind, and withdraws it from its just and upright intention in managing the affairs of the state. But he would have done better, if he had cast out of his soul avarice and contention, and cleansed himself from envy and malice. For cities want not men that are friendless and unaccompanied, but such as are good and temperate. Now he indeed drove away his friends; but a hundred heads of fawning flatterers were, as the comedian speaks, licking about him;* and being harsh and severe to those that were civil, he again debased himself to court the favor of the multitude, doing all things to humor them in their dotage, and taking rewards at every man's hand,† and joining himself with the worst and most distempered of the people against the best. But Themistocles, on the

* Aristoph. Pac. 756   † See Aristoph. Eq. 1009.

contrary, said to one who told him that he would govern well if he exhibited himself alike to all: May I never sit on that throne on which my friends shall not have more power with me than those who are not my friends. Neither did he well in pinning the state to his friendship, and submitting the common and public affairs to his private favors and affections. And farther, he said to Simonides, when he requested somewhat that was not just: Neither is he a good poet or musician, who sings against measure; nor he an upright magistrate, who gratifies any one against the laws. And it would really be a shameful and miserable thing, that the pilot should choose his mariners, and the master of a ship the pilot,

> Who well can rule the helm, and in good guise
> Hoist up the sails, when winds begin to rise,

and that an architect should make choice of such servants and workmen as will not prejudice his work, but take pains in the best manner to forward it; but that a statesman — who, as Pindar has it,

> The best of artists and chief workman is
> Of equity and justice —

should not presently choose himself like-affected friends and ministers, and such as might co-inspire into him a love of honesty; but that one or other should be always unjustly and violently bending him to other uses. For then he would seem to differ in nothing from a carpenter or mason who, through ignorance or want of experience, uses such squares, rules, and levels as will certainly make his work to be awry. Since friends are the living and intelligent instruments of statesmen, who ought to be so far from bearing them company in their slips and transgressions, that they must be careful they do not, even unknown to them, commit a fault.

And this it was, that disgraced Solon and brought him into disrepute amongst his citizens; for he, having an intention to ease men's debts and to bring in that which was called at Athens the Seisachtheia (for that was the name given by way of extenuation to the cancelling of debts), communicated this design to some of his friends, who thereupon did a most unjust act; for having got this inkling, they borrowed abundance of money, and the law being a little after brought to light, they appeared to have purchased stately houses, and great store of land with the wealth they had borrowed; and Solon, who was himself injured, was accused to have been a partaker of their injustice. Agesilaus also was most feeble and mean-spirited in what concerned the suits of his friends, being like the horse Pegasus in Euripides,

> Who, frighted, bowed his back, more than his rider would,*

so that, being more ready to help them in their misfortunes than was requisite, he seemed to be privy to their injustices. For he saved Phoebidas, who was accused for having without commission surprised the castle of Thebes, called Cadmea, saying that such enterprises were to be attempted without expecting any orders. And when Sphodrias was brought to trial for an unlawful and heinous act, having made an incursion into Attica at such time as the Athenians were allies and confederates of the Spartans, he procured him to be acquitted, being softened by the amorous entreaties of his son. There is also recorded a short epistle of his to a certain prince, written in these words: If Nicias is innocent, discharge him; if he is guilty, discharge him for my sake; but however it is, discharge him. But Phocion (on the contrary) would not so much as appear in behalf of his son-in-law Charicles, when he was accused for having taken money of Harpalus; but having said, Only for acts of justice have I made you my son-in-law, — went his way. And Timoleon the Corinthian, when he

---

* Eurip. Bellerophon, Frag. 311.

could not by admonitions or requests dissuade his brother from being a tyrant, confederated with his destroyers. For a magistrate ought not to be a friend even to the altar (or till he comes to the point of being forsworn), as Pericles sometime said, but no farther than is agreeable to all law, justice, and the utility of the state; any of which being neglected brings a great and public damage, as did the not executing of justice on Sphodrias and Phoebidas, who did not a little contribute to the engaging of Sparta in the Leuctrian war.

Otherwise, reason of state is so far from necessitating one to show himself severe on every peccadillo of his friends, that it even permits him, when he has secured the principal affairs of the public, to assist them, stand by them, and labor for them. There are, moreover, certain favors that may be done without envy, as is the helping a friend to obtain an office, or rather the putting into his hands some honorable commission or some laudable embassy, such as for the congratulating or honoring some prince or the making a league of amity and alliance with some state. But if there be some difficult but withal illustrious and great action to be performed, having first taken it upon himself, he may afterwards assume a friend to his assistance, as did Diomedes, whom Homer makes to speak in this manner:

> Since a companion you will have me take,
> How can I think a better choice to make,
> Than the divine Ulysses?*

And Ulysses again as kindly attributes to him the praise of the achievement, saying:

> These stately steeds, whose country you demand,
> Nestor, were hither brought from Thracian land,
> Whose king, with twelve of his best friends, lies dead,
> All slain by th' hand of warlike Diomed.†

* Il. X. 242.   † Il. X. 558.

For this sort of concession no less adorns the praiser than the praised; but self-conceitedness, as Plato says, dwells with solitude. He ought moreover to associate his friends in those good and kind offices which are done by him, bidding those whom he has benefited to love them and give them thanks, as having been the procurers and counsellors of his favors to them. But he must reject the dishonest and unreasonable request of his friends, yet not churlishly but mildly, teaching and showing them that they are not beseeming their virtue and honor. Never was any man better at this than Epaminondas, who, having denied to deliver out of prison a certain victualler, when requested by Pelopidas, and yet a little after dismissing him at the desire of his miss, said to his friend, These, O Pelopidas, are favors fit for wenches to receive, and not for generals. Cato on the other side acted morosely and insolently, when Catulus the censor, his most intimate and familiar friend, interceded with him for one of those against whom he, being quaestor, had entered process, saying: It would be a shame if you, who ought to reform young men for us, should be thrust out by our servants. For he might, though in effect refusing the requested favor, have yet forborne that severity and bitterness of speech; so that his doing what was displeasing to his friend might have seemed not to have proceeded from his own inclination, but to have been a necessity imposed upon him by law and justice. There are also in the administration of the state methods, not dishonorable, of assisting our poorer friends in the making of their fortune. Thus did Themistocles, who, seeing after a battle one of those which lay dead in the field adorned with chains of gold and jewels, did himself pass by him; but turning back to a friend of his, said, Do you take these spoils, for you are not yet come to be Themistocles. For even the affairs themselves do frequently afford a statesman such opportunities of benefiting his friends; for every man is not a Menemachus. To one therefore give the patronage of a cause, both just and beneficial; to another recommend some rich man, who stands in need of management and protection; and help a third to be employed in some public work, or to some gainful and profitable farm. Epaminondas bade a friend of his go to a certain rich man, and ask him for a talent by the command of Epaminondas, and when he to whom the message was sent came to enquire the reason of it; Because, said Epaminondas, he is a very honest man and poor; but you, by converting much of the city's wealth to your own use, are become rich. And Xenophon reports, that Agesilaus delighted in enriching his friends, himself making no account of money.

14. Now since, as Simonides says, all larks must have a crest, and every eminent office in a commonweal brings enmities and dissensions, it is not a little convenient for a statesman to be forewarned also of his comportment in these rencounters. Many therefore commend Themistocles and Aristides, who, when they were to go forth on an embassy or to command together the army, laid down their enmity at the confines of the city, taking it up again after their return. Some again are highly pleased with the action of Cretinas the Magnesian. He, having for his rival in the government one Hermias, a man not powerful and rich, but ambitious and high-spirited, when the Mithridatic war came on, seeing the city in danger, desired Hermias either to take the government upon himself and manage the affairs whilst he retired, or, if he would have him take the command of the army, to depart himself immediately, lest they should through their ambitious contention destroy the city. The proposal pleased Hermias, who, saying that Cretinas was a better soldier than himself, did with his wife and children quit the city. Cretinas then escorted him as he went forth, furnishing him out of his

own estate with all such things as are more useful to those that fly from home than to those that are besieged; and excellently defending the city, unexpectedly preserved it, being at the point to be destroyed. For if it is generous and proceeding from a magnanimous spirit to cry out,

> I love my children, but my country more,

why should it not be readier for every one of them to say, I hate this man, and desire to do him a diskindness, but the love of my country has greater power over me? For not to condescend to be reconciled to an enemy for those very causes for which we ought to abandon even a friend, is even to extremity savage and brutish. But far better did Phocion and Cato, who grounded not any enmity at all on their political differences, but being fierce and obstinate only in their public contests not to recede from any thing they judged convenient for the state, did in their private affairs use those very persons friendly and courteously from whom they differed in the other. For one ought not to esteem any citizen an enemy, unless it be one like Aristion, Nabis, or Catiline, the disease and plague of the city: but as for those that are otherwise at discord, a good magistrate should, like a skilful musician, by gently setting them up or letting them down, bring them to concord; not falling angrily and reproachfully upon those that err, but mildly reprehending them in such like terms as these of Homer's,

> Good friend, I thought you wiser than the rest; *

and again,

> You could have told a better tale than this; †

nor yet repining at their honors, or sparing to speak freely in commendation of their good actions, if they say or do any thing advantageous to the public. For thus will our reprehension, when it is requisite, be credited, and we shall render them averse to vice, increasing their virtue, and

* Il. XVII. 171 † Il. VII. 358.

showing, by comparing them, how much the one is more worthy and beseeming them than the other.

But I indeed am also of opinion, that a statesman should in just causes give testimony to his enemies, stand by them when they are accused by sycophants, and discredit imputations brought against them if they are repugnant to their characters; as Nero himself, a little before he put to death Thraseas, whom of all men he both most hated and feared, when one accused him for giving a wrong and unjust sentence, said: I wish Thraseas was but as great a lover of me, as he is a most upright judge. Neither is it amiss for the daunting of others who are by Nature more inclined to vice, when they offend, to make mention of some enemy of theirs who is better behaved, and say, Such a one would not have spoken or acted thus. And some again, when they transgress, are to be put in mind of their virtuous progenitors. Thus Homer says,

> Tydeus has left a son unlike himself.*

And Appius, contending in the Comitia with Scipio Africanus, said, How deeply, O Paulus, wouldst thou sigh amongst the infernal shades, wert thou but sensible that Philonicus the publican guards thy son, who is going to stand for the office of censor. For such manner of speeches do both admonish the offender, and become their admonishers. Nestor also in Sophocles, being reproached by Ajax, thus politicly answers him:

> I blame you not, for you act well, although
> You speak but ill.

And Cato, who had opposed Pompey in his joining with Caesar to force the city, when they fell to open wars, gave his opinion that the conduct of the state should be committed to Pompey, saying, that those who are capable to do the greatest mischiefs are fittest to put a stop to them.

* Il. V. 800.

For reprehension mixed with praise, and accompanied not with opprobriousness but liberty of speech, working not animosity but remorse and repentance, appears both kind and salutary; but railing expressions do not at all beseem statesmen. Do but look into the speeches of Demosthenes against Aeschines, and of Aeschines against him; and again into what Hyperides has written against Demades, and consider whether Solon, Pericles, Lycurgus the Lacedaemonian, or Pittacus the Lesbian would have spoken in that manner. And yet Demosthenes used this reproachful manner of speaking only in his juridical orations or pleadings; for his Philippics are clean and free from all scoffing and scurrility. For such discourses do not only more disgrace the speakers than the hearers, but do moreover breed confusion in affairs, and disturb counsels and assemblies. Wherefore Phocion did excellently well, who, having broken off his speech to give way to one that railed against him, when the other with much ado held his peace, going on again where he had left off, said: You have already heard what has been spoken of horsemen and heavy armed foot; I am now to treat of such as are light armed and targeteers.

But since many persons can hardly contain themselves on such occasions, and since railers have often their mouths not impertinently stopped by replies; let the answer be short and pithy, not showing any indignation or bitterness of anger, but mildness joined with raillery and gracefulness, yet somewhat tart and biting. Now such especially are the retortings of what has been spoken before. For as darts returning against their caster seem to have been repulsed and beaten back by a certain strength and solidity in that against which they were thrown; so what was spoken seems by the strength and understanding of the reproached to have been turned back upon the reproacher. Such was that reply of Epaminondas to Callistratus, who upbraided the Thebans with Oedipus, and the Argives with Orestes,—one of which had killed his father and the other his mother,—Yet they who did these things, being rejected by us, were received by you. Such also was the repartee of Antalcidas the Spartan to an Athenian, who said to him, We have often driven you back and pursued you from the Cephissus; But we (replied Antalcidas) never yet pursued you from the Eurotas. Phocion also, when Demades cried out, The Athenians if they grow mad, will kill thee; elegantly replied, And thee, if they come again to their wits. So, when Domitius said to Crassus the orator, Did not you weep for the death of the lamprey you kept in your fish-pond?—Did not you, said Crassus to him again, bury three wives without ever shedding a tear? These things therefore have indeed their use also in other parts of a man's life.

15. Moreover, some, like Cato, thrust themselves into every part of polity, thinking a good citizen should not omit any care or industry for the obtaining authority. And these men greatly commend Epaminondas; for that being by the Thebans through envy and in contempt appointed telearch, he did not reject it, but said, that the office does not show the man, but the man also the office. He brought the telearchate into great and venerable repute, which was before nothing but a certain charge of the carrying the dung out of the narrow streets and lanes of the city, and turning of watercourses. Nor do I doubt but that I myself afford matter of laughter to many who come into this our city, being frequently seen in public employed about such matters. But that comes into my assistance which is related of Antisthenes; for, when one wondered to see him carry a piece of stock-fish through the market, 'Tis for myself, said he. But I, on the contrary, say to those who upbraid me for being present at and overseeing the measuring of tiles, or the bringing in and unloading of clay and

stones: It is not for myself, but for my country, that I perform this service. For though he who in his own person manages and does many such things for himself may be judged mean-spirited and mechanical, yet if he does them for the public and for his country, he is not to be deemed sordid; but on the contrary, his diligence and readiness, extending even to these small matters, is to be esteemed greater and more highly to be valued. But others there are, that hold Pericles's manner of acting to have been more magnanimous and august; amongst which Critolaus the Peripatetic, who is of opinion that, as at Athens the Salaminian ship and the Paralus were not launched forth for every service, but only on necessary and great occasions, so a statesman ought to employ himself in the chiefest and greatest affairs, like the King of the universe, who, as Euripides says,

> Reserves great things for his own government,
> But small things leaves to Fortune's management.

For neither do we approve the excessively ambitious and contentious spirit of Theagenes, who, having obtained the victory not only through the whole course of public games, but also in many other contests, and not only in wrestling but in buffeting and running of long races, at last, being at the anniversary festival supper of a certain hero, after every one was served, according to the custom, he started up, and fell to wrestling, as if it were necessary that no other should conquer when he was present; whence he got together twelve hundred coronets, most of which one would have taken for rubbish.

Now nothing do they differ from him, who strip themselves for every public affair, and render themselves reprehensible by many, becoming troublesome, and being, when they do well, the subject of envy, and when they do ill, of rejoicing. And that industry which was at the beginning admired turns afterwards to contempt and laughter. In this manner it was said; Metiochus leads forth the army, Metiochus oversees the highways, Metiochus bakes the bread, Metiochus bolts the meal, Metiochus does all things, Metiochus shall suffer for it at last. This Metiochus was a follower of Pericles, and made use, it seems, of the power he had with him invidiously and disdainfully. For a statesman ought to find the people when he comes to them (as they say) in love with him, and leave in them a longing after him when he is absent; which course Scipio Africanus also took, dwelling a long time in the country, at the same time both removing from himself the burthen of envy, and giving those leisure to breathe, who seemed to be oppressed by his glory. But Timesias the Clazomenian, who was otherwise a good commonwealths-man, was ignorant of his being envied and hated for doing all things by himself, till the following accident befell him. It happened that, as he passed by where certain boys were striking a cockal-bone out of an hole, some of them said, that the bone was still left within; but he who had stricken it cried out, I wish I had as certainly beaten out Timesias's brains, as this bone is out of the hole. Timesias, hearing this, and thereby understanding the envy and spite borne him by every one, returned home, where he imparted the matter to his wife, and having commanded her to pack up all and follow him, immediately left both his house and the city. And Themistocles seems to have been in some such condition amongst the Athenians, when he said: How is it, O ye blessed ones, that you are tired with the frequent re ceiving of benefits?

Now some of those things have indeed been rightly spoken, others not so well. For a statesman ought not to withdraw his affection and providential care from any public affair whatever, nor reserve himself sacred, like the anchor in a ship, for the last necessities and hazards of the state. But as the masters of ships do some things with their own hands, and perform others, sitting afar off, by other instruments, turning and winding them by the hands of others, and making use of mariners, boatswains, and mates, some of which they often call to the stern, putting the helm into their hands; so it is convenient for a statesman sometimes to yield the command to his companions, and to invite them kindly and civilly to the tribunal, not managing all the affairs of the commonweal by his own speeches, decrees, and actions, but having good and faithful men, to employ every one of them in that proper and peculiar station which he finds to be most suitable for him. Thus Pericles used Menippus for the conduct of the armies, by Ephialtes he humbled the council of the Areopagus, by Charinus he passed the law against the Megarians, and sent Lampon to people the city of Thurii. For not only is the greatness of authority less liable to be envied by the people, when it seems to be divided amongst many; but the business also is more exactly done. For as the division of the hand into fingers has not weakened it, but rendered it more commodious and instrumental for the uses to which it serves; so he who in the administration of a state gives part of the affairs to others renders the action more efficacious by communicating it. But he who, through an unsatiable desire of glory or power, lays the whole burthen of the state upon his own shoulders, and applies himself to that for which he is neither fitted by nature nor exercise, — as Cleon did to the leading forth of armies, Philopoemen to the commanding of navies, and Hannibal to haranguing the people, — has no excuse for his errors; but hears that of Euripides objected against him,

> Thou, but a carpenter, concernd'st thyself
> With works not wrought in wood; —

being no good orator, you went on an embassage; being of a lazy temper, you thrust yourself into the stewardship; being ignorant in keeping accounts, you would be treasurer; or, being old and infirm, you took on you the command of the army. But Pericles divided his authority with Cimon, reserving to himself the governing within the city, and committing to him the manning of the navy and making war upon the barbarians; for the other was naturally fitted for war, and himself for civil affairs. Eubulus also the Anaphlystian is much commended, that, having credit and authority in matters of the greatest importance, he managed none of the Grecian affairs, nor betook himself to the conducting of the army; but employing himself about the treasure, he augmented the public revenues, and greatly benefited the city by them. But Iphicrates, practising to make declamations at his own house in the presence of many, rendered himself ridiculous; for though he had been no bad orator but an excellently good one, yet ought he to have contented himself with the glory got by arms, and abstaining from the school, to have left it to the sophisters.

16. But since it is incident to every populacy to be malicious and desirous to find fault with their governors, and since they are apt to suspect that many, even useful things, if they pass without being opposed or contradicted, are done by conspiracy, and since this principally brings societies and friendships into obloquy; they must not indeed leave any real enmity or dissension against themselves, as did Onomademus, a demagogue of the Chians, who, having mastered a sedition, suffered not all his adversaries to be expelled the city; lest, said he, we should begin to differ with our friends, when we are wholly freed from our enemies; for this would be indeed a folly. But when the multitude shall have conceived a suspicion against any important beneficial project, they must not, as if it were by confederacy, all deliver the same opinion; but two or three of them must dissent, and mildly oppose their friend, and afterwards, as if they were convinced by reason,

change their sentiments; for by this means they draw along with them the people, who think them moved by the beneficialness of the thing. But in small matters, and such as are of no great consequence, it is not amiss to suffer his friends really to differ, every one following his own private reason; that so in the principal and greatest concerns, they may not seem to act upon design, when they shall unanimously agree to what is best.

17. The politician therefore is by nature always the prince of the city, as the king among the bees; and in consideration of this, he ought always to have the helm of public affairs in his hand. But as for those dignities and offices to which persons are nominated and chosen by the suffrages of the people, he should neither too eagerly nor too often pursue them, — the seeking after offices being neither venerable nor popular, — nor yet should he reject them, when the people legally confer them on him and invite him to them, but even though they are below his reputation, he should accept them and willingly employ himself in them; for it is but just that they who have been honored by offices of greater dignity should in return grace those of inferior rank. And in those more weighty and superior employs, such as are the commanding of the armies in Athens, the Prytania in Rhodes, and the Boeotarchy amongst us, he should carry himself with such moderation as to remit and abate something of their grandeur, adding somewhat of dignity and venerableness to those that are meaner and less esteemed, that he may be neither despised for these nor envied for those.

Now it behooves him that enters upon any office, not only to have at hand those arguments of which Pericles put himself in mind when he first received the robe of state: Bethink thyself, Pericles, thou govern'st freemen, thou govern'st Grecians, yea, citizens of Athens; but farther also, he ought to say thus with himself: Thou, being a subject, govern'st a city which is under the obedience of Caesar's proconsul or lieutenant. Here is no fight in a fair field, this is not the ancient Sardis, nor is this the puissance of the Lydians. Thou must make thy robe scantier, look from the pavilion to the tribunal, and not place too great confidence in thy crown, since thou see'st the Roman's shoes over thy head. But in this the stage-players are to be imitated, who add indeed to the play their own passionate transports, behavior, and countenance, suitable to the person they represent, but yet give ear to the prompter, and transgress not the rhyme and measures of the faculty granted them by their masters. For an error in government brings not, as in the acting of a tragedy, only hissing and derision ; but many have by this means subjected themselves to that

> Severe chastiser, the neck-cutting axe.

As it befell your countryman Pardalas, when he forgot the limits of his power. Another, being banished from home and confined to a little island, as Solon has it,

> Became at last from an Athenian
> A Pholegandrian or Sicinitan.

For we laugh indeed, when we see little children endeavoring to fasten their father's shoes on their own feet, or setting their crowns on their own heads in sport. But the governors of cities, foolishly exhorting the people to imitate those works, achievements, and actions of their ancestors which are not suitable to the present times and affairs, elevate the multitude, and although they do things that are ridiculous, they yet meet with a fate which is not fit to be laughed at, unless they are men altogether despised. For there are many other facts of the ancient Greeks, the recital of which to those who are now living may serve to form and moderate their manners; as would be the relating at Athens, not the warlike exploits of their progenitors, but (for example) the decree of amnesty after the expulsion of the Thirty Tyrants; the fining of Phrynicus, who represented in a tragedy the taking of Miletus; how they wore garlands on their heads when Cassander rebuilt Thebes; how, having intelligence of the Scytalism (or slaughter) at Argos in which the Argives put to death fifteen hundred of their own citizens, they commanded a lustration (or expiatory sacrifice) to be carried about in a full assembly; and how, when they were searching of houses for those that were confederated with Harpalus, they passed by only one, which was inhabited by a man newly married. For by the imitating of such things as these, they may even now resemble their ancestors; but the fights at Marathon, Eurymedon, and Plataea, and whatever examples vainly puff up and heighten the multitude, should be left to the schools of the sophisters.

18. Now a statesman ought not only to exhibit himself and his country blameless to the prince, but also to have always for his friend some one of those that are most powerful above, as a firm support of polity; for the Romans are of such a disposition, that they are most ready to assist their friends in their political endeavors. It is good also, when we have received benefit from friendship with princes, to apply it to the advancement of our country; as did Polybius and Panaetius, who through the favor of Scipio to them greatly advantaged their countries for the obtaining felicity. So Caesar Augustus, when he had taken Alexandria, made his entry into it, holding Arius by the hand, and discoursing with him alone of all his familiars; after which he said to the Alexandrians, who expecting the utmost severity supplicated his favor, that he pardoned them first for the greatness of their city, secondly for its builder, Alexander, and thirdly, added he, to gratify this my friend. Is it then fit to compare to this benefit those exceeding gainful commissions and adminis-

trations of provinces, in the pursuit of which many even grow old at other men's doors, leaving their own domestic affairs in the mean time unregarded? Or should we rather correct Euripides, singing and saying that, if one must watch and sue at another's court and subject one's self to some great man's familiarity, it is most commendable so to do for the sake of one's country; but otherwise, we should embrace and pursue friendships on equal and just conditions.

19. Yet ought not he who renders and exhibits his country obsequious to potent princes to contribute to the oppressing of it, nor having tied its legs to subject also its neck, as some do who, referring all things both great and little to these potentates, upbraid it with servitude, or rather wholly take away the commonwealth, rendering it astonished, timorous, and without command of any thing. For as those who are accustomed neither to sup nor bathe without the physician do not make so much use of their health as Nature affords them; so they who introduce the prince's judgment into every decree, council, favor, and administration, necessitate the princes to be more masters of them than they desire. Now the cause of this is principally the avarice and ambition of the chief citizens. For either, by injuring their inferiors, they compel them to fly out of the city; or in such things wherein they differ from one another, disdaining to be worsted by their fellow-citizens, they bring in such as are more powerful, whence both the council, people, courts of judicature, and whole magistracy lose their authority. But he ought to appease private citizens by equality, and mightier men by mutual submissions, so as to keep peace within the commonweal, and coolly to determine their affairs; making for these things, as it were for secret diseases, a certain political medicine, both being himself rather willing to be vanquished amongst his fellow-citizens, than to get the better

by the injury and dissolution of his country's rights, and requesting the same of every one else, and teaching them how great a mischief this obstinacy in contending is. But now, rather than they will with honor and benignity mutually yield to their fellow-citizens, kinsmen, neighbors, and colleagues in office, they do, with no less prejudice than shame, carry forth their dissensions to the doors of the pleaders, and put them into the hands of pragmatical lawyers.

Physicians indeed turn and drive forth into the superficies of the body such diseases as they are not able utterly to extirpate; but a statesman, though he cannot keep a city altogether free from internal troubles, yet should, by concealing its disturbance and sedition, endeavor to cure and compose it, so that it may least stand in need of physicians and medicines from abroad. For the intention of a statesman should be fixed upon the public safety, and should shun, as has been said, the tumultuous and furious motion of vain-glory; and yet in his disposition there should be magnanimity,

> And undaunted courage, — as becomes
> The men, who are for their dear country's right
> Prepared till death 'gainst stoutest foes to fight,*

and who are bravely resolved, not only to hazard their lives against the assaults of invading enemies, but also to struggle with the most difficult affairs, and stem the torrent of the most dangerous and impetuous times. For as he must not himself be a creator of storms and tempests, so neither must he abandon the ship of the state when they come upon it; and as he ought not to raise commotions and drive it into danger, so is he obliged, when it is tossed and is in peril, to give it his utmost assistance, putting forth all his boldness of speech, as he would throw out a sacred anchor when affairs are at the greatest extremity.

* See Il. XVII. 156.

Such were the difficulties that befell the Pergamenians under Nero, and the Rhodians lately under Domitian, and the Thessalians heretofore in the time of Augustus, when they burned Petraeus alive.

> You shall not in this case demurring see,*

or starting back for fear, any one who is truly a statesman; neither shall you find him accusing others and withdrawing himself out of harm's way; but you shall have him rather going on embassies, sailing to foreign parts, and not only saying first,

> We're here, Apollo, who the murther wrought,
> No longer plague our country for our fault,

but also ready to undergo perils and dangers for the multitude, even though he has not been at all partaker of their crime. For this indeed is a gallant action; and besides its honesty, one only man's virtue and magnanimity has often wonderfully mitigated the anger conceived against a whole multitude, and dissipated the terror and bitterness with which they were threatened. Such an influence with a king of Persia had the deportment of Sperchis and Bulis, two noble Spartans; and equally prevalent was the speech of Stheno with Pompey, when, being about to punish the Mamertines for their defection, he was told by Stheno, that he would not act justly if he should for one guilty person destroy abundance of innocents; for that he himself had caused the revolt of the city, by persuading his friends and forcing his enemies to that attempt. This speech did so dispose Pompey, that he both pardoned the city and courteously treated Stheno. But Sylla's host, having used the like virtue towards an unlike person, generously ended his days. For when Sylla, having taken the city of Praeneste, determined to put all the rest of the inhabitants to the sword, and to spare only him for the hospitality that

---

* See Il. IV. 223

had been between them, he, saying that he would not be indebted for his preservation to the destroyer of his country, thrust himself in amongst his fellow-citizens, and was massacred with them. We ought therefore indeed to deprecate such times as these, and hope for better things.

20. Moreover, we should honor, as a great and sacred thing, every magistracy and magistrate. Now the mutual concord and friendship of magistrates with one another is a far greater honor of magistracy than their diadems and purple-garded robes. Now those who lay for a foundation of friendship their having been fellow-soldiers or having spent their youth together, and take their being joint commanders or co-magistrates for a cause of enmity, cannot avoid being guilty of one of these three evils. For either, regarding their colleagues in government as their equals, they brangle with them; or looking on them as their superiors, they envy them; or esteeming them their inferiors, they despise them; whereas, indeed, one ought to court his superior, advance his inferior, honor his equal, and love and embrace all, as having been made friends, not by eating at the same table, drinking in the same cup, or meeting at the same solemn feast, but by a common and public bond, and having in some sort an hereditary benevolence derived from their country. Scipio therefore was ill spoken of in Rome, for that, making a feast for his friends at the dedication of a temple to Hercules, he invited not to it his colleague Mummius; for, though in other things they took not one another for friends, yet in such occurrences as these they should have mutually honored and caressed each other, for the sake of their common magistracy. If then the omission of so small a civility brought Scipio, who was otherwise an admirable man, under a suspicion of arrogancy; how can he who seeks to impair the dignity of his colleague, or to obfuscate the lustre of his actions, or through insolency to draw and attribute all things to

himself, taking them wholly from his companion, be esteemed reasonable and moderate? I remember that, when I was yet but a young man, being jointly with another sent on an embassy to the proconsul, and my companion — I know not on what occasion — stopping by the way, I went on alone and performed the affair. Now when at my return I was to render an account of my charge, my father, taking me aside, admonished me not to say *I went* but *We went*, not *I spoke* but *We spoke*, and so through all the rest to make my report by associating my companion, and rendering him a sharer in my actions. For this is not only decent and courteous, but also takes from glory what is offensive, that is, envy. Whence it is that great men generally co-ascribe their most glorious actions to their Daemon or Fortune; as did Timoleon, who having destroyed the tyrannies in Sicily, consecrated a temple to Chance; and Python, when, being admired and honored by the Athenians for having slain Cotys, he said, God did this, making use of my hand. But Theopompus, king of the Lacedaemonians, when one said that Sparta was preserved because its kings were well skilled in governing, replied: 'Tis rather because the people are well versed in obeying.

21. These two things then are affected by each other; yet most men both say and think that the business of political instruction is to render the people pliable to be governed. For there are in every city more governed than governors, and every one who lives in a democracy rules only a short time, but is subject all his life, so that it is the most excellent and useful lesson we can learn, to obey those who are set over us, though they are less furnished with authority and reputation.

For it is absurd that a Theodorus or a Polus, the principal actor in a tragedy, should often obey a hireling who plays the third part, and speak humbly to him because he wears a diadem and a sceptre; and that in real actions and in the government of the state, a rich and mighty man should undervalue and contemn a magistrate because he is simple and poor, thus injuring and degrading the dignity of the commonweal by his own; whereas he should rather by his own reputation and authority have increased and advanced that of the magistrate. As in Sparta the kings rose up out of their thrones to the ephors, and whoever else was sent for by them did not slowly obey, but running hastily and with speed through the forum, gave a pattern of obedience to his fellow-citizens, whilst he gloried in honoring the magistrates; not like to some ill-bred and barbarous persons, who, priding themselves in the abundance of their power, affront the judges of the public combats, revile the directors of the dances in the Bacchanals, and deride military commanders and those that preside over the exercises of youth, neither knowing nor understanding that to honor is sometimes more glorious than to be honored. For to a man of great authority in a city, his accompanying and attending on the magistrate is a greater grace than if he were himself accompanied and attended on by him; or rather this indeed would bring trouble and envy, but that brings real glory, and such as proceeds from kindness and good-will. And such a man, being seen sometimes at the magistrate's door, and saluting him first, and giving him the middle place in walking, does, without taking any thing from himself, add ornament to the city.

22. It is also a popular thing and wins greatly on the multitude, to bear patiently the reproaches and indignation of a magistrate, saying either with Diomedes,

Great glory soon will follow this,*

or this, which was sometime said by Demosthenes, — that he is not now Demosthenes only, but a magistrate, or a director of public dances, or a wearer of a diadem. Let us therefore lay aside our revenge for a time; for

* Il. IV. 415.

either we shall come upon him when he is dismissed from his office, or shall by delaying gain a cessation of anger.

23. Indeed one should in diligence, providence, and care for the public always strive with every magistrate, advising them, — if they are gracious and well behaved, — of such things as are requisite, warning them, and giving them opportunities to make use of such things as have been rightly counselled, and helping them to advance the common good; but if there is in them any sloth, delay, or ill-disposedness to action, then ought one to go himself and speak to the people, and not to neglect or omit the public on pretence that it becomes not one magistrate to be curious and play the busybody in another's province. For the law always gives the first rank in government to him who does what is just and knows what is convenient. "There was," says Xenophon,* "one in the army named Xenophon, who was neither general nor inferior commander;" but yet this man, by his skill in what was fit and boldness in attempting, raising himself to command, preserved the Grecians. Now of all Philopoemen's deeds this is the most illustrious, that Agis† having surprised Messene, and the general of the Achaeans being unwilling and fearful to go and rescue it, he with some of the forwardest spirits did without a commission make an assault and recover it. Yet are we not to attempt innovations on every light or trivial occasion; but only in cases of necessity, as did Philopoemen, or for the performance of some honorable actions, as did Epaminondas when he continued in the Boeotarchy four months longer than was allowed by the law, during which he brake into Laconia and re-edified Messene. Whence, if any complaint or accusation shall on this occasion happen, we may in our defence against

---

* Xen. Anab. III. 1, 4.
† Probably a mistake for *Nabis*. See Plutarch's Life of Philopoemen, § 12. (G.)

such accusation plead necessity, or have the greatness and gallantry of the action as a comfort for the danger.

24. There is recorded a saying of Jason, monarch of the Thessalians, which he always had in his mouth when he outraged or molested any, that there is a necessity for those to be unjust in small matters who will act justly in great ones. Now that speech one may presently discern to have been made by a despot. But more political is this precept, to gratify the populacy with the passing over small things, that we may oppose and hinder them when they are like to offend in greater. For he that will be exact and earnest in all things, never yielding or conniving, but always severe and inexorable, accustoms the people to strive obstinately, and behave themselves perversely towards him.

> But when the waves beat high, the sheet should be
> A little slackened, —

sometimes by unbending himself and sporting graciously with them, as in the celebrating of festival sacrifices, assisting at public games, and being a spectator at the theatres, and sometimes by seeming neither to see nor hear, as we pass by the faults of such children in our houses; that the faculty of freely chastising and reprehending, being — like a medicine — not antiquated or debilitated by use, but having its full vigor and authority, may more forcibly move and operate on the multitude in matters of greater importance.

Alexander, being informed that his sister was too familiarly acquainted with a certain handsome young man, was not displeased at it, but said, that she also must be permitted to have some enjoyment of the royalty; acting in this concession neither rightly nor as beseemed himself; for the dissolution and dishonoring of the state ought not to be esteemed an enjoyment. But a statesman will not to his power permit the people to injure any private citizens, to confiscate other men's estates, or to share the public stock amongst them ; but will by persuading, instructing, and threatening oppugn such irregular desires, by the feeding and increasing of which Cleon caused many a stinging drone, as Plato says, to breed in the city. But if the multitude, taking occasion from some solemn feast of the country or the veneration of some God, shall be inclined either to exhibit some show, to make some small distribution, to bestow some courteous gratification, or to perform some other magnificence, let them in such matters have an enjoyment both of their liberality and abundance. For there are many examples of such things in the governments of Pericles and Demetrius ; and Cimon adorned the market-place by planting rows of plane-trees and making of walks. Cato also, seeing the populacy in the time of Catiline's conspiracy put in a commotion by Caesar, and dangerously inclined to make a change in the government, persuaded the senate to decree some distributions of money amongst the poor, and this being done appeased the tumult and quieted the sedition. For, as a physician, having taken from his patient great store of corrupt blood, gives him a little innocent nourishment ; so a statesman, having taken from the people some great thing which was either inglorious or prejudicial, does again by some small and courteous gratuity still their morose and complaining humor.

25. It is not amiss also dexterously to turn aside the eager desires of the people to other useful things, as Demades did when he had the revenues of the city under his management. For they being bent to send galleys to the assistance of those who were in rebellion against Alexander, and commanding him to furnish out money for that purpose, he said to them: You have money ready, for I have made provision against the Bacchanals, that every one of you may receive half a mina ; but if you had rather

have it employed this way, make use as you please of your own. And by this means taking them off from sending the fleet, lest they should be deprived of the dividend, he kept the people from offending Alexander. For there are many prejudicial things to which we cannot directly put a stop, but we must for that end make use of turning and winding; as did Phocion, when he was required at an unseasonable time to make an incursion into Bocotia. For he immediately caused proclamation to be made, that all from sixteen years of age to sixty should prepare to follow him; and when there arose upon it a mutiny amongst the old men, he said: There is no hardship put upon you, for I, who am above fourscore years old, shall be your general. In this manner also is the sending of embassies to be put off, by joining in the commission such as are unprepared; and the raising of unprofitable buildings, by bidding them contribute to it; and the following of indecent suits, by ordering the prosecutors to appear together and go together from the court. Now the proposers and inciters of the people to such things are first to be drawn and associated for the doing them; for so they will either by their shifting it off seem to break the matter, or by their accepting of it have their share in the trouble.

26. But when some great and useful matter, yet such as requires much struggling and industry, is to be taken in hand, endeavor to choose the most powerful of your friends, or rather the mildest of the most powerful; for they will least thwart you and most co-operate with you, having wisdom without a contentious humor. Nevertheless, thoroughly understanding your own nature, you ought, in that for which you are naturally less fit, rather to make choice of such as are of suitable abilities, than of such as are like yourself; as Diomedes, when he went forth to spy, passing by the valiant, took for his companion one that was prudent and cautious. For thus are actions better coun-

terpoised, and there is no contention bred betwixt them, when they desire honor from different virtues and qualities. If therefore you are yourself no good speaker, choose for your assistant in a suit or your companion in an embassy an eloquent man, as Pelopidas did Epaminondas; if you are unfit to persuade and converse with the multitude, being too high-minded for it, as was Callicratidas, take one that is gracious and courtly; if you are infirm of body and unable to undergo fatigues, make choice of one who is robust and a lover of labor, as Nicias did of Lamachus. For thus Geryon would have become admirable, having many legs, hands, and eyes, if only they had been all governed by one soul. But it is in the power of statesmen — by conferring together, if they are unanimous, not only their bodies and wealth, but also their fortunes, authorities, and virtues, to one common use — to perform the same action with greater glory than any one person; not as did the Argonauts, who, having left Hercules, were necessitated to have recourse to female subtleties and be subject to enchantments and sorceries, that they might save themselves and steal away the fleece.

Men indeed entering into some temples leave their gold without; but iron, that I may speak my mind in a word, they never carry into any. Since then the tribunal is a temple common to Jupiter the counsellor and protector of cities, to Themis, and to Justice, from the very beginning, before thou enterest into it, stripping thy soul of avarice and the love of wealth, cast them into the shops of bankers and usurers,
And from them turn thyself,*
esteeming him who heaps up treasures by the management of public affairs to rob the temples, plunder graves, and steal from his friends, and enriching himself by treachery and bearing of false witness, to be an unfaithful counsellor.

* Odyss. V. 350.

a perjured judge, a bribe-taking magistrate, and in brief, free from no injustice. Whence it is not necessary to say much concerning this matter.

27. Now ambition, though it is more specious than covetousness, brings yet no less plagues into a state. For it is usually more accompanied with boldness, as being bred, not in slothful and abject spirits, but chiefly in such as are vigorous and active; and the vogue of the people, frequently extolling it and driving it by their praises, renders it thereby headstrong and hard to be managed. As therefore Plato advised, that we should even from our infancy inculcate into young people, that it is not fit for them to wear gold about them abroad nor yet to be possessors of it, as having a peculiar treasure of their own, immixed with their souls, — enigmatically, as I conceive, insinuating the virtue propagated in their natures from the race or stock of which they are descended, — so let us also moderate our ambition by saying, that we have in ourselves uncorrupted gold, that is, honor unmixed, and free from envy and reprehension, which is still augmented by the consideration and contemplation of our acts and jests in the service of the commonweal. Wherefore we stand not in need of honors painted, cast, or engraven in brass, in which what is most admired frequently belongs to another. For the statue of a trumpeter or halberdier is not commended or esteemed for the sake of the person whom it is made to represent, but for that of the workman by whom it is made. And Cato, when Rome was in a manner filled with statues, would not suffer his to be erected, saying, I had rather men should ask why my statue is not set up, than why it is. For such things are subject to envy, and the people think themselves obliged to those who have not received them; whereas those who have received them are esteemed burthensome, as seeking public employs for a reward. For as he does no great or glorious act who, having without

danger sailed along the Syrtis, is afterwards cast away in the harbor; so he who, having kept himself safe in passing through the treasury and the management of the public revenues, is caught with a presidency or a place in the Prytaneum, not only dashes against an high promontory, but is likewise drowned.

He then is best, who desires none of these things, but shuns and refuses them all. But if perhaps it is not easy wholly to decline a favor or testimonial of the people's amity, when they are fully bent to bestow it, yet for those who have in the service of the state contended not for silver or presents, but have fought a fight truly sacred and deserving a crown, let an inscription, a tablet, a decree, or a branch of laurel or olive suffice, such as Epimenides received out of the castle of Athens for having purified the city. So Anaxagoras, putting back the other honors that were given him, desired that on the day of his death the children might have leave to play and intermit their studies. And to the seven Persians who killed the Magi it was granted that they and their posterity should wear their turban on the fore part of the head; for this, it seems, they had made the signal, when they went about that attempt. The honor also which Pittacus received had something political; for being bid to take what portion he would of the land he had gotten for his citizens, he accepted as much as he could reach with the cast of his dart. So Cocles the Roman took as much as he himself, being lame, could plough in a day. For the honor should not be a recompense of the action, but an acknowledgment of gratitude, that it may continue also long, as those did which we have mentioned. But of the three hundred statues erected to Demetrius Phalereus, not one was eaten into by rust or covered with filth, they being all pulled down whilst himself was yet alive; and those of Demades were melted into chamber-pots. Many other honors also have undergone the like fate, being regarded with an ill eye, not only for the wickedness of the receiver, but also for the greatness of the gift. A moderation in the expense is therefore the best and surest preservative of honors; for such as are great, immense, and ponderous are like to unproportioned statues, soon overthrown.

28. Now I here call those honors which the people,

Whose right it is, so name; with them I speak:

as Empedocles has it; since a wise statesman will not despise true honor and favor, consisting in the good-will and friendly disposition of those who gratefully remember his services; nor will he contemn glory by shunning to please his neighbors, as Democritus would have him. For neither the fawning of dogs nor the affection of horses is to be rejected by huntsmen and jockeys; nay, it is both profitable and pleasant to breed in those animals which are brought up in our houses and live with us, such a disposition towards one's self as Lysimachus's dog showed to his master, and as the poet relates Achilles's horses to have had towards Patroclus.* And I am of opinion that bees would fare better if they would make much of those who breed them and look after them, and would admit them to come near them, than they do by stinging them and driving them away; for now their keepers punish them by smothering them with smoke; so they tame unruly horses with short bits; and dogs that are apt to run away, by collaring them and fastening them to clogs. But there is nothing which renders one man so obsequious and submissive to another, as the confidence of his good-will, and the opinion of his integrity and justice. Wherefore Demosthenes rightly affirmed, that the greatest preservative of states against tyrants is distrust. For the part of the soul by which we believe is most apt to be caught. As there-

---

* See Il. XIX. 404.

fore Cassandra's gift of prophecy was of no advantage to the citizens of Troy, who would not believe her:

> The God (says she) would have me to foretell
> Things unbelieved; for when the people well
> Have smarted, groaning under pressures sad,
> They style me wise, till then they think me mad;

so the confidence the citizens had in Archytas, and their good-will towards Battus, were highly advantageous to those who would make use of them through the good opinion they had of them.

Now the first greatest benefit which is in the reputation of statesmen is the confidence that is had in them, giving them an entrance into affairs; and the second is, that the good-will of the multitude is an armor to the good against those that are envious and wicked; for,

> As when the careful mother drives the flies
> From her dear babe, which sweetly sleeping lies,*

it chases away envy, and renders the plebeian equal in authority to the nobleman, the poor man to the rich, and the private man to the magistrates; and in a word, when truth and virtue are joined with it, it is a strange and favorable wind, directly carrying men into government. And on the other side behold and learn by examples the mischievous effects of the contrary disposition. For those of Italy slew the wife and children of Dionysius, having first violated and polluted them with their lusts; and afterwards burning their bodies, scattered the ashes out of the ship into the sea. But when one Menander, who had reigned graciously over the Bactrians, died afterwards in the camp, the cities indeed by common consent celebrated his funeral; but coming to a contest about his relics, they were difficultly at last brought to this agreement, that his ashes being distributed, every one of them should carry away an equal share, and they should all erect monuments

* II. IV. 180.

to him. Again, the Agrigentines, being got rid of Phalaris, made a decree, that none should wear a blue garment; for the tyrant's attendants had blue liveries. But the Persians, because Cyrus was hawk-nosed, do to this day love such men and esteem them handsomest.

29. That is of all loves the strongest and divinest, which is by cities and states borne to any man for his virtue. But those false-named honors and false testimonials of amity, which have their rise from stage-plays, largesses, and fencings, are not unlike the flatteries of whores; the people always with smiles bestowing an unconstant and short-lived glory on him that presents them and gratifies them.

He therefore who said, the people were first overthrown by him which first bestowed largesses on them, very well understood that the multitude lose their strength, being rendered weaker by receiving. But these bestowers must also know that they destroy themselves, when, purchasing glory at great expenses, they make the multitude haughty and arrogant, as having it in their power to give and take away some very great matter.

30. Yet are we not therefore to act sordidly in the distribution of honorary presents, when there is plenty enough. For the people more hate a rich man who gives nothing of his own, than they do a poor man that robs the public treasury; attributing the former to pride and a contempt of them, but the latter to necessity. First, therefore, let these largesses be made gratis, for so they more oblige the receivers, and strike them with admiration; then, on some occasion that has a handsome and laudable pretence, with the honor of some God wholly drawing the people to devotion; for so there is at the same time bred in them a strong apprehension and opinion that the Deity is great and venerable, when they see those whom they honor and highly esteem so bountifully and readily expending their wealth upon his honor. As therefore Plato forbade

young men who were to be liberally educated to learn the Lydian and Phrygian harmony, — one of which excites the mournful and melancholy part of our soul, whilst the other increases its inclination to pleasure and sensual delight, — so do you, as much as possibly you can, drive out of the city all such largesses as either foster and cherish brutality and savageness, or scurrility and lasciviousness; and if that cannot be, at least shun them, and oppose the many when they desire such spectacles; always making the subjects of our expenses useful and modest, having for their end what is good and necessary, or at least what is pleasant and acceptable, without any prejudice or injury.

31. But if your estate be but indifferent, and by its centre and circumference confined to your necessary use, it is neither ungenerous nor base to confess your poverty and give place to such as are provided for those honorary expenses, and not, by taking up money on usury, to render yourself at the same time both miserable and ridiculous by such services. For they whose abilities fall short cannot well conceal themselves, being compelled either to be troublesome to their friends, or to court and flatter usurers, so that they get not any honor or power, but rather shame and contempt by such expenses. It is therefore always useful on such occasions to call to mind Lamachus and Phocion. For Phocion, when the Athenians at a solemn sacrifice called upon him, and often importuned him to give them something, said to them, I should be ashamed to give to you, and not pay this Callicles, — pointing to an usurer who was standing by. And as for Lamachus, he always put down in his bill of charges, when he was general, the money laid out for his shoes and coat. And to Hermon, when he refused the undertaking of an office because of his poverty, the Thessalians ordained a puncheon of wine a month, and a bushel and a half of meal every four days. It is therefore no shame to confess one's

poverty; nor are the poor in cities of less authority than those who feast and exhibit public shows, if they have but gotten freedom of speech and reputation by their virtue.

A statesman ought therefore chiefly to moderate himself on such occasions, and neither, being himself on foot, go into the field against well-mounted cavaliers, nor, being himself poor, vie with those that are rich about race matches, theatrical pomps, and magnificent tables and banquets; but he should rather strive to be like those who endeavor to manage the city by virtue and prudence, always joined with eloquence; in which there is not only honesty and venerableness, but also a gracefulness and attractiveness,

> Far more to be desired than Croesus' wealth.

For a good man is neither insolent nor odious; nor is a discreet person self-conceited,

> Nor with a look severe walks he amongst
> His fellow-citizens;

but he is, on the contrary, courteous, affable, and of easy access to all, having his house always open, as a port of refuge to those that will make use of him, and showing his care and kindness, not only by being assistant in the necessities and affairs of those that have recourse to him, but also by condoling with those that are in adversity, and congratulating and rejoicing with such as have been successful; neither is he troublesome or offensive by the multitude and train of domestics attending him at bath, or by taking up of places in the theatres, nor remarkable by things invidious for luxury and sumptuousness; but he is equal and like to others in his clothes, diet, education of his children, and the garb and attendance of his wife, as desiring in his comportment and manner of living to be like the rest of the people. Then he exhibits himself an intelligent counsellor, an unfeed advocate and courteous arbitrator between men and their wives, and friends at variance amongst themselves; not spending a small part of the day for the service of the commonweal at the tribunal or in the hall of audience, and employing all the rest, and the whole remainder of his life, in drawing to himself every sort of negotiations and affairs, as the northeast wind does the clouds; but always employing his cares on the public, and reputing polity (or the administration of the state) as a busy and active life, and not, as it is commonly thought, an easy and idle service; he does by all these and such like things turn and draw the many, who see that all the flatteries and enticements of others are but spurious and deceitful baits, when compared to his care and providence. The flatterers indeed of Demetrius vouchsafed not to give the other potentates of his time, amongst whom Alexander's empire was divided, the title of kings, but styled Seleucus master of the elephants, Lysimachus treasurer, Ptolemaeus admiral, and Agathocles governor of the isles. But the multitude, though they may at the beginning reject a good and prudent man, yet coming afterwards to understand his veracity and the sincerity of his disposition, esteem him a public-spirited person and a magistrate; and of the others, they think and call one a maintainer of choruses, a second a feaster, and a third a master of the exercises. Moreover, as at the banquets made by Callias or Alcibiades, Socrates only is heard, and to Socrates all men's eyes are directed; so in sound and healthy states Ismenias bestows largesses, Lichas makes suppers, and Niceratus provides choruses; but it is Epaminondas, Aristides, and Lysander that govern, manage the state, and lead forth the armies. Which if any one considers, he ought not to be dejected or amazed at the glory gotten amongst the people from theatres, banqueting-halls, and public buildings; since it lasts but a short time, being at an end as soon as the prizes and plays are over, and having in them nothing honorable or worthy of esteem.

32. Those that are versed in the keeping and breeding of bees look on that hive to be healthiest and in best condition, where there is most humming, and which is fullest of bustle and noise; but he to whom God has committed the care of the rational and political hive, reputing the felicity of the people to consist chiefly in quietness and tranquillity, will receive and to his power imitate the rest of Solon's ordinances, but will doubt and wonder what it was that induced him to decree, that he who, when there arises a sedition in the city, adheres to neither party should be reputed infamous. For in the body, the beginning of its change from sickness to health is not wrought by the parts that are infected with the disease, but when the temperature of such parts as are sound, growing powerful, drives away what is contrary to nature; and in a state, where the people are disturbed by a sedition not dangerous and mortal, but which will after a while be composed and allayed, it is of necessity that there be a mixture of much that is uninfected and sound, and that it continue and cohabit in it. For thither flows from the wise what is fit and natural, and passes into the part that is diseased. But when cities are in an universal commotion, they are in danger of being utterly destroyed, unless, being constrained by some necessity and chastisement from abroad, they are by the force of their miseries reduced to wisdom. Yet does it not become you in the time of a sedition to sit as if you were neither sensible nor sorry, praising your own unconcernedness as a quiet and happy life, and taking delight in the error of others. But on such occasions chiefly should you put on the buskin of Theramenes, and conferring with both parties, join yourself to neither. For you will not seem a stranger by not being a partaker in injustice,

but a common friend to them all by your assistance; nor will you be envied for your not sharing in the calamity, when you appear equally to condole with every one of them. But the best is, by your providential care to prevent the raising of any sedition; and in this consists the greatest and most excellent point, as it were, of the political art. For you are to consider that, the greatest benefits a city can enjoy being peace, liberty, plenty, abundance of men, and concord, the people have at this time no need of statesmen for the procuring of peace; since all war, whether with Greeks or barbarians, is wholly taken away and banished from us. As for liberty, the people have as much as the emperors think fit to grant them, and more perhaps would not be expedient. The prudent man therefore will beg the Gods to grant to his fellow-citizens the unenvied plenty of the earth, and the kind temper of the seasons, and that wives may bear " children like to their parents,"* and also safety for all that is born and produced.

There remains therefore to a statesman, of all those things that are subject to his charge, this alone, which is inferior to none of the other benefits, the keeping of those who are co-inhabitants of the same city in perpetual concord and friendship, and the taking away of all contentions, animosities, and heart-burnings. In which he shall, as in the differences between friends, so converse with the party appearing to be most injured, as if he himself seemed also a sharer in the injury and equally offended at it, endeavoring afterwards so to appease him, by showing him how much those who pass by injuries excel such as strive to contend and conquer, not only in good-nature and sweetness of disposition, but also in prudence and magnanimity; and how, by remitting a little of their right in small matters, they get the better in the greatest and most important. He shall afterwards admonish them both in general and

* Hesiod, Works and Days, 235.

apart, instructing them in the weakness of the Grecian affairs, which it is better for intelligent men to make the best of, and to live in peace and concord, than to engage in a contest for which fortune has left no reward. For what authority, what glory is there remaining for the conquerors? What power is there, which the least decree of a proconsul cannot abolish or transfer elsewhere, and which, though it should continue, would yet have any thing worth our pains? But since, as a conflagration in a town does not frequently begin in sacred and public places, but a lamp negligently left in a house, or the burning of a little trash or rubbish, raises a great fire and works a common mischief; so sedition in a state is not always kindled by contentions about public affairs, but oftentimes the differences arising from private concerns and jangles, being propagated into the public, have disturbed a whole city. It is no less becoming a statesman to remedy and prevent all these, so that some of them may never have any being, others may quickly be extinguished, and others hindered from increasing or taking hold of the public, and confined amongst the adversaries themselves. And as himself ought to take care for this, so should he advertise others, that private disturbances are the occasion of public ones, and little of great ones, if they are neglected and suffered to proceed without taking care to apply fit remedies to them in the beginning.

In this manner is the greatest and most dangerous disturbance that ever happened in Delphi said to have been occasioned by Crates, whose daughter Orgilaus, the son of Phalis, being about to marry, it happened that the cup they were using in the espousals brake asunder of itself; which he taking for an ill omen, left his bride, and went away with his father. Crates a little after, charging them with taking away a certain golden vessel, used in the sacrifices, caused Orgilaus and his brother, unheard, to be precipitated from the top of a rock to the bottom, and afterwards slew several of their most intimate friends, as they were at their devotions in the temple of Providence. After many such things were perpetrated, the Delphians, putting to death Crates and his companions in the sedition, out of their estates which they called excommunicated, built the temples in the lower part of the town. In Syracuse also there were two young men, betwixt whom there was an extraordinary intimacy, one of which, having taken into his custody his friend's catamite, vitiated him in his absence. The other at his return, by way of retaliation, debauched his companion's wife. Then one of the ancient senators, coming into the council, proposed the banishing of them both before the city was ruined by their filling it with enmity. Yet did not he prevail; but a sedition arising on this occasion by very great calamities overturned a most excellently constituted commonweal. You have also a domestical example in the enmity between Pardalus and Tyrrhenus, which wanted little of destroying Sardis by embroiling it in revolt and war on little and private differences. A statesman therefore is not to slight the little offences and heart-burnings which, as diseases in a body, pass speedily from one to another, but to take them in hand, suppress, and cure them. For, as Cato says, by attention and carefulness great matters are made little, and little ones reduced to nothing. Now there is no better artifice of inuring men to this, than the showing one's self easily pacified in his own private differences, persisting without rancor in matters of the first importance, and managing none with obstinacy, contending wrath, or any other passion, which may work sharpness or bitterness in necessary disputes. For as they bind certain round muffles about the hands of those who combat at buffets, that in their contests there may not arrive any fatal accident, the blows being soft and such as can do no great harm; so in such suits and processes with one's fellow-citizens, it is best to manage the dispute by making use of pure and simple pretences, and not by sharpening and empoisoning matters, as if they were weapons, with calumnies, malice, and threats, to render them pernicious, great, and public. For he who in this manner carries himself with those with whom he has affairs will have others also subject to him. But contentions about public matters, where private grudges are taken away, are soon appeased, and bring no difficult or fatal mischiefs.

WHICH ARE THE MOST CRAFTY, WATER-ANIMALS OR THOSE CREATURES THAT BREED UPON THE LAND?

AUTOBULUS, SOCLARUS, OPTATUS, PHAEDIMUS, ARISTOTIMUS, HERACLEO.

1. AUTOBULUS. Leonidas, being asked the question what he thought of Tyrtaeus, made answer, that he was a good poet to whet minds of young men; as a person who, by the vigor and spirit of his poetical raptures, kindled that wrathful indignation and ambition of honor, which emboldened them in combat to the contempt of death and danger. Which makes me afraid, my dearest friends, lest the encomium of hunting yesterday recited may have inflamed our young gentlemen beyond the bounds of moderation, so as to deem all other things fruitless and of little worth, while they rendezvous from all parts to this exercise. So much the rather, because I myself, when I was but very young, even beyond the strength of my age, seemed to be more than became me addicted to this sport, and to be over desirous with Phaedra in Euripides,

> With hounds and horn and merry hollow,
> The spotted hart and hind to follow.

So did that discourse affect me, fortified with many and probable arguments.

SOCLARUS. You say very truly, Autobulus. For that same poet seems to me to have awakened the force of rhetoric, for a long time lulled asleep, to gratify the inclinations of the youthful gentry, and to make himself their spring companion. But I am most pleased with him for introducing the example of single combatants, from whence he takes occasion to praise the sport of hunting, as being that which for the most part draws to itself whatever is natural in us, or what we have by use acquired, of that delight which men take in fighting with single weapons one against another, thus affording an evident prospect of artifice and daring courage, endued with understanding, encountering brutish force and strength, and applauding that of Euripides:

> Small is the nerveless strength of feeble man,
> Yet through the cunning of his reaching brain,
> By various slights and sundry stratagems,
> Whatever land or th' Ocean breeds he tames.*

2. AUTOBULUS. And hence it was, as they say, my dearest Soclarus, that men at first became insensible and inhuman, having once tasted of murder, and being all accustomed, by hunting and following the chase, not only to behold without remorse the wounds and blood of wild beasts, but to rejoice at their being killed and slaughtered. Afterwards, as at Athens, some sycophant was by the Thirty Tyrants set apart for death, as a proper object of capital punishment, then a second, and a third; till, proceeding by degrees, they seized upon good men, and at length spared not the best and most worthy citizens. In like manner the first that slew a bear or a wolf obtained applause, then the ox and hog were appointed to be killed, under pretence of having tasted the sacred things that lay before them. Next to them deer, hares, and goats were made use of for food, and in some places the flesh of sheep, dogs, and horses grew familiar to human taste. The tame goose also and pigeon, man's familiar domestic, according to Sophocles, — not for nourishment or to assuage hunger,

---

* Eurip. Hippol. 218.

as cats and weasels do, but to indulge voluptuous appetites,
— they dressed and mangled to pieces. This gave strength
and vigor to whatever was in nature bloodthirsty and
savage, and rendering the disposition of man inflexible
to pity, had almost erased out of his breast whatever was
inclinable to humanity and mildness. Whereas, on the other
side, the Pythagoreans, that they might accustom men to
the love of humanity and compassion, still inculcated into
their minds a particular care of being mild and gentle
towards beasts. For there is nothing more powerful than
custom to win upon all the affections of man, and to
draw them from moderation to extremity. But I know not
how it comes to pass, that being entered into this discourse, we have forgot not only the subject we were yesterday upon, but what we had also this day agreed to
make the theme of our colloquy. For yesterday, as you
well know, having thrown out a proposition, that all creatures were in some manner partakers of understanding
and reason, we gave an occasion to you, young huntsmen,
for a fair dispute, which of the two excelled in craft and
cunning, the land animals, or the creatures that breed in
the sea? Which, if you please, we will determine this
day, if Aristotimus and Phaedimus will stand to their
agreement; of which two gentlemen, the one has offered
himself to his friends to be the patron of the land animals,
the other reserves the honor of being more crafty to those
of the sea.

SOCLARUS. They will be as good as their words, I assure
you, Autobulus, and will be here presently; for I saw them
both early this morning preparing for the combat. In the
mean time, if you please, before they begin, let us resume
something of what was yesterday not so fully discoursed
of for want of time, or not so carefully argued in our
wine, as it ought to have been. For there seemed a dispute to resound in my ears from the Stoics' portico, that,

as immortal is opposite to mortal, incorruptible to corruptible, incorporeal to corporeal, in like manner things void of reason ought to be opposed to those beings that are endued with reason, lest among so many pairs of contraries this alone should be found maimed and imperfect.

3. AUTOBULUS. Good now, friend Soclarus, who was he that maintained that, because there are certain beings endued with reason, therefore there is nothing void of reason? For we abound with examples in all things that are destitute of a soul; nor do we want any other antithesis to irrational, but only to oppose whatever is deprived of a soul — as being void of reason and understanding — to that which is endued with reason and understanding together with a soul. But if any one will assert, that Nature is not defective, and that therefore animated Nature is partly rational, partly without reason; another may at the same time allege, that animated Nature is partly endued with imagination, partly deprived of it; partly sensible, partly insensible; to the end that Nature may not want these opposite habits and privations, as it were, equally balanced in the same kind. For, as it would be absurd to expect to find some living creatures sensible and others without sense, and equally ridiculous to grant imagination to some living creatures and not alllow it to others, — since there is no living creature that comes into the world but what is presently endued with sense and imagination, — thus would he be as much out of the way, who should require one living creature to be rational and another void of reason, and that too when he is disputing with men who hold that nothing whatever can partake of sense which does not also partake of understanding, and that there is no animal not endued by Nature with opinion and ratiocination, as well as with sense and instinct. For Nature, which, as they truly say, made all things for the sake of something and to some end, did not make a sensible

creature to be merely sensible of barely suffering something; but since there are many things familiar and agreeable, and other things as baneful and pernicious, no one of them could survive for a moment, did they not learn to avoid some things and covet the use and benefit of others. Sense it is, therefore, that affords to every creature the knowledge both of useful and hurtful; but the discretion which accompanies the said sense, choosing and seizing upon things profitable, and discerning and avoiding things pernicious or troublesome, can never be thought to reside in any creature not capable to reason, to judge, remember, and consider. Therefore, if you will deprive the creatures of expectation, memory, design, preparation, hope, fear, desire, and grief, you must at the same time deny them the use either of eyes or ears, and indeed of all sense and imagination; which it is better for them to be without, since they cannot make use of them, than to labor under grief and pain, with no means present of averting them.

There is an oration of Strato the philosopher, demonstrating that without sense there can be no understanding. For many times letters cursorily glanced upon by the eye, and speeches little regarded by the ear, escape our knowledge, our minds being intent on other matters. Afterwards by recollection the same things return into our mind, for us to run through and pursue them in our thoughts as we please. Whence we say proverbially, "The mind sees, the mind hears; all other things are deaf and blind," in regard there can be no sense in the eyes and ears, if understanding be wanting. Therefore King Cleomenes, after great commendations given to a copy of verses recited at a banquet where he was present, being asked whether it were not an admirable piece, bid them that heard it give their judgment, for that his mind was in the Peloponnesus. Therefore of necessity, whatever creatures are capable of sense must also be capable of understanding, if we can no otherwise be sensible than by the force of understanding.

But suppose we should grant that sense has no need of the understanding for the performance of the duty incumbent upon it; nevertheless, when that same sense which has shown an animal the difference between what is grateful and what is averse to Nature has departed, where is that faculty which retains this difference in the memory, — dreading things that are abominable, and longing after things that are useful, and if they are wanting, seeking means to compass them, — which provides animals receptacles and places of refuge, that they may look out after their prey, and avoid the snares and gins of the hunters? And yet those very authors inculcate these things in their introductions, even to the teasing our ears: defining purpose to be an indication that something is to be brought to completion; design to be an impulse before an impulse; preparation to be an action before an action; memory to be the comprehension of some certain past impression, which at first was apprehended by sense. In all which things there is nothing which may not rightly be said to partake of reason, and yet all these things are common to all creatures; as indeed are certainly all cogitations; which, while they lie concealed in the brain, we call thoughts, but when they come to be in motion, we name conceptions. In the mean time they acknowledge all passions and perturbations of the mind to be false judgments and erroneous opinions; so that it is a wonder to me, that the same men should oversee so many operations and motions, some of desire, others of fear, nay, by Jupiter, many times of envy and emulation itself. And many times they themselves punish their dogs and horses when they commit a fault, and this not to no purpose, but to chastise them by causing in them through pain that trouble of mind which we call repentance. Now the tickling the ear by pleasing sounds is called enchantment, but the bewitching the eye is called bewitching; both which we make use of in the domesticating of wild beasts. Harts and horses are allured by the sounds of pipes and flutes. And there are a sort of crabs which are charmed out of their holes by fifes; and it is reported that the shadfish are drawn to show themselves above water by singing and clapping of hands. The otus also, which is a bird not much unlike a night-raven, is taken by allurement of the sight; for that while he stands staring upon the fowlers dancing before him in measure and figure, and out of affection will be striving to act his part by aping their motions with his wings and shoulders, he is frequently surprised and taken.

But as for those that more foolishly affirm that beasts are not affected with joy or anger or fear, that the swallow does not build, that the bee does not remember, that the lion is not angry, that the hart is not timorous, but that they do all these things only as it were and apparently; I would fain know what answer they will make to those who say, that beasts neither see nor hear, but as it were see and as it were hear; that they neither neigh nor bleat, but as it were send forth a certain sound; lastly, that they do not absolutely live, but live as it were? For, in my opinion, to aver this is as contrary to plain demonstration as the rest.

4. SOCLARUS. Well then, Autobulus, suppose me to be one of those that affirm these things. For it is great folly for men to compare the actions of beasts with the customs, actions, and manner of living men, and above all, to deny that beasts have the least inclination or aim at any progress towards virtue, to which we bent our discourse. Indeed, I doubt whether Nature gave them a beginning or no, since they are so incapable to attain the end.

AUTOBULUS. Why truly, Soclarus, this is not a thing that

seems so absurd to those men. For that while they assert the extreme love of parents towards their children to be the principle of society and justice, and find at the same time this virtue apparent and surpassing in brute animals, yet they will not allow them in the least to partake of justice; like mules, which, though they are furnished with genital parts, as wanting neither privities nor wombs, and mixing with delight and pleasure, yet cannot attain the end of generation. But then again I would have you consider, whether they be not ridiculous, that affirm Socrates or Plato to be no less vicious than the meanest of slaves, — nay more, that they were fools, intemperate, and unjust, — and then find fault with the nature of beasts, as being impure and no way accurately framed for the reception of virtue; as if this were proof of utter want of reason, and not of depravedness and imbecility of reason. And all the while, they acknowledge that there are vices of reason, of which all brute beasts are guilty; many of which we plainly find to be intemperate, fearful, malicious, and unjust. Therefore he that denies that reason exists by Nature in a creature, because it is not framed by Nature to attain to the perfection of reason, little differs from one that should deny a monkey to partake of deformity by Nature, or a tortoise of slowness, as being neither susceptible of beauty or swiftness. Nor do they observe the distinction that lies before their eyes. For reason is in the creature by Nature, but right and perfect reason is attained by industry and education; so that naturally all creatures may be said to be rational. But if they look for perfection of reason and true wisdom, they will hardly find those perfections in any man whatever. For as there is a difference between sight and sight, and between flight and flight, — for hawks and grasshoppers do not see alike, neither do eagles and partridges fly with equal swiftness, — so neither in all rational creatures is there to be found the same perfection of cunning and acuteness. For as there are many examples to be produced of several brute creatures, excelling in the observance of society, fortitude, and foresight as to their particular economy and making provision for themselves; so on the other side, there may be found among them as many of injustice, cowardice, and folly. Which is evident from the present contest wherein these young gentlemen have engaged themselves, while the one has undertaken to maintain that land-animals, the other that creatures bred in the sea, are most inclined to virtue. Which is plainly demonstrated by comparing river-horses with storks. For the one support and cherish their fathers, the others kill them that they may enjoy their dams. So likewise, if you compare doves with partridges. For the cock partridge will not suffer the hen to sit, but breaks her eggs and throws them out of the nest if she refuses to be trod. But the cock pigeon takes upon him part of the female's duty, in brooding over the eggs and feeding the young ones; and if the hen happens to be too long absent, he corrects her with his bill, till he forces her to return to her nest. So that, while Antipater found fault with sheep and asses for their nastiness, I wonder how he came to pass by lynxes and swallows, of which the one are so cleanly that they always remove and hide their excrements, the others teach their young ones to turn their tails out of their nest, before they let fall their defilement. And indeed, why may we not say that one tree is more docible than another, as dogs are more docible than sheep; or one pot-herb more timorous than another, as harts are more fearful than lions? Or otherwise, as among things immovable, there is not one thing slower in motion than another; nor among things that are mute, one thing more vocal than another; so neither, among things to which Nature has not afforded a faculty of understanding, is there one thing more timorous, more slothful, or more intemperate than another. But as to those creatures where that faculty is present, the difference is manifest in the degrees of more or less.

5. SOCLARUS. However, it is a wonderful thing to observe, how much man differs from all other creatures in probity of manners, in industry, and in all those things that relate to justice and common society.

AUTOBULUS. Nevertheless, my dear friend, this cannot be denied, that there are many brute beasts that surpass men both in bulk and swiftness, others that far surpass him in strength of sight and exactness of hearing; and yet for all this we are not to say that man is blind, without strength, or wants ears. For Nature has not deprived us either of hands or eyes or strength or bulk, though we must not compare with camels or elephants. In like manner we must not say that brute beasts are altogether deprived of reason and understanding, because they are more dull of understanding, and not so quick at ratiocination as we are, as only enjoying a weak and muddy sort of reason, like a dim and clouded eye. And did I not presently expect these young gentlemen, being persons both studious and learned, to bring together an infinite number of examples in reference to both land and sea-animals, I could produce a thousand examples of docility and a thousand more of good nature in beasts, which the famous city of Rome has given us an opportunity to fetch from her imperial theatres; but we will leave these things fresh and untouched, for them to embellish with their eloquent discourse.

In the mean time I have something to offer by the by, which is this, that I am of opinion that there is a mutilation, disease, and defect peculiar to every part and faculty, — as blindness of the eye, lameness of the leg, and stuttering of the tongue, — which defects cannot be appropriated to any other members. For that blindness can never be attributed to that which was never created to see, nor lameness to that which never could go, nor can any thing be said to stammer that wants a tongue, or to lisp or stutter that has not a vocal utterance. And nothing can be said to be a changeling or beside his wits or mad, to which Nature never gave the use of thought, reason, and understanding; for it is impossible to be so without some faculty that can suffer either privation or mutilation or some other defect. But you have seen dogs that were mad, and I have seen horses under the same predicament; and some there are who say that bulls and foxes will be mad. But the example of dogs is sufficient, which is unquestionable. This makes it evident, that those creatures have a sort of reason and understanding not to be despised, which being once confused and troubled, the affection arises which is called madness. For we do not find either their sight or their hearing diminished. Now, as when a man is affected with hypochondriac melancholy, or in a delirium, it would be absurd to say that he was not beside himself, or that his sense, reason, and memory were not disturbed, — for custom tells that they who are in a raving condition are not in their right senses, but are fallen from their reason, — so whoever believes that there is any other cause why dogs run mad, but only that their natural senses, reason, and memories are disturbed, while they cease to know faces the most familiar to them before, and abandon their most usual food, and overlook what is just before their eyes, such a man, I say, seems to me either to overlook what is just before his eyes, or else, seeing the conclusions that follow, to fight against the truth itself.

6 Soclarus. You seem to me to be very much in the right, for the Stoics and Peripatetics are led to affirm the contrary upon this supposition, that justice could have no certain original, but would be altogether incomprehensible and inexistent if all brute creatures should partake

of reason. For either of necessity we must do a very great piece of injustice when we devour and feed upon them; or if we forbear the use of them, it will be impossible for us to live, or rather we shall in some measure live the lives of beasts, rejecting the use of brute creatures. I pass by those innumerable myriads of nomades and Troglodytes that know no other food but flesh. But as for us that seem to live lovingly and in friendship together, what necessity would there be of laboring on the earth, toiling upon the sea, or mining in the mountains, what ornament would there be in our life, if it were so that we must be bound to live, as it would then become us, not only without injury but rather with all civility and humanity toward all the sorts of beasts, as being our fellow rational creatures? We have no cure, no remedy for an unquestionable necessity that deprives us either of life or justice, unless we observe that ancient bound and dispensation which, according to Hesiod, distinguishing natures and separating every kind by themselves, commands

> The fish, wild beasts, and all the winged fowl,
> To prey upon their kinds without control,
> For among them no law nor justice reigns;
> Only by justice man from man abstains.*

And therefore, as brutes can extend no act of justice to us, so neither can we commit any act of injustice against them. Which argument they who reject have left us no benefit of life, nor any the smallest entrance for justice into the world.

7. AUTOBULUS. These things, dear friend, you utter as the opinion of those people. But we are not to allow philosophers a remedy to procure easy delivery, as they do to women that are subject to hard labors, merely that they may bring us forth justice without any pain or trouble. For the same persons, even in the greatest matters, will

---

* Hesiod, Works and Days, 275.

not allow to Epicurus so small and pitiful a thing as the slightest inclination of one only atom, for to make way for the stars and living creatures and Fortune to come into the world, and that thereby our free will might be saved. For we ought either to prove what is doubtful or to assume what of itself is manifest; so we ought not to take for granted this doctrine touching beasts as regards justice, unless it is either confessed or otherwise proved by demonstration. For justice has another way to establish itself, neither so steep nor so slippery, nor leading to the subversion of evident truths; but which, according to Plato's instruction, my son and thy friend, Soclarus, has showed to such as are not captiously contentious but willing to learn. For certain it is, that both Empedocles and Heraclitus held it for a truth, that man could not be altogether cleared from injustice in dealing with beasts as he now does; often bewailing and exclaiming against Nature, as if she were nothing else but necessity and war, having neither any thing unmixed nor any thing truly pure, but still arriving at her end by many, and those unjust and unlawful passions. Whence they affirm that generation itself originally proceeded from injustice by the conjunction of immortal with mortal, and that the thing engendered is still contrary to Nature delighted with the parts of that which engenders, dismembered from the whole. But this seems to be too luxuriant and severe an accusation of Nature. For there is yet a more moderate excuse, which does not altogether deprive the beasts of reason, yet justifies the necessary and convenient use of them; which when the ancients introduced, they detested and utterly discountenanced voracious and voluptuous gluttony. Pythagoras also resumed the argument, teaching how we might reap the benefit of the creatures without doing injustice. For they do no injustice, that chastise and kill such savage beasts that are both hurtful to man and never will be tame. But taming such as are gentle and loving to men, they thereby make them assistant in the several uses to which they were ordained, —

> The horse and ass, that backs to load resign,
> And race of bulls,

which, as Prometheus in Aeschylus * observes,

> Kind Heaven vouchsafed to men by toil distrest,
> With servile limbs his labors to assist.

Thus we make use of dogs to guard our goats and sheep, while they are milked and shorn. For life does not presently forsake a man unless he have his platters of fish or livers of geese, or unless he may kill whole oxen or kids to supply his banquets, or unless — that he may disport himself in the theatre or take his pleasure in hunting — he may compel some beasts to be daring and to fight against their wills, and kill others whom Nature has not armed to defend themselves. For, in my opinion, he that is for sport and pastime ought to seek out for such as will sport and be merry with him. And as it was the saying of Bion, that, though boys throw stones at frogs in sport, yet the frogs do not die in sport but in earnest; so in hunting and fishing, the fault is in the men delighting in the torments and cruel deaths of beasts, and tearing them without compassion from their whelps and their young ones. For it is not in the making use of beasts that men do them wrong, but in the wastefully and cruelly destroying them.

8. SOCLARUS. Contain yourself, my dearest Autobulus, and forbear these accusations; for here are several gentlemen coming, all great huntsmen, whom it will be very difficult to bring over to your opinion; neither is it convenient to offend them.

AUTOBULUS. You give me good advice. However, I

---

* In the lost tragedy, Prometheus Unbound, Frag. 188 (Nauck). (G.)

know Eubiōtus very well, and my kinsman Ariston; nor am I less acquainted with Aeacides and Aristotimus, the sons of Dionysius the Delphian, as also with Nicander the son of Euthydamus, all expert in the chase by land, as Homer expresses it; and therefore likely to take part with Aristotimus. On the other side, yonder comes Phaedimus too, bringing along with him the islanders and neighbors to the sea, Heracleon of Megara, and Philostratus of Euboea,

>Whose whole delight is all the day
>The toilsome pastime of the sea.*

But as for Optatus, our equal in years (like Tydides),—

>Which of the sides to range him well,
>So versed in both, we cannot tell.†

For he is one that offers as well the first-fruits of his fishery to Dictynna, as of his forest spoils to Diana; so that it is apparent he comes among us as one that intends not to be partial to one side more than the other; or else our conjecture is amiss, dear Optatus, that your design is only to be an impartial umpire between these young gentlemen.

OPTATUS. You conjecture very truly, Autobulus. For the ancient law of Solon is out of date, that punished those who stood neuters and refused to adhere to either side.

AUTOBULUS. Seat yourself then here by us, that if there should be any occasion for a testimony, we may not be troubled to run to Aristotle's writings, but acquiescing in your experience, may give our suffrages according to what you aver for truth.

OPTATUS. Go to then, young gentlemen: are ye agreed upon the method and order of the dispute?

PHAEDIMUS. Truly, worthy Soclarus, that very thing

---

* See Odyss. XII. 116. † Il. V. 85

occasioned a great debate among us; but at length, according to that of Euripides,

> The child of Fortune, Chance, the point agreed,
> And fixed the method how we should proceed,

by giving the precedence to the land animals to plead their cause before marine creatures.

SOCLARUS. Then, Aristotimus, it is high time for you to speak and for us to hear.

9. ARISTOTIMUS. The court is open to all concerned in the controversy. . . . Others there are that kill their young ones by leaping the females at the very instant of their bringing forth. There are a sort of mullets, called pardiae, that feed upon their own slime. But the polypus sits all the winter feeding upon itself,

> In fireless house, and domicils forlorn;*

so slothful, or so stupid, or so given to his gut he is, or else so abandoned to all those vices together. And therefore Plato again and again forbids, or rather makes it his wish, in his laws, that young men might not be permitted to addict themselves to marine fishery, wherein there is no exercise of strength, no cogitation of wisdom, nor any thing that contributes to fortitude, swiftness, or agility, in combating against pikes, congers, or scates; whereas, in the chase of wild beasts, the fiercer sort accustom the huntsman to contempt of danger, the more subtle sort exercise and sharpen his wit and cunning, the swifter sort exercise his strength, and render him more apt to endure labor. These are the advantages that accrue to a man by hunting; but in fishing, there is nothing worth his while. For never any of the Gods got honor by the surname of a conger-killer; as Apollo was surnamed the wolf-slayer; never any of the Deities gloried in being a darter of mullets, as Diana is honored with the addition of hart-darting.

* Hesiod, Works and Days, 525.

And what wonder is it, when it is accounted more noble for a man to kill than to buy a wild boar, a hart, a goat, or a hare, but more honorable to buy a tunny, a lobster, or an amy, than to kill one? And therefore, because there is nothing in fishing that is noble, no using of gins and slight of cunning, it is accounted a sorry, pitiful exercise, not worth a man's labor.

10. In general then, since the usual arguments by which philosophers demonstrate that beasts partake of reason are these following, — purpose, contrivance, memory, passions, care of their young ones, gratefulness to those from whom they receive kindnesses, and the remembrance of shrewd turns, to which we may add the search after and choice of what is needful and beneficial for them, together with apparent shows of virtue, as of fortitude, society, continence, and magnanimity, — if we consider the marine creatures, we shall not find that our strictest observation can perceive in them any of these excellences, or at best they are such obscure and imperfect glimmerings as are scarce discernible. But in terrestrial and land animals, there is not any man but may behold the most luculent, the most evident and uncontrollable demonstrations in the world of all that has been said. In the first place, observe the designs and preparations of bulls provoked to combat, and of wild boars whetting their teeth. Again, elephants — since, by digging up or tearing down the trees which they intend to feed upon, they blunt and wear out their tushes — make use of only one for those purposes, but reserve the other strong and sharp for their own defence. The lion also always walks with his feet inverted, hiding his claws withinside his paw, to prevent the hunter from tracing him easily by his footing. For the track of a lion's claw is not easily to be found, so that the hunters are frequently at a loss, and wander after the obscure and scarce discernible footsteps of those beasts. You have heard also, I sup-

pose, of the ichneumon, how that he arms himself as completely as a soldier with his breastplate and cuirass prepared for battle; in such a manner does that creature surround and wrap himself about with a coat of mail, when he attacks the crocodile.

Admirable are the preparations of swallows before they go to lay their eggs, how they place the more solid stubble for foundations, and upon that build up the slighter straws; and if they perceive that the nest wants mud to serve as glue, you may observe how they fly to the next lake or sea, and after they have skimmed the superficies of the water with their wings, — so as to make them moist, yet not heavy with wet, — they lick up the dust, and so daub and bind together the loose and ill-cohering parts of the nest. As for the form of their architecture, it is composed neither of angles nor of many sides, but smooth and, as much as may be, spherical; for that such a figure is lasting and capacious, and not easily affording entrance to creatures that lie in wait for their destruction from without.

Who is there that does not admire, for more reasons than one, the labor of the spiders, which seems as pattern for the threads that women spin and the nets that are used in hunting? For the extraordinary fineness of the spinning, and the evenness of the thread, not discontinued or snapped off like the yarn upon a quill, but having the smooth and subtle texture of a thin membrane, and knit and spun together with a certain clammy moisture imperceptibly mixed; besides the tincture of it, causing a kind of airy and misty color, the better to deceive; but above all, the conduct and governing of this little engine, in which when any thing happens to be entangled, you see how presently, like an expert huntsman, the subtle artist contracts her net and binds her prey within it; — all this, being every day obvious to our sight and contemplation, gives credit to my discourse, which otherwise might be accounted no less fabulous than what is reported of certain Libyan crows, that, when they are a-thirsty, throw stones into the water, by that means to raise it to such a height that they may be able to reach it with their bills. Then again, when I saw a ship dog, in the absence of the seamen, putting in stones in a half-empty jar of oil, it was to me a wonder how that dog should understand that the pressure of the heavier weight would make the lighter rise.

And the same artifices are reported of Cretan bees and Cilician geese. For the first of these, being to take their flight about some windy promontory, ballast themselves with little stones, to prevent their being carried away by the stronger blasts. And as for the geese, they being afraid of the eagles, every time they cross the mountain Taurus, carry great stones in their mouths, to the end that by that means (as it were) bridling their gaggling tongues, they may cross the mountain in silence, without alarming their enemies.

Extraordinary also is the caution which the cranes observe in their flight. For they fly, when the wind is very high and the air very tempestuous, not as in fair weather, all afront or in manner of the half-moon; but forming a triangular body, with the sharp angle of that figure they penetrate the wind that ruffles round about them, and by that means preserve their order unbroken. On the other side, when they fall upon the ground, those that are upon the night-watch stand with the whole weight of their bodies upon one leg, holding a stone in the claw of the other foot. For the holding of the stone keeps them awake for a long time together, and wakes them again with the noise of the fall if they happen to drop asleep. So that it was no wonder that Hercules laid his quiver under his arm-pit, and with his strenuous arm embracing his bow,

> Slept all the night, where'er he laid his load,
> With his right-handed weight upon the wood.

Nor do I so much admire at him who was the first that hit upon the way to open an oyster, when I meet with and consider the artifices of the herons. For a heron, when he has swallowed a closed oyster, endures the trouble and vexation of it for so long time, till he perceives it soften and relaxed by the heat of his stomach; then casting it up again gaping and divided, he takes out that which is fit for food.

11. But as it is a task of great labor accurately to relate the economy and contrivances of the emmets, so it would argue too much of negligence to pass them over in silence. For there is not in Nature a smaller creature; and yet it is a most absolute mirror of the greatest and most noble performances, and (as it were) in a transparent drop the appearance of all virtue. There is friendship to be discerned in their mutual society. There is the image of fortitude in the patient undergoing of labor. In them are to be seen many seeds of continence, many of wisdom and justice. Insomuch that Cleanthes, who denied that beasts were endued with reason, could not forbear reporting how he met with the following accident of a crowd of emmets, that came to another ant-hill, bringing along with them a dead emmet. Presently other emmets ascending out of their ant-hill seemed (as it were) to meet them, and then disappeared again; and this was done twice or thrice. Till at length the one side brought up from under ground a worm, as the price of the dead emmet's redemption, which the other party of pismires receiving, delivered the dead emmet, and so departed. But that which is apparent to all is their equity to each other when they meet one another, while they that carry nothing always give way to those that are burdened; nor are their divisions and partitions of things too weighty for single carriage less re-

markable, to the end the burdens may be divided among many. But when they bring forth their little eggs and expose them to the cold, Aratus makes it a sign of rainy weather.

> When from her hollow cells th' industrious ant
> Her hidden store of eggs brings forth.

For in that sense many read ἴα (*provision*) for ὤεα (*eggs*), referring it to the providence of those little creatures, who, when they find their provision in their magazines to begin to taint and grow rotten, bring it forth and expose it to the open air, to prevent the progress of the putrefaction. But that which above all things demonstrates the surpassing excellency of their understanding is their pre-apprehension of the germinating of wheat. For the wheat does not remain dry and void of putrefaction, but grows moist and turns into a kind of milky substance, when it changes from seed to become an herb. For fear therefore that preserving the quality it should become useless for food, they eat out the very principal part of the grain, from whence the wheat sends forth its blossom. I must confess, I do not approve of those who dig up ant-hills on purpose to improve their learning (as it were) by anatomy. However, they tell us by virtue of that cruel information, that the passage or descent from the top of the hill to the nest is not directly straight nor easily penetrated by any other creature, but intercepted with several turnings and windings, leading through several underminings and perforations into three cavities; of which the one is the common place of feeding and converse for the whole community, the next is the general magazine of their provision, and the third is the apartment where they dispose of their dead.

12. I am afraid you may deem me too impertinent in joining elephants with pismires, and yet I cannot but think it seasonable to show the nature and force of under-

standing, as well in the smallest as in the greatest bodies, neither obscured in the one nor deficient in the other.

Some there are that admire in an elephant his aptness to learn and to be taught, and the many various postures and alterations of movement which he shows upon the theatres, not easily to be equalled by human assiduity, as subtle and abounding in memory and retention as man is. But for my part, I rather choose to prove his evident understanding from the passions and inclinations of the creature, that were never taught him, but only infused by Nature, as being altogether unmixed and pure without the help of art.

At Rome, not very long ago, there were many elephants that were taught many dangerous postures, many windings and turnings and circular screwings of their bulky bodies, hard to be expressed; among which there was one, which, being duller than the rest, and therefore often rated and chastised for his stupidity, was seen in the night-time, by moonlight, without being forced to it, to practise over his lessons with all the industry imaginable.

Agno tells a story of an elephant in Syria, that was bred up in a certain house, who observed that his keeper took away and defrauded him every day of half the measure of his barley; only that once, the master being present and looking on, the keeper poured out the whole measure; which was no sooner done, but the elephant, extending his proboscis, separated the barley and divided it into two equal parts, thereby ingeniously discovering, as much as in him lay, the injustice of his keeper.

Another in revenge that his keeper mixed stones and dirt with his barley, as the keeper's meat was boiling upon the fire, took up the ashes and flung them into the pot.

Another being provoked by the boys in Rome, that pricked his proboscis with the sharp ends of their writing-steels, caught one of them in his proboscis, and mounted him up into the air, as if he intended to have squashed out his guts; but upon the loud outcries of the spectators, set him gently down again upon his feet, and so went on, believing he had sufficiently punished the boy in scaring him. Many other things are reported of the wild elephants that feed without control, but nothing more to be admired than their passing of great rivers. For first of all the youngest and the least flounces into the stream; whom the rest beholding from the shore, if they see that the less bulky leader keeps steady footing with his back above water, they are then assured and confident that they may boldly adventure without any danger.

13. Having thus far proceeded in our discourse, I cannot think it well done to pass by the cunning of the fox, by reason of the similitude it has with the former. The mythologists tell us that the dove which Deucalion sent out of his ark, returning back again, was to him a certain sign of the storm not ceased; but of serene and fair weather, when she flew quite away. But the Thracians to this day, when they design to pass a river that is frozen over, make use of a fox to try whether the ice will bear or no. For the fox, treading gently, lays his ear to the ice, and if he perceive by the noise of the water that the stream runs very close underneath, conjecturing from thence that the congelation is not deep but thin, and no way steadfastly solid, he makes a stop, and if he be suffered, returns back again; but if he perceive no noise, he goes on boldly. Nor can we say that this is only an exquisiteness of sense without reason; but it is a syllogistical deduction from sense, concluding that whatever makes a noise is moved; whatever is moved, cannot be frozen; what is not frozen, is moist; what is moist, gives way. The logicians say that a dog, making use of the argument drawn from many disjunctive propositions, thus reasons with himself, in places where several highways meet: Either the wild beast is

gone this way, or that, or that way; but not that way, nor that way, therefore this way: the force of sense affording nothing but the minor premise, but the force of reason affording the major proposition, and inferring the conclusion of the assumption. But a dog stands in no need of any such testimonial; in regard it is both false and adulterate. For sense itself shows which way the beast is fled, by his tracks and footsteps, bidding farewell to disjunctive and copulative propositions. The nature of dogs is palpably to be discerned by many other actions, affections, and dutiful service, neither the effects of hearing or seeing, but practicable only by reason and understanding. It would be ridiculous for me to discourse of the continence, obedience, and industry of dogs in hunting, to you that are so well confirmed in the knowledge of those things by daily experience and practice.

There was a Roman named Calvus, slain in the civil wars, whose head nobody durst cut off before they killed the dog that guarded his body and fought in defence of his master. It happened that King Pyrrhus, travelling one day, lit upon a dog watching over the carcass of a person slain; and hearing that the dog had been there three days without meat or drink, yet would not forsake his dead master, ordered that the man should be buried, but that the dog should be preserved and brought to him. A few days after, there was a muster of the soldiers, so that they were forced to march all in order by the king, with the dog quietly lying by him for a good while. But when he saw the murderers of his master pass by him, he flew upon them with a more than ordinary fury, barking and baying and tearing his throat, and ever and anon turning about to the king; which did not only rouse the king's suspicion, but the jealousy of all that stood about him. Upon which the men were presently apprehended; and though the circumstances were very slight which otherwise appeared against them, yet they confessed the fact and were executed.

The same thing is reported to have been done by a dog that belonged to Hesiod, surnamed the wise, which discovered the sons of Ganyctor the Naupactian, by whom Hesiod was murdered. But that which came to the knowledge of our parents, when they were students at Athens, is yet more evident than any thing we have said. For a certain person getting into the temple of Aesculapius, after he had stolen all the massy offerings of gold and silver, made his escape, not believing he was discovered. But the dog which belonged to the temple, who was called Capparus, when he found that none of the sacristans took any notice of his barking, pursued himself the sacrilegious thief; and though at first the fellow pelted him with stones, he could not beat him off. So soon as it was day, the dog still followed him, though at such a distance that he always kept him in his eyes. When the fellow threw him meat he refused it; when the thief went to bed, the dog watched at his door; and when he rose in the morning, the dog still followed him, fawning upon the passengers on the road, but still barking and baying at the heels of the thief. These things when they who were in pursuit of the sacrilegious person heard, and were told withal by those they met the color and bigness of the dog, they were the more vigorous in the pursuit; and by that means overtaking the thief, brought him back from Crommyon, while the dog ran before, leaping and capering and full of joy, as it were challenging to himself the praise and reward of apprehending the temple-robber. And indeed the Athenians were so grateful to him, that they decreed him such a quantity of meat to be publicly measured to him, and ordered the priests to take care to see it done; in imitation of the kindness of the ancient Athenians in rewarding the mule.

For when Pericles built the temple Hecatompedon (or Parthenon) in the tower of Athens, it so fell out that the stones were to be fetched every day many furlongs off, and a world of carriages were made use of for that purpose. Among the rest of the mules that labored hard in this employment, there was one that, though dismissed by reason of age, would still go down to the Ceramicus, and meeting the carts that brought the stones, would be always in their company running by their sides, as it were by the way of encouragement and to excite them to work cheerfully. So that the people, admiring the zeal of the mule, ordered him to be fed at the public charge, as they were wont to decree public alms to the superannuated wrestlers.

14. And therefore they who deny that there is any thing of justice due from us towards dumb animals may be said to speak true, so far as concerns them that live in the sea and haunt the abysses of the deep. For those kind of creatures are altogether unsociable, without affection for their young ones, void of all softness of disposition; and therefore it was well said of Homer, speaking to a person whom he looked upon as a mere savage,

> But as for thee, so little worth,
> The gleaming sea did bring thee forth; *

in regard the sea brings forth nothing friendly, nothing mansuete or gentle. But he that uses the same discourse and arguments against land animals is himself a brute and savage creature; unless any man will affirm that there was nothing of justice due from Lysimachus to the Hyrcanian dog, that would not stir from the body of his deceased master, and when he saw his master's carcass burning, ran and threw himself into the flames. The same is reported to have been done by the dog Astus, that was kept by one Pyrrhus, not the king, but a private person of that name. For upon the death of his master, he would not stir from

* Il. XVI. 34.

the body, but when it was carried forth, leaped upon the bier, and at length threw himself into the funeral pile, and was burnt alive with his master's body.

The elephant also which carried King Porus, when the king was wounded in the battle against Alexander, pulled out several darts out of his wounds with his proboscis, with no less tenderness and care than the chirurgeon could have done; and though the elephant himself was but in a very bad condition, yet would he not give over till he perceived the king was ready to reel and sink down by reason of the blood which he had lost; and then fearing lest the king should fall, he stooped down gently, to ease the king in sliding to the ground.

Such was the humor of Bucephalus, who, before he was accoutred, would suffer his groom to back him, but when he had all his royal trappings and housings about him, would permit nobody but Alexander to bestride him. But if any other persons approached him in curiosity to try what they could do, he encountered them open-mouthed, and neighing out his fury, leaped upon their shoulders, bore them down, and trampled them under his feet, unless prevented by keeping at a distance or by speedy flight.

15. Nor am I ignorant but that there is something of variety in every one of these examples, which you must acknowledge. And indeed it is not easy to find out the natural dexterity of any one ingenious and docible animal, which is not accompanied with more than one single virtue. Thus, where there is affection toward their young ones, there is desire of praise. Where there is generosity, there is also moderation of anger. Cunning likewise and understanding are rarely parted from daring boldness and fortitude. But as for those that rather choose to divide and distinguish every one of these virtues particularly by themselves, they shall find in dogs a fair demonstration of a gentle and yet lofty mind at the same time, in turning away

from such as sit quietly upon the ground ; according to that of Homer,

> With hideous noise the dogs upon him flew ;
> But sly Ulysses, who the danger knew,
> Sate husht and still, and from his royal hand
> His sceptre dropt, as useless in command.*

For dogs never bite or worry those that prostrate themselves at their mercy and put on a face of humility. Thus they say the bravest of those Indian dogs that fought against Alexander never stirred or so much as looked about them upon the letting loose of a hart, a boar, and a bear; but when they saw a lion, then they began to rouse, to shake, and prepare themselves for the combat. By which it was plain that they thought only the lion an antagonist worthy of their courage, but despised all the rest as below their anger.

Your hounds that usually hunt hares, if they kill the hares themselves, take great delight in tearing them to pieces and lapping up the blood. But if the hare despairing of her life, as many times it happens, runs herself to death, the hounds finding her dead will never touch her, but stand wagging their tails, as if they did hunt not so much for the love of the food as for victory and triumph's sake.

16. There are many examples of cunning and subtlety abounding in land creatures ; but to omit slights and artifices of foxes, cranes, and jackdaws, of which I shall say nothing, because they are things already so well known, I shall make use of the testimony of Thales, the ancientest of our philosophers, who is reported to have chiefly admired the most excellent in any art or cunning.

A certain mule that was wont to carry salt, in fording a river, by accident happened to stumble, by which means the water melting away the salt, when the mule rose again he felt himself much lighter ; the cause of which the mule

---

* Odyss. XIV. 30.

was very sensible of, and laid it up in his memory, insomuch that every time he forded the same river, he would always stoop when he came into the deepest part, and fill his vessels with water, crouching down, and leaning sometimes to one side, sometimes to the other. Thales hearing this, ordered the vessels to be well filled with wool and sponges, and to drive the mule laden after that manner. But then the mule, as he was wont, filling his burthens with water, reasoned with himself that he had ill consulted his own benefit, and ever afterwards, when he forded the same river, was so careful and cautious, that he would never suffer his burthens so much as to touch the water by accident.

Another piece of cunning, joined with an extraordinary affection to their young ones, is to be observed in partridges, which instruct their young ones, ere they are able to fly, when they are pursued by the fowlers, to lay themselves upon their backs, their breasts covered with some clod of earth or little heap of dirt, under which they may lie concealed. On the other side, the old partridges do deceive the fowlers, and draw them quite a contrary way, make short flights from one place to another, thereby enticing the fowlers to follow them; till thus allured from their young ones, the fowlers give over all hopes of being masters of their game.

In like manner, hares returning to their forms dispose their leverets one to one place, another to another, at the distance many times of an acre of ground; so that, upon the tracing either of men or hounds, they are sure not to be all in danger at one time, — themselves in the mean time not easy to be tracked, by reason of the various windings and turnings which they make, until at length, by giving a large leap, they discontinue the print of their feet, and so betake themselves to their rest.

A bear, when she perceives her winter sleep coming

upon her, before she grows stiff and unwieldy, cleanses the place where she intends to conceal herself, and in her passage thither lifts up her paws as high as she can, and treads upon the ground with the top of her toes, and at length turning herself upon her back, throws herself into her receptacle.

Your hinds generally calve at a distance from all places frequented by flesh-devouring beasts; and stags, when they find themselves unwieldy through surplusage of flesh and fat, get out of the way and hide themselves, hoping to secure themselves by lurking, when they dare not trust to their heels.

The means by which the land hedge-hogs defend and guard themselves occasioned the proverb,

> Many sly tricks the subtle Reynard knows,
> But one the hedge-hog greater than all those.

For the hedge-hog, as Ion the poet says,* when he spies the fox coming,

> Round as a pine-nut, or more sphere-like ball,
> Lies with his body palisaded all
> With pointed thorns, which all the fox's slight
> Can find no way to touch, much less to bite.

But the provision which the hedge-hogs make for their young ones is much more ingenious. For when autumn comes, they creep under vines, and shake off the grapes with their feet; which done they roll themselves up and down, and take them up with their prickles, so that when they creep away again, you would think it a walking cluster (and this we have looked on and seen them do); after which returning to their holes, they lay themselves down for their young ones to feed. Their holes have two openings, one to the south, the other to the north. So that when they perceive the alteration of the air, like pilots shifting their sails, they stop up that which lies to the

* Fragment 38.

wind and open the other. Which a certain person that lived at Cyzicus observing, took upon him from thence at any time to tell in what corner the wind would sit.

17. As for love and observance of society joined with understanding and prudence, Juba produces many examples of it in elephants. For it is the usual practice of the elephant-hunters to dig large pits in the elephants' walks, and cover them slightly over with dry twigs or other materials; into which if any elephant happens to fall, the rest fetch wood and stones to fill up the cavity of the pit, that the other may the more easily get out again. And some report of the elephants, that they make prayers to the Gods by natural instinct, that they perform divine ceremonies to the sea, and worship the rising sun, lifting up the proboscis to heaven instead of hands. For which reason they are creatures the most beloved of any by the Gods, as Ptolemy Philopator testified. For having vanquished Antiochus, and being desirous to pay a more than ordinary honor to the Deity, among many other oblations of thanksgivings for his victory, he sacrificed four elephants. After which being terrified with a dream, which threatened him with the wrath of the Deity for that prodigious sacrifice, he sought out several ways to expiate his offence, and among the rest by way of propitiation, he erected four elephants of brass to atone for the four elephants he had slaughtered.

Examples not inferior of the observance of society are to be found among lions. For the younger carry forth the slow and aged, when they hunt abroad for their prey. When the old ones are weary and tired, they rest and stay for the younger that hunt on; who, when they have seized upon any thing, call to the old ones, making a noise like the bleating of a calf. They presently hear, and so meeting all together, they feed in common upon the prey.

18. In the amours of many animals there is much vari-

ety. Some are furious and mad; others observe a kind of human decency, and tricking of themselves to set off their beauty, not without a courtly kind of conversation. Such was the amour of the elephant at Alexandria, that rivalled Aristophanes the grammarian. For they were both in love with a girl that sold garlands; nor was the elephant's courtship less conspicuous than the other's. For as he passed through the fruit-market, he always brought her apples, and stayed with her for some time, and thrusting his proboscis within her waistcoat, instead of a hand, took great delight in gently feeling her breasts.

No less remarkable was the serpent in love with the Aetolian woman. He came to her in the night, and getting under her garments to her very skin, embraced her naked body; and never either willingly or unwillingly did he do her any harm, but always about break of day departed; which the kindred of the woman observing to be the common custom of the animal, removed her a great way off. After that, the serpent came not again for three or four days together, being all the while, as it seemed, wandering about in search of her. But at length, having with much ado found her out, he did not approach her with that mildness as he was wont to do, but after a rougher manner; with his folds having first bound her hands to her body, with the end of his tail he lashed the calves of her legs; expressing thereby a gentle and loving anger, which had more in it of indulgent expostulation than punishment.

I say nothing of a goose in Egypt in love with a boy, nor of the ram in love with Glauce who played on the harp; for the stories are in all people's mouths. And besides, I am apt to think you are satiated with examples of this nature.

19. But as for starlings, magpies, and parrots, that learn to talk, and afford their teachers such a spirit of voice, so well tempered and so adapted for imitation, they seem to

me to be patrons and advocates in behalf of other creatures, by their talent of learning what they are taught; and in some measure to teach us that those creatures also, as well as we, partake of vocal expression and articulate sound. From whence I conclude it a most ridiculous thing in them that would compare these creatures with a sort of mute animals, I mean the fish, that have not voice enough to howl or make a mournful noise. Whereas, in the natural and untaught notes of these creatures, what music, what a charming grace do we observe! To which the famous poets and choicest singers among men bear testimony, while they compare their sweetest odes and poems to the singing of swans and melody of nightingales. Now in regard there is more of reason in teaching than in learning, we are to believe Aristotle,[*] who assures us that terrestrial animals do that likewise, in regard that nightingales have been observed instructing their young ones to sing. Of which this may be a sufficient proof, that such nightingales are known to sing worse that are taken very young from the nest and deprived of the education of the old one. For they both learn and are taught from the old one, not for hire or to get reputation, but merely out of a delight in mixing their notes together, and because they have a greater love for that which is excellent and curious in the voice than for what is profitable. Concerning which I have a story to tell you, which I heard from several Greeks and Romans, who were eye-witnesses of the thing.

A certain barber in Rome, who had a shop right against the temple which is called the Greeks' Market, bred in his house a kind of a prodigy of a magpie, whose tongue would be always going with the greatest variety imaginable, sometimes imitating human speech, sometimes chattering her wild notes, and sometimes humoring the sounds

[*] History of Animals, IV. 9, 19.

of wind instruments; neither was this by any constraint, but as she accustomed herself, with a more than ordinary ambition, to leave nothing unspoken, nothing that her imitation should not master.

It happened a certain person of the wealthier sort, newly dead in the neighborhood, was carried forth to be buried with a great number of trumpets before him. Now in regard it was the custom of the bearers to rest themselves before the barber's shop, the trumpeters being excellent in their art, and withal commanded so to do, made a long stop, sounding all the while.

After that day the magpie was altogether mute, not so much as uttering her usual notes by which she called for what she wanted, insomuch that they who before admired as they passed to and fro at the chattering and prating of the bird now much more wondered at her sudden silence; and many suspected her to have been poisoned by some that affected peculiar skill in teaching this kind of birds. But the greatest number were of opinion, that the noise of the trumpets had stupefied her hearing, and that by the loss of her hearing the use of her voice was likewise extinguished. But her unusual silence proceeded from neither of these causes, but from her retiring to privacy, by herself to exercise the imitation of what she had heard, and to fit and prepare her voice as the instrument to express what she had learned. For soon after she came of a sudden to sight again, but had quitted all her former customary imitations, and sounded only the music of the trumpets, observing all the changes and cadences of the harmony, with such exactness of time as was not to be imagined; an argument, as I have said before, that the aptness in those creatures to learn of themselves is more rational than readiness to be taught by others. Nor do I think it proper to pass by in silence one wonderful example of the docility of a dog, of which I myself was a spectator at Rome. This dog belonged to a certain mimic, who at that time had the management of a farce wherein there was great variety of parts, which he undertook to instruct the actors to perform, with several imitations proper for the matters and passions therein represented. Among the rest there was one who was to drink a sleepy potion, and after he had drunk it, to fall into a deadly drowsiness and counterfeit the actions of a dying person. The dog, who had studied several of the other gestures and postures, more diligently observing this, took a piece of bread that was sopped in the potion, and after he had ate it, in a short time counterfeited a trembling, then a staggering, and afterwards a drowsiness in his head. Then stretching out himself, he lay as if he had been dead, and seemed to proffer himself to be dragged out of the place and carried to burial, as the plot of the play required. Afterwards understanding the time from what was said and acted, in the first place he began gently to stir, as it were waking out of a profound sleep, and lifting up his head, he gazed about him. Afterwards to the amazement of the beholders, he rose up, and went to his master to whom he belonged, with all the signs of gladness and fawning kindness, insomuch that all the spectators, and even Caesar himself (for old Vespasian was present in Marcellus's theatre) were taken with the sight.

20. But perhaps we may seem ridiculous for signalizing beasts in this manner because they learn, since we find that Democritus affirms us to have been their scholars in the greatest matters; — of the spider, in weaving and repairing what we tear or wear out; of the swallow, in building houses; and of the mournful swan and nightingale, in singing and imitation. Moreover in others we observe a threefold practice of physic, both natural and inbred. For tortoises make use of marjoram and weasels eat rue, when they have devoured a serpent; and dogs

purge themselves from abounding gall with a certain sort of grass. The dragon quickens the dimness of his sight with fennel; and the bear, coming forth of her cave after long emaciation, feeds upon the wild arum, for the acrimony of that herb opens and separates her guts when clung together. At other times, being overcloyed with food, she repairs to the emmet-hills, and thrusting forth her tongue all soft and unctuous, by reason of the sweet kind of slime that all besmears it, till it be crowded with emmets, at length swallows them down her throat, and so recovers. And it is reported that the Egyptians observe and imitate the bird called ibis, in purging and cleansing her bowels with the briny sea-water. For which reason the priests, when they hallow themselves, make use of the water of which the ibis has drunk; for that those birds will not drink the water, if it be medicinal or otherwise infected. Some beasts there are that cure themselves by abstinence; as wolves and lions, who, when they are gorged with flesh, lie still and digest their crudities by the warmth of one another's bodies. It is reported also of the tiger, that if a kid be thrown to her, she will not eat in two days; but growing almost famished the third day, if she be not supplied with another, she will tear down the cage that holds her, if she have strength enough; yet all this while she will not meddle with the first kid, as being her companion and fellow-housekeeper.

More than this, the elephants are said to make use of chirurgery; for that being brought to persons wounded, they will draw forth the heads of spears and arrows out of their bodies with little pain, and without dilacerating and mangling the flesh.

The Cretan goats, which by eating dittany expel the arrows shot into their bodies, taught women with child to understand the virtue of that herb, so prevalent to expel the birth. For those goats being wounded seek no other cure, but presently seek out and hunt for dittany.

21. But these things, though wonderful, are not so much to be admired as are those beasts that understand the use of numbers and have the power of reckoning, like the oxen about Susa. For there are oxen in that place that water the king's gardens with portable buckets, of which the number is fixed. For every ox carries a hundred buckets every day, and more you cannot force them to take or carry, would you never so fain; insomuch that, when constraint has been used for experiment's sake, nothing could make them stir after they had carried their full number. Such an accurate account do they take, and preserve the same in their memory, as Ctesias the Cnidian relates it.

The Libyans deride the Egyptians for the fables which they report of the oryx, which, as they say, makes a great noise upon the same day, at the very hour, when the Dog-star, which they call Sothes, rises. However, this is certain, that all their goats, when that star rises truly with the sun, turn themselves and stand gazing toward the east; which is a most unquestionable argument of that star's having finished its course, and agrees exactly with the astronomer's observations.

22. But that my discourse may draw to a conclusion, let us (as the saying is) move the stone over the sacred line, and add something concerning the divinity and prophetic nature with which our terrestrial creatures are endued. Which when we consider, we shall find that that part of soothsaying which is founded upon the observation of birds is not the meanest or most ignoble, but very ancient and in great esteem. For the smartness and intelligible faculty of birds, together with their capability to receive all impressions of fancy, afford the Deity a convenience to make use of those faculties as instruments, that he may turn them into motion, sounds, chirpings, and forms, now to stop and stay, anon to drive forward like the winds; by

means of some of these stopping short, by the means of others directing to their end, the actions and impetuous impulses of men. Therefore Euripides in general calls birds the criers of the Gods; and particularly Socrates styles himself a fellow-servant with the swans. As among princes, Pyrrhus was pleased with the surname of Eagle; and Antiochus loved to be called Antiochus the Falcon. But they who deride men as insipid and void of ingenuity call them by the names of fish. And whereas we can produce millions of things and accidents which are foretold us by land and flying creatures, there is not any one such example that the patrons of water-animals can produce in their behalf; but being all void of hearing, perfectly sottish, and without any sight, discerning, or providence, they are all thrown apart into that same place, unblest and hideous, called the sea, as it were into the region of the ungodly, where the rational and intellectual part of the soul is extinguished; being animated with only some diminutive portion, the lowest that may be imagined, of a confused and overwhelmed sense, so that they rather seem to palpitate than breathe.

23. HERACLEO. Pluck up your brows then, friend Phaedimus; after all this, it is time to rouse thyself in the defence of the islanders, and others that live by the seaside. For this has been no frivolous discourse, but a hard fought contest, and a continued piece of rhetoric that wanted only lattices and a pulpit to give it the honor it deserved.

PHAEDIMUS. Therefore, you see, it is plain here has been foul play and treachery in the case, for a person sober and upon premeditation to set upon us when we were stomach-sick and dozed with our last night's compotation. But there is no way to avoid the combat; for that, being an imitator of Pindar, it shall never be said of me,

Combats refused, when nobly set upon,
Have virtue into deepest darkness thrown.

For we have leisure enough, as having not only allowed ourselves a vacation from jollity and balls, but our hounds and horses a relaxation from their labors, and withal having hung up our drag-nets and spears, as having also this day granted, for disputation's sake, a general truce to all creatures, as well upon the land as in the sea. However, fear not; for I will use it moderately, without producing either the opinions of philosophers or the fables of the Egyptians, or the relations either of the Indians or Libyans, wanting testimony; but such as shall be verified by good witnesses, who have made it their business to toil upon the ocean, and such as are evident to the eye. For to say truth, there is not any one of those examples produced from the land which is not apparent and openly manifested to our sense. Whereas the sea affords few but such as are difficult to be discerned, as concealing the generation and nourishment of most of her creatures, their antipathies, and ways of preserving themselves; in reference to which many acts of understanding, memory, and community are unknown to us, so that we cannot be so copious in our discourse. Then again, land animals, by reason of their familiarity and cohabitation, being in some measure accustomed to the conditions of men, become capable of their nutriture, education, and imitation; which sweetens and allays all their acerbity and moroseness, like the mixture of fresh water with sea brine, and awakening that which is slow and disordered in them, inflames it with human motions. Whereas the living of sea animals being by many degrees remote from the converse of men, and having nothing adventitious or that may be said to be acquired by custom and familiarity, is altogether peculiar, genuine, and unmixed with manners strange and foreign to them; which proceeds not from Nature, but from the place itself. For Nature, receiving and cherishing whatever knowledge comes to herself, affords it also to fish, and makes many eels tame and familiar to men, which for that reason are called sacred, like those in the fountain Arethusa; so that in many places there are fish that will hear and obey when called by their names, as the story goes of Crassus's mullet, upon the death of which he wept. For which when Domitius twitted him in these words, Did not you weep when your mullet died? — he retorted upon him again, Did you not bury three wives and never weep at all? The crocodiles belonging to the priests not only know the voices of those that call them, and suffer themselves to be stroked and handled, but gaping hold out their teeth to be cleansed and wiped by the hands of the priests.

Lately Philinus, after he had been long travelling in Egypt, returning to us, told us how he saw, in the city which derives its name from Anteus, an old woman sleeping by the side of a crocodile, upon a low soft bed well and decently dressed up.

In ancient histories we find that when King Ptolemy called the sacred crocodile, and when the crocodile neither vouchsafed to appear at his call nor would answer to the earnest expostulations of the priests, it was looked upon as a prognostication of the death of the king, which happened soon after. Which shows that the race of water-animals is neither without a share of that inestimable thing called prophetic signification, nor undeserving those honors ascribed to land creatures. For that about Sura, which is a village in Lycia between Phellus and Myra, I have heard it credibly reported, that there are certain persons who make it their business to watch the turns, flights, and pursuits of the fish, whence, by a certain art which they have, they gather predictions, as others from the observation of birds.

24. But let these examples suffice to show, that fish are not altogether strangers to mankind, nor altogether void of human affection. But for a great and common demon-

stration of their unmixed and natural understanding, we find that there is not any fish that swims, unless they be such as stick and cling to the rocks, which is so easily taken by men, as asses are seized by wolves, bees by bee-eaters, grasshoppers by swallows, serpents by harts. And these last are therefore called ἔλαφοι, not from their swiftness (ἐλαφρότης), but from a faculty which they have of drawing serpents to them (ἕλκειν ὄφεις). So sheep call the wolf by the sound of their feet, and the panther allures to her paws both apes and other creatures by the fragrant smell of her body. But so suspicious is the sense of all water animals, and so watchful are they to avoid all baits and treacheries against them, by reason of their extraordinary cunning, that fishing thereby becomes no easy or single labor, but a toil that requires various instruments and many tricks of human cunning and deceit. This is apparent from examples near at hand. For no man desires an angling-rod too thick, though strong enough to hold against the twitches of the fish when taken; but rather they require it slender, lest by casting too great a shadow upon the water, it should frighten the suspicious creature. In the next place, they never knit too many knots in the line, but make it as smooth as may be, for that would too much discover the deceit; and then for the hairs which are next the hook, they endeavor to get the whitest they can meet with; for so, by reason of the likeness of color, they lie the more easily concealed in the water. Therefore some there are who, wrongly expounding the following verses of Homer,*

> She to the bottom quickly sinks, like lead,
> Which fixt to horn † of rustic ox descends,
> And brings destruction to the greedy fish,

believe that the ancients made use of ox-hair for their lines with which they angled, alleging that κέρας then signified

* Il. XXIV. 80. † κέρας.

hair, — from whence κείρασθαι, *to be shaved*, and κουρά, *shaving*, — and that κεροπλάστης in Archilochus signified one who takes delight in trimming and decking the hair. But this is an error. For they made use of horse-hair, more especially that of male horses. For mares, by moistening their tails with their urine, render the hair weak and brittle. Though Aristotle will not allow any thing to be said in all this that requires such extraordinary subtlety. Only he says, that the lower piece of the line was fortified with a little hollow piece of horn, lest the fish should come at the line itself and bite it off; moreover, that they made use of round hooks to catch mullets and tunnies, in regard they had but small mouths, for that they were afraid of a straight hook. He also further says, that the mullet many times suspecting the round hook, will swim round about it, flapping the bait with his tail, and then turning round, secures to himself so much as he has broken off. Or if he cannot do that, he shuts his mouth close, and with the extremities of his lips nibbles off some part of the bait.

The fish called labrax behaves himself more stoutly than the elephant; for when he perceives himself struck with the hook, without assistance he sets himself at liberty, widening the wound by flinging his head to and fro, and enduring the painful twingings of the hook, till he have freed himself from it with the loss of his flesh. The sea fox (or the fish called alopex) seldom bites, but avoids the deceit; but if he chance to be taken, he presently turns the inside of his body outward. For by reason of the strength and moisture of his body, he has a peculiar faculty to turn it so that, the inside coming to be outermost, the hook falls off. These things demonstrate understanding, and a subtle and extraordinary use of it in the nick and juncture of time.

25. Other examples there are which show not only this same understanding and knowledge, but the community

and mutual affection of fish. Thus, if one scate happen to swallow the hook, all the rest of the scates that are in the same shoal presently crowd together and bite the line in pieces. The same scates, if any of their companions fall into the net, give the prisoners their tails to take hold of with their teeth, and so draw them forth by main force.

But the fish called anthiae with far more courage assist their fellows in distress. For getting under the line with their backs, and setting up their fins, with these, as with sharp saws, they endeavor to cut it in two.

Now we know no land animal that will assist and defend his kind in danger; neither the bear, nor the wild boar, nor the lion, nor the panther. True it is that, when they are in herds together, they will gather into a circle and defend each other in common; but no single land animal either knows or cares to assist a single companion, but flies and shifts for himself as far off as he can from the beast that is wounded and lies a dying. For as for that old story of elephants filling up the ditches with heaps of adjoining materials, whether wood or earth, for the unfortunate elephant the more easily to get up again, this, my good friend, is extremely uncouth and foreign to us, as if we were bound to believe Juba's books by virtue of a royal edict. However, if it is true, it does but serve to show that many of the marine creatures are nothing inferior in understanding and community to the most intelligent of the land animals. But as for their mutual society, we shall discourse apart of that by itself.

26. Now the fishermen, observing how that most fish avoided the casts of their hooks by cunning or by striving with the tackling, betook themselves to force, — as the Persians use to serve their enemies in their wars,* —

* That is, by joining hands and sweeping across an island. See the description in Herod. VI. 31, and σαγηνεύω in Liddell and Scott. (G.)

making use of nets, that there might be no escape for those that were caught either by the help of reason or subtlety. Thus mullets and the fish called julides are taken with sweep-nets and drag-nets, as are also several other sorts of fish called mormuri, sargi, gobii, and labraces; those that are called casting-nets catch the mullet, the gilthead, and the scorpion fish; and therefore Homer calls this sort of net παναγρα, or the *all-sweeper*.* And yet there are some fish that are too cunning for these nets. Thus the labrax, perceiving the drawing of the sweep-net, with the force of his body beats a hollow place in the mud, where he lays himself close till the net be gone over him. But as for the dolphin, when he finds himself taken and in the midst of the net, he remains there without being in the least perplexed, but falls to with a great deal of joy, and feasts upon the numerous fry within the meshes; but so soon as he comes near the shore, he bites his way through the net with his teeth and swims away. Or if he chance to be taken, the fishermen do him no other harm the first time, but only sew a sort of large bulrush to the finny crown upon his head, and so let him go. If they take him a second time, they punish him with stripes, well knowing him again by the prints of the needle. But that rarely happens. For having got pardon the first time, for the most part of them, they acknowledge the favor, and abstain from spoil for the future.

Moreover, among the many examples that make evident the wariness of fish in avoiding the deceits and craft of the fishermen, it would not be convenient to pass by that of the cuttle-fish. For this fish, carrying near his neck a certain black and inky sort of liquor, so soon as he perceives himself discovered, throws that liquor forth, and darkens all the water round about him in such a manner that, the fisherman losing sight of him, by that means he

---

* See Il. V. 487.

makes his escape; imitating therein Homer's Deities, who, when they had a mind to save any of their heroes, hid them in an azure cloud. But of this enough.

27. Now for the extraordinary subtlety of fish in hunting and catching their own prey, we shall meet with several examples of it in several fish. Particularly the star-fish, understanding his own nature to be such that whatever he touches dissolves and liquefies, readily offers his body, and permits himself to be touched by all that come near him.

You know yourself the property of the torpedo or cramp fish, which not only benumbs all those that touch it, but also strikes a numbness through the very net into the hands of them that go about to take him. And some that have had greater experience of this fish report that, if it happen to fall alive upon the land, they that pour water upon it shall presently perceive a numbness seizing upon their hands and stupefying their feeling, through the water affected with the quality of the fish. And therefore, having an innate sense of this faculty, it never makes any resistance against any thing, nor ever is it in danger. Only swimming circularly about his prey, he shoots forth the effluviums of his nature like so many darts, and first infects the water, then the fish through the water, which is neither able to defend itself nor to escape, being (as it were) held in chains and frozen up.

The fish called the fisherman is well known to many, who has his name given him from his manner of catching fish; whose art, as Aristotle writes, the cuttle-fish makes use of, for he lets down, like a line, a certain curl which Nature has given him, so ordered as to let it run out at length or draw it to him again, as he sees occasion. This, when he sees any of the lesser fish approach, he offers them to bite, and then by degrees pulls the curl nearer and nearer by virtue of the bait, till he has drawn his prey within the reach of his mouth. And as for the polypus's changing his color, Pindar has made it famous in these words:

> In any city may that man expose
> His safety, who well knows
> Like sea-bred polypus to range,
> And vary color upon every change.

In like manner Theognis:

> Change manners with thy friends, observing thus
> The many-colored, cunning polypus;
> Who let him stick to whatsoever rock,
> Of the same color does his body look.*

It is true the chameleon changes color, not out of any design or to conceal himself, but out of fear, being naturally timorous and trembling at every noise he hears. And this is occasioned by the extraordinary abundance of breath which he enjoys, as Theophrastus affirms. For the whole body of this creature wants but little of being nothing else but lungs; which demonstrates him to be full of spirits, and consequently apt to change. But this same change of the polypus is no product of any affection of the mind, but a kind of action. For he changes on purpose, making use of this artifice to escape what he fears, and to get the food which he lives by. For by fraud, those things that he will take never avoid him, and those things he will escape pass him by without taking any notice of him. For that he devours his own claws is an untruth, but that he is afraid of the lamprey and conger is certain; for by these he is ill treated, not being able to return them any injury, by reason of their being so slippery. Though on the other side the crawfish, having once got them within his claws, holds them with ease. For slenderness affords no help against roughness; but when the polypus comes to thrust his horns into the body of the crawfish, then also the crawfish dies. And this same vicissitude of avoiding

---

* Theognis, vs. 215.

and pursuing one another has Nature infused into them on purpose to exercise their subtlety and understanding.

28. Then again we have heard Aristotimus relating how the land hedge-hog had a perception of the rising of the wind, and praising the trigonal flight of cranes. But for my part, I produce no particular hedge-hog of Cyzicus or Byzantium, but all the sea hedge-hogs in general; who, when they perceive a storm coming, ballast themselves with little stones, lest they should be overturned by reason of their lightness or carried away by the rolling of the waves, which they prevent by the weight of their little stones.

On the other side, the cranes' order in their flight against the wind is not of one sort. But this is a general notion among all fish, that they always swim against the waves and the tide, and always take care lest the wind being in their tails should force their fins from their backs, and leave their naked bodies exposed to the cold and other inconveniences; and therefore they still oppose the prows of their bodies against the waves. For that while they thus cleave the waves at the top, the sea keeps their fins close, and lightly flowing over the superficies of their bodies, becomes less burdensome, besides that it suffers not their scales to rise.

This, I say, is common to all fish, except that fish which is called ellops; which, as they report, always swims with the wind and tide, not minding the erection or opening of the scales, which do not lie towards the tail, as in other fish.

29. Moreover, the tunny is so sensible of the equinoxes and solstices, that he teaches even men themselves without the help of any astrological table. For where the winter solstice overtakes him, there he remains till the vernal equinox.

As for that same artifice of the cranes, that keep themselves waking by clutching a stone in their claws, how much more cunningly done is that of the dolphin, for whom it is not lawful to stand still or to be out of motion. For it is the nature of the dolphins to be always in motion; so that, when they cease to move, they also cease to live. And therefore when sleep seizes them, they raise their bodies to the superficies of the sea, and so sinking down again with their bellies upward, are carried along with the tide till they touch again the shore. Wakened in that manner, with an impetuous noise they mount upward again, designing thus a kind of rest still intermixed with motion. And the same thing is reported of the tunnies for the same reason.

Having thus concluded their mathematical foreknowledge of the mutations of the sun, of which Aristotle gives testimony, let me now relate their skill in arithmetic; but first of all, their knowledge in optics, of which Aeschylus seems not to have been altogether ignorant. For these are his words:

>Casting a squint-eye like the tunny.

For tunnies seem to be dim-sighted of one eye. And therefore, when they enter the Euxine Sea, they coast along the land on the right side, and contrariwise when they come forth; prudently committing the care of their bodies to the best eye.

But wanting arithmetic in order to the preservation of mutual love and society one with another, they arrive in such a manner to the perfection of that science, that, in regard they are extremely desirous to enjoy the society of each other, they always make up their whole fry into the form of a cube, and make a solid of the whole number consisting of six equal planes; and then they swim in such order as to present an equal front in each direction. So then, if the observer of the tunnies does but exactly take the number of the side that he sees, he knows the whole number of the shoal; well knowing that the depth is equal to the breadth and length.

30. The fish amiae, which are another sort of tunnies, are so called, because they swim in shoals, as also the pelamydes or summer whitings. As for the rest that are seen to swim in shoals and to observe a mutual society, their number is not to be expressed. And therefore let us proceed to those that observe a kind of private and particular society one with another. Among which is the pinoteras of Chrysippus, upon which he has expended so much ink, that he gives it the precedency in all his books, both physical and ethical. For Chrysippus never knew the spongotera, for he would not have passed it over out of negligence.

The pinoteras is so called, from watching the fish called pina or the nacre, and in shape resembles a crab; and cohabiting with the nacre, he sits like a porter at his shellside, which he lets continually to stand wide open until he spies some small fishes gotten within it, such as they are wont to take for their food. Then entering the shell, he nips the flesh of the nacre, to give him notice to shut his shell; which being done, they feed together within the fortification upon the common prey.

The sponge is governed by a certain little creature more like a spider than a crab. For the sponge wants neither soul nor sense nor blood; but growing to the stones, as many other things do, it has a peculiar motion from itself and to itself, which nevertheless stands in need as it were of a monitor or instructor. For being otherwise of a substance loose and open, and full of holes and hollowness, by reason of the sloth and stupidity of it the sponge-watcher assists to give notice when any thing of food enters the cavities of it, at which time the sponge contracts itself and falls to feeding.

But if a man approach and touch it, being nipped and admonished by the sponge-watcher, it seems to shudder and shut up the body of it, closing and condensing it in such a manner as makes it no easy thing to cut it from the place where it grows.

The purple shellfish also, called porphyrae, clustering together in a kind of mutual society, build up little combs for themselves like bees, wherein they are said to generate; and culling out the choicest substance of the moss and seaweed that stick to their shells, they seem to be in a circular commons among themselves, feeding the one upon the other's nourishment.

31. But why should we admire society in these creatures, when the most savage and most unsociable of all creatures which either lakes, rivers, or the ocean nourishes, the crocodile, shows himself the most sociable and grateful of water monsters in the banquets which he bestows upon the trochilus? For the trochilus is a bird that haunts marshes and rivers, and he guards and watches over the crocodile, not as one that feeds at his table, but as one that lives upon his scraps and leavings only. For when this bird observes the crocodile asleep, and the ichneumon ready to assail him, smeared with mud for the conflict like a wrestler covered with dust, he never leaves crying and pecking him with his beak, till he rouse the drowsy monster. In return of which the crocodile is so tame and gentle towards this bird, that he permits him to enter his yawning chaps, and is pleased with his pecking out and cleansing away with his beak the remainders of the devoured flesh that sticks between his teeth. And when the monster has an inclination to shut his mouth, he gives the bird notice by a gentle lowering of his jaw, nor will he close his chaps till he finds that the bird is flown away. The fish which the Greeks call hegemon (or the captain or leader) is a small fish, in bigness and shape not much unlike a gudgeon, but by reason of the roughness of his scales is said to resemble a bird when she shakes her feathers. This

fish always keeps company with one of the huge whales, and swims before him to direct his course, lest he should bruise himself upon the shallows, or fall into any marshy place or narrow haven whence he could not easily get out again. Therefore the whale follows him, as the ship follows the helm, directing his course with confidence. All other things whatever, whether skiff, whether beast or stone, that chance to light into the gaping gulf of the whale's mouth, immediately perish, being swallowed by the monster; but acknowledging his conductor, he receives him and lodges him, like an anchor, safely in his jaws. There he sleeps; and all the while he takes his rest, the whale lies still, as if he were at anchor; and when his guide comes forth again, the whale proceeds, never forsaking him night or day; or if he wander without his leader, the monster shipwrecks, like a vessel cast upon a rock without a helm. And this we saw not long ago near Anticyra, where they report that in former times a whale being cast and putrefying caused a pestilence.

Is it worth while then to compare these observations of community and association with those sympathies which, as Aristotle relates, exist between foxes and serpents because the eagle is an enemy to both? Or with those of the horn-owls with horses, whose dung they love to scrape about the field? For my part I observe no such care of one another in bees and emmets, which, by reason of their multitude, carry on and perfect their work in common, but have no particular care or consideration one of another.

32. We shall observe this difference more evidently, if we direct our discourses upon the most ancient and greatest works of common society, which are the works of generation and procreation of offspring. For in the first place, those fish that frequent the shores next adjoining to vast lakes or great rivers, when they are near their time of bringing forth, retire up into those places, seeking the

fresh waters which are more gentle and void of brine. For tranquillity is most convenient for such as bring forth, and there is most safety in rivers and lakes for their young ones, as being freest from the devouring monsters of the sea. Which is the reason that there is the greatest plenty of fish about the Euxine Sea, where there are no whales, but only small sea-calves or little dolphins. Besides, the mixture of rivers, many in number, and those very large, that fall into the Pontus, make the temperature more kindly and proper for breeding and bringing forth. And that is most wonderful which is reported of the anthias, which Homer * calls the sacred fish, though some interpret sacred to signify great in that place, as we call a certain great bone *os sacrum*, and the epilepsy, being a great disease, the *sacred disease*, though others interpret that to be sacred which ought not to be touched, as being dedicated to holy use. And Eratosthenes seems to take the gilthead, so called from the golden hair about his eyes, for the sacred fish; though many believe it to be the ellops, — a fish seldom seen and difficult to be caught, yet many times it appears in the rivers of Pamphylia. So they that catch them are crowned, and their boats are also adorned with garlands, and as they pass along they are received and honored with loud shouts and clapping of hands. However it be, most people take the anthias to be a sacred fish, because that where the anthias appears, there are no sea-monsters, but the sponge-cutters dive boldly, and the fish as fearlessly spawn, as having a pledge for their security. And the reason is twofold, either because the sea-monsters dread the anthias, as elephants dread a hog, and lions a cock; or else it is a sign that there are no sea-monsters in those places, which the anthias knows and observes, as being an intelligent fish, endued with sense and a good memory.

* Il. XVI. 407.

33. Then again, the care of their young is common to both sexes. For the males never devour their offspring, but remain and abide constantly by the spawn, protecting it with a diligent watchfulness, as Aristotle relates; and those that accompany the females moisten the spawn with a small quantity of milky seed; for that otherwise the spawn will not grow, but remains imperfect and never arrives at the due proportion. Particularly the fish called phycides make themselves nests in the seaweed to preserve their spawn from the waves.

But the love of the galeus toward her young ones is beyond the affection and clemency of any the tamest of creatures; for they lay an egg, which being hatched, they nourish and carry the young about not outwardly, but within their own bowels, as if they could not breed their young without a second birth.

When the young ones are somewhat grown, they put them forth again, and teach them to swim close by themselves, then resume them again through their mouths into their bellies, and afford them nourishment and safe retirement in their bodies, till they are able to shift for themselves.

No less admirable is the care of the tortoise, as to the bringing forth and preserving her young. For she retires out of the sea to lay; but not being able to stay long upon the land, she hides her eggs in the sand, covering them over gently with the lightest of the gravel; and when she has thus sufficiently and assuredly concealed them, some report that she marks and streaks the place with her feet, that she may be able to know it again; others affirm that the female, being turned upon her back upon the sand by the male, leaves her particular marks and signatures behind her. However it be, this is most wonderful, that after waiting forty days (for in so many the eggs come to break) she returns, and knowing where the treasure lies, as well as any man understands where he hides his gold, she opens them with great joy and alacrity.

34. Many observations like to these are made of the crocodile. But such is its skill in choosing a place for breeding, that no man can explain it by reason or conjecture. Whence it comes that the foreknowledge of this creature is imputed more to divinity than reason. For neither farther nor nearer, but just so far as the Nile that year will increase and cover the land, thither she goes forth and lays her eggs; which the countrymen finding, are able to tell one another how far the river will overflow that year. So truly does that animal measure for herself, that though she live in the water, she may lay her eggs dry. But the young ones being hatched, whichsoever of them, so soon as they are come to life, does not seize whatever comes next — either upon a fly, or a worm, or a straw, or a tuft of grass — with his mouth, the dam presently tears him to pieces with her teeth. But those that are fierce and active she loves and cherishes, according to the judgment of the wisest men, imparting her affection by the rules of judgment, not by the sway of passion.

The sea-calves also bring forth upon the dry lands; but then fetching out their young ones by degrees, they give them a taste of the sea-water, and presently lead them out again; and this they often do, till custom has made them bold, and brought them to love a sea life.

Frogs when they couple use a certain croaking invitation, which is commonly called ololygon; and when the male has thus enticed the female, they abide together all night. For in the water they cannot, and in the daytime they are afraid to engender upon the land, which in the night-time they do without control. At other times they croak more shrill and loud; and this is a sign of rain, and holds among the most assured prognostics of wet weather.

35. But what absurdity, dearest Neptune, would this passion of mine lead me into! How ridiculous should I appear, if trifling among sea-calves and frogs, I should omit one of the marine animals, the wisest and most beloved by the Gods! For what nightingales are to be compared with the halcyon for music? or who will presume to prefer the swallow's love of offspring, the dove's love of her mate, or the art and curiosity of the bees, to those virtues ascribed to the halcyon? One only island, as history tells us, received and entertained Latona when she gave birth; which island, floating before, was then made firm land. But when the halcyon brings forth, about the winter solstice, the whole ocean remains calm and undisturbed without the wrinkle of a wave. So that there is not any other creature for which man has so great an affection, seeing that for her sake for seven days and seven nights together, in the depth of winter, they sail without fear of shipwreck, and make their voyages upon the sea with greater safety than they travel upon the land.

But if it be required that we should make a brief recital of her particular virtues, she is so great an example of conjugal affection, that she does not keep company with her mate for a single season, but for the whole year together, and that not for wantonness (for she never couples but with her own), but out of affection and friendship, like a truly virtuous married wife. And when her mate through age becomes infirm and not able to bear her company, she takes care of him, and feeds and carries him about in his old age, never forsaking nor leaving him alone, but taking him upon her shoulders, carries him from place to place, never abandoning him till death.

As to her affection towards her young ones and care of their preservation, so soon as she perceives herself near the time of her bringing forth, she presently betakes herself to the making of her nest. For the building of which, she neither makes use of mud and dirt nor props it up with walls and rafters, like the swallows; nor does she use several members of her body to work with, like the bees, that employ their whole body to enter the wax and open their cells, with their six feet fashioning their six-sided apartments. For the halcyon having but one single instrument, one single tool, which is her bill, nor any other help to assist her in labor and her care of her young ones, what a wonderful master-piece of workmanship does she erect? Insomuch that it is a difficult thing for them that have not well considered it to believe their eyesight; her workmanship seeming rather the art of a shipwright than of a common builder; of all inventions being the only form not to be overwhelmed and washed by the waves. To this purpose she gathers together the thorns of the sea-needle — some straight, others oblique, like the woof in the loom — and twists and binds them where the thread and yarn are interwoven one within another, till she has framed a nest round and oblong, resembling the usual fisher-boats. This when she has finished she launches into the sea, where the waves beating gently upon it direct to reform what is amiss, by consolidating the loose and ill compacted parts, where the water has forced any entrance; insomuch that at length she fastens and strengthens what she has put together in such a manner, that it is not to be broken or pierced either by stones or steel. Nor is the symmetry and form of the inside and cavity of the nest less to be admired. For it is so contrived as only to receive herself; the entrance into it not being to be found by any other creature, nor can the sea itself find a way into it. I am apt to believe that there is none of you who never saw this nest. But for my own part, that have often seen and handled one of them, I may safely say, that I

> In Delos' temple near Apollo's shrine,
> Something like this, a fabric most divine,

have seen. That is to say, the horned altar, celebrated for one of the seven wonders of the world, which without the help of parget, glue, soder, paste, or any other binding, is framed only of horns that grew on the right side of the head of the beast.

Now may the Deity that is somewhat musical and an islander be propitious to me, . . . while I deride the questions which those scoffers put, — wherefore Apollo may not be called mullet-shooter, when we find that Venus is called the mullet-protectrix; for which reason she is honored with temples adjoining to the sea, and sacred rights; and certain it is, that she is displeased when any mullet is killed. Therefore at Leptis the priests of Neptune never eat any thing that breeds in the sea; and you know the mullet is in great veneration among the professors of the Eleusinian mysteries; moreover, that the priestess of Juno at Argos abstains from the same fish; and the reason is because the mullets kill and destroy the sea-hare, which is pernicious to man, and therefore they spare those creatures that are kind and beneficial to him.

36. Then again, we find among many of the Greeks temples and altars frequently dedicated to Diana Dictynna (so called from δίκτυον, *a net*) and Delphinian Apollo. And that same place which Apollo has peculiarly chosen for himself was first of all inhabited by Cretans, having a dolphin for their leader. For the Deity did not swim before his army in another shape (as the mythologists dream), but sending a dolphin to direct them in their course, the dolphin brought them to Cirrha. Story also tells us that Soteles and Dionysius, who were sent to Sinope by Ptolemy Soter to fetch from thence Serapis, were driven by contrary winds beyond Cape Malea, having the Peloponnesus upon their right hands; while they were thus wandering and out of their course, a dolphin appeared before the prow of the headmost vessel, and (as it were) kindly inviting

them, conducted them into safe harbors and roads, till by his good guidance and leading them he at length brought the whole fleet to Cirrha. There, when they came to offer the usual sacrifices for their safe landing, they came to understand that, of two statues which were in the place, they were to take that of Pluto and carry it along with them; but as for that of Proserpina, they were only to take the mould and leave the statue itself behind. Probable it is that the Deity had a kindness for the dolphin, considering how much he delights in music. For which reason Pindar likens himself to the dolphin, and confesses himself to be moved in the same manner as that noble creature,

> Which flutes' beloved sound
> Excites to play,
> Upon the calm and placid sea.

Though it is very probable that his affection to men is more pleasing to the Deity, he being the only creature that bears an affection to man as man. For as for the land animals, some kinds there are that fly him altogether, and the tamest and most gentle follow him and are familiar with him, only for the benefit and nourishment which they receive from him; as the dog, the horse, and elephant. The swallows, by necessity constrained, build in houses, seeking shade and security, but are no less afraid of men than of the wild beasts. Only to the dolphin has Nature bequeathed that excellent quality, so much sought for by the best of philosophers, to love for no advantage; for that having no need at all of man, he is a kind friend to all men, and has lent his assistance to many. There is no man that is ignorant of the famous story of Arion. And you, my dear friend, have seasonably put us in mind of Hesiod; but

> Thou didst not by a legal course
> Rightly conclude thy long discourse.*

---

* Il. IX. 56. See above, chap. 13.

For when you had spoken so much in praise of the dog, you should not have passed by the dolphin. For it would have been a blind story of the dog that barked and flew with violence upon the murderers, had it not been for the dolphins, that took the carcass of Hesiod, floating in the sea near Nemeum, and readily receiving it from one another, landed it at Rhium, whereby the murder came to be known.

Myrtilus the Lesbian writes, that Enalus the Aeolian, being in love with the daughter of Phineus, who, by the command of the oracle of Amphitrite was cast into the sea by the Penthilidae, when he understood it, threw himself also into the sea, but was saved by a dolphin, and carried to Lesbos.

But the gentleness and kindness of the dolphin towards the lad of Jasus was so extraordinary that it might be said to amount even to amorous love. For he played and swam with him in the daytime, and suffered himself to be handled and bestrid by him; nor did he swim away with him, but joyfully carried him which way soever the lad by the motion of his body turned him, while the Iasians flocked from all parts to the shore to behold the sight. At length the lad, being thrown from the dolphin's back by a terrible shower of rain and hail, was drowned. Which the dolphin perceiving took up the dead youth, and threw himself upon the land together with the body, from which he never stirred till he died out of his own element; deeming it but just to partake of that end of which he seemed to have been the occasion to his friend and playfellow. Nor can the Iasians forget the accident, but keep it still in remembrance by the stamp upon their coin, which is a lad upon a dolphin's back.

And from hence it was that the fabulous stories of Coeranus gained credit. He was a Parian by birth, who residing at Byzantium, when a draught of dolphins caught in a net were exposed to sale and in danger of slaughter, bought them up all, and put them into the sea again. It happened not long after that Coeranus took a voyage in a vessel of fifty oars, carrying, as the story goes, several pirates. But between Naxos and the Bay of Paros he suffered shipwreck; and when all the rest were drowned, he alone was taken up by a dolphin that hastened to his succor, and carried to Sicynthus, and set ashore near the cave which to this day bears the name of Coeraneum. Upon which Archilochus is said to have made these lines:

> Of fifty men, great Neptune gentle grown
> Left courteous Coeranus alive alone.

Some years after Coeranus dying, his relations burnt his body near the seaside; at what time several dolphins appeared near the shore, as if they had come to his funeral; nor would they stir till the funeral was over. Moreover Stesichorus writes that Ulysses bore a dolphin painted upon his shield; and for what reason the Zacynthian records tell us, as Critheus testifies. For they say that Telemachus, when he was but a boy, falling into the sea, was saved by the dolphins that took him up and set him ashore. And therefore he made use of a dolphin for the impression of his seal and the ornament of his shield. But having promised before that I would produce no fabulous stories, and yet being carried, I know not how, to discourse beyond probability of dolphins by this repetition of the stories of Coeranus and Ulysses, I will do justice upon myself by concluding here.

37. ARISTOTIMUS. Now, gentlemen, it lies on your part that are judges, to pronounce sentence.

SOCLARUS. Assuredly then, for our parts, we shall give the same judgment in this, as Sophocles did in another case:

> Discourse upon discording arguments
> Is then determined best, when what was said
> Is duly weighed and stated on both sides.

For thus comparing what you have both discoursed one against another, it will be found that you have acquitted yourselves on both sides like true champions against those that would deprive brute animals of sense and understanding.

THAT BRUTE BEASTS MAKE USE OF REASON

ULYSSES, CIRCE, GRYLLUS.

1. ULYSSES. All these things, Circe, I believe that I have learned and well remember. But I would willingly ask thee, whether thou hast any Grecians here, which being men thou hast transformed into wolves and lions.

CIRCE. Very many, dearest Ulysses, but wherefore do you ask the question?

ULYSSES. Because in good truth I am of opinion I should gain a high reputation among the Greeks, if by thy favor I could restore these men to human shape again, and not suffer them through any negligence of mine to wax old in the bodies of beasts, where they lead a miserable and ignominious life.

CIRCE. Surely, this man, fool as he is, believes it requisite that his ambition should be unfortunate not only to himself and his friends, but to those that nothing belong to him.

ULYSSES. Thou art now jumbling and mixing another villanous potion of twittle twattle, and wouldst plainly turn me into a beast too, if thou couldst make me believe that it were a misfortune to be transformed from a beast to a man.

CIRCE. What hast thou made thyself better than a beast, who, forsaking an immortal life, free from the miseries of old age, with me, art making such haste through a thousand threatening calamities to a mortal and (as I may say) old wife, pursuing an empty good and a shadow instead of real truth, and all this, thinking to be more conspicuous and famous than thou art.

Ulysses. Well, Circe, let it be as thou sayest; for why should we be always contending about the same thing? However, do me the favor to restore these men, and give them into my custody.

Circe. By Hecate, not so fast neither; these are no ordinary fellows. But ask them first whether they are willing. If they refuse, do you, being such an eloquent gentleman, discourse them and persuade them; if you cannot persuade them, being too hard for ye at your own weapon, then let it suffice ye that you have ill consulted your own and the good of your friends.

Ulysses. Blessed woman, wherefore dost thou mock me thus? For how can they either talk or hear reason, so long as they are asses, hogs, and lions?

Circe. Be of good comfort, most ambitious of men; I will so order the business, that they shall both understand and discourse; or rather, let one suffice to hear and return answers instead of all the rest. Look ye, here is one at hand; pray talk to him.

Ulysses. Prithee, Circe, by what name shall we call him? Who is this fellow of all the men in the world?

Circe. What's this to the purpose? Call him Gryllus, if you please; and for my part, I'll leave ye together, that ye may not suspect him for speaking contrary to his mind to please me.

2. Gryllus. Save ye, Mr. Ulysses.

Ulysses. And you too, by Jove, Mr. Gryllus.

Gryllus. What is't your worship would have with me?

Ulysses. Knowing you were all born men, I pity the condition ye are now in; and I pity ye the more, for that being Greeks ye are fallen under this misfortune; and therefore I made it my request to Circe that she would restore ye again to your former shape, as many of you as were desirous, to the end ye might return home again with us.

GRYLLUS. Hold, Mr. Ulysses, not a word more of this, I beseech your worship. For we all contemn thee, as one that none but fools call cunning, and as vainly vauntest thyself to be wiser than other men, and yet art afraid of being changed from worse to better; like children that are frightened at physician's doses and hate going to school, although the medicines and the precepts make them healthy and learned of diseased and fools; just so thou refusest to be transformed out of one thing into another. And now thy bones rattle in thy skin for dread of living with Circe, lest she should transform thee into a hog or a wolf; and thou wouldst persuade us living in plenty of all enjoyments not only to forsake these blessings, but to abandon her that has so well provided for us, to sail along with thee, and to become men again, the most miserable of all creatures.

ULYSSES. In my opinion, Gryllus, this same wicked cup has not only deprived thee of thy shape, but of thy sense and reason too; or else thou art got drunk with those opinions which are everywhere exploded as nasty and villanous, unless some voluptuous pleasure of custom and habit has bewitched thee to this body.

GRYLLUS. Neither of these, O king of the Cephallenians. But if thou art come hither to dispute, and not to rail and swagger, we shall soon convince thee, having experience of both manners of living, that our way is to be preferred before that which thou so much applaudest.

ULYSSES. Nay, then go on; I'll listen with both ears to hear this paradox discussed.

3. GRYLLUS. Have at ye then, sir. But it behooves us

to begin first with those virtues which you so presumptuously assume to yourselves, and for which you so highly advance yourselves before the beasts, such as justice, prudence, fortitude, &c. Now answer me, thou the wisest among mortals; for I have heard thee telling a story to Circe of the territory of the Cyclops, that being neither ploughed nor planted by any person, it is so fertile and generously productive, that it bears all sorts of fruits and herbs spontaneously Now which do you prefer, this country, or your own goat-feeding stony Ithaca, which being cultivated with great labor and hardship, yet answers the expectations of the husbandmen with only a mean and scanty return? Now take it not amiss that I forewarn ye lest your love to your country sway ye to give an answer contrary to truth.

ULYSSES. No, no, I will not lie for the matter; I must confess I love and honor my own country more; but I applaud and admire theirs far beyond it.

GRYLLUS. Hence we must conclude that it is so as the wisest of men has affirmed; that there are some things to be praised and approved, others to be preferred by choice and affection. And I suppose you believe the same concerning the soul. For the same reasons hold in reference to the soul as to the ground; that such a soul should be the best, that produces virtue like spontaneous fruit, without labor and toil.

ULYSSES. Grant all this.

GRYLLUS. Then you confess that the souls of beasts are the more perfect, and more fertilely endued for the production of virtue; seeing that without any command or instruction — as it were without sowing or ploughing — it produces and increases that virtue which is requisite for every one.

ULYSSES. Prithee, Gryllus, don't rave, but tell me what those virtues are that beasts partake of?

4. Gryllus. Rather what virtues do they not partake of in a higher degree than the wisest of men? Look upon fortitude in the first place, of which you vaunt and brag to have such a terrible share, being not ashamed of the magnificent titles of Ulysses the bold and city-stormer, when indeed, like a pitiful knave as thou art, thou dost only circumvent by tricks and artifices men that understand only the simple and generous way of making war, ignorant altogether of fraud and faith-breaking, and by that means coverest thy deceit with the name of virtue, which never admits of any such coney-catching devices. But do you observe the combats and warfare of beasts, as well one against another as against yourselves, how free from craft and deceit they are, and how with an open and naked courage they defend themselves by mere strength of body; and how, neither afraid of the law that calls them forth to battle nor the severe edicts against deserters, but only out of scorn to be overcome, they fight with obstinacy to the last for conquest and victory. For they are not vanquished when their bodies are worsted, neither does despair cowardize them, but they die upon the spot. And you shall see many times that the strength of many, while they are expiring, being retired and crowded together in some part of the body, still makes resistance against the victor, and pants and fumes till at length it fails like extinguished fire that goes out for want of fuel. But there is no crying for quarter, no begging of mercy, no acknowledgment of being beaten; nor will the lion be a slave to the lion, nor the horse to the horse, as one man is a slave to another, willingly and patiently embracing servitude, which derives its name (δουλεία) from that of cowardice (δειλία). On the other side, such beasts as men by nets and treacherous snares get into their power, if fully grown, rather choose to die than serve, refusing nourishment and suffering extremity of drought. But as for their young

ones, — being tractable and supple by reason of their age, and fed with the deceitful mixtures and food that men provide for them, their inbred fierceness languishing through the taste of preternatural delights, — they suffer that which is called domestication, which is only an effeminating of their natural fury.

Whence it is apparent that beasts are naturally inclined to be courageous and daring, but that the martial confidence of men is preternatural. Which, most noble Ulysses, you may chiefly observe from hence; for that in beasts Nature keeps an equal balance of strength; so that the female, being but little inferior to the male, undergoes all necessary toils, and fights in defence of her young ones. And thus you hear of a certain Cromyonian sow, which, though a female, held Theseus tack, and found him work sufficient. Neither had the wisdom of that same female Sphinx that sat on Phicium, with all her riddles and enigmas, availed her, had she not far excelled the Cadmeans in strength and fortitude. Not far from whence the Telmesian fox had his den, a great propounder of questions also; not to omit the female serpent that fought with Apollo for his oracle at Delphi. Your king also took the mare Aetha from the Sicyonian, as a bribe to discharge him from going to the wars; and he did well, thereby showing how much he esteemed a valiant and generous mare above a timorous coward. You yourself have also seen female panthers and lionesses little inferior to the males in strength and courage; when your own wife, though a Lacedaemonian, when you were hectoring and blustering abroad, sat at home in the chimney-corner, not daring to do so much as the very swallows in encountering those who plagued both her and her family. Why need I still speak of the Carian and Maeonian women? Whence it is apparent that fortitude is not natural to men, for then the women would partake of the same strength with men.

So that the fortitude which you exercise is only constrained by law, not natural and voluntary, but subservient to the manners of the place and enslaved to reproach, a thing made up only of glorious words and adventitious opinion. And you undergo labor and throw yourself into danger, not out of real valor and boldness, but because ye are more afraid of other things. Therefore, as among thy own companions he that first makes haste to snatch up the light oar does it not because he contemns it, but because he is loath to be troubled with the more heavy; so he that endures a blow to avoid a wound, and defends himself against an enemy to preserve himself from wounds and death, does it not out of daring courage against the one, but out of fear of the other. Thus your fortitude is only a prudent fear; and your courage a knowing timidity, which understandingly does one thing to avoid another.

In short, if you believe yourselves superior to the beasts in fortitude, why do your poets call those that behave themselves most valiantly against their enemies wolf-breasted, lion-hearted, and compare them to wild boars; but never call the courage of lions man-like, or resemble the strength of a wild boar to that of a man? But as they call the swift wind-footed, and the beautiful Godlike-formed, hyperbolizing in their similes; so when they extol the gallantry of the stout in battle, they derive their comparisons from the superior in bravery. The reason is, because courage is as it were the tincture and edge of fortitude; which the beasts make use of unmixed in their combats, but in you being mixed with reason, like wine diluted with water, it gives way to danger and loses the opportunity. And some of you there are who deny that courage is requisite in battle, and therefore laying it aside make use of sober reason; which they do well for their preservation, but are shamefully beside the cushion, in point of strength and revenge. How absurd is it therefore for you to complain of Nature, because she did not furnish your bodies with goads and teeth and crooked claws to defend yourselves, when at the same time you would disarm the soul of her natural weapons?

5. ULYSSES. In good truth, Gryllus, you are grown, in my conceit, a notable sophister, to discourse at this rate out of a hog's snout, and yet to handle your argument so strenuously. But why have you not all this while spoke a word of temperance?

GRYLLUS. Because I thought you would have contradicted first what I have already said. But you are in haste to hear what I have to say concerning temperance, because that, being the husband of a most temperate and chaste wife, you believe you have set us an example of temperance by abstaining from Circe's embraces. And yet in this you differ nothing from all the beasts; for neither do they desire to approach their superiors, but they pursue their pleasures and amours among those of their own tribe. No wonder is it then, if — like the Mendesian goat in Egypt, which is reported to have been shut up with several most beautiful women, yet never to have offered copulation with them, but when he was at liberty, with a lustful fury flew upon the she-goats — so thou, though a man addicted greatly to venereal pleasures, yet being a man, hast no desire to sleep with a goddess. And for the chastity of thy Penelope, the ten thousand rooks and daws that chatter it abroad do but make it ridiculous and expose it to contempt, there being not one of those birds but, if she loses her mate, continues a widow, not for a small time, but for nine ages of men; so that there is not one of those female rooks that does not surpass in chastity thy fair Penelope above nine times.

6. But because thou believest me to be a sophister, I shall observe a certain order in my discourse, first giving thee the definition of temperance, and then dividing desire

according to the several kinds of it. Temperance then is the contracting and well governing our desires, pruning off those that are superfluous and encroaching upon our wills, and ruling those that are necessary by the standards of reason and moderation. Now in desires you observe a vast number of distinctions. For it is both natural and necessary to drink; but as for venereal desires, which derive their originals from Nature, there is a time when they may be restrained without any inconvenience; these are therefore called natural but not necessary. But there is another sort, which are neither natural nor necessary, but infused from without by vain opinion through the mistake of right and true; and it is these that want but very little of ruining all your natural desires with their number, like a multitude of foreigners outnumbering the natives and expelling them from their habitations. But the beasts, having their souls unmixed and not to be overcome by these adventitious passions, and living lives as distant from vain opinion as from the sea, are inferior to you in living elegantly and superfluously, but they are extremely wary in preserving temperance and the right government of their desires, as being neither troubled with many, nor those foreign to their natures. And therefore formerly I was no less smitten with the glister of gold than thou art now, as believing nothing else that a man could possess to be comparable to it. Silver also and ivory inveigled me with the same desires; and he that enjoyed these things in the greatest measure seemed to be a man most happy and beloved of God, whether a Phrygian or a Carian, whether more meanly descended than Dolon or more miserable than Priam. From thenceforward being altogether swayed by my desires, I reaped no other pleasure nor delight in any other blessings of my life, with which I abounded, believing that I wanted still and missed my share of those that were the chiefest and the greatest. Therefore, I remember, when I beheld thee in Crete, at some solemnity, most pompously attired, I neither envied thy wisdom nor thy virtue; but the extraordinary fineness and exquisite workmanship of thy tunic, and the glistering of thy purple upper garment, and the beauty of the ornaments struck me with admiration. And the golden clasp, methought, was a pretty toy that had something of extraordinary graving in it; and bewitched with these baubles, I followed thee as the women did. But now being altogether estranged from those vain opinions, and having my understanding purified, I tread both gold and silver under my feet as I do the common stones; nor did I ever sleep more soundly upon thy carpets and tapestries, than now I do, rolled over head and ears in the deep and soft mud. None of those adventitious desires reside in our souls, but for the most part our manner of living is accustomed to necessary pleasures and desires; and as for those pleasures which are not necessary but only natural, we make such a use of them as is neither without order nor moderation.

7. And therefore let us consider these in the first place. The pleasure then that affects the sense of smelling with sweet odors and fragrant exhalations, besides that it has something in it which is pure in itself, and as it were bestowed upon us gratis, contributes also in some measure to the distinction of nourishment. For the tongue is said to be the judge of sweet, sour, and tart, only when the juices have come to be mingled and concorporate with the tasting faculty, and not before. But our smell, before the taste, becoming sensible of the virtue and qualities of every thing, and being more accurate than the tasters attending upon princes, admits what is familiar to Nature, and expels whatever is disagreeable to it; neither will it suffer it to touch or molest the taste, but accuses and declares the offensiveness of the thing smelt, before it do any harm. As to other things, it troubles us not at all as it does you,

whom it constrains for the sake of the sweet scents of cinnamon nard, malobathrum, and Arabian reed, to seek out for things dissimilar, and to jumble them together with a kind of apothecary's or perfumer's art, and at vast expense to purchase an unmanly and effeminate delight, for nothing profitable or useful. Now being such, this sense of smelling has not only corrupted all the female sex but the greatest part of men, insomuch that they care not to converse with their own wives, unless perfumed with precious ointments and odoriferous compositions. Whereas sows, she-goats, and other females attract the boars, he-goats, and the males of their own kind, by their own proper scents; and smelling of the pure dew, the meadows, and the fresh grass, they are incited to copulation out of common affection; the females without the coynesses of women, or the practice of little frauds and fascinations, to inflame the lust of their mates; and the males, not with amorous rage and frenzy stimulated, and enforced to purchase the act of generation with expensive hire or servile assiduity, but enjoying their seasonable amours without deceit or purchase of the satisfaction of their venery. For Nature in the spring-time, even as she puts forth the buds of plants, likewise awakens the desires of animals, but presently quenches them again, neither the female admitting the male nor the male attempting the female after conception. And thus pleasure has but a small and slender esteem among us; but Nature is all in all. So that even to this very day, we beasts were never yet tainted with coupling male with male, and female with female. Of which nevertheless there are many examples to be produced among the greatest and most celebrated persons; for I pass by those not worth remembrance.

Agamemnon hunted all Boeotia in pursuit of Argynnus, who fled his embraces; and after he had falsely accused the sea and winds, bravely flung himself into the lake Copais, to quench his love and free himself from the ardor of his lust.

Hercules in like manner pursuing his beardless friend, forsook his choicest associates and abandoned the fleet.

In the vaulted room belonging to Apollo surnamed Ptous, one of you men secretly wrote this inscription, Achilles the fair; when Achilles at that time had a son. [And I hear the inscription is still remaining.]* Yet if a cock tread a cock in the absence of the hen, he is burned alive, upon the signification of the soothsayer that it portends some fatal calamity. This is a plain confession in men themselves, that the beasts excel them in chastity, and that force is not to be put upon Nature for the sake of pleasure. But your incontinence is such, that Nature, though she have the law to assist her, is not able to keep it within bounds; insomuch that, like a rapid inundation, those inordinate desires overwhelm Nature with continual violence, trouble, and confusion. For men have copulated with she-goats, sows, and mares; and women have run mad after male beasts. And from such copulations sprang the Minotaurs and Silvans, and, as I am apt to believe, the Sphinxes and Centaurs. It is true, that sometimes, constrained by hunger, a dog or a bird has fed upon human flesh; but never yet did any beast attempt to couple with human kind. But men constrain and force the beasts to these and many other unlawful pleasures.

8. Now being thus wicked and incontinent in reference to the aforesaid lustful desires, it is no less easy to be proved that men are more intemperate than beasts, even in those things which are necessary, that is to say, in eating and drinking, the pleasure of which we always enjoy with some benefit to ourselves. But you, pursuing the pleasures of eating and drinking beyond the satisfaction of nature,

---

* It seems incredible that Plutarch could have put this into the mouth of Gryllus, even by carelessness. (G.)

are punished with many and tedious diseases, which, arising from the single fountain of superfluous gormandizing, fill your bodies with all manner of wind and vapors not easy for purgation to expel. In the first place, all sorts of beasts, according to their kind, feed upon one sort of food, which is proper to their natures; some upon grass, some upon roots, and others upon fruits. They that feed upon flesh never mind any other sort of food. Neither do they rob the weaker animals of their nourishment. But the lion suffers the hart, and the wolf the sheep, to feed upon what Nature has provided for them. But man, such is his voracity, falls upon all, to satisfy the pleasures of his appetite; tries all things, tastes all things; and, as if he were yet to seek what was the most proper diet and most agreeable to his nature, among all the creatures is the only all-devourer. And first he makes use of flesh, not for want, as having the liberty to take his choice of herbs and fruits, the plenty of which is inexhaustible; but out of luxury and being cloyed with necessaries, he seeks after inconvenient and impure diet, purchased by the slaughter of living creatures; by that means showing himself more cruel than the most savage of wild beasts. For blood, murder, and flesh are proper to nourish the kite, the wolf, and dragon; but to men they are delicious viands. Then making use of all, he does not do like the beasts, which abstain from most creatures and are at enmity only with a few, and that only compelled by the necessities of hunger; but neither fowl nor fish nor any thing that lives upon the land escapes your tables, though they bear the epithets of human and hospitable.

9. Let it be so, that nothing will serve ye but to devour whatever comes near ye, to pamper and indulge your voracious appetites. Yet where is the benefit and pleasure of all this? But such is the prudence of the beasts, as not to admit of any vain and unprofitable arts. And as

for those that are necessary, they do not acquire them, as being introduced by others or taught for reward; neither do they make it their study to soder and fasten one contemplation to another, but they are supplied by their own prudence with such as are true-born and genuine. It is true, we hear the Egyptians are generally physicians. But the beasts are not only every one of them notionally endued with knowledge and art which way to cure themselves, but also to procure their food and repair their strength, to catch their prey by slight and cunning, to guard themselves from danger; neither are some of them ignorant how to teach the science of music so far as is convenient for them. For from whom did we hogs learn to run to the rivers, when we are sick, to search for crawfish? Who taught the tortoises, when they have eaten vipers, to physic themselves with origanum? Who taught the Cretan goats, when shot with arrows that stick in their bodies, to betake themselves to dittany, which they have no sooner eaten, but the heads of the darts fall out of the wound? Now if you say that Nature is the schoolmistress that teaches them these things, you acknowledge the prudence of beasts to be derived from the chiefest and wisest original of understanding; which if you think not proper to call reason and wisdom, it is time for ye to find out a more glorious and honorable name for it. Indeed by its effects it shows itself to be greater and more wonderful in power; not illiterate or without education, but instructed by itself and wanting nothing from without; not weak and imperfect, but, through the vigor and perfection of its natural virtue, supporting and cherishing that natural contribution of understanding which others attain to by instruction and education. So that, whatever men acquire and contemplate in the midst of their luxury and wantonness, those things our understanding attains to through the excellency of our apprehensions, even contrary to the nature of the body. For not to speak of whelps that learn to draw dry foot, and colts that will practise figure-dances; there are crows that will speak, and dogs that will leap through hoops as they turn around. You shall also see horses and bulls upon the theatres lie down, dance, stop, and move their bodies after such a manner as would puzzle even men to perform the same things; which, though they are of little use, yet being learned and remembered by beasts, are great arguments of their docility.

If you doubt whether we learn arts, be convinced that we teach them. For partridges teach their young ones to hide themselves by lying upon their backs just before a clod of earth, to escape the pursuit of the fowlers. And you shall observe the old storks, when their young ones first begin to take wing, what care they take to instruct them upon the tops of houses. Nightingales also teach their young ones to sing; insomuch that nightingales taken young out of the nest, and bred up by hand in cages, sing worse, as being deprived of their instructors before their time. So that after I had been a while transformed into this shape, I admired at myself, that I was so easily persuaded by idle arguments of the sophisters to believe that all other creatures were void of sense and reason except man.

10. ULYSSES. What then, Gryllus? Does your transmutation inform ye also that sheep and asses are rational creatures?

GRYLLUS. From these very creatures, most worthy and best of men, Ulysses, the nature of beasts is chiefly to be discerned to be as it is, neither void of reason nor understanding. For as one tree is neither more or less than another without a soul, but all are together in the same condition of insensibility (for there is no tree that is endued with a soul); so neither would one animal seem to be more slow to understand or more indocible than another, if all did not partake of reason and understanding, though some in a less, some in a greater measure. For you must consider that the stupidity and slothfulness of some is an argument of the quickness and subtlety of others, which easily appears when you compare a fox, a wolf, or a bee with a sheep or ass; as if thou shouldest compare thyself to Polyphemus, or thy grandfather Autolycus with the Corinthian [mentioned in] Homer. For I do not believe there is such difference between beast and beast, in point of reason and understanding and memory, as between man and man.

ULYSSES. Have a care, Gryllus; it is a dangerous thing to allow them reason that have no knowledge of a Deity.

GRYLLUS. Must we then deny that thou, most noble Ulysses, being so wise and full of stratagems as thou art, wast begotten by Sisyphus? . . .

OF THE FACE APPEARING WITHIN THE ORB OF THE MOON.

LAMPRIAS, APOLLONIDES, LUCIUS, PHARNACES, SYLLA, ARISTOTELES, THEON, MENELAUS.

[*The beginning of this discourse is lost.*]

1. THESE things then, said Sylla, agree with my story, and are taken thence. But I should first willingly ask, what need there is of making such a preamble against these opinions, which are at hand and in every man's mouth, concerning the face that is seen within the orb of the moon. Why should we not, said I, being, by the difficulty there is in these discourses, forced upon those? For, as they who have long lain lingering under chronical diseases, after they have been worn out and tired with experimenting all ordinary remedies and the usual rules of living and diet, have at last recourse to lustrations and purifications, to charms and amulets fastened about the neck, and to the interpretation of dreams; so in such obscure and abstruse questions and speculations, when the common, apparent, and ordinary reasons are not satisfactory, there is a necessity of trying such as are more extravagant, and of not contemning but enchanting ourselves (as one may say) with the discourses of the ancients, and endeavoring always to find out the truth.

2. For you see at the very first blush, how impertinent his opinion is who said, that the form appearing in the moon is an accident of our sight, by its weakness giving way to her brightness, which we call the dazzling of our

eyes; for he perceives not that this should rather befall our looking against the sun, whose lustre is more resplendent, and whose rays are more quick and piercing; as Empedocles also in a certain passage of his has not unpleasantly noted the difference of these two planets, saying,

> The sharp-rayed sun, and gently shining moon.

For thus does he call her alluring, favorable, and harmless light. No less absurd appears the reason he afterwards gives why dull and weak eyes discern no difference of form in the moon, her orb appearing to them plain and smooth, whereas those whose sight is more acute and penetrating better descry the lineaments and more perfectly observe the impressions of a face, and more evidently distinguish its different parts. For it should, in my opinion, be quite contrary, if this were a fancy caused by the weakness of the vanquished sight; so that where the patient's eye is weaker, the appearance would be more express and evident. Moreover, the inequality every way confutes this reason; for this face is not seen in a continuance and confused shadow, but the poet Agesianax not unelegantly describes it, saying,

> With shining fire it circled does appear,
> And in the midst is seen the visage clear
> Of a young maid, whose eyes more gray than blue,
> Her brow and cheeks a blushing red do show.

For indeed dark and shady things, encompassed with others that are bright and shining, sink underneath and reciprocally rise again, being repelled by them; and in a word, they are so interlaced one within another, that they represent the figure of a face painted to the life; and there seems to have been great probability in that which was spoken against your Clearchus, my dear Aristotle. For he appears not inconveniently to be called yours, for he was intimately acquainted with the ancient Aristotle, although he perverted many of the Peripatetic doctrines.

3. Then Apollonides taking up the discourse, and asking what that opinion of Clearchus was; It would more, said I, beseem any man than you to be ignorant of this discourse, as being grounded on the very fundamental principles of geometry. For he affirms, that what we call a face, is the image and figure of the great ocean, represented in the moon as in a mirror. For the circumference of a circle, when it is reflected back,* is wont in many places to touch objects which are not seen in a direct line. And the full moon is for evenness and lustre the most beautiful and purest of all mirrors. As then you hold, that the heavenly bow appears, when the ray of light is reflected back towards the sun, in a cloud which has got a little liquid smoothness and consistence; so, said he, there is seen in the moon the surface of the sea, not in the place where it is situated, but from whence the reflection gives a sight of it by its reverberated and reflexed light, as Agesianax again says in another passage,

> This flaming mirror offers to your eyes
> The vast sea's figure, as beneath it lies
> Foaming with raging billows.

4. Apollonides therefore, being delighted with this, said. A singular opinion indeed is this of his, and (to speak in a word) strangely and newly invented by a man sufficiently presumptuous, but not void of learning and wit. But how, I pray, was it refuted?

First, said I, the superficies of the sea is all of a nature, the current of it being uniform and continuous; but the appearance of those black and dark spots which are seen in the face of the moon is not continued, but has certain

---

* See the account of various ancient doctrines of vision and the reflection of light in the treatise on the Opinions of Philosophers, Book IV. Chapters 13 and 14. The idea that vision was caused by something proceeding from the eye to the object is especially to be noticed. (G.)

isthmuses or partitions clear and bright, which divide and separate what is dark and shady. Whence every place being distinguished and having its own limits apart, the conjunctions of the clear with the obscure, taking a resemblance of high and low, express and represent the similitude of a figure seeming to have eyes and lips; so that we must of necessity suppose, either that there are main oceans and main seas, distinguished by isthmuses and continents of firm land, which is evidently absurd and false; or that if there is but one, it is not credible its image should appear so distracted and dissipated into pieces. And as for this, there is less danger in asking than in affirming in your presence, whether, since the habitable earth has both length and breadth, it is possible that the sight of all men, when it is reflected by the moon, should equally touch the ocean, even of those that sail and dwell in it, as do the Britons; especially since the earth, as you have maintained, has but the proportion of a point, if compared to the sphere of the moon. This therefore, said I, it is your business to observe, but the reflection of the sight against the moon belongs neither to you nor Hipparchus. And yet, my friend Lamprias, there are many naturalists, who approve not this doctrine of his touching the driving back of the sight, but affirm it to be more probable that it has a certain obedient and agreeing temperature and compactness of structure, than such beatings and repercussions as Epicurus feigned for his atoms.* Nor am I of opinion that Clearchus would have us suppose the moon to be a massy and weighty body, but a celestial and light-giving star, as you say it is, which must have the property of breaking and turning aside the sight; so that all this reflection would come to nothing. But if we are desired to receive and admit it, we shall ask why this face or image of the sea is to be seen only in the body of the

* The text in this passage is defective, and the sense chiefly conjectural. (G.)

moon; and not in any of the other stars? For the laws of probability require that the sight should suffer this equally in all, or else in none.

But pray, sir, said I, casting mine eyes upon Lucius, call a little to mind what was said at first by those of our party.

5. Nay rather, answered he, — lest we should seem too injurious to Pharnaces, in thus passing by the opinion of the Stoics, without opposing any thing against it, — let us make some reply to this man, who supposes the moon to be wholly a mixture of air and mild fire, and then says that, as in a calm there sometimes arises on a sudden a breeze of wind which curls and ruffles the superficies of the sea, so, the air being darkened and rendered black, there is an appearance and form of a face.

You do courteously, Lucius, said I, thus to veil and cover with specious expressions so absurd and false an opinion. But so did not our friend; but he said, as the truth is, that the Stoics disfigured and mortified the moon's face, filling it with stains and black spots, one while invocating her by the name of Diana and Minerva, and another while making her a lump and mixture of dark air and charcoal-fire, not kindling of itself or having any light of its own, but a body hard to be judged and known, always smoking and ever burning, like to those thunders which by the poets are styled lightless and sooty. Now that a fire of coals, such as they would have that of the moon to be, cannot have any continuance nor yet so much as the least subsistence, unless it meets with some solid matter fit to maintain it, keep it in, and feed it, has, I think, far better than it is by these philosophers, been understood by those poets who in merriment affirm that Vulcan was therefore said to be lame because fire can no more go forward without wood or fuel than a cripple without a crutch. If then the moon is fire, whence has it so much air? For that region above, which is with a continual motion carried round, consists not of air, but some more excellent substance, whose nature it is to subtilize and set on fire all other things. And if it has been since engendered there, how comes it that it does not perish, being changed and transmuted by the fire into an ethereal and heavenly substance? And how can it maintain and preserve itself, cohabiting so long with the fire, as a nail always fixed and fastened in one and the same place? For being rare and diffused, as by Nature it is, it is not fitted for permanency and continuance, but for change and dissipation. Neither is it possible that it should condense and grow compact, being mixed with fire, and utterly void of water and earth, the only two elements by which the nature of the air suffers itself to be brought to a consistency and thickness. And since the swiftness and violence of motion is wont to inflame the air which is in stones, and even in lead itself, as cold as it is; much more will it that which, being in fire, is with so great an impetuosity whirled about. For they are displeased with Empedocles for making the moon a mass of air congealed after the manner of hail, included within a sphere of fire. And yet they themselves say, that the moon, being a globe of fire, contains in it much air dispersed here and there, — and this, though it has neither ruptures, concavities, nor depths (which they who affirm it to be earthly admit), but the air lies superficially on its convexity. Now this is both against the nature of permanency, and impossible to be accorded with what we see in full moons; for it should not appear separately black and dark, but either be wholly obscured and concealed or else co-illuminated, when the moon is overspread by the sun. For with us the air which is in the pits and hollows of the earth, whither the rays of the sun cannot penetrate, remains dark and lightless; but that which is spread over its exterior parts has clearness and a lightsome color. For it is by reason of its rarity easily transformed into every quality and faculty, but principally that of light and brightness, by which, being never so little touched, it incontinently changes and is illuminated. This reason therefore, as it seems greatly to help and maintain the opinion of those who thrust the air into certain deep valleys and caves in the moon, so confutes you, who mix and compose her sphere, I know not how, of air and fire. For it is not possible that there should remain any shadow or darkness in the superficies of the moon, when the sun with his brightness clears and enlightens whatsoever we can discern of her and ken with our sight.

6. Whilst I was yet speaking, Pharnaces interrupting my discourse said: See here again the usual stratagem of the Academy brought into play against us, which is to busy themselves at every turn in speaking against others, but never to afford an opportunity for reproving what they say themselves; so that those with whom they confer and dispute must always be respondents and defendants, and never plaintiffs or opponents. You shall not therefore bring me this day to give you an account of those things you charge upon the Stoics, till you have first rendered me a reason for your turning the world upside down.

Then Lucius smiling said: This, good sir, I am well contented to do, provided only that you will not accuse us of impiety, as Cleanthes thought that the Greeks ought to have called Aristarchus the Samian into question and condemned him of blasphemy against the Gods, as shaking the very foundations of the world, because this man, endeavoring to save the appearances, supposed that the heavens remained immovable, and that the earth moved through an oblique circle, at the same time turning about its own axis. As for us therefore, we say nothing that we take from them. But how do they, my good friend, who suppose the moon to be earth, turn the world upside down more than you, who say that the earth remains here hanging in the air, being much greater than the moon, as the mathematicians measure their magnitude by the accidents of eclipses, and by the passages of the moon through the shadow of the earth, gathering thence how great a space it takes up? For the shadow of the earth is less than itself, by reason it is cast by a greater light. And that the end of this shadow upwards is slender and pointed, they say that Homer himself was not ignorant, but plainly expressed it when he called the night θοή (that is, *acute*) from the sharp-pointedness of the earth's shadow. And yet the moon in her eclipses, being caught within this point of the shadow, can scarce get out of it by going forward thrice her own bigness in length. Consider then, how many times the earth must needs be greater than the moon, if it casts a shadow, the narrowest point of which is thrice as broad as the moon. But you are perhaps afraid lest the moon should fall, if it were acknowledged to be earth; but as for the earth, Aeschylus has secured you, when he says that Atlas

> Stands shouldering the pillar of the heaven and earth,
> A burden onerous.*

If then there runs under the moon only a light air, not firm enough to bear a solid burthen, whereas under the earth there are, as Pindar says, columns and pillars of adamant for its support, therefore Pharnaces himself is out of all dread of the earth's falling, but he pities the Ethiopians and those of Taprobane, who lie directly under the course of the moon, fearing lest so ponderous a mass should tumble upon their heads. And yet the moon has, for an help to preserve her from falling, her motion and the impetuosity of her revolution; as stones, pebbles, and other weights, put into slings, are kept from dropping out, whilst they are swung round, by the swiftness of their motion. For every body is carried according to its natural

---

* Aesch. Prom. 849.

motion, unless it be diverted by some other intervening cause. Wherefore the moon does not move according to the motion of her weight, her inclination being stopped and hindered by the violence of a circular revolution. And perhaps there would be more reason to wonder, if the moon continued always immovable in the same place, as does the earth. But now the moon has a great cause to keep herself from tending hither downwards; but for the earth, which has no other motion, it is probable that it has also no other cause of its settlement but its own weight. For the earth is heavier than the moon, not only because it is greater, but also because the moon is rendered lighter by the heat and inflammation that is in it. In brief, it appears by what you say, if it is true that the moon is fire, that it stands in need of earth or some other matter, which it may rest on and cleave to, for the maintaining and nourishing of its power. For it is not possible to imagine how a fire can be preserved without some combustible matter. And you yourselves say that the earth continues firm without any basis or pedestal to support it.

Yes surely, said Pharnaces, being in its proper and natural place, the very middle and centre of the universe. For this it is to which all heavy and ponderous things do from every side naturally tend, incline, and aspire, and about which they cling and are counterpoised. But every superior region, though it may perhaps receive some earthly and weighty thing sent by violence up into it, immediately repels and casts it down again by force, or (to speak better) lets it follow its own proper inclination, by which it naturally tends downwards.

7. For the refutation of which, being willing to give Lucius time for the calling to mind his arguments, I addressed myself to Theon, and asked him which of the tragic poets it was who said that physicians

With bitter med'cines bitter choler purge.

And Theon having answered me that it was Sophocles;
This, said I to him, we must of necessity permit them to
do ; but we are not to give ear to those philosophers who
would overthrow paradoxes by assertions no less strange
and paradoxical, and for the oppugning strange and extravagant opinions, devise others yet more wonderful and
absurd ; as these men do, who broach and introduce this
doctrine of a motion tending towards the middle, in which
what sort of absurdity is there not to be found ? Does it
not thence follow, that the earth is spherical, though we
nevertheless see it to have so many lofty hills, so many
deep valleys, and so great a number of inequalities ? Does
it not follow that there are antipodes dwelling opposite to
another, sticking on every side to the earth, with their
heads downwards and their heels upwards, as if they were
woodworms or lizards ? That we ourselves go not on the
earth straight upright, but obliquely and bending aside
like drunken men ? That if bars and weights of a thousand talents apiece should be let fall into the hollow of
the earth, they would, when they were come to the centre,
stop and rest there, though nothing came against them or
sustained them ; and that, if peradventure they should by
force pass the middle, they would of themselves return
and rebound back thither again ? That if one should saw
off the two trunks or ends of a beam on either side of the
earth, they would not be always carried downwards, but
falling both from without into the earth, they would equally
meet, and hide themselves together in the middle ? That
if a violent stream of water should run downwards into
the ground, it would, when it came to the centre of the
earth, which they hold to be an incorporeal point, there
gather together, and turn round like a whirlpool, with a
perpetual and endless suspension ? Some of which positions are so absurd, that none can so much as force his
imagination, though falsely, to conceive them possible.

For this is indeed to make that which is above to be below; and to turn all things upside down, by making all that is as far as the middle to be *downwards*, and all that is beyond the middle to be *upwards;* so that if a man should, by the sufferance and consent of the earth, stand with his navel just against her centre, he would by this means have his feet and head both upwards; and if one, having digged through that place which is beyond the middle, should come to pull him out from thence, that part which is below would at one and the same time be drawn upwards, and that which is above, downwards. And if another should be imagined to stand the contrary way, their feet, though the one's were opposite to the other's, would both be and be said to be upwards.

8. Bearing then upon their shoulders, and drawing after them, I do not say a little bag or box, but a whole pack of juggler's boxes, full of so many absurdities, with which they play the hocus-pocus in philosophy, they nevertheless accuse others of error for placing the moon, which they hold to be earth, on high, and not in the middle or centre of the world. And yet, if every heavy body inclines towards the same place, and does from all sides and with every one of its parts tend to its own centre, the earth certainly will appropriate and challenge to itself these ponderous masses — which are its parts — not because it is the centre of the universe, but rather because it is the whole; and this gathering together of heavy bodies round about it will not be a sign showing it to be the middle of the world, but an argument to prove and testify that these bodies which had been plucked from it and again return to it have a communication and conformity of nature with the earth. For as the sun draws into himself the parts of which he is composed, so the earth receives a stone as a part belonging to it, in such manner that every one of such things is in time united and incorporated with it.

And if peradventure there is some other body which was not from the beginning allotted to the earth nor has been separated from it, but had its own proper and peculiar consistence and nature apart, as these men may say of the moon, what hinders but it may continue separated by itself, being kept close, compacted, and bound together by its own parts? For they do not demonstrate that the earth is the middle of the universe; and this conglomeration of heavy bodies which are here, and their coalition with the earth, show us the manner how it is probable that the parts which are assembled in the body of the moon continue also there. But as for him who drives and ranges together in one place all earthly and ponderous things, making them parts of one and the same body, I wonder that he does not attribute also the same necessity and constraint to light substances, but leaves so many conglomerations of fire separated one from another; nor can I see why he should not amass together all the stars, and think that there ought to be but one body of all those substances which fly upwards.

9. But you mathematicians, friend Apollonides, say that the sun is distant from our upper sphere infinite thousands of miles, and after him the day-star or Venus, Mercury, and other planets, which being situated under the fixed stars, and separated from one another by great intervals, make their revolutions; and in the mean time you think that the world affords not to heavy and terrestrial bodies any great and large place or distance one from another. You plainly see, it would be ridiculous, if we should deny the moon to be earth because it is not seated in the lowest region of the world, and yet affirm it to be a star, though so many thousands of miles remote from the upper firmament, as if it were plunged into some deep gulf. For she is so low before all other stars, that the measure of the distances cannot be expressed, and you mathematicians

want numbers to compute and reckon it; but she in a manner touches the earth, making her revolution so near the tops of the mountains, that she seems, as Empedocles has it, to leave even the very tracks of her chariot-wheels behind her. For oftentimes she surpasses not the shadow of the earth, which is very short through the excessive greatness of the sun that shines upon it, but seems to turn so near the superficies, and (as one may say) between the arms and in the bosom of the earth, that it withholds from her the light of the sun, because she mounts that shady, earthly, and nocturnal region which is the lot and inheritance of the earth. And therefore I am of opinion, we may boldly say that the moon is within the limits and confines of the earth, seeing she is even darkened by the summits of its mountains.

10. But leaving the stars, as well erring as fixed, see what Aristarchus proves and demonstrates in his treatise of magnitudes and distances; that the distance of the sun is above eighteen times and under twenty times greater than that of the moon from us. And yet they who place the moon lowest say that her distance from us contains six and fifty of the earth's semidiameters, that is, that she is six and fifty times as far from us as we are from the centre of the earth; which is forty thousand stadia, according to those that make their computation moderately. Therefore the sun is above forty millions and three hundred thousand stadia distant from the moon; so far is she from the sun by reason of her gravity, and so near does she approach to the earth. So that if substances are to be distinguished by places, the portion and region of the earth challenges to itself the moon, which, by reason of neighborhood and proximity, has a right to be reputed and reckoned amongst the terrestrial natures and bodies. Nor shall we, in my opinion, do amiss if, having given so vast an interval and distance to these bodies which are said to be above, we

leave also to those which are below some space and room to turn them in, such as is that between the earth and the moon. For neither is he who calls only the utmost superficies of the heaven *above* and all the rest *beneath* moderate or tolerable; nor is he to be endured who confines *beneath* only to the earth, or rather to its centre; seeing the vast greatness of the world may afford means for the assigning farther to this lower part some such space as is necessary for motion. Now against him who holds that whatever is above the earth is immediately high and sublime, there is presently another opposition to encounter and contradict it, that whatever is beneath the sphere of the fixed stars ought to be called low and inferior.

11. In a word, how is the earth said to be the middle, and of what is it the middle? For the universe is infinite; and infiniteness having neither beginning nor end, it is convenient also that it should not have any middle; for the middle is a certain end or limit, but infiniteness is a privation of all sorts of limits. Now he that affirms the earth to be the middle, not of the universe but of the world, is certainly a pleasant man, if he does not think that the world itself is subject to the same doubts and difficulties. For the universe has not left a middle even to the very world, but this being without any certain seat or foundation, it is carried in an infinite voidness to no proper end; or if perhaps it has stopped, it has met with some other cause or stay, not according to the nature of the place. As much may be conjectured of the moon, that by the means of another soul and another Nature, or (to say better) of another difference, the earth continues firm here below, and the moon moves. Besides this, see whether they are not ignorant of a great inconvenience and error. For if it is true that all which is without the centre of the earth, however it be, is above, there will then be no part of the world below; but the earth and all that is upon it

will be above; and in brief, every body that shall be placed about the centre will be above, and there will be nothing below or underneath, but one only point which has no body, which will of necessity make head against and oppose all the rest of the world's nature, if *above* and *beneath* are naturally opposite to one another. Nor is this the only absurdity that will follow; but all heavy and ponderous bodies will also lose the cause for which they move and tend downwards hither, for there will be no body below to which they should move; and as for that which is incorporeal, it is not probable, neither will they themselves allow, that it should be so forcible as to draw and retain all things about itself. But if it is unreasonable and contrary to Nature that the whole world should be above, and that there should be nothing below but an incorporeal and indivisible term or limit, then is this, as we say, yet more reasonable, that the region above and that below being divided the one from the other, have nevertheless each of them a large and spacious room.

12. Nevertheless, supposing, if you please, that it is against Nature for earthly bodies to have any motions in heaven, let us consider leisurely and mildly — and not violently, as is done in tragedies — that this is no proof of the moon's not being earth, but only that earth is in a place where by nature it should not be; for the fire of Mount Aetna is indeed against nature under ground, nevertheless it ceases not to be fire. And the wind contained within bottles is indeed of its own nature light and inclined to ascend, but is yet by force constrained to be there where naturally it should not be. And is not our very soul, I beseech you in the name of Jupiter, which, as yourselves say, is light, of a fiery substance, and imperceptible to sense, included within the body, which is heavy, cold, and palpable? Yet do we therefore say that the soul does not belong to the body; or that it is not a divine substance

under a gross and heavy mass, or that it does not in a moment pass through heaven, earth, and sea, pierce into the flesh, nerves, and marrow, and into the humors which are the cause of a thousand passions? And even your Jupiter, such as you imagine him and depaint him to be, is he not of his own nature a great and perpetual fire? Yet now he submits, is pliable, and transformed into all things by several mutations. Take heed therefore, good sir, lest, by transferring and reducing every thing to the place assigned it by Nature, you so philosophize as to bring in a dissolution of the whole world, and put all things again into that state of enmity mentioned by Empedocles, or (to speak more properly) lest you raise up again those ancient Titans and Giants to put on arms against Nature, and endeavor to introduce again that fabulous disorder and confusion, where all that is heavy goes one way apart, and all that is light another;

> Where neither sun's bright face is seen,
> Nor earth beheld, spread o'er with green,
> Nor the salt sea,

as Empedocles has it. Then the earth felt no heat, nor the sea any wind; no heavy thing moved upwards, nor any light thing downwards; but the principles of all things were solitary, without any mutual love or dilection one to another, not admitting any society or mixture together; but shunning and avoiding all communication, moving separately by particular motions, as being disdainful, proud, and altogether carrying themselves in such manner as every thing does from which (as Plato says) God is absent; that is, as those bodies do in which there is neither soul nor understanding; till such time as, by Divine Providence, desire coming into Nature engendered mutual amity, Venus, and Love, — as Empedocles, Parmenides, and Hesiod have it, — to the end that changing their natural places, and reciprocally communicating their faculties, some being by necessity bound to motion, others to quiet and rest, and all tending to the better, every thing remitting a little of its power and yielding a little from its place, . . . they might make at length a harmony, accord, and society together.

13. For if there had not been any other part of the world against Nature, but every thing had been in the same place and quality it naturally ought to be, without standing in need of any change or transposition or having had any occasion for it from the beginning, I know not what the work of Divine Providence is or in what it consists, or of what Jupiter has been the father, creator, or worker. For there would not in a camp be any need of the art of ranging and ordering of battles, if every soldier of himself knew and understood his rank, place, and station, and the opportunity he ought to take and keep; nor would there be any want of gardeners or builders, if water were of itself framed to flow where it is necessary, and irrigate such plants as stand in need of watering, or if bricks, timber, and stones would of their own inclinations and natural motion range and settle themselves in due and fitting places and orders. Now if this discourse manifestly takes away Providence, and if the ordering and distinction of things that are in the world belongs to God, why should we wonder at Nature's having been so disposed and ordained by him, that the fire should be here, and the stars there, and again the earth should be situated here below, and the moon above, lodged in a prison found out by reason, more sure and straight than that which was first ordained by Nature? For if it were of absolute necessity that all things should follow their natural instinct and move according to the motion given them by Nature, neither the Sun, Venus, nor any other planet would any more run a circular course; for light and fiery substances have by Nature their motion directly upwards. And if

perhaps Nature itself receives this permutation and change by reason of the place, so that fire should here in a direct line tend upwards, but being once arrived at heaven, should turn round with the revolution of the heavens; what wonder would it be, if heavy and terrestrial bodies, being in like manner out of their natural place, were vanquished by the ambient air, and forced to take another sort of motion? For it cannot with any reason be said that heaven has by Nature the power to take away from light things the property of mounting directly upwards, and cannot likewise have the force to overcome heavy things and such as tend downwards; but that sometimes making use of this power, and sometimes of the proper nature of the things, it still orders every thing for the best.

14. But if, laying aside those servile habits and opinions to which we have enslaved ourselves, we must frankly and fearlessly deliver our judgment, it seems clear to me, that there is not any part of the universe which has a peculiar and separate rank, situation, or motion, that can simply be said to be natural to it. But when every thing exhibits and yields up itself to be moved, as is most profitable and fit for that for whose sake it was made and to which it is by Nature appointed, — suffering, doing, or being disposed, as is most expedient and meet for the safety, beauty, and power of the same, — then it appears to have its place, motion, and disposition according to Nature. As a proof of this, we may observe that man, who, if any thing in the world be so, is made and disposed according to Nature, has upwards, especially about his head, heavy and terrestrial things, and about the middle of his body such as are hot and participate of fire; of his teeth also some grow upwards and some downwards, and yet neither the one nor the other are contrary to Nature; neither is the fire which shines in his eyes according to Nature, and that which is in his heart and stomach against it; but it is in

each place properly and beneficially seated. Moreover, consider the nature of all shell-fishes; and, that I may use the words of Empedocles,

> Look on the crabs, the oysters of the sea,
> And shell-fish all, which heavy coats enfold,
> The tortoise too with arched back, whom we
> Covered with crust, as hard as stone, behold.
> View them but well, and plain it will appear,
> They hardened earth above their bodies bear.

And yet this crust, stone-like, hard, and heavy, as it is thus placed over their bodies, does not press and crush their natural habit, nor on the contrary does their heat fly upwards by reason of its lightness, and vanish away, but they are mingled and composed one with another, according to the nature of each one.

15. Wherefore it is also probable that the world, if it is an animal, has in many parts of its body earth, and in as many fire and water and air, not thrust and driven into it by force, but ordered and disposed by reason. For neither was the eye by its lightness forced into that part of the body where it is, nor the heart by its gravity pressed down into the breast; but both the one and the other were thus placed because it was better and more expedient. In like manner we ought not to think of the parts of the world, either that the earth settled where it is, being beaten down thither by its ponderosity; or that the sun was carried upwards by its levity, like a bottle or bladder full of wind (which, being plunged into the bottom of the water, immediately rises up again), as Metrodorus of Chios was persuaded; or that the other stars, as if they had been put into a balance, were swayed this way or that way, according to their weight or lightness, and so mounted higher or lower to the places they now possess. But reason having prevailed in the constitution of the world, the stars have, like to glittering eyes, been fixed in the firmament, as it were in the face of the universe, there to turn continually

about; and the sun, having the force and vigor of the heart, sends and distributes its heat and light, like blood and spirits, throughout all; the earth and sea are in the world, as the paunch and bladder in the body of a living creature; and the moon placed between the sun and the earth, as the liver, or some other soft entrail between the heart and the belly, transmits down thither the heat of the superior bodies, and draws round about her the vapors which arise from hence, subtilizing them by way of concoction and purification. And whether its solid and terrestrial quality has any other property serving for some profitable use, is indeed unknown to us; but everywhere that which is better prevails over what is by necessity. For what probability can we draw from that which they affirm? They say, that the most subtile and luminous part of the air, by reason of its rarity, became heaven; but what was thickened and closely driven together was made into stars, of which the moon being the heaviest is compacted of the grossest and muddiest matter. And yet it is plainly to be seen, that the moon is not separated or divided from the air, but moves and makes her revolution through that which is about her, to wit, the region of the winds, and where the comets are engendered and keep their course. These bodies then were not by a natural inclination thus placed and situated as they are, but have by some other reason been so ordered and disposed.

16. These things being said, as I was giving Lucius his turn to follow and continue the discourse, — there being nothing left to be added but the demonstrations of this doctrine, — Aristotle smiling said: I am a witness, that you have directed all your contradictions and all your refutations against those who, supposing the moon to be half fire, affirm in general that all bodies do of their own accord tend either upwards or downwards; but if there is

any one who holds that the stars have of their own nature a circular motion, and that they are of a substance wholly different from the four elements, you have not thought of saying any thing, so much as accidentally or by the way, against him; and therefore I am wholly unconcerned in your discourse.

Indeed, good sir, said Lucius, if you should suppose the other stars, and the whole heaven apart, to be of a pure and sincere nature, free from all change and alteration of passion, and should bring in also a circle, in which they make their motion by a perpetual revolution, you would not perhaps find any one now to contradict you, though there are in this infinite doubts and difficulties. But when the discourse descends so far as to touch the moon, it cannot maintain in her that perfection of being exempt from all passion and alteration, nor that heavenly beauty of her body. But to let pass all other inequalities and differences, the very face which appears in the body of the moon necessarily proceeds from some passion of her own substance or the mixture of another; for what is mixed suffers, because it loses its first purity, being filled by force with that which is worse. Besides, as for the slowness and dulness of her course, her feeble and inefficacious heat, by which, as Ion says,

<blockquote>The black grape comes not to maturity,</blockquote>

to what shall we attribute them but to her weakness and passion, if an eternal and celestial body can be subject to passion?

In brief, my friend Aristotle, if the moon is earth, she is a most fair and admirable thing, and excellently well adorned; but if you regard her as a star or light or a certain divine and heavenly body, I am afraid she will prove deformed and foul, and disgrace that beautiful appellation, if of all bodies, which are in heaven so numerous, she alone stands in need of light borrowed of another, and, as Parmenides has it,

<blockquote>Looks always backwards on the sun's bright rays.</blockquote>

Our friend therefore indeed, having in a lecture of his demonstrated this proposition of Anaxagoras, that the sun communicates to the moon what brightness she has, was well esteemed for it. As for me, I will not say what I have learned of you or with you, but having taken it for granted, will pass on to the rest. It is then probable that the moon is illuminated, not like a glass or crystal, by the brightness of the sun's rays shining through her, nor yet again, by a certain collustration and conjunction of light and brightness, as when many torches set together augment the light of one another. For so she would be no less full in her conjunction or first quarter than in her opposition, if she did not obstruct or repel the rays of the sun, but let them pass through her by reason of her rarity, or if he did by a contemperature shine upon her and kindle the light within her. For we cannot allege her declinations and aversions in the conjunction or new moon, as when it is half-moon or when she appears crescent or in the wane; but being then perpendicularly (as Democritus says) under him that illuminates her, she receives and admits the sun; so that then it is probable she should appear, and he shine through her. But this she is so far from doing, that she is not only then unseen, but also often hides the sun, as Empedocles has it:

<blockquote>The sun's bright beams from us she turns aside,
And of the earth itself as much doth hide,
As her orb's breadth can cover;</blockquote>

as if the light of the sun fell not upon another star, but upon night and darkness. And as for what Posidonius says, that the depth of the moon's body is the cause why the light of the sun cannot pierce through her to us, this is evidently refuted; for the air, which is infinite and of a far greater depth than the body of the moon, is nevertheless all over illustrated and enlightened by the rays of the sun.

It remains then that, according to the opinion of Empedocles, the light of the moon which appears to us comes from the repercussion and reflection of the sun's beams. And for this reason it comes not to us hot and bright, as in all probability it would, if her shining proceeded either from inflammation or the commixtion of two lights. But as voices reverberated cause an echo more obscure and less express than the speech that was pronounced, and as the blows of darts and arrows, rebounding from some wall against which they are shot, are more mild and gentle;

So Titan's lustre, smiting the moon's orb,

yields but a faint and feeble reflection and repercussion of brightness upon us, its force being abated and weakened by the refraction.

17. Sylla then, taking up the discourse, said: There is indeed a great deal of probability in all that you have spoken. But as to the strongest objection that is brought against it, has it, think you, been any way weakened by this discourse? Or has our friend quite passed it over in silence?

What opposition do you mean, said Lucius? Is it the difficulty about the moon, when one half of her appears enlightened?

The very same, answered Sylla. For there is some reason, seeing that all reflection is made by equal angles, that when the half-moon is in the midst of heaven, the light proceeding from her should not be carried upon the earth, but glance and fall beyond and on one side of it. For the sun, being placed in the horizon, touches the moon with its beams; which, being equally reflected, will therefore necessarily fall on the other bound of the horizon, and not send their light down hither; or else there will be a great distortion and difference of the angle, which is impossible.

And yet, by Jupiter, replied Lucius, this has not been forgotten or overpassed, but already spoken to. And casting his eye, as he was discoursing, upon the mathematician Menelaus; I am ashamed, said he, in your presence, dear Menelaus, to attempt the subverting and overthrowing of a mathematical position, which is supposed as a basis and foundation to the doctrine of the catoptrics concerning the causes and reasons of mirrors. And yet of necessity I must. For it neither appears of itself nor is confessed as true, that all reflections are at equal angles; but this position is first checked and contradicted in concave mirrors, when they represent the images of things, appearing at one point of sight, greater than the things themselves. And it is also disproved by double mirrors, which being inclined or turned one towards the other, so that an angle is made within, each of the glasses or plain superficies yields a double resemblance; so that there are four images from the same face, two answerable to the object without on the left side, and two others obscure and not so evident on the right side in the bottom of the mirror. Of which Plato renders the efficient cause; for he says, that a mirror being raised on the one and the other side, the sight varies the reflection, falling from one side to the other. And therefore, since of the views or visions some immediately have recourse to us, and others, sliding to opposite parts of the mirror, do again return upon us from thence, it is not possible that all reflections should be made at equal angles. Though those who closely impugn our opinion contend that, by these reflections of light from the moon upon the earth, the equality of angles is taken away, thinking this to be much more probable than the other.

Nevertheless, if we must of necessity yield and grant

thus much to our dearly beloved geometry, first, this should in all likelihood befall those mirrors which are perfectly smooth and exquisitely polished; whereas the moon has many inequalities and roughnesses, so that the rays proceeding from a vast body, and carried to mighty altitudes, receive one from another and intercommunicate their lights, which, being sent to and fro and reciprocally distributed, are refracted and interlaced all manner of ways, and the counter-lights meet one another, as if they came to us from several mirrors. And then, though we should suppose these reflections on the superficies of the moon to be made at equal angles, yet it is not impossible that the rays, coming down unto us by so long an interval, may have their flexions, fractions, and delapsions, that the light being compounded may shine the more. Some also there are who prove by lineary demonstration, that many lights send a ray down by a line drawn below the line of reflection; but to make the description and delineation of it publicly, especially where there were many auditors, would not be very easy.

18. But in brief, said he, I wonder how they come thus to allege against us the half-moon, there being the same reason when she is gibbous and crescent. For if the sun enlightened the moon, as a mass of ethereal or fiery matter, he would never surely leave one hemisphere, or half of her globe always appearing dark and shadowy to sense, as it is seen to be; but how little soever he touched her superficies, it would be agreeable to reason that it should be wholly replenished and totally changed by that light of his, which by reason of its agility and swiftness so easily spreads and passes through all. For, since wine touching water only in one point, or one drop of blood falling into any liquor, dyes and colors it all with a red or purple color; and since they say, that the very air is altered and changed with light, not by any defluxions or beams intermingled,

but by a sudden conversion and change made in one only point; how can they imagine that one star touching another star, and one light another light, should not be immediately mingled, nor make any thorough confusion or change, but only exteriorly illuminate that whose superficies it touches? For that circle which the sun makes by fetching a compass and turning towards the moon, — sometimes falling upon the very line that distinguishes her visible part from her invisible, and sometimes rising up directly, so that it cuts her in two and is reciprocally cut by her, causing in her, by several inclinations and habitudes of the luminous to the dark, those various forms by which she appears gibbous and crescent, — that more than any thing else demonstrates, that all this illumination of the moon is not a mixture, but only a touching; nor a conflux or gathering together of sundry lights, but only an illustration round about.

But forasmuch as she is not only enlightened herself, but also sends back hither the image of her illumination, this confirms us yet further in what we say touching her substance. For reflections and reverberations are not made upon any thing which is rare, and of thin and subtile parts; nor is it easily to be imagined how light can rebound from light, or one fire from another. But that which is to make the reverberation or reflection must be solid and firm, that a blow may be given against it and a rebounding made from it. As a proof of this, we see that the air transmits the sun, and gives him a way to pierce quite through it, not obstructing or driving back his rays; but on the contrary from wood, stones, or clothes put in the sun, there are made many reflections of light and many illuminations round about. So we see that the earth is illuminated by him, not to the very bottom, as the water, nor thoroughly and all over, as the air, through which the beams of the sun have a clear passage; but just such a circle as surrounds the moon surrounds also the earth ; and as much of the earth as this circle includes, so much does the sun enlighten, the rest being left without light; for what is illuminated both in the one and in the other is little more than an hemisphere. Permit me therefore now to conclude after the manner of geometricians by proportions. If there are three things which the light of the sun approaches, the air, the moon, and the earth, and if we see that the moon is enlightened by him, not as the air, but as the earth, it is of necessity that those two things must have one and the same nature, which of one and the same cause suffer the same effects.

19. Now when all the company began highly to commend Lucius's harangue ; This is excellently well done of you, Lucius (said I to him), that you have to so fine a discourse added as fine a proportion, for you must not be defrauded of that which is your due.

Then Lucius, smiling, thus went on : I have yet a second proportion to be added to the former, by which we will clearly demonstrate that the moon altogether resembles the earth, not only because they suffer and receive the same accidents from the same cause, but because they work the same effect on the same object. For you will without difficulty, I suppose, grant me that, of all the accidents which befall the sun, there is none so like to his setting as his eclipse, especially if you but call to mind that recent conjunction which, beginning at noonday, showed us many stars in many places of the heavens, and wrought a temperature in the air like that of the twilight. But if you will not grant me this, our friend Theon here will bring us a Mimnermus, a Cydias, an Archilochus, and besides these, a Stesichorus and a Pindar, lamenting that in eclipses the world is robbed of its brightest light, and saying that night comes on in the midst of the day, and that the rays of the sun wander in the path of darkness ; but above all he will produce Homer, saying that the faces of men are in eclipses seized upon by night and darkness, and the sun is quite lost out of heaven by the conjunction of the moon. And . . . it is natural that this should happen,

When one moon's going, and another comes.

For the rest of the demonstration is, in my opinion, as certain and exactly concluding, as are the acute arguments of the mathematics. As night is the shadow of the earth, so the eclipse of the sun is the shadow of the moon, when it stands in the way of our sight. For the sun is at his setting kept from our sight by the interposition of the earth, and at his eclipse by that of the moon. Now both of these are obscurations; but that of his setting is from the earth, and that of his being eclipsed from the moon, their shadows intercepting our sight. Now the consequences of these things are easily understood. For if the effect is alike, the efficient causes are also alike; because it is of necessity that the same effects, happening in the same subjects, proceed from the same efficients. Now if the darkness in eclipses is not so profound, nor does so forcibly and entirely seize the air, as does the night, we are not to wonder at it; for the substance of the body which makes the night, and of that which causes the eclipse, is indeed the same, though their greatness is not equal. For the Egyptians, if I am not mistaken, hold that the moon is in bigness the two and seventieth part of the earth; and Anaxagoras says, she is as big as Peloponnesus. And Aristarchus shows the overthwart line or diameter of the moon to have a proportion to that of the earth which is less than if sixty were compared to nineteen, and somewhat greater than an hundred and eight compared to forty and three. Whence it happens that the earth, by reason of its greatness, wholly withdraws the sun from our sight;

for it is a great obstacle and opposition, and lasts all the night. But although the moon sometimes hides all the sun, yet that eclipse continues not so long nor is so far extended, but there always appears about the circumference a certain brightness, which permits not the darkness to be black, deep, and perfectly obscure.

And Aristotle (I mean the ancient philosopher of that name) rendering the reason why there are oftener seen to happen eclipses of the moon than of the sun, among other causes alleges this, that the sun is eclipsed by the interposition of the moon, and the moon by that of the earth, which is much greater and consequently oftener opposes itself. And Posidonius thus defines this accident: The eclipse of the sun is the conjunction of the sun and moon, the shadow of which darkens our sight.* For there is no eclipse except to those whose sight the shadow of the moon intercepting hinders them from seeing the sun. Now in confessing that the shadow of the moon descends down to us, I know not what he has left himself to say. It is certainly impossible for a star to cast a shadow; for that which is not enlightened is called a shadow, and light makes no shadow, but on the contrary drives it away.

20. But what arguments, said he, were alleged after this?

The moon, answered I then, suffered the same eclipse.

You have done well, replied he, to put me in mind of it. But would you have me go on and prosecute the rest of the discourse, as if you had already supposed and granted that the moon is eclipsed, being intercepted within the shadow of the earth? Or shall I take for the subject of a declamation the making a demonstration of it, by rehearsing to you all the arguments, one after another?

Nay, by Jove, said Theon, let this be the argument of your discourse. For I indeed stand in need of some per

---

* Here again the text is defective, and the sense conjectural. (G.)

suasion, having only heard that when these three bodies, the earth, the moon, and the sun, are in a direct line, then eclipses happen; for that either the earth takes the sun from the moon, or the moon takes him from the earth. For the sun suffers an eclipse when the moon, and the moon when the earth, is in the midst of the three; of which the one happens in the conjunction or new moon, and the other in the opposition or when the moon is full.

Then said Lucius: These are the principal points, and the summary of what is said. But in the first place, if you please, take the argument drawn from the form and figure of the shadow. For this is a cone, as it must be when a great fire or light that is spherical encompasses a mass that is also globular but less; whence it comes that, in the eclipses of the moon, the circumscriptions of the black and dark from the clear and luminous have their sections always round. For the sections given or received by one round body applied to another, which way soever they go, do by reason of the similitude always keep a circular form. Now as for the second argument, I suppose you understand that the first part which is eclipsed in the moon is always that which looks towards the east, and in the sun that which regards the west. Now the shadow of the earth moves from the east to the west, but the sun and moon from the west eastward. The experience of the appearances gives us a visible knowledge of this, nor is there need of many words to make us fully understand it; and from these suppositions the cause of the eclipse is confirmed. For, inasmuch as the sun is eclipsed by being overtaken, and the moon by meeting that which makes the eclipse, it probably or rather necessarily follows that the one is surprised behind, and the other before. For the obstruction begins on that side whence that which causes it first approaches. Now the moon comes upon the sun from the west, as striving in course with him and hastening after him; but the shadow of the earth comes from the east, as that which has a contrary motion.

The third argument is taken from the time and greatness of the eclipses. For the moon, if she is eclipsed when she is on high in her apogee (or at her farthest distance from the earth), continues but a little while in her defect or want of light; but when she suffers the same accident being low and in her perigee (or near the earth), she is very much oppressed, and slowly gets out of the shadow; and yet, when she is low, she moves swifter, and when high, slower. But the cause of the difference is in the shadow, which is, like pyramids, broadest at the bottom or basis; and, growing still narrower by little and little, terminates in a sharp point at the top. Whence it comes, that when she is low, she is embarrassed within greater circles, traversing the bottom of the shadow and what is most obscure and dark; but when she is high, being through the narrowness of the shadow (as it were) but in a shallow puddle, by which she is sullied, she immediately gets out again. I omit what was said particularly about the bases and disposition of parts, for these admit of a rational explanation, so far as this is possible; but I return to the subject properly before us, which has its foundation in our senses. For we see that fire shines forth and appears brighter out of a dark and shady place, through the thickness of the caliginous air, which admits no effluxions or diffusions of the fire's virtue, but keeps in and contains its substance within itself. Or rather, — if this is a passion of the senses, — as hot things, when near to cold ones, are felt to be hotter, and pleasures immediately after pains are found more vehement, so things that are bright appear better when they are near to such as are obscure, the imagination being more strained and extended by means of different passions. But there seems to be a greater appearance of probability in the first reason. For in the sun, all the nature of fire not only loses its faculty of illuminating, but is also rendered duller and more unapt to burn, because the heat of the sun dissipates and scatters all its force.

If it were then true that the moon, being, as the Stoics say, a muddy and troubled star, has a weak and duskish fire, it would be meet that she should suffer none of these accidents which she is now seen to suffer, but altogether the contrary; to wit, that she should be seen when she is hidden, and absconded when she appears; that is, she should be concealed all the rest of the time, being obscured by the environing air, and again shine forth and become apparent and manifest for six months together, and afterwards disappear again five months, entering into the shadow of the earth. For of four hundred and sixty-five revolutions of ecliptic full moons, four hundred and four are of six months' duration, and the rest of five. The moon then should all this time appear shining in the shadow; but on the contrary we see, that in the shadow she is eclipsed and loses her light, and recovers it again after she is escaped and got forth of the shadow. Nay, she appears often in the daytime, so that she is rather any thing else than a fiery and starry body.

21. As soon as Lucius had said these things, Pharnaces and Apollonides ran both together upon him, to oppugn and refute his discourse; and then Apollonides giving him way, Pharnaces said: This it is that principally shows the moon to be a star and of a fiery nature, that in her eclipses she is not wholly obscured and disappearing, but shows herself with a certain coal-resembling color, terrible to the sight, yet such as is proper to her.

As for Apollonides, he insisted much in opposition to the word shadow, saying, that the mathematicians always give that name to the place which is not enlightened, and that heaven admits no shadow.

To this I thus answered: This instance is rather alleged obstinately against the name, than naturally or mathematically against the thing. For if one will not call the place obfuscated by the opposition of the earth a shadow, but a place deprived of light, yet be it what it will, you must of necessity confess that the moon being there becomes obscure; and every way, said I, it is a folly to deny that the shadow of the earth reaches thither from whence the shadow of the moon, falling upon our sight here on earth, causes the eclipse of the sun. And therefore I now address myself to you, Pharnaces; for this coal-like and burnt color of the moon, which you affirm to be proper to her, belongs to a body that has thickness and depth. For there is not wont to remain any relic, mark, or print of flame in a body that is rare, nor can a coal be made where there is not a solid body which may receive into it the heat of the fire; as Homer himself shows in a certain passage, where he says,

> Then, when the languid flames at length subside,
> He strows a bed of glowing embers wide.*

For the coal seems not properly a fire, but a body enkindled and altered by the fire, which stays and remains in a solid firmly rooted mass; and whereas flames are the setting on fire and fluxions of a nutriment and matter, which is of a rare substance, and by reason of its weakness quickly dissolved and consumed; so that there could not be any more evident and plain argument to demonstrate that the moon is solid and earthly, than if her proper color were that of a coal. But it is not so, my friend Pharnaces; but in her eclipses she diversely changes her colors, which the mathematicians, determining with respect to the time and hour, thus distinguish. If she is eclipsed in the evening, she appears horribly black until the middle of the fourth hour of the night; if about midnight, she

* Il. IX. 212.

sends forth this reddish and fire-resembling color, and after the middle of the eighth hour, the redness disappears; and finally, if about the dawning of the morning, she takes a blue or grayish color; which is the cause why she is by the poets, and particularly by Empedocles, called Glaucopis.

Since then they clearly see that the moon changes into so many colors in the shadow, they do ill to attribute to her only that of a burning coal, which may be said to be less proper to her than any other, being only a small remnant and semblance of light, appearing and shining through a shadow, her own proper color being black and earthy. And since that here below, red and purple garments, and rivers and lakes, which receive the rays of the sun, cause neighboring shady places to take the same appearances of colors and to be illuminated by them, casting and sending back by reason of reflections several rebated splendors; what wonder is it if a copious flux of shadow, falling as it were into an immense celestial sea of light, not steady and quiet, but agitated by innumerable stars, and besides admitting several mixtures and mutations in itself, takes from the moon the impression sometimes of one color, sometimes of another, and sends them hither to us? For it is not to be denied but that a star of fire cannot appear in a shadow black, gray, or violet; but there are seen upon hills, plains, and seas, several various resemblances of colors, caused by the reflection of the sun, which are the very tinctures that brightness mixed with shadows and mists, as if it were with painters' colors, brings upon them. And as for the tincture or colors of the sea, Homer has indeed in some sort endeavored to name and express them, when he sometimes terms the sea violet-colored or red as wine, at other times the waves purple, and again the sea blue, and the calm white. As for the diversities of tinctures and colors appearing upon the earth, he has, I suppose, omitted them, because they are in number infinite. Now it is not probable that the moon has but one superficies all plain and even, as the sea; but rather that of its nature it principally resembles the earth, of which old Socrates in Plato seemed to mythologize at his pleasure; whether it were, that under covert and enigmatical speeches he meant it of the moon, or whether he spake it of some other. For it is neither incredible nor wonderful, if the moon, having in herself nothing corrupt or muddy, but enjoying a pure and clear light from heaven, and being full of heat, not of a burning and furious fire, but of such as is mild and harmless, has in her places admirably fair and pleasant, resplendent mountains, purple-colored cinctures or zones, and store of gold and silver, not dispersed here and there within her bowels, but flourishing in great abundance on the superficies of her plains, or spread all over her smooth hills and mountains.

And if the sight of all these things comes to us through a shadow, sometimes in one manner and sometimes in another, by reason of the diversity and different change of the ambient air, the moon does not therefore lose the venerable persuasion that is had of her, or the reputation of divinity; being esteemed by men a heavenly earth, or rather (as the Stoics say) a troubled, thick, and dreggish fire. For even the fire itself is honored with barbarian honors among the Assyrians and Medes, who through fear serve and adore such things as are hurtful, hallowing them even above such things as are of themselves indeed holy and honorable. But the very name of the earth is truly dear and venerable to every Greek, and there is through all Greece a custom received of adoring and revering it, as much as any of the Gods. And we are very far from thinking that the moon, which we hold to be a heavenly earth, is a body without soul and spirit, exempt and deprived of all that is to be offered to the Gods. For both by law we yield her recompenses and thanksgivings, for that we receive of her and by nature we adore what we acknowledge to be of a more excellent virtue and a more honorable power; and therefore we do not think that we offend in supposing the moon to be earth.

Now as to the face which appears in her, as this earth on which we are has in it many great sinuosities and valleys, so it is probable that the moon also lies open, and is cleft with many deep caves and ruptures, in which there is water or very obscure air, to the bottom of which the sun cannot reach or penetrate, but failing there, sends back a dissipated reflection to us here below.

22. Here Apollonides, taking up the discourse, said: Tell me then, I beseech you, good sir, even by the moon herself, do you think it possible that there should be there shadows of caves and chinks, and that the sight of them should come even to our eyes? Or do you not regard what will come of it? And must I tell you what it is? But hearken to me, although you are not ignorant of it. The diameter of the moon, according to that bigness which appears to us when she is in her mean and ordinary distances, is twelve digits, and every one of these black and shady spots is above half a digit, that is above the four and twentieth part of the diameter. Now if we suppose the circumference of the moon to be only thirty thousand stadia; and the diameter according to that supposition to be ten thousand, every one of these shadowy marks within her will not be less than five hundred stadia. Consider then, first, whether there can possibly be in the moon such great gaps and such inequalities as may make such a shadow? And then how is it possible that, being so great, they are not seen by us?

At this I, smiling upon him, said: You have done me a pleasure, dear Apollonides, in having found out such a demonstration by which you will prove that you and I shall be bigger than those giant sons of Aloeus,* — not indeed every hour of the day, but principally morning and evening, — if indeed you think that, when the sun makes our shadows so long, he suggests to our minds this goodly argument; if that which is shadowed is great, that which shadows must of necessity be yet excessively greater. I know well that neither you nor I have ever been in Lemnos; yet we have often heard that Iambic verse, so frequent in every one's mouth:

> Mount Athos' shade shall hide the Lemnian cow.

For the shadow of that mountain falls, as it seems, on the image of a brazen heifer which is in Lemnos, extending itself in length over the sea not less than seven hundred stadia. . . . The mountain which makes the shadow causes it, because the distance of the light renders the shadow of bodies manifoldly greater than the bodies themselves. Consider then here, that when the moon is in the full, and shows us the form of a visage most expressly, by reason of the profundity of the shadow, it is then that she is most remote from the sun; for it is the distance of the light that makes the shadow bigger, and not the greatness of the inequalities which are on the superficies of the moon. And you moreover see, that the brightness of the sun's beams suffers not the tops of the mountains to be discerned in open day; but on the contrary, the deep hollow and shadowy parts appear from afar. It is not therefore any way absurd or strange, if we cannot so exactly see how the illumination of the moon and her reception of the sunbeams take place, while yet the conjunction of things that are obscure and dark to such as are clear and shining is by reason of this diversity apparent to our sight.

23. But this, said I, seems rather to refute and check

---

* Otus and Ephialtes.

the reflection and reverberation which is said to rebound from the moon; because those who are within retorted rays do not only see that which is enlightened, but also that which enlightens. For when, at the resulting of light from water upon a wall, the sight falls upon the place which is thus illuminated by the reflection, the eye there beholds three things, to wit, the ray or light that is driven back, the water which makes the reflection, and the sun himself, whose light, falling on the superficies of the water, is repulsed and sent back. This being confessed, as what is evidently seen, it is required of those who say that the earth is enlightened from the moon by the reflections of the sun's rays upon it, that they show us by night the sun appearing upon the superficies of the moon, in the same manner as he may be seen by day appearing in the water on which he shines when there is the said reflection of his beams. But since the sun does not so appear, they thence infer that the moon receives her illumination by some other means, and not by reflection; and if there is no reflection, the moon then is not earth.

What answer then is to be made them, said Apollonides? For the argument of this objection against reflection is common also to us.

It is indeed, answered I, in some sort common, and in some sort not. But first consider the comparison, how perversely and against the stream they take it. For the water is here below on the earth, and the moon there above in heaven. So that the reflected and reverberated rays make the form of their angles quite opposite one to the other, the one having their point upwards towards the superficies of the moon, and the other downwards toward the earth. Let them not then require that from every form of mirror, nor that from every distance and remoteness, there should be a like and semblable reflection; for so doing, they would repugn notorious and apparent evidence. And as for those who hold the moon to be a body not smooth, even, and subtile as the water, but solid, massy, and terrestrial, I cannot conceive why they should require to see the image of the sun in her as in a glass. For neither does milk itself render such peculiar images, nor cause reflection of the sight, by reason of the inequality and ruggedness of its parts. How then is it possible that the moon should send back the sight from her superficies, as mirrors do that are more polished? And if in these also there is any scratch, filth, or dulness on their superficies whence the reflected sight is wont to receive a form, they are dimmed, and although the mirrors may be seen, they yield no counterlight. He then who requires that either the sun should appear in the moon, or else the moon should not reflect the sun's light to us, might as well require that the eye be the sun, the sight light, and man heaven. For it is probable, that the reflection of the sun's beams which is made upon the moon does, by reason of their vehemence and great brightness, rebound with a stroke upon us. But our sight being weak and slender, what wonder is it, if it neither give such a stroke as may rebound, or if it rebounds, that it does not maintain its continuity, but is broken and fails, as not having such abundance of light that it should not disgregate and be dissipated within those inequalities and asperities? For it is not impossible, that the reflection upon water or other sorts of mirrors, being yet strong, powerful, and near its origin, should from thence return upon the eye; but though there may perhaps from the moon be some glimmerings, yet they still will be weak and obscure, and will fail in the way, by reason of so long a distance. For otherwise hollow and concave mirrors send back the reverberated and reflected rays stronger than they came, so that they frequently burn and set on fire; and those that are convex and embossed like a bowl, because they beat them not back on all sides, render them dark and feeble. You see for certain, when two rainbows appear together in the heaven, one cloud comprehending another, that the rainbow which outwardly environs the other yields dim colors, and such as are not sufficiently distinguished and expressed, because the exterior cloud, being more remote, makes not a strong and forcible reflection. And what needs there any more to be said, seeing that the very light of the sun, reverberated and sent back by the moon, loses all its heat; and of his brightness, there comes to us with much ado but a small remainder, and that very languishing and weak? Is it then possible, that our sight, turning the same course, should bring back any part of the solar image from the moon? I for my part think it is not. But consider, I said, yourselves, that if our sight were in one and the same manner affected and disposed towards the water and towards the moon, the full moon would of necessity represent to us the images of the earth, plants, men, and stars, as is done by the water and all other sorts of mirrors. And if there is no such reflection of our sight as to bring us back these images, either by reason of our said sight's weakness, or through the rugged inequality of the moon's superficies, let us no longer require that it should rebound against the sun.

24. We have then, said I, related, as far as our memory would carry it away, whatever was there said. It is now time to desire Sylla, or rather to exact of him, that he would make us his narration, as being on such condition admitted to hear all this discourse. If you think good therefore, let us give over walking, and sitting down on these seats, make him a quiet and settled audience.

Every one approved this motion. And therefore, when we had seated ourselves, Theon thus began: I am indeed, O Lamprias, as desirous as any of you can be to hear what shall be said; but I would gladly first understand something concerning those who are said to dwell in the moon; not whether there are any persons inhabiting it, but whether it is impossible there should be any; for if it is not possible for the moon to be inhabited, it is also unreasonable to say that she is earth; otherwise she would have been created in vain and to no end, not bearing any fruits, not affording a place for the birth or education of any men, for which causes and ends this earth wherein we live was made and created, being (as Plato says) our nurse and true guardian, producing and distinguishing the day from the night. Now you know, that of this matter many things have been said, as well merrily and in jest as seriously and in earnest. For of those who dwell under the moon, it is said that she hangs over their heads, as if they were so many Tantaluses; and on the contrary, of those who inhabit her, that being tied and bound to her, like a sort of Ixions, they are with violence turned and whirled about. Nor is the moon indeed moved by one only motion, but is, as they were wont to call her, Trivia, or Three-wayed; performing her course together according to length, breadth, and depth in the Zodiac; the first of which motions mathematicians call a direct revolution, the second volutation, or an oblique winding and wheeling in and out; and the third (I know not why) an inequality; although they see that she has no motion uniform, settled, and certain, in all her circuits and reversions. Wherefore it is not greatly to be admired, if through violence of her motion there sometime fell a lion from her into Peloponnesus, but it is rather to be wondered, that we do not daily see ten thousand falls of men and women and shocks of other animals tumbling down thence with their heels upwards on our heads; for it would be a mockery to dispute about their habitation there, if they can have there neither birth nor existence. For seeing the Egyptians and the Troglodytes, over whose heads the sun directly stands only one moment of one day in the solstice, and then presently retires, can hardly escape being burnt, by reason of the air's excessive dryness; is it credible that those who are in the moon can bear every year twelve solstices, the sun being once a month just in their zenith, when the moon is full? As for winds, clouds, and showers, without which the plants can neither come up nor, when they are come up, be preserved, it cannot be so much as imagined there should be any, where the ambient air is so hot, dry, and subtile; since even here below, the tops of mountains never feel those hard and bitter winters, but the air, being there pure and clear, without any agitation, by reason of its lightness, avoids all that thickness and concretion which is amongst us; unless, by Jupiter, we will say that, as Minerva instilled nectar and ambrosia into the mouth of Achilles, when he received no other food, so the moon, which both is called and indeed is Minerva, nourishes men, producing for them and sending them every day ambrosia, with which, as old Pherecydes was wont to say, the Gods themselves are fed. For as touching that Indian root, which, as Megasthenes says, some people in those parts, who neither eat nor drink, but have pure mouths, burn and smoke, living on the smell of its perfume; whence should they have any of it there, the moon not being watered or refreshed with rain?

25. When Theon had spoken these things; You have very dexterously and gently, said I to him, by this facetiousness of yours smoothed as it were the brow, and taken off the chagrin and sourness of this discourse; which encourages and emboldens us to return an answer, since, however we may chance to fail, we expect not any severe or rigorous chastisement. For, to speak the truth, they who are extremely offended with these things and wholly discredit them, not being willing mildly to consider what probability and possibility there may be in them, are not much less in

fault than those that are too excessively persuaded of them.
First then, I say, it is not necessary that the moon must
have been made in vain and to no end or purpose, if there
are not men who dwell in it; for we see that this very
earth here is not all cultivated or inhabited, but that only
a small part of it, like so many promontories or demi-
islands arising out of the deep, engenders, brings forth,
and breeds plants and animals; the rest being through
excessive cold or heat wholly desert and barren, or (which
is indeed the greatest share of it) covered and plunged
under the vast ocean. But you, who are always so great a
lover and admirer of Aristarchus, give no ear to Crates
when he reads in Homer,

> The sea, which gave to Gods and men their birth,
> Covers with waves the most part of the earth.*

And yet those parts are far from having been made in vain.
For the sea exhales and breathes out mild vapors; and the
snow, leisurely melting from the cold and uninhabited
regions, sends forth and spreads over all our countries
those gentle breezes which qualify the scorching heat of
summer; and in the midst, as Plato says, is placed the
faithful guardian and operator of night and day. There is
then nothing to hinder but that the moon may be withouᵗ
living creatures, and yet give reflections to the light that is
diffused about her, and afford a receptacle to the rays of
the stars, which have their confluence and temperature in
her, for to digest the evaporation rising from the earth and
moderate the over-violent and fiery heat of the sun. And
attributing much to ancient fame, we will say that she is
styled Diana, as being a virgin and fruitless, but otherwise
greatly salutary, helpful, and profitable to the world.
Moreover, of all that has been said, my friend Theon, there
is nothing which shows it impossible for the moon to be

---

* See Il. XIV. 246. The second of these verses is not found in the present text of the Iliad, but was probably defended by Crates against Aristarchus. (G.)

inhabited. For her turning about, being gentle, mild, and calm, dulcifies and polishes the ambient air, and distributes it in so good order about her, that there is no occasion to fear the falling or slipping out of those who live in her. And as to the diversity and multiplicity of her motion, it proceeds not from any inequality, error, or uncertainty, but the astrologers show in this an admirable order and course, enclosing her within circles, which are turned by other circles; some supposing that she herself stirs not, others making her always move equally, smoothly, and with the same swiftness. For it is these ascensions of divers circles, with their turnings and habitudes, one towards another and with respect to us, which most exactly make those heights, depths, and depressions, that appear to us in her motion, and her digressions in latitude, all joined with the ordinary revolution she makes in longitude. As to the great heat and continual inflammation of the sun, you will cease to fear it, if first to the eleven estival conjunctions you oppose the full moons, and then to the excesses the continuity of change which permits them not to last long, reducing them to a proper and peculiar temperature, and taking from them both what is over much; for the middle, or what is between them, it is probable, has a season most like to the spring. And, moreover, the sun sends his beams to us through a gross and troubled air, and casts on us an heat fed by exhalation; whereas the air, being there subtile and transparent, dissipates and disperses his lustre, which has no nourishment nor body on which it may settle. Trees and fruits are here nourished by showers; but elsewhere, as in the higher countries with you about Thebes and Syene, the earth drinking in not aerial but earth-bred water, and being assisted with refreshing winds and dew, will not (such is the virtue and temperature of the soil) yield the first place for fertility to the best watered land in the world. And the same sorts of trees which in our country, having suffered a long and sharp winter, bring forth abundance of good fruit, are in Africa and with you in Egypt soon offended with cold and very fearful of the winter. And the provinces of Gedrosia and Troglodytis, which lie near the ocean sea, being by reason of drought barren and without any trees, there grow nevertheless in the adjacent sea trees of a wonderful height and bigness, and green even to the very bottom; some of which they call olive-trees, others laurels, and others the hair of Isis. And those plants which are named anacampserotes, being hanged up after they are plucked out of the ground, not only live, but — which is more — bud and put forth green leaves. Some seeds are sown in winter; and others in the heat of summer, like sesame and millet. And thyme or centaury, if it is sown in a rich and fat earth, and there well drenched and watered, degenerates from its natural quality and all its virtue, because it loves dryness and thrives in its own proper natural soil. Others cannot bear so much as the least dew, of which kind are the most part of the Arabian plants, and if they are but once wet, they wither, fade, and die. What wonder is it then, if there grow in the moon roots, seeds, and plants which have no need of rains or winter colds, and are appropriated to a dry and subtile air, such as is that of summer? And why may it not be probable that the moon sends forth warm winds, and that her shaking and agitation, as she moves, is accompanied by comfortable breezes, fine dews, and gentle moistures, which are everywhere dispersed to furnish nutriment for the verdant plants? — seeing she is not of her temperature ardent or parched with drought, but rather soft, moist, and engendering all humidity. For there come not from her to us any effects of dryness, but many of a feminine moisture and softness, such as are the growing of plants, the putrefaction of flesh, the changing and flatness of wines, the tenderness and rotting of wood, and the easy deliveries of child-bearing women. But because I am afraid of irritating again and provoking Pharnaces — who all this while speaks not a word — if I should allege the flowing and ebbing of the great ocean (as they themselves say), and the increasings of the friths and straits, which swell and rise by the moon augmenting the moisture; therefore I will rather turn myself to you, my friend Theon. For you, interpreting this verse of the poet Alcman,

> Such things as dew, Jove's daughter and the moon's,
> Does nourish,

tell us, that in this place he calls the air Jupiter, which, being moistened by the moon, is by Nature changed into dew. For she seems, my good friend, to be of a nature almost wholly contrary to the sun, not only in that she is wonted to moisten, dissolve, and soften what he thickens, dries, and hardens; but moreover, in that she allays and cools his heat, when it lights upon her and is mingled with her.

Those then who think the moon to be a fiery and burning body are in an error; and in like manner those who would have all such things to be necessary for the generation, life, food, and entertainment of the animals dwelling there as are requisite to those that are here below, consider not the vast diversity and inequality there is in Nature; in which there are found greater varieties and differences between animals and animals, than there are between animals and other subjects that are not animated. There are surely not in the world any men of such pure mouths that they feed only on smells. . . . But that power of Nature which Ammonius himself has shown us, and which Hesiod has obscurely signified in these words,

> Nor how great virtue is in asphodels and mallows,*

Epimenides has made plain to us in effect, teaching us that

---

* Hesiod, Works and Days, 41.

Nature sustains a living creature with very little food, and that, provided it has but the quantity of an olive, it stands in need of no other nourishment. Now, if any, those surely who dwell within the moon should be active, light, and easy to be nourished with any thing whatsoever; since they affirm that the moon herself, as also the sun, which is a fiery animal, and manifoldly greater than the earth, is nourished and maintained by the moistures that come from the earth, as are also all the other stars, whose number is in a manner infinite; such light and slender animals do they assign to the upper region, and with so small necessaries do they think them contented and satisfied. But we neither see these things, nor consider that a quite different region, nature, and temperature is accommodated to those lunar men.

As therefore, if we were unable to come near and touch the sea, but could only see it at a distance, and had heard that its water is brackish, salt, and undrinkable, any one who should tell us that there are in its depths many and great animals of various forms and shapes, and that it is full of great and monstrous beasts who make the same use of the water as we do of the air, would be thought only to relate a parcel of strange and uncreditable stories, newly found out and invented for delight and amusement; in the same manner we seem to be affected and disposed towards the moon, not believing that there are any who inhabit it. And I am of opinion, that they themselves do much more wonder, when they behold the earth, — which is, as it were, the dregs and mud of the universe, appearing to them through moist and foggy clouds and mists, a little place, a low, abject, and immovable thing without any brightness or light whatever,— how this pitiful inconsiderable thing should be able to produce, nourish, and maintain animals that have motion, respiration, and heat. And if peradventure they had ever heard these verses of Homer,

> A filthy squalid place, abhorred even by
> The Gods themselves;*

and again,

> Hell is as far beneath, as heaven above
> The earth;†

they would certainly think them to have been written of this place where we live, and that here is hell and Tartarus, and that the earth which is equally distant from heaven and hell is only the moon.

26. I had not well ended my discourse, when Sylla interrupting me said: Forbear Lamprias, and put a stop to your discourse, lest running (as they say) the vessel of your story on ground, you confound and spoil all the play, which has at present another scene and disposition. I myself therefore shall be the actor, but shall, before I enter upon my part, make known to you the poet or author; beginning, if there is nothing to hinder, with that of Homer,

> An isle Ogygia lies in Ocean's arms,‡

distant about five days' sail westward from Britain; and before it there are three others, of an equal distance from one another and also from that, bearing north-west, where the sun sets in summer. In one of these the barbarians feign that Saturn is detained prisoner by Jupiter, who, as his son, having the guard or keeping of those islands and the adjacent sea, named the Saturnian, has his seat a little below; and that the continent, by which the great sea is circularly environed, is distant from Ogygia about five thousand stadia, but from the others not so far, men using to row thither in galleys, the sea being there low and ebb, and difficult to be passed by great vessels because of the mud brought thither by a multitude of rivers, which, coming from the mainland, discharge themselves into it, and raise there great bars and shelves that choke up the river

---
* Il. XX. 65.   † Il. VIII. 16.   ‡ Odyss. VII. 244.

and render it hardly navigable; whence anciently there arose an opinion of its being frozen. Moreover, the coasts of this continent lying on the sea are inhabited by the Greeks about a bay not much smaller than the Macotic, the mouth of which lies in a direct line over against that of the Caspian Sea. These name and esteem themselves the inhabitants of the firm land, calling all us others islanders, as dwelling in a land encompassed round about and washed by the sea. And they think that those who heretofore came thither with Hercules and were left there by him, mixing themselves with the people of Saturn, raised up again the Greek nation, which was well near extinguished, brought under and supplanted by the language, laws, and manners of the barbarians, and made it again flourish and recover its pristine vigor. And therefore in that place they give the first honor to Hercules, and the second to Saturn. Now when the star of Saturn, by us called Phaenon and by them Nycturus, comes to the sign of Taurus, as it does once in the time of thirty years, they, having been a long time preparing what is necessary for a solemn sacrifice and a long voyage or navigation, send forth those on whom the lots fall to row in that vast sea, and make their abode for a great while in foreign countries. These men then, being embarked and departed, meet with different adventures, some in one manner, others in another. Now such as have in safety passed the danger of the sea go first ashore in those opposite islands, which are inhabited by the Greeks, where they see that the sun is scarce hidden one full hour during the space of thirty days, and that this is their night, of which the darkness is but small, as having a twilight from the going down of the sun not unlike the dawning of the day; that having continued there ninety days, during which they are highly caressed and honored, as being reputed and termed holy men, they are afterwards conducted by the winds, and transported into the isle of Saturn, where there are no other inhabitants but themselves and such as have been sent thither before them. For though it is lawful for them, after they have served Saturn thirty years, to return home to their own countries and houses, yet most of them choose rather to remain quietly there; some, because they are already accustomed to the place; others, because without any labor and trouble they have abundance of all things, as well for the offering of sacrifices and holding festival solemnities, as to support the ordinary expenses of those who are perpetually conversant in the study of learning and philosophy. For they affirm the nature of the island and the mildness of the air which environs it to be admirable; and that there have been some persons who, intending to depart thence, have been hindered by the Divinity or Genius of the place showing himself to them, as to his familiar friends and acquaintance, not only in dreams and exterior signs, but also visibly appearing to them by the means of familiar spirits discoursing and conversing with them. For they say, that Saturn himself is personally there, lying asleep in the deep cave of an hollow rock, shining like fine gold, Jupiter having prepared sleep instead of fetters and shackles to keep him from stirring; but that there are on the top of this rock certain birds, which fly down and carry him ambrosia; that the whole island is filled with an admirable fragrancy and perfume, which is spread all over it, arising from this cave, as from an odoriferous fountain; that these Daemons serve and minister to Saturn, having been his courtiers and nearest attendants when he held the empire and exercised regal authority over men and Gods; and that having the science of divining future occurrences, they of themselves foretell many things; but the greatest and of the highest importance, when they return from assisting Saturn, and reveal his dreams; for whatever Jupiter premeditates, Saturn dreams; but his awakenings are Titanical passions or perturbations of the soul in him, which sleep altogether controls, in order that the royal and divine nature may be pure and incontaminate in itself.

This stranger then, having been brought thither, and there serving the God in repose and at his ease, attained to as great skill in astrology as it is possible for any one to do that has made the greatest progress in geometry; as for the rest of philosophy, having given himself to that which is called natural, he was seized with an extraordinary desire and longing to visit and see the great island; for so they call the continent inhabited by us. After therefore his thirty years were passed and his successors arrived, having taken leave of all his relations and friends, he put to sea, in other respects soberly and moderately equipped, but having good store of voyage-provision in vessels of gold. Now one day would not suffice to relate unto you in particular what adventures befell him, how many nations he visited, through how many countries he passed, how he searched into sacred writings, and was initiated in all holy confraternities and religious societies, as he himself recounted it to us, exactly particularizing every thing. But give ear, I pray you, to what concerns the present dispute. For he continued no small time at Carthage, a city not a little also esteemed by us, where he found certain sacred skins of parchment, which had been secretly conveyed thither when the old town was sacked, and had there long lain hidden under ground. Now he told me that, of all the Gods which appear to us in heaven, we ought chiefly to honor the Moon, and earnestly exhorted me to be diligent in venerating of her, as having the principal influence and dominion over our life.

27. At these things when I was amazed, and entreated him to declare and explain them a little more fully to me, he said: The Greeks, O Sylla, deliver many things con-

cerning the Gods, but they are not always in the right. For first, when they tell us that there is a Ceres and a Proserpine, they say well; but not so well, when they put them both in one and the same place. For one, to wit Ceres, is on the earth, and the lady and mistress of all earthly things. The other, to wit Proserpine, is in the moon, and the mistress of all lunar things; and she is called both Cora and Persephone; Persephone, as being a bringer of light and brightness, and Cora, because the apple of the eye, in which the image of him who looks into it is represented, as the brightness of the sun appears in the moon, is by the Greeks called κόρη. And as to what they say concerning the wandering about of Ceres and Proserpine, and their mutual seeking of one another, there is in it somewhat of truth, for they long after each other, being separated, and often embrace in shadow. And that Cora is sometimes in heaven and light, and sometimes in darkness and night, is not untrue; only there is some error in the computation of the time. For we see her not six whole months, but every sixth month, caught in the shadow by the earth, as by her mother; and this rarely happens within five months, because it is impossible she should forsake Pluto (Hades), being herself the bound or limit of Hades; which Homer also covertly but not unelegantly signified, when he said,

> Into th' Elysian fields, earth's utmost bounds,
> The Gods will bring thee;*

for he has there placed the end and boundary of the earth, where the shadow ceases and goes no farther. Now into that place no wicked or impure person can have access. But good folks, being after their decease carried thither, lead there indeed an easy and quiet, but yet not a blessed and divine life, till the second death.

28. But what is that, O Sylla? said I. Ask me not, he

* Odyss. IV. 563.

replied, for I am of myself going to declare it to you.
The common opinion, which most persons hold, is that
man is a compound subject, and this they have reason to
believe. But they are mistaken in thinking him to be
compounded of two parts only. For they imagine that the
understanding is a part of the soul, but they err in this no
less than those who make the soul to be a part of the
body; for the understanding as far exceeds the soul, as the
soul is better and diviner than the body. Now this composition of the soul with the understanding makes reason;
and with the body, passion; of which the one is the beginning or principle of pleasure and pain, and the other
of virtue and vice. Of those three parts conjoined and
compacted together, the earth has given the body, the moon
the soul, and the sun the understanding to the generation
of man, . . . as therefore brightness to the moon. Now
of the deaths we die, the one makes man two of three,
and the other one of two. And the former indeed is in
the region and jurisdiction of Ceres, whence the name
given to her mysteries (τελεῖν) resembles that given to death
(τελευτᾶν). The Athenians also heretofore called the deceased sacred to Ceres. As for the other death, it is in the
moon, or region of Proserpine. And as with the one the
terrestrial, so with the other the celestial Mercury doth
dwell. This suddenly and with force and violence plucks
the soul from the body; but Proserpine mildly and in a
long time disjoins the understanding from the soul. And
for this reason is she called Μονογενής, that is, *only begotten*,
or rather, *begetting one alone;* for the better part of man
becomes alone when it is separated by her. Now both
the one and the other happens thus according to Nature.
It is ordained by Fate that every soul, whether with or
without understanding, when gone out of the body, should
wander for a time, though not all for the same, in the
region lying between the earth and the moon. For those

that have been unjust and dissolute suffer there the punishments due to their offences; but the good and virtuous are there detained till they are purified, and have by expiation purged out of them all the infections they might have contracted from the contagion of the body, as if from [1] foul breath, living in the mildest part of the air, called the meadows of Pluto, where they must remain for a certain perfixed and appointed time. And then, as if they were returning from a wandering pilgrimage or long exile into their country, they have a taste of joy, such as they principally receive who are initiated in sacred mysteries, mixed with trouble, admiration, and each one's proper and peculiar hope. For the moon drives and chases out many souls which already long after it. And some who are already come thither, and yet take pleasure in things below, are seen descending down as it were into an abyss. But those that are got on high, and are there securely seated, first go about as victors, crowned with garlands called the wings of constancy, because in their lives they restrained the unreasonable and passible part of their soul, rendering it subject and obedient to the curb of reason. Secondly, they are like to the rays of the sun in appearance, and like to fire in their soul, which is borne aloft by the clear air which is about the moon, — like fire here on the earth, — from which they gather strength and solidity, as iron and steel do by their being tempered and plunged in water. For that which was hitherto rare and loose is compacted and made firm, and becomes bright and transparent; so that it is nourished with the least exhalation in the world. And this is what Heraclitus meant, when he said that the souls in Pluto's region have their smell exceeding quick.

29. Now they first see the moon's greatness, beauty, and nature, which is not simple nor unmixed, but a composition as it were of earth and star. For as the earth mixed

with wind and moisture becomes soft, and as the blood tempered with the flesh gives it sense; so they say that the moon, being mingled with an ethereal quintessence even to the very bottom, is animated, becomes fruitful, and generative, and is equally counterpoised with ponderosity and lightness. For even the world itself, being composed of some things naturally moving upwards and others by nature tending downwards, is exempt from all local motion or change of place. These things also Xenocrates seems by a certain divine reasoning to have understood, having taken his first light from Plato. For Plato it was who first affirmed that every star is compounded of fire and earth, by the means of certain intermediate natures given in proportion; forasmuch as nothing can be an object of human sense which has not in some proportion a mixture of earth and light. Now Xenocrates says that the stars and the sun are composed of fire and the first or primitive solid; the moon of the second solid and its own peculiar air; and the earth, of water, fire, and the third solid. For neither is the solid alone by itself, nor the rare alone by itself, capable or susceptible of a soul. And let thus much suffice for the substance of the moon.

Now as to her breadth and magnitude, it is not such as the geometricians deliver, but manifoldly greater. And she seldom measures the shadow of the earth by her greatness, not because she is small, but because she adds to her motion by heat, that she may quickly pass the shady place, carrying with her the souls of the blessed, which make haste and cry. For when they are in the shadow, they can no longer hear the harmony of the heavenly bodies. And withal, the souls of the damned are from below presented to them, lamenting and wailing through this shadow. Wherefore also in eclipses,.many are wont to ring vessels of brass, and to make a noise and clattering to be heard by these souls. Moreover, that which is called the face of the moon affrights them when they draw near it, seeming to them a dreadful and terrible sight; whereas indeed it is not so. But as our earth has deep and great bays, one here running between Hercules's pillars into the land to us, and others without, as the Caspian, and those about the Red Sea; so in the moon also there are hollows and great depths. Now of these, the greatest they call the gulf of Hecate, where the souls punish or are punished according to the evils they suffered or did whilst they were Daemons. The two others are long passages, through which the soul must go sometimes to that part of the moon which is towards heaven, and sometimes to that which is towards earth. Now that part of the moon which is towards heaven is called the Elysian fields; and that which is towards the earth, the fields of Proserpine that is opposite to the earth.

30. The Daemons do not always stay in the moon, but sometimes descend down here below, to have the care and superintendency of oracles. They are assistant also, and join in celebrating the sublimest ceremonies, having their eye upon misdeeds, which they punish, and preserving the good as well in perils of war as of the sea. And if in the performance of this charge they commit any fault, either through anger, envy, or any unjust grace or favor, they smart for it; for they are again thrust down to the earth, and tied to human bodies. Now those who were about Saturn said, that themselves were some of the better of these Daemons; as were formerly those that were heretofore in Crete called Dactyli Idaei, the Corybantes in Phrygia, and the Trophoniades in Lebadea, a city of Boeotia, and infinite others in several places of the habitable earth, whose names, temples, and honors continue to this day. But the powers of some fail, being by a most happy change translated to another place; which translations some obtain sooner, others later, when the under-

standing comes to be separated from the soul; which separation is made by the love and desire to enjoy the image of the sun, in which and by which shines that divine, desirable, and happy beauty, which every other nature differently longs after and seeks, one after one manner, another after another. For the moon herself continually turns, through the desire she has to be joined with him. But the nature of the soul remains in the moon, retaining only some prints and dreams of life. And of this I think it to have been well and truly said,

> The soul, like to a dream, flies quick away;*

which it does not immediately, as soon as it is separated from the body, but afterwards, when it is alone and divided from the understanding. And of all that Homer ever writ, there is not any passage more divine than that in which, speaking of those who are departed this life, he says,

> Next these, I saw Alcides' image move;
> Himself is with th' immortal Gods above.†

For every one of us is neither courage, nor fear, nor desire, — no more than flesh or humors, — but the part by which we think and understand. And the soul being moulded and formed by the understanding, and itself moulding and forming the body, by embracing it on every side, receives from it an impression and form; so that although it be separated both from the understanding and the body, it nevertheless so retains still its figure and semblance for a long time, that it may with good right be called its image.

And of these souls (as I have already said) the moon is the element, because souls resolve into her, as the bodies of the deceased do into earth. Those indeed who have been virtuous and honest, living a quiet and philosophical life without embroiling themselves in troublesome affairs, are quickly resolved; because being left by the understand-

* Odyss. XI. 221. † Odyss. XI. 601.

ing, and no longer using corporeal passions, they incontinently vanish away. But the souls of the ambitious and such as have been busied in negotiations, of the amorous and such as have been addicted to corporeal pleasures, as also of the angry and revengeful, calling to mind the things they did in their lives, as dreams in their sleep, walk wandering about here and there, like that of Endymion; because their inconstancy and their being over-subject to passions transports them, and draws them out of the moon to another generation, not letting them rest, but alluring them and calling them away. For there is nothing small, staid, constant, and accordant, after that being forsaken by the understanding, they come to be seized by corporeal passions. And of such souls, destitute of reason and suffering themselves to be carried away by the proud violence of passion, were bred the Tityi and Typhons; and particularly that Typhon who, having by force and violence seized the city of Delphi, overturned the sanctuary of the oracle there. Nevertheless, after a long tract of time the moon receives those souls and recomposes them; and the sun inspiring again and sowing understanding in them, the moon receives them by its vital power, and makes them new souls; and the earth in the third place gives them a body. For she gives nothing . . . after death of all that she takes to generation. And the sun takes nothing, but reassembles and receives again the understanding which he gave. But the moon gives and receives, joins and disjoins, unites and separates, according to divers faculties and powers; of which the one is named Ilithyia or Lucina (to wit, that which joins), and the other Artemis or Diana (to wit, that which separates and divides). And of the three fatal Goddesses or Parcae, she which is called Atropos is placed in the sun, and gives the principle of generation; and Clotho, being lodged in the moon, is she who joins, mingles, and unites; and the last, named Lachesis, is on the earth, where she adds her helping hand, and with her does Fortune very much participate. For that which is without a soul is weak in itself and liable to be affected by others. The understanding is sovereign over all the rest, and cannot be made to suffer by any. Now the soul is a certain middle thing mixed of them both; as the moon was by God made and created a composition and mixture of things high and low, having the same proportion to the sun as the earth has to her.

This (said Sylla) is what I understood from this guest of mine, who was a stranger and a traveller; and this he said he learned from the Daemons who served and ministered to Saturn. And you, O Lamprias, may take my relation in such part as you please.

OF FATE.*

I WILL endeavor, my dearest Piso, to send you my opinion concerning Fate, written with all the clearness and compendiousness I am capable of; since you, who are not ignorant how cautious I am of writing, have thought fit to make it the subject of your request.

1. You are first then to know that this word Fate is spoken and understood two manner of ways; the one as it is an energy, the other as it is a substance. First therefore, as it is an action, Plato † has under a type described it, saying thus in his dialogue entitled Phaedrus: "And this is a sanction of Adrastea (or an inevitable ordinance), that whatever soul being an attendant on God," &c. And in his treatise called Timaeus: "The laws which God in the nature of the universe has established for immortal souls." And in his book of a Commonweal he calls Fate "the speech of the virgin Lachesis, who is the daughter of Necessity." By which sentences he not tragically but theologically shows us what his sentiments are in this matter. Now if any one, translating the fore-cited passages, would have them expressed in more familiar terms, the description in Phaedrus may be thus explained: That Fate is a divine sentence, intransgressible because its cause

---

* "This little Treatise is so pitiously torne, maimed, and dismembred thorowout, that a man may sooner divine and guess thereat (as I have done) than translate it. I beseech the readers therefore, to hold me excused, in case I neither please my selfe, nor content them, in that which I have written." — HOLLAND.

† See Plato, Phaedrus, p. 248 C; Timaeus, p. 41 E; Republic, X. p. 617 D.

cannot be divested or hindered. And according to what he has said in his Timaeus, it is a law ensuing on the nature of the universe, according to which all things that are done are transacted. For this does Lachesis effect, who is indeed the daughter of Necessity, — as we have both already related, and shall yet better understand by that which will be said in the progress of our discourse. Thus you see what Fate is, when it is taken for an action.

2. But as it is a substance, it seems to be the universal soul of the world, and admits of a threefold distribution; the first destiny being that which errs not; the second, that which is thought to err; and the third that which, being under the heaven, is conversant about the earth. Of these, the highest is called Clotho, the next Atropos, and the lowest, Lachesis; who, receiving the celestial influences and efficacies of her sisters, transmits and fastens them to the terrestrial things which are under her government. Thus have we declared briefly what is to be said of Fate, taken as a substance; what it is, what are its parts, after what manner it is, how it is ordained, and how it stands, both in respect to itself and to us. But as to the particularities of these things, there is another fable in his Commonweal, by which they are in some measure covertly insinuated, and we ourselves have, in the best manner we can, endeavored to explain them to you.

3. But we now once again turn our discourse to Fate, as it is an energy. For concerning this it is that there are so many natural, moral, and logical questions. Having therefore already in some sort sufficiently defined what it is, we are now in the next place to say something of its quality, although it may to many seem absurd. I say then that Fate, though comprehending as it were in a circle the infinity of all those things which are and have been from infinite times and shall be to infinite ages, is not in itself infinite, but determinate and finite; for neither law, reason,

nor any other divine thing can be infinite. And this you will the better understand, if you consider the total revolution and the whole time in which the revolutions of the eight circles (that is, of the eight spheres of the fixed stars, sun, moon, and five planets), having (as Timaeus* says) finished their course, return to one and the same point, being measured by the circle of the Same, which goes always after one manner. For in this order, which is finite and determinate, shall all things (which, as well in heaven as in earth, consist by necessity from above) be reduced to the same situation, and restored again to their first beginning. Wherefore the habitude of heaven alone, being thus ordained in all things, as well in regard of itself as of the earth and all terrestrial matters, shall again (after long revolutions) one day return; and those things that in order follow after, and being linked together in a continuity are maintained in their course, shall be present, every one of them by necessity bringing what is its own. But for the better clearing of this matter, let us understand that whatever is in us or about us is not wrought by the course of the heavens and heavenly influences, as being entirely the efficient cause both of my writing what I now write, and of your doing also what you at present do, and in the same manner as you do it. Hereafter then, when the same cause shall return, we shall do the same things we now do, and in the same manner, and shall again become the same men; and so it will be with all others. And that which follows after shall also happen by the following cause; and in brief, all things that shall happen in the whole and in every one of these universal revolutions shall again become the same. By this it appears (as we have said before) that Fate, being in some sort infinite, is nevertheless determinate and finite; and it may be also in some sort seen and comprehended, as we have farther said, that it is as it were a

* Plato, Tim. p. 89 D.

circle. For as a motion of a circle is a circle, and the time that measures it is also a circle; so the order of things which are done and happen in a circle may be justly esteemed and called a circle.

4. This therefore, though there should be nothing else, almost shows us what sort of thing Fate is; but not particularly or in every respect. What kind of thing then is it in its own form? It is, as far as one can compare it, like to the civil or politic law. For first it commands the most part of things at least, if not all, conditionally; and then it comprises (as far as is possible for it) all things that belong to the public in general; and the better to make you understand both the one and the other, we must specify them by an example. The civil law speaks and ordains in general of a valiant man, and also of a deserter and a coward; and in the same manner of others. Now this is not to make the law speak of this or that man in particular, but principally to propose such things as are universal or general, and consequently such as fall under them. For we may very well say, that it is legal to reward this man for having demeaned himself valiantly, and to punish that man for flying from his colors; because the law has virtually — though not in express terms and particularly yet in such general ones as they are comprehended under, — so determined of them. As the law (if I may so speak) of physicians and masters of corporal exercises potentially comprehends particular and special things within the general; so the law of Nature, determining first and principally general matters, secondarily and consequently determines such as are particular. Thus, general things being decreed by Fate, particular and individual things may also in some sort be said to be so, because they are so by consequence with the general. But perhaps some one of those who more accurately examine and more subtly search into these things may say, on the

contrary, that particular and individual things precede the composition of general things, and that the general exist only for the particular, since that for which another thing is always goes before that which is for it. Nevertheless, this is not the proper place to treat of this difficulty, but it is to be remitted to another. However, that Fate comprehends not all things clearly and expressly, but only such as are universal and general, let it pass for resolved on at present, as well for what we have already said a little before, as for what we shall say hereafter. For that which is finite and determinate, agreeing properly with divine Providence, is seen more in universal and general things than in particular; such therefore is the divine law, and also the civil; but infinity consists in particulars and individuals.

After this we are to declare what this term "conditionally" means; for it is to be thought that Fate is also some such thing. That then is said to be conditionally, which is supposed to exist not of itself or absolutely, but as really dependent upon and joined to another; which signifies a suit and consequence. "And this is the sanction of Adrastea (or an inevitable ordinance), that whatever soul, being an attendant on God, shall see any thing of truth, shall till another revolution be exempt from punishment; and if it is always able to do the same, it shall never suffer any damage."* This is said both conditionally and also universally. Now that Fate is some such thing is clearly manifest, as well from its substance as from its name. For it is called εἱμαρμένη as being εἰρομένη, that is, dependent and linked; and it is a sanction or law, because things are therein ordained and disposed consequentially, as is usual in civil government.

5. We ought in the next place to consider and treat of

---

* This is the whole passage from Plato's Phaedrus, p. 248 C, of which part is quoted in § 1. (G.)

mutual relation and affection; that is, what reference and respect Fate has to divine Providence, what to Fortune, what also to "that which is in our power," what to contingent and other such like things; and furthermore we are to determine, how far and in what it is true or false that all things happen and are done by and according to Fate. For if the meaning is, that all things are comprehended and contained in Fate, it must be granted that this proposition is true; and if any would farther have it so understood, that all things which are done amongst men, on earth, and in heaven are placed in Fate, let this also pass as granted for the present. But if (as the expression seems rather to imply) the "being done according to Fate" signifies not all things, but only that which is an immediate consequent of Fate, then it must not be said that all things happen and are done by and according to Fate, though all things are so according to Fate as to be comprised in it. For all things that the law comprehends and of which it speaks are not legal or according to law; for it comprehends treason, it treats of the cowardly running away from one's colors in time of battle, of adultery, and many other such like things, of which it cannot be said that any one of them is lawful. Neither indeed can I affirm of the performing a valorous act in war, the killing of a tyrant, or the doing any other virtuous deed, that it is legal; because that only is proper to be called legal, which is commanded by the law. Now if the law commands these things, how can they avoid being rebels against the law and transgressors of it, who neither perform valiant feats of arms, kill tyrants, nor do any other such remarkable acts of virtue? And if they are transgressors of the law, why is it not just they should be punished? But if this is not reasonable, it must then be also confessed that these things are not legal or according to law; but that legal and according to law is only that which is particularly prescribed and expressly commanded by the law, in any action whatsoever. In like manner, those things only are fatal and according to Fate, which are the consequences of causes preceding in the divine disposition. So that Fate indeed comprehends all things which are done; yet many of those things that are comprehended in it, and almost all that precede, should not (to speak properly) be pronounced to be fatal or according to Fate.

6. These things being so, we are next in order to show, how " that which is in our power " (or free will), Fortune, possible, contingent, and other like things which are placed among the antecedent causes, can consist with Fate, and Fate with them; for Fate, as it seems, comprehends all things, and yet all these things will not happen by necessity, but every one of them according to the principle of its nature. Now the nature of the possible is to presubsist, as the genus, and to go before the contingent; and the contingent, as the matter and subject, is to be presupposed to free will; and our free will ought as a master to make use of the contingent; and Fortune comes in by the side of free will, through the property of the contingent of inclining to either part. Now you will more easily apprehend what has been said, if you shall consider that every thing which is generated, and the generation itself, is not done without a generative faculty or power, and the power is not without a substance. As for example, neither the generation of man, nor that which is generated, is without a power; but this power is about man, and man himself is the substance. Now the power or faculty is between the substance, which is the powerful, and the generation and the thing generated, which are both possibles. There being then these three things, the power, the powerful, and the possible; before the power can exist, the powerful must of necessity be presupposed as its subject, and the power must also necessarily subsist before the possible. By this

deduction then may in some measure be understood what is meant by possible; which may be grossly defined as "that which power is able to produce;" or yet more exactly, if to this same there be added, "provided there be nothing from without to hinder or obstruct it." Now of possible things there are some which can never be hindered, as are those in heaven, to wit, the rising and setting of the stars, and the like to these; but others may indeed be hindered, as are the most part of human things, and many also of those which are done in the air. The first, as being done by necessity, are called necessary; the others, which may fall one way or other, are called contingent; and they may both thus be described. The necessary possible is that whose contrary is impossible; and the contingent possible is that whose contrary is also possible. For that the sun should set is a thing both necessary and possible, forasmuch as it is contrary to this that the sun should not set, which is impossible; but that, when the sun is set, there should be rain or not rain, both the one and the other is possible and contingent. And then again of things contingent, some happen oftener, others rarely and not so often, others fall out equally or indifferently, as well the one way as the other, even as it happens. Now it is manifest that those are contrary to one another, — to wit, those which fall out oftener and those which happen but seldom, — and they both for the most part depend on Nature; but that which happens equally, as much one way as another, depends on ourselves. For that under the Dog it should be either hot or cold, the one oftener, the other seldomer, are both things subject to Nature; but to walk and not to walk, and all such things of which both the one and the other are submitted to the free will of man, are said to be in us and our election; but rather more generally to be in us. For there are two sorts of this "being in our power;" the one of which proceeds from some sudden passion and motion of the mind, as from anger or pleasure; the other from the discourse and judgment of reason, which may properly be said to be in our election. And some reason there is to believe that this possible and contingent is the same thing with that which is said to be in us and according to our free will, although differently named. For in respect to the future, it is styled possible and contingent; and in respect of the present, it is named "in our power" and "in our free will." So that these things may thus be defined: The contingent is that which is itself—as well as its contrary—possible; and "that which is in our power" is one part of the contingent, to wit, that which now takes place according to our will. Thus have we in a manner declared, that the possible in the order of Nature precedes the contingent, and that the contingent subsists before free will; as also what each of them is, whence they are so named, and what are the qualities adjoined or appertaining to them.

7. It now remains, that we treat of Fortune and casual adventure, and whatever else is to be considered with them. It is therefore certain that Fortune is a cause. Now of causes, some are causes by themselves, and others by accident. Thus for example, the proper cause by itself of an house or a ship is the art of the mason, the carpenter, or the shipwright; but causes by accident are music, geometry, and whatever else may happen to be joined with the art of building houses or ships, in respect either of the body, the soul, or any exterior thing. Whence it appears, that the cause by itself must needs be determinate and one; but the causes by accident are never one and the same, but infinite and undetermined. For many — nay, infinite — accidents, wholly different one from the other, may be in one and the same subject. Now the cause by accident, when it is found in a thing which not merely is done

for some end but has in it free will and election, is then called Fortune; as is the finding a treasure while one is digging a hole to plant a tree, or the doing or suffering some extraordinary thing whilst one is flying, following, or otherwise walking, or only turning about, provided it be not for the sake of that which happens, but for some other intention. Hence it is, that some of the ancients have declared Fortune to be a cause unknown, that cannot be foreseen by the human reason. But according to the Platonics, who have approached yet nearer to the true reason of it, it is thus defined: Fortune is a cause by accident, in those things which are done for some end, and which are of our election. And afterwards they add, that it is unforeseen and unknown to the human reason; although that which is rare and strange appears also by the same means to be in this kind of cause by accident. But what this is, if it is not sufficiently evidenced by the oppositions and disputations made against it, will at least most clearly be seen by what is written in Plato's Phaedo, where you will find these words:

PHAED. Have you not heard how and in what manner the judgment passed? ECH. Yes indeed; for there came one and told us of it. At which we wondered very much that, the judgment having been given long before, it seems that he died a great while after. And what, Phaedo, might be the cause of it? PHAED. It was a fortune which happened to him, Echecrates. For it chanced that, the day before the judgment, the stern of the galley which the Athenians send every year to the isle of Delos was crowned.*

In which discourse it is to be observed, that the expression *happened to him* is not simply to be understood by *was done* or *came to pass*, but it much rather regards what befell him through the concurrence of many causes

* Plato, Phaedo, p. 58 A.

together, one being done with regard to another. For the priest crowned the ship and adorned it with garlands for another end and intention, and not for the sake of Socrates; and the judges also had for some other cause condemned him. But the event was strange, and of such a nature that it might seem to have been effected by the providence of some human creature, or rather of some superior powers. And so much may suffice to show with what Fortune must of necessity subsist, and that there must be first some subject of such things as are in our free will: its effect is, moreover, like itself called Fortune.

But chance or casual adventure is of a larger extent than Fortune; which it comprehends, and also several other things which may of their own nature happen sometimes one way, sometimes another. And this, as it appears by the derivation of its name, which is in Greek αὐτόματον, *chance*, is that which happens of itself, when that which is ordinary happens not, but another thing in its place; such as cold in the dog-days seems to be; for it is sometimes then cold. . . . Once for all, as " that which is in our power" is a part of the contingent, so Fortune is a part of chance or casual adventure; and both the two events are conjoined and dependent on the one and the other, to wit, chance on contingent, and Fortune on " that which is in our power," — and yet not on all, but on what is in our election, as we have already said. Wherefore chance is common to things inanimate, as well as to those which are animated; whereas Fortune is proper to man only, who has his actions voluntary. And an argument of this is, that to be fortunate and to be happy are thought to be one and the same thing. Now happiness is a certain well-doing, and well-doing is proper only to man, and to him perfect.

8. These then are the things which are comprised in Fate, to wit, contingent, possible, election, " that which is

in our power," Fortune, chance, and their adjuncts, as are the things signified by the words *perhaps* and *peradventure;* all which indeed are contained in Fate, yet none of them is fatal. It now remains, that we discourse of divine Providence, and show how it comprehends even Fate itself.

9. The supreme therefore and first Providence is the understanding or (if you had rather) the will of the first and sovereign God, doing good to every thing that is in the world, by which all divine things have universally and throughout been most excellently and most wisely ordained and disposed. The second Providence is that of the second Gods, who go through the heaven, by which temporal and mortal things are orderly and regularly generated, and which pertains to the continuation and preservation of every kind. The third may probably be called the Providence and procuration of the Daemons, which, being placed on the earth, are the guardians and overseers of human actions. This threefold Providence therefore being seen, of which the first and supreme is chiefly and principally so named, we shall not be afraid to say, although we may in this seem to contradict the sentiments of some philosophers, that all things are done by Fate and by Providence, but not also by Nature. But some are done according to Providence, — these according to one, those according to another, — and some according to Fate; and Fate is altogether according to Providence, while Providence is in no wise according to Fate. But let this discourse be understood of the first and supreme Providence. Now that which is done according to another, whatever it is, is always posterior to that according to which it is done; as that which is according to the law is after the law, and that which is according to Nature is after Nature, so that which is according to Fate is after Fate, and must consequently be more new and modern. Wherefore supreme

OF FATE. 305

Providence is the most ancient of all things, except him whose will or understanding it is, to wit, the sovereign author, maker, and father of all things. " Let us therefore," says Timaeus, " discourse for what cause the Creator made and framed this machine of the universe. He was good, and in him that is good there can never be imprinted or engendered any envy against any thing. Being therefore wholly free from this, he desired that all things should, as far as it is possible, resemble himself. He therefore, who admits this to have been chiefly the principal original of the generation and creation of the world, as it has been delivered to us by wise men, receives that which is most right. For God, who desired that all things should be good, and nothing, as far as possibly might be, evil, taking thus all that was visible, — restless as it was, and moving rashly and confusedly, — reduced it from disorder to order, esteeming the one to be altogether better than the other. For it neither was nor is convenient for him who is in all perfection good, to make any thing that should not be very excellent and beautiful."* This, therefore, and all that follows, even to his disputation concerning human souls, is to be understood of the first Providence, which in the beginning constituted all things. Afterwards he speaks thus: " Having framed the universe, he ordained souls equal in number to the stars, and distributed to each of them one ; and having set them, as it were, in a chariot, showed the nature of the universe, and appointed them the laws of Fate." † Who then will not believe, that by these words he expressly and manifestly declares Fate to be, as it were, a foundation and political constitution of laws, fitted for the souls of men? Of which he afterwards renders the cause.

As for the second Providence, he thus in a manner explains it, saying : " Having prescribed them all these laws,

* Plato, Timaeus, p. 29 D. † Plato, Timaeus, p. 41 D.

to the end that, if there should afterwards happen any fault, he might be exempt from being the cause of any of their evil, he dispersed some of them upon the earth, some into the moon, and some into the other instruments of time. And after this dispersion, he gave in charge to the young Gods the making of human bodies, and the making up and adding whatever was wanting and deficient in human souls; and after they had perfected whatever is adherent and consequent to this, they should rule and govern, in the best manner they possibly could, this mortal creature, so far as it should not be the cause of its own e ils."* For by these words, "that he might be exempt from being the cause of any of their evil," he most clearly signifies the cause of Fate; and the order and office of the young Gods manifests the second Providence; and it seems also in some sort to have touched a little upon the third, if he therefore established laws and ordinances that he might be exempt from being the cause of any of their evil. For God, who is free from all evil, has no need of laws or Fate; but every one of these petty Gods, drawn on by the providence of him who has engendered them, performs what belongs to his office. Now that this is true and agreeable to the opinion of Plato, these words of the lawgiver, spoken by him in his Book of Laws, seems to me to give sufficient testimony: "If there were any man so sufficient by Nature, being by divine Fortune happily engendered and born, that he could comprehend this, he would have no need of laws to command him. For there is not any law or ordinance more worthy and powerful than knowledge; nor is it fitting that Mind, provided it be truly and really free by Nature, should be a subject or slave to any one, but it ought to command all."†

10. I therefore do for mine own part thus understand and interpret this sentence of Plato. There being a three-

* Plato, Timaeus, p. 42 D. † Plato, Laws, IX. p. 875 C.

fold Providence, the first, as having engendered Fate, does in some sort comprehend it; the second, having been engendered with Fate, is with it totally comprehended and embraced by the first; the third, as having been engendered after Fate, is comprehended by it in the same manner as are free will and Fortune, as we have already said. "For they whom the assistance of a Daemon's power does aid in their intercourse with me" says Socrates, declaring to Theages what is the almost inevitable ordinance of Adrastea "are those whom you also mean; for they grow and come forward with speed."* In which words, what he says of a Daemon's aiding some is to be ascribed to the third Providence, and the growing and coming forward with speed, to Fate. In brief, it is not obscure or doubtful but that this also is a kind of Fate. And perhaps it may be found much more probable that the second Providence is also comprehended under Fate, and indeed all things that are done; since Fate, as a substance, has been rightly divided by us into three parts, and the fable of the chain comprehends the revolutions of the heavens in the number and rank of those things which happen conditionally. But concerning these things I will not much contend, to wit, whether they should be called conditional, or rather conjoined with Fate, the precedent cause and commander of Fate being also fatal.

11. Our opinion then, to speak compendiously, is such. But the contrary sentiment does not only include all things in Fate, but affirms them all to be done by and according to Fate. It accords indeed in all things to the other (the Stoic) doctrine; and that which accords to it, 'tis clear, is the same thing with it. In this discourse therefore we have first spoken of the contingent; secondly, of "that which is in our power;" thirdly, of Fortune and chance, and whatever depends on them; fourthly, of praise, blame,

* Plato, Theages, p. 129 E.

and whatever depends on them; the fifth and last of all may be said to be prayers to the Gods, with their services and ceremonies.

For the rest, as to those which are called idle and reaping arguments, and that which is named the argument against destiny, they are indeed but vain subtleties and captious sophisms, according to this discourse. But according to the contrary opinion, the first and principal conclusion seems to be, that there is nothing done without a cause, but that all things depend upon antecedent causes; the second, that the world is governed by Nature, and that it conspires, consents, and is compatible with itself; the third seems rather to be testimonies, — of which the first is divination, approved by all sorts of people, as being truly in God; the second is the equanimity and patience of wise men, who take mildly and bear patiently whatever befalls, as happening by divine ordinance and as it ought; the third is the speech so common and usual in every one's mouth, to wit, that every proposition is true or false. Thus have we contracted this discourse into a small number of short articles, that we might in few words comprehend the whole matter of Fate; into which a scrutiny ought to be made, and the reasons of both opinions to be weighed with a most exact balance. But we shall hereafter come to discuss particulars.

CONCERNING THE FIRST PRINCIPLE OF COLD.

1. Is there then, Favorinus, any first or principal power or existence of cold, as fire is the principle of heat, by the presence and imparting of which all other things of the same nature become cold? Or rather is not cold the privation of heat, as they say darkness is the privation of light, and rest the privation of motion? In regard that cold seems to be firm and stable, and heat always in motion; and for that the refrigeration of hot things is not caused by the presence of any active power, but by the departure of the heat. For we find the heat go off in great quantity, and then that which remains grows cold. Thus the vapor which boiling water sends forth ceases also when the heat is gone. Therefore refrigeration, expelling the heat, diminishes the quantity, while nothing supplies the place of it.

2. First, we might question this way of arguing, as being that which would abolish several manifest faculties, as being neither qualities nor habits, but the privations of habits and qualities; so as to make ponderosity the privation of levity, hardness the privation of softness, black of white, bitter of sweet, and so with other things which are naturally opposed to each other in their power and not as a privation to a habit. Or else for this reason, because all privation is a thing altogether sluggish and without action, as blindness, deafness, silence, and death; for they are the

departure of forms, and the utter defacings of substances, not being natures nor substances of themselves; but cold, wherever it resides, causes no less affections and alterations in bodies than heat. For many things are congealed by cold, many things thereby condensed. So that whatever is solid in it and difficult to be moved cannot be said to be sluggish and void of action, but firm and ponderous, as being supported by its own strength, which is endued with a power to preserve it in its proper station. Wherefore privation is the deficiency and departure of the opposite power, but many things are subject to be cold, though abounding with heat within themselves. And there are some things which cold the more condenses and consolidates the hotter they are, as iron quenched in water. The Stoics also affirm, that the spirit which is in the bodies of infants is quickened by refrigeration, and changing its Nature, turns to a soul. But this is a thing much to be disputed. Neither is it rational to believe that cold, which is the productive agent in many other things, can be a privation.

3. Besides, no privation is capable of more and less. Neither can any man say, that one among those that cannot see is more blind than another, or that one among those that cannot speak is more silent than another, or that any thing is more dead than another among those things that never had life. But in cold things there is more and less, and excess and diminution to several degrees; in a word, there is both intensity and remission as well as in hot things; because the matter suffers in some things more violently, in others more languidly, and therefore some things are hotter, some things colder than others, according to the nature of the matter. For there is no mixture of habit with privation. Neither does any power admit of privation opposite to it, nor associate with it in the same subject, but it withstands it altogether. Hot things allow themselves to be mixed

with cold things to a certain degree, as black with white, heavy with light, and sour with sweet, — this community and harmony of colors, sounds, medicaments, and sauces generating several tastes and pleasures grateful to the senses. But the opposition of privation and habit is an antipathy never to be reconciled; the being of the one enforcing the destruction of the other. Which destruction, if it fall out seasonably, according to the opposition of contrary powers, the arts make great use of, but chiefly Nature, not only in her other creations, but especially in the alterations of the air, and in all other things of which the Deity being the adorner and dispenser obtains the attribute of harmonical and musical. Not that those attributes are given him for the disposal of deep and shrill, black and white, so as to make them agree together; but for his governing in the world the sympathies and antipathies of cold and heat in such a manner that they may unite and separate again, and for reducing both to a decent order, by taking that which we called "the overmuch" from both.

4. Then again, we find that there is the same sense and feeling of cold as of heat; but privation is neither to be seen, heard, or felt, neither is it known to any of the other senses. For the object of sense is substance; but where no substance appears, there we understand privation to be, — which is a negation of substance, as blindness of sight, silence of voice, and vacuity of corporeal substance. For there is no sense or perception of vacuity by feeling; but where there is no body to be felt, there a vacuity is implied. Neither do we hear silence; but where we do not hear any thing at all, there we imply silence. In like manner we have no perception of blindness, nakedness, or being unarmed; but we know them from the negation of our sense. Therefore if cold were a privation of heat, there would be no being sensible of cold; but

only where heat ceased to be, there cold would be implied But if, as heat is perceptible by the warmth and laxative softness of the flesh, so cold is no less perceptible by the contraction and condensation of it, it is from thence apparent, that there is some peculiar original and fountain of cold as well as heat.

5. Further then, privation of every kind is something single and simply particular; but in substances there are several differences and efficacies. For silence is a thing but of one sort; but of sounds there are great variety, sometimes molesting, sometimes delightful to the sense. There are also the same differences in colors and figures, which vary as they occur to the senses. But that which is not to be felt, which is without color and void of quality, can never be distinguished, but is always like itself.

6. Is cold therefore to be numbered among those privations that are not distinguished in their action? Rather the contrary, in regard that pleasures very great and beneficial to our bodies arise from cold things; as no less terrible mischiefs, pains, and stupefaction on the other side; which the heat does not always avoid and give way to, but many times enclosed within the body, withstands and opposes. Which contention of theirs is called quivering and shaking, at what time, if the cold overcome the heat, thence proceed numbness and stiffness of the limbs; but if the cold be vanquished by the heat, there follow a pleasing warmth and opening of the skin, which Homer expresses by the word ἰαίνεσθαι. These things are past dispute; and chiefly by these passive qualities it is, that we find cold to be opposite to heat, as substance to substance, or passive quality to passive quality, not as negation or privation; neither is it the destruction or abolishing of hot, but a kind of nature and power tending to its destruction. Otherwise we should exempt the winter out of the seasons, and the north winds out of the number of the winds, as

being privations of the warmer seasons and the southern gales, and not having any proper original.

7. Now in regard there are four first bodies in the universe, which, by reason of their number, their being uncompounded, and their efficacy, are allowed for the most part to be the principles and beginnings of all other, — that is to say, fire and water, air and earth, — is there not the same necessity that there should be as many first and uncompounded qualities? And what are they but heat and cold, drought and moisture, by virtue of which it comes to pass that all the principles act and suffer? Thus, as there are in grammar lengthenings and shortenings of sounds, in music, deep and acute sounds, though not one of them is the privation of the other; we must leave the dry opposed to the moist principles, and the hot to the cold, if we intend to have the effects answerable to reason and what is visible in Nature. Unless, as it was the opinion of the ancient Anaximenes, we will not allow either cold or hot to be in substance, but only to be common passive qualities accompanying the alterations of the matter. For he affirms the contraction and condensation of the matter to be cold; but the rarefication and laxation of it (for by that word he calls it) to be hot. Whence it may not be improperly said, that a man breathes hot and cold at once. For the breath grows cold being compressed and thickened by the lips, but coming out of the open mouth it is hot, as being rarefied by that emission. But for this, Aristotle convinces the same person of ignorance; for that when we blow with the mouth open, we blow hot from our own bodies; but when we blow with compressed lips, we do not breathe forth the air from ourselves, but the air that is before our mouths, being cold, is thrust forward, and lights upon what is next it.

8. But if we must grant that both heat and cold are substances, let us proceed a little farther in our discourse, and

enquire what sort of substance is cold, and what is its first principle and nature.

They then who affirm that there are certain irregular triangular figures in our body, and tell us also that shuddering, trembling, and quivering, and whatever else we suffer of the same nature, proceed from the roughness of those figures, if they mistake in the parts, nevertheless derive the beginning from whence they ought. For we ought to begin the question — as it were from Vesta — from the substance of all things. By which it chiefly appears wherein a philosopher differs from a physician, a husbandman, or a piper. For it is sufficient for these to contemplate the last causes. For if the consideration of the nearest causes of the affection go no farther than to find that the cause of a fever is intenseness of heat, or the lighting of some humor where it ought not to be, that the cause of blasting is the scorching heat of the sun after rain, and that the cause why pipes give a bass sound is the inclination of the pipes or the bringing them near one to another; this is enough for the artist to know in reference to his business. But when a philosopher for contemplation's sake scrutinizes into the truth, the knowledge of remote causes is not the end but the beginning of his proceeding in search of the first and ultimate causes. Wherefore Plato and Democritus, enquiring after the cause of heat and gravity, did not stop at the consideration of earth and fire, but bringing things perceptible to sense to beginnings intelligible only by the mind, they went on even to the smallest, as it were the seeds of what they sought for.

9. But it is much the better way for us in the first place to move forward upon those things which are perceptible to sense, wherein Empedocles, Strato, and the Stoics placed the substances of active qualities; the Stoics ascribing primitive cold to the air, Empedocles and Strato

to the water ; and perhaps there might be somebody else who might affirm the earth to be the substance of cold. But first let us consider the opinions of those already named.

Seeing then that fire is both hot and bright, therefore there must be something opposite to fire which is cold and dark. For as dark is opposite to light, so is cold to hot. Besides, as dark confounds the sight, so cold confounds the feeling. But heat diffuses the sense of feeling, as light diffuses the sense of seeing. Therefore that which is first dark in nature is first cold. Now that the air is first dark, was not unknown to the poets ; for that they call the air darkness :

> The thickened air the fleet with darkness covered,
> Nor could the moonlight be from heaven discovered.*

And again :

> Then darkness scattered and the fog dispelled,
> The sun brake forth, and all the fight beheld.†

They also call the air, when it is without light κνεφας, as being as it were κενὸν φάους (*void of light.*) The air collected and condensed into a cloud is called νέφος, from its negation of light (νή-φάος). The words also ἀχλύς and ὁμίχλη (*mist*), and whatever else restrains the perception of light from the sense, are but distinctions of the air ; insomuch that the same part of it which is invisible and without color (ἀειδές and ἀχρωστον) is called Hades and Acheron. So that, as the air grows dark when the splendor of it fails, in like manner when heat fails, that which is left is no more than cold air, which by reason of its coldness is called Tartarus. And this Hesiod makes manifest, when he calls it Τάρταρον ἠερόεντα (or *cloudy Tartarus*); and when a man quakes and shivers for cold, he is said to tartarize. And so much for this.

* Odyss. IX. 144.   † Il. XVI. 649.

10. But in regard corruption is the alteration of those things that are corrupted into that which is contrary to every one of them, let us consider whether it be a true saying, " The death of fire is the generation of air." For fire dies like a living creature, being quenched by force or going out of its own accord. Now quenching makes the alteration of it into air more conspicuous. For smoke is a sort of air, or, according to Pindar, a fuliginous vapor and exhalation, "lashing the air with steaming smoke."* On the other side, when fire goes out for want of fuel, as in candles, you shall observe a thick and cloudy air ascending from the top of them. Moreover, the vapor steaming from our bodies upon the pouring of cold water after hot bathing or sweating sufficiently declares the alteration of extinguished heat into air, as being naturally opposite to air; whence it follows that the air was at first dark and cold.

11. Then again, congelation, which is the most forcible and violent of all things that befall our bodies by reason of cold, is the affection of water, but the action of air. For water of itself is easily diffused, loose in its parts, and not readily congealed together; but it is thickened and compressed by the air, by reason of the coldness of it. Which is the reason of the proverb:

> But if the southern wind provoke the north,
> Snow straight will cover all the earth.

For the southern wind preparing the moisture as matter, presently the north wind receives and congeals it. And this is manifest from the consideration of snow; for ere it falls, you shall observe a thin and sharp cold air breathing before it. Aristotle also tells us, that whetstones of lead [?] will melt and run in the winter through excess of freezing cold, merely upon the setting of the water near

---

* Pind. Isthm. IV. 112.

them. For it is probable that the air compresses and gripes the bodies so close together, that at length it breaks and crumbles them in pieces.

12. And therefore water drawn from a fountain soonest congeals; for the more of cold in the air overcomes the less of cold in the water. Thus if a man takes cold water out of a well and puts it into a vessel, and then lets the vessel down again into the well, so that it may not touch the water but hang for some time in the air, the water will be much colder. Whence it is apparent, that the coldness of the water is not the first cause of coldness, but the coldness of the air. For you do not find that any of your great rivers are ever thoroughly frozen, by reason of their depth. For the air doth not pierce through the whole; only so much as it can seize and embrace with its cold quality generally freezes, and no more. Therefore the barbarians never cross over frozen rivers till they have sent a fox before to try the depth of the ice. For if the ice be not very thick, but only superficial, the fox, perceiving it by the noise of the water floating underneath, returns. And some there are that melt the ice with hot water to make way for their lines, when they go to catch fish in winter. So that nothing suffers from cold in the depth of the water. Nevertheless, so great has been the alteration of the upper parts of the water by congelation, that several vessels riding in the stream have been bruised and broken by the forcible compressure and griping of the congelation; as we have heard from them who lately had their winter quarters with Caesar upon the Danube. And indeed, what happens to ourselves is sufficient to demonstrate the truth of this. For after hot bathings and sweatings, we are most sensible of cold, at what time, our bodies being open and the skin relaxed, we give a freer entrance to the cold together with the ambient air. And after the very same manner the water itself suffers. For

it sooner freezes if it be first heated, as being thereby rendered more easy for the air to work upon. And therefore they who lade out scalding water, and let it fall again from a good height in the air, do it to no other purpose than to mix it with a great deal of air. And therefore, Favorinus, the arguments that attribute the first power of cold to the air are grounded upon these probabilities.

13. Those that allow it to water lean upon principles of the same nature. And this was intimated by Empedocles, where he says:

> Behold the sun, how warm he is,
> And shining everywhere;
> But rain and tempests cold and dark
> With horror fill the air.

And thus opposing cold to heat, and dark to bright, he gives us to understand that black and cold are both of the same substance, as also are bright and hot. Now that black is proper to the water and not to the air, sense itself bears witness, nothing being darkened by the air, all things being clouded and blackened by water. So that if you throw the whitest wool that is, or a white garment into the water, it comes out black, and so remains, till the moisture be dried up again by the heat, or squeezed forth by presses or weights. Also when the ground is watered, the places that receive the drops grow black, the rest retaining their former color. And therefore the deepest waters, by reason of their quantity, always appear blackest, but the parts which are next the air afford a lovely and smiling brightness. But of all liquids, oil is the most transparent, because of the great quantity of air that is in it. And of this, the lightness of it is an unquestionable proof; the reason why it swims above all things, as carried upward by the air. Being poured forth upon the waves, it will cause calmness upon the sea, not because it is so slippery that the winds can have no power over it, as Aristotle thought, but because the waves will fall and sink when smitten by any moist body. And this is also peculiar to oil, that it shines and causes a transparency at the bottom of the water, while the watery humors are dispersed by the air. For being spurted out of the mouth into the sea, not only by those that sail in the night, but also by those that dive for sponges to the bottom of the sea, it will cast a light in the water. Water therefore has more of blackness than the air, but less of cold. Oil therefore, partaking more of air than most liquid things, is least cold, nor will it easily or suddenly freeze; for the air which is mixed with it will not suffer the congelation to grow hard. And therefore, as for needles, steel buckles, and such sort of small iron and steel wares, they never quench them in water but in oil, fearing lest the over-coldness of the water should make them too brittle. And indeed the truth is more truly enquired into from the consideration of these experiments, than those of colors. For hail, snow, and ice, as they are most transparent, so are most cold; and pitch, as it is hotter, so it is blacker and darker than honey.

14. This makes me admire at those who affirm the air to be cold because it is dark and obscure, unless it be because they find others affirming it to be hot because it is light. For dark is not so proper and familiar to cold, as heavy and stable; for many things that are void of heat partake of splendor and light, but there is nothing cold that is light, nimble, or apt to ascend upward. Even the clouds themselves, while they preserve the nature of air, tower aloft in the sky; but changing into moisture, they presently fall down, and having admitted coldness, they lose their lightness as well as their heat. And so on the other side, having regained their heat, they again return to motion, their substance being carried upward as soon as it is changed into air.

Neither is the argument produced from corruption true. For nothing that perishes is corrupted *into* what is opposite, but *by* what is opposite to it; as fire extinguished by water changes into air. And therefore Aeschylus spake not merely like a tragedian but like a philosopher, when he said,

> The water curb, that punishment of fire.

In like manner Homer opposed in battle Vulcan to the river, and Apollo to Neptune, more like a philosopher than a poet or mythologist. And Archilochus spoke not amiss of a woman whose thoughts were contrary to her words, when he said,

> She, weaving subtle trains and sly vagaries,
> Fire in one hand, in th' other water carries.

Among the Persians there were several customs of supplication, of which the chiefest, and that which would admit of no refusal, was when the suppliant, taking fire in his hand and entering into a river, threatened, if his supplications were denied, to throw the fire into the water. But though his suit were granted him, yet he was punished for threatening, as being against the law and contrary to Nature. And this is a vulgar proverb in everybody's mouth, to mix fire with water, spoken of those that would attempt impossibilities; to show that water is an enemy to fire, and being extinguished thereby, is destroyed and punished by it, — not by the air, which, upon the change and destruction of it, receives and entertains the substance of it. For if that into which the thing destroyed is changed be contrary to it, why does fire seem contrary to air more than water? For air changes into water by condensation, but into fire by dissipation; as, on the other side, water is turned into air by separation, into earth by condensation. Which, in my opinion, happens by reason of the propriety and near affinity between both, not from any thing of contrariety and hostility one to another. Others there are, that, which way soever they maintain it, spoil the argument. For it is most irrational to say that water is congealed by the air, when they never saw the air congealed in their lives. For clouds, fogs, and mists are no congelations, but thickenings and condensations of the air moist and full of vapors; but a dry air void of moisture never undergoes refrigeration to such a degree. For there are some mountains that never admit of a cloud, nor dew, nor mist, their tops being so high as to reach into an air that is pure and void of moisture. Whence it is manifest that it is the condensation and consistency below, which contributes that cold and moisture to the air which is mixed with it.

15. Now that great rivers never freeze downwards is but consentaneous to reason. For those parts which are frozen above transmit no exhalation outward; for this, being penned up within and forced downward, affords heat to the moisture at the bottom. A clear demonstration of which is this, that when the ice is dissolved, you may observe a steam arising out of the water upwards in a very great quantity. And therefore the bodies of living creatures are warmest within in the winter, for that the heat is driven inward by the ambient cold. Now those upward exhalations and ascensions of the vapors deprive the waters not only of their heat but of their coolness. And therefore they that vehemently desire their drink to be cold never move the snow nor the moisture that is pressed out of it; for motion would deprive them both of the virtue which is required from them.

Now that this virtue is not the virtue of air, but of water, a man may collect by reasoning thus from the beginning. First, it is not probable that the air, which is next the sky, and touching the fiery substance is also touched by it, should be endued with a contrary virtue; for otherwise it is not possible that the extremities of the one should touch and be contiguous to the extremities of the other. Nor is it agreeable to reason that Nature should constitute that which is corrupted next in order to that which corrupts, as if she were not the author of community and harmony but of combat and contention. For she makes use of contrary things in sustaining the universe; but she does not use them pure and unmixed, nor so that they will be in hostility; but she uses such as have alternately a certain position and order which is not destructive, but which inclines them to communicate and co-operate one with another, and to effect a harmony between the opposing qualities. And this is the nature of the air, being expanded under the fire above the water, contingent and adhering to both, neither hot in itself nor cold, but containing an intermixture and communion of hot and cold, harmlessly intermixed in herself; and lightly cherishing the contrary extremities.

16. Therefore the air is of an equal temper in all places, but winter is not in all places alike nor equally cold; but some parts of the habitable world are cold and moist, others hot and dry, not by chance, but because there is but one substance of heat and dryness. For the greatest part of Africa is hot and without water. But they that have travelled Scythia, Thrace, and the Pontic regions report them to be full of vast lakes, and large and deep rivers. And as for those regions lying between, those parts that join upon lakes and marshes are most cold by reason of the exhalations from the water. Posidonius therefore, affirming the freshness and moistness of the air of marshes to be the cause of its cold, has no way disturbed the probability of our argument, but rather added to the strength of it; for the air would not always be the colder the fresher it is, unless cold has its original from moisture. And therefore Homer much more truly shows us the fountain of cold, when he says,

> Chill from the river blows the wind
> Before the coming morn.*

Then again it many times happens that our sense deceives us. So that when we feel cold garments or cold wool, we believe we feel them to be moist, by reason of the substance which is common to both, and of their natures which are coherent and familiar one with another. But in climates where the cold is extreme, it oftentimes breaks and cracks both pots and vessels, whether made of earth or brass, — none empty, but all full, the cold giving force and might to the liquor within, — which made Theophrastus say, that the air breaks those vessels, making use of the cold as of a hammer; whether more eloquently or more truly spoken, I leave you to judge. For then vessels full of pitch or milk should be more subject to be broken by the air.

But water seems to be cold of itself, and that primitively too; for in respect of the coldness of it, it is opposite to the heat of the fire; as to drought in respect of its moisture, and to ponderosity in regard of its lightness. Lastly, fire is altogether of a dissipating and dividing nature; water, of a nature to fasten and contain, holding and joining together by virtue of its moisture. Which was the reason why Empedocles called fire "a pernicious contention," but water a "tenacious friendship." For the nourishment of fire is that which changes into fire, and it changes that which is as it were of kin and familiar to it. What is contrary to it, as water, cannot be changed by it, or at least only with great difficulty. True it is, that as for itself, as I may so say, it cannot be burned; but as for green wood and wet straw, it overcomes them with much struggling, while the heat and cold contending together, by reason of their moisture and their natural antipathy,

---

* Odyss. V. 469.

produce only a dull flame, clouded with smoke, that makes little progress upon the materials.

17. Compare these arguments with theirs, and consider them well. But Chrysippus, believing the air to be the primitive cold, because it is dark, makes mention only of those that say the water lies at farther distance from the sky than the air. And being desirous to give some answer to them, "If so," says he, "we may as well affirm the earth to be primitively cold, because it is the farthest distant from the sky;" rejecting that, as altogether improbable and absurd. But for my part, I am of opinion that there might be many probable and rational arguments brought for the earth; beginning with that which Chrysippus chiefly makes use of for the air. What is this? First, that it is dark. For if he, assuming these two contrarieties of faculties, believes that the one follows the other of necessity, then there might be produced a thousand oppositions and repugnances of the earth in respect of the sky, which would of necessity follow upon this which we have mentioned. For it is not to be opposed only as heavy to light, or as that which tends downward to that which moves upward, or as slow and stable to swift and full of motion; but as that which is heaviest to that which is most thin, or lastly, as that which is immovable of itself to that which moves spontaneously, and as possessing the middle space to that which is in a perpetual circular motion. Would it not be absurd to aver that the opposition of heat to cold is accompanied with so many and such remarkable contrarieties? But fire is bright, the earth is dark, nay, the very darkest and most void of light of all things. The air first of all participates of light, is soonest altered, and being replenished with radiancy, diffuses the splendor of it far and near, and shows itself a vast body of light. For the sun rising, as one of the dithyrambic authors writes,

> Presently doth fill
> The spacious house of the air-prancing winds.

From thence the descending air disposes a part of her brightness to the sea and lakes, and the hidden depths of profound rivers laugh and smile so far as the air penetrates into them. Only the earth of all bodies remains without light, and impenetrable to the beams of the sun and moon. But it is cherished and comforted by them, and suffers a small part of it to be warmed and softened by entrance of the heat. But the solidness of it will not admit the brightness of light, only the surface of it is enlightened; but the innermost parts of it are called by the names of Darkness, Chaos, and Hades; and Erebus is nothing else but that same perpetual darkness and horror in the body of the earth. Besides, the mythologists tell us that Night was the daughter of the Earth; and the mathematicians show that it is the shadow of the earth eclipsing the body of the sun. For the air is filled with darkness by the earth, as with light by the sun; and that part of the air which is void of all light is that same length of the night which is caused by the shadow of the earth. And therefore both men and many beasts make use of the exterior air, and ramble in the dark, guided only by some footsteps of light and certain effluxes of a dim twinkling that are scattered through it; but he that keeps house and shuts himself up in his chamber, as being encompassed by the earth, remains altogether blind and without light. Also the hides and horns of beasts will not admit of light by reason of their solidness; but being burnished and shaved, they become transparent, the air being intermixed with them. Moreover, I am of opinion that the earth is everywhere by the poets said to be black, by reason of the darkness of it and want of light. So that the antithesis of light and darkness is much more remarkable in reference to the earth, than in respect of the air.

18. But this is nothing to the question. For we have shown that there are many cold things which are bright and transparent, and many hot things which are obscure and dark. But ponderosity, stability, density, and immutability are qualities more properly belonging to cold, of none of which the air partakes, but of all of which the earth has a far greater share than the water. And yet in all these things cold, by the judgment of sense itself, appears to be hard, to cause hardness, and to make resistance. For Theophrastus tells us of fish that have been frozen by extremity of cold, when they have chanced to bounce ashore, that their bodies have been broken and crumbled to pieces like a vessel of glass or potter's clay. You yourself have heard at Delphi, how that certain persons ascending to the top of Parnassus to succor the Thyades that were overtaken with a violent storm of wind and hail, their coats were frozen so hard and into a substance so like wood, that being spread upon the ground they broke and crumbled to pieces. It also stiffens the nerves and deprives the tongue of motion, congealing the moist and softer parts of the body.

19. This being obvious to sight, let us consider the effect. Every faculty, wherever it prevails, changes into itself whatever it overcomes. Thus whatever is overcome by heat is set on fire; that which is vanquished by wind is changed into air. That which falls into water becomes well moistened, unless quickly saved. Of necessity, therefore, those things which are violently affected by cold must be changed into the primitive cold. For freezing is an excess of refrigeration; which congelation ends in alteration and petrifaction, when the cold, prevailing every way, congeals the liquid substance and presses forth the heat; so that the bottom of the earth is, as it were, a kind of congelation, and altogether ice. For there the cold inhabits simple and unmixed, and removed hard and rigid at

the greatest distance from the sky. But as for those things which are conspicuous, as rocks and precipices, Empedocles believes them to be thrust forth and supported by the fire that burns in the bottom of the earth. Which appears the more, in regard that, wherever the heat is pressed forth and vanishes away, all those things are congealed or stiffened by the cold; and therefore congelations are called πάγοι (*stiffened*). And the extremities of many things where heat fails, growing black, make them look like brands when the fire is out. For cold congeals some things more, some things less; more especially such things wherein it is primitively existent. For as, if it be the nature of hot to render light, that which is hottest is lightest; if of moist to soften, that which is moistest is softest; so if it be the nature of cold to congeal, of necessity that which is coldest must be most congealed, — that is to say the earth, — and that which is most cold must be that which is by nature and primitively cold, which is no more than what is apparent to sense. For mud is colder than water, and earth being thrown upon fire puts it out. Your smiths also, when their iron is melted and red hot, strew upon it the dust of marble to cool it and stop the running of it too fluidly. Dust also cools the bodies of the wrestlers, and dries up their sweat.

20. To go no farther, what means our own yearly practice to alter our lodgings and habitations, while we remove in the winter so far as we can into the upper parts of our buildings, but in the summer descend again and seek convenient refuge in the lower edifices, sometimes enjoying ourselves under ground in the very arms of the earth? Do we not do it, as being guided by our senses for coolness's sake to the earth, and thereby acknowledging that to be the seat of primitive cold? And certainly our coveting to live near the sea in winter may be thought to be a kind of flight from the earth, since we seem to forsake it,

as far as we can, by reason of the nipping frosts, and run to encircle themselves with the air of the sea for warmth's sake; and then again in the summer, by reason of the scorching heat, we desire the earth-born upland air, not because it is cold of itself, but because it had its original and blossomed from the primitive natural cold, and is imbued with that power which is in the earth, as iron is imbued with the virtue of the water wherein it is quenched. Then again, of river waters we find those are the coldest that flow upon gravel and stones and fall down from mountains; and of well-waters, those which are in the deepest wells. For with these the exterior air is no longer mixed, by reason of the depth of the wells, and the other arise out of the pure and unmixed earth; like the river that falls from the mountain Taenarum, which they call the water of Styx, rising out of a rock with a parsimonious spring, but so cold that no other vessel except the hoof of an ass will hold it; for all other sorts of vessels it breaks and cracks to pieces.

21. The physicians also tell us that the nature of all sorts of earth is binding and restrictive; and they number up several sorts of metals which are made use of in physic by reason of their styptic and binding qualities. For the element of earth is fit neither to cut nor to move, neither has it any points, neither is it subject to be softened or melted, but is firm and stable like a cube; and therefore it has both ponderosity and coldness, and the faculty to thicken and condense moist things; and it causes tremblings and quiverings in bodies by reason of its inequality; and if it get the better by the utter expulsion and extinguishing of the heat, it occasions a frozen and deadly habit of body. Therefore earth either does not consume by burning, or else burns with a very slow and difficult progress. But the air many times darts forth flame from itself; and being once set on fire, it grows fluid and flashes

out in lightning. Heat also feeds upon moisture; for it is not the solid part of the wood, but the moist and oily part, that is combustible; which being consumed, the solid and dry is left behind in the ashes. Neither do they arrive at their mark, who, pretending to burn the ashes also, sprinkle them with oil and grease; for when the liquid is consumed, the earthy part remains, do what they can. Therefore, because the earth is not only of a nature not to be moved from its station, but also unalterable in its substance and always abiding in the habitation of the Gods, the ancients well called it Hestia or Vesta (from *standing*), by reason of its immobility and concretion; of which cold is the bond or ligament, as Archelaus the philosopher termed it, which nothing is able to unloosen or soften, as not being capable of heat and warmth.

As for those who say they have been sensible of the cold of air and water, but never felt the earth so cold, they consider only the surface of the earth, which is a mixture of air, water, sun, and heat. They are no better than people who deny the aether to be naturally and primitively hot, but believe it to be either scalding water or red hot iron, because they feel and handle the one, but are not sensible of the pure and celestial fire. In like manner, neither do they see the earth which lies concealed at the bottom, though that be what is chiefly to be taken for the earth, separated from all other things. We may see some token of this lower earth in these rocks here about us, which from their depths send forth a cold vapor so sharp and vehement that it is hard to be endured. They also that desire cool drink throw small flint stones into water. For it becomes denser and quicker to the taste, through the cold which is carried upward fresh and unmixed from the stones.

22. Therefore it was the opinion of the ancient philosophers and learned men, that terrestrial and celestial things

were not to be mixed together, not so much out of a local consideration of uppermost and lowermost, in respect of place, but with a respect to the difference of faculties, attributing hot and splendent, swift and light to the immortal and sempiternal Nature, but believing dark and cold and slow to be the unhappy portion of the dead under the shackles of corruption. Since the body of a living creature, while it breathes and flourishes (as the poets say), enjoys both heat and life; but being deprived of these, and only the terrestrial parts remaining, presently cold and stiffness take place, as if heat were naturally existent in every thing else but only the earth.

23. These things, dear Favorinus, compare with what has been said by others; and if they neither come too short of probability nor too much exceed it, bid all their opinions farewell, as believing it much more becoming a philosopher to pause in dubious matters, rather than over hastily to side with any one particular party.

WHETHER WATER OR FIRE BE MOST USEFUL.

1. "WATER is the best of things, but gold is like burning fire," says Pindar.* Therefore he positively assigns the second place to fire; with whom Hesiod agrees, where he says,

First of all Chaos being had.†

For most believe that by the word chaos he meant water, from χύσις, signifying *diffusion*. But the balance of argument as to this point seems to be equal. For there are some who will have it that fire is the principle of all things, and that like sperm it begets all things out of itself, and resolves all things again by conflagration. Therefore, not to mention the persons, let us consider the arguments on both sides, which are to us the most convincing.

2. Now then, is not that the most useful to us, which in all places and always and most of all we stand in need of, — like a piece of household-stuff or a tool, nay, like a friend that is ready at all hours and seasons? But fire is not always useful; for sometimes it is a prejudice to us and we avoid it if we can. But water is useful, winter and summer, to the healthy and sick, night and day; neither indeed is there any time but that a man has need of it. Therefore it is that the dead are called *alibantes*, as being without moisture (λιβάς) and by that means deprived of life; and man may be without fire, but never

* Pindar, Olymp. I. 1.   † Hesiod, Theog. 116.

was any man without water. Besides, that which was existent from the beginning and with the first creation of man must be thought more useful than what was afterwards invented. From whence it is apparent, that Nature bestowed the one upon us as a thing absolutely necessary, the other fortune and art found out for superfluity of uses. Nor was the time ever known when man lived without water, nor was it an invention of any of the Gods or heroes; for it was present almost at their generation, and it made their creation possible. But the use of fire was a late invention of Prometheus, at what time life was without fire, but not without water. And that this is no poetical fiction is demonstrable from this, that there are many sorts of people that live without fire, without houses, and without hearths, in the open air. And Diogenes the Cynic made no use of fire; so that after he had swallowed a raw fish, "This hazard," said he, "do I run for your sakes." But without water no man ever thought it convenient or possible to live.

3. But why do I so meanly confine my discourse to the nature of men, seeing there are many, nay, infinite sorts of creatures? The race of man is almost the only one that knows the use of fire; the others live and feed without fire. Indeed, beasts, birds, and creeping things live upon roots, fruits, and raw flesh, without fire; but without water neither fish nor fowl nor land animals can subsist. For all beasts that feed upon flesh, of which there are some (as Aristotle reports) that never drink, nevertheless support life and being merely by moisture. So that of necessity that must be most profitable without which no sort of life can subsist or endure.

4. Let us therefore make a step from animals that eat to things that we ourselves make use of, such are plants and fruits; of which some are altogether void of heat, others enjoy it but imperfectly and obscurely. But moist-

ure causes all things to germinate, increase, and bring forth. Why should I stand to reckon up wine and oil, milk and honey, and whatever else we reap and bring forth and see before our eyes, when wheat itself, which is looked upon as a dry nourishment, grows by alteration, putrefaction, and corruption of the moist matter?

5. Then again, that is most useful which is no way detrimental. Now fire easily becomes most pernicious, but the nature of water is never prejudicial. In the next place, that is most useful which affords the benefit which it brings with least expense, and without any preparation. But the benefit of fire requires cost and materials, and therefore the rich make more use of it than the poor, and princes than private persons; but water has that kindness for mankind, that it freely offers itself to all alike, a benefit perfect in itself, indigent of nothing, and wanting neither tools nor implements.

6. Moreover, that which by augmentation loses its benefit is of least use. Such is fire, which like a devouring beast ravages all before it, useful rather by art and skilful moderation, than of its own nature. But from water there is nothing to be feared. Furthermore, that is most useful which may be joined with another. But fire will not admit of water, neither is it any way profitable by conjunction with it. But water becomes profitable by joining with fire; and therefore hot waters are wholesome, and sensibly cure several diseases. Neither shall you ever find moist fire; but water both cold and hot is profitable for the body of man.

7. Then again, there being four elements, water produces a fifth out of itself, which is the sea, no less beneficial than the rest, as well for commerce as for many other things. So that it may be said, this element united and perfected our manner of living, which before was wild and unsociable, correcting it by mutual assistance, and

creating community of friendship by reciprocal exchanges of one good turn for another. And as Heraclitus said, If there were no sun, it would be perpetual night; so may we say, If there were no sea, man would be the most savage and shameless of all creature. But the sea brought the vine from India into Greece, and out of Greece transmitted the use of corn to foreign parts; from Phoenicia translated the knowledge of letters, the memorials that prevent oblivion; furnished the world with wine and fruit, and prevented the greatest part of mankind from being illiterate and void of education. How is it possible then but that water should be the most useful, when it thus furnishes us with an entirely new element?

8. Or can any man speak as follows in defence of the contrary? We say then that God, as a master workman, had before him the four elements, to complete the fabric of the universe; and these again were different one from another. But earth and water were placed at the foundation, like matter, to be formed and fashioned, participating of form and order and of power to procreate and bring forth, so far as they are assisted by air and fire, — the great artificers that mould them into various shapes, — and lying dead till roused by them to act and generate. Of these two latter, fire is the ruling agent. This is manifest by induction. For earth without warmth and heat is altogether barren and unfruitful; but fire, by virtue of its rousing and inflaming quality, renders it diffusive, and swells it into generation. Nor can any man find out any other cause why rocks and the dry tops of mountains are not productive, but because they participate either nothing at all or very little of fire.

9. Then generally for water, it is so far from being sufficient of itself for the generation and preservation of other things, that it is itself destroyed for want of fire. But fire is that which upholds every thing in its proper being, and

preserves it in its proper substance, as well water itself as all other things; so that when fire leaves it, water will stink, and it may be said that the want of fire is the death and destruction of water. And thus we find in regard to pools and all manner of standing waters, and such as are settled in pits and holes without issue, what an offensive and dead stench they send forth, and all for want of motion ; for this kindles and preserves heat in all things, and more especially in running waters and swift streams, which being thus agitated and enlivened by heat, we commonly say such waters "live." Why then should not that be accounted the most useful of the two, that affords to the other the cause of its being, as fire does to water? Moreover, that is the most useful, of which if an animal be wholly deprived, it must perish ; for it is evident, that anything without which an animal cannot live affords the reason and cause why it exists. There is moisture also in things after they are dead, nor are they altogether dried up ; for otherwise moist bodies would never putrefy ; since putrefaction is the alteration of dry into moist, or rather the corruption of moisture in flesh. Neither is death any other than an absolute defect and want of heat, and therefore dead carcasses are the coldest of all ; so that if you do but touch them with a razor, they will blunt the edge of it through excess of coldness. Also in living creatures, those parts that least partake of heat are most insensible, as the bones and hair, and those parts which are most distant from the heart. Nay, to some of the most important things the absence of fire and the presence of water are destructive. For plants and fruits are not produced by moisture, but by the warmth of the moisture ; and cold waters are most certainly either less productive, or altogether barren. For if water were fruitful in itself, it would always, and that spontaneously too, bear fruit. But the contrary is apparent, and it is rather baneful to **generation.**

10. Let us begin anew. As to the use of fire, considered as fire, we have no need of water. Rather the contrary is to be made out; for water extinguishes fire. And as for water, there is no use to be made of it in most things without fire. For water heated becomes more useful, whereas otherwise it is prejudicial. So that, of the two, that is to be accounted best which is profitable of itself without the assistance of another. Besides, water is beneficial only to the feeling, when you either wash with it or touch it; but fire is profitable to all the senses, being not only felt, but also seen at a distance; so that you may add this to the rest of the virtues of it, that its uses are manifold.

11. Then to say that man did once subsist without fire is a mistake, it being impossible that man should be without it. But we must acknowledge there are differences in this kind, as well as in other things. Thus heat has rendered the sea more beneficial, as having a greater portion of heat in it than other waters, from which it otherwise differs not at all. And as for those that have no need of outward fire, they do not avoid it because they do not want it, but because they abound in heat within themselves. So that the use of fire seems to be more excellent in this, that water is never in such a condition as not to want external aids, but fire, endued with manifold virtues, contents itself with its own sufficiency. Therefore, as he is the best commander who so manages the affairs of his city as not to have any need of foreign assistance, so that element excels that supplies us in such a manner as to want the least of other helps from without. And this is to be said of other creatures that have no need of external heat.

Now, to argue on the other side, a man may say thus, that whatever we singly and alone make use of is more profitable, since we are by our reason best fitted to choose what is best. For what is more useful and beneficial to us than reason?... And yet brute animals want fire. What then? Is it the less profitable, because found out by foresight of a higher power?

12. And since our discourse has brought us to it, what is more beneficial to life than art? Yet fire invented and preserves all manner of arts. And therefore Vulcan is feigned to be the prince of all artificers. Man has allowed him but a little time to live; and as Aristo said, sleep, like a toll-gatherer, deprives him of the one-half of that too. I would rather say that the darkness does this; for a man may watch all night. But he would have no benefit of his watchfulness unless fire afforded him all the benefit of the light of day, and removed the difference between night and day. Since then there is nothing more beneficial to man than life, and this is prolonged by fire, why should not fire be accounted the most beneficial of all things?

13. Lastly, that is to be thought most profitable, of which the temperament of the senses participates most. Now do you find that there is any of the senses, which of itself makes use of moisture without an intermixture of air and fire? But every sense partakes of fire, as being that which quickens the vital faculty; more especially the sight, which is the most acute of all the senses in the body, being a certain fiery efflux, that gave us our first light into the belief of a Deity, and by virtue of which we are able, as Plato says, to conform our souls to the motions of the celestial bodies.

AGAINST COLOTES, THE DISCIPLE AND FAVORITE OF EPICURUS.

1. Colotes, whom Epicurus was wont diminutively and by way of familiarity or fondness, to call Colotaras and Colotarion, composed, O Saturninus, and published a little book which he entitled, "That according to the opinions of the other philosophers one cannot so much as live." This he dedicated to King Ptolemy. Now I suppose that it will not be unpleasant for you to read, when set down in writing, what came into my mind to speak against this Colotes, since I know you to be a lover of all elegant and honest treatises, and particularly of such as regard the science of antiquity, and to esteem the bearing in memory and having (as much as possible may be) in hand the discourses of the ancient sages to be the most royal of all studies and exercises.

2. Not long since therefore, as this book was reading, Aristodemus of Aegium, a familiar friend of ours (whom you well know to be one of the Academy, and not a mere thyrsus-bearer, but one of the most frantic celebrators of Plato's orgies),* did, I know not how, keep himself contrary to his custom very still all the while, and patiently gave ear to it even to the end. But the reading was scarce well over, when he said: Well then, whom shall we cause

---

* See Plato, Phaed. p. 69 C, and Stallbaum's note. Here the proverb occurs, — Ναρθηκοφόροι μὲν πολλοί, Βάκχοι δέ τε παῦροι, the thyrsus-bearers are many, but the true priests of Bacchus are few. (G.)

to rise up and fight against this man, in defence of the philosophers? For I am not of Nestor's opinion, who, when the most valiant of those nine warriors that presented themselves to enter into combat was to be chosen, committed the election to the fortune of a lot.

Yet, answered I, you see he so disposed himself in reference to the lot, that the choice might pass according to the arbitrament of the wisest man;

> And th' lot drawn from the helmet, as they wished,
> On Ajax fell.

But yet since you command me to make the election,

> How can I think a better choice to make
> Than the divine Ulysses? *

Consider therefore, and be well advised, in what manner you will chastise this man.

But you know, replied Aristodemus, that Plato, when highly offended with his boy that waited on him, would not himself beat him, but requested Speusippus to do it for him, saying that he himself was angry. As much therefore may I say to you; Take this fellow to you, and treat him as you please; for I am in a fit of choler.

When therefore all the rest of the company desired me to undertake this office; I must then, said I, speak, since it is your pleasure. But I am afraid that I also shall seem more vehemently transported than is fitting against this book, in the defending and maintaining Socrates against the rudeness, scurrility, and insolence of this man; who, because Socrates affirmed himself to know nothing certainly, instead of bread (as one would say) presents him hay, as if he were a beast, and asks him why he puts meat into his mouth and not into his ear. And yet perhaps some would make but a laughing matter of this, considering the mildness and gentleness of Socrates; " but

* Il. VII. 182; X. 243.

for the whole host of the Greeks," that is, of the other philosophers, amongst which are Democritus, Plato, Stilpo, Empedocles, Parmenides, and Melissus, who have been basely traduced and reviled by him, it were not only a shame to be silent, but even a sacrilege in the least point to forbear or recede from freedom of speech in their behalf, who have advanced philosophy to that honor and reputation it has gotten.

And our parents indeed have, with the assistance of the Gods, given us our life; but to live well comes to us from reason, which we have learned from the philosophers, which favors law and justice, and restrains our concupiscence. Now to live well is to live sociably, friendly, temperately, and justly; of all which conditions they leave us not one, who cry out that man's sovereign good lies in his belly, and that they would not purchase all the virtues together at the expense of a cracked farthing, if pleasure were totally and on every side removed from them. And in their discourses concerning the soul and the Gods, they hold that the soul perishes when it is separated from the body, and that the Gods concern not themselves in our affairs. Thus the Epicureans reproach the other philosophers, that by their wisdom they bereave man of his life; whilst the others on the contrary accuse them of teaching men to live degenerately and like beasts.

3. Now these things are scattered here and there in the writings of Epicurus, and dispersed through all his philosophy. But this Colotes, by having extracted from them certain pieces and fragments of discourses, destitute of any arguments whatever to render them credible and intelligible, has composed his book, being like a shop or cabinet of monsters and prodigies; as you better know than any one else, because you have always in your hands the works of the ancients. But he seems to me, like the Lydian, to open not only one gate against himself, but to involve

Epicurus also in many and those the greatest doubts and difficulties. For he begins with Democritus, who receives of him an excellent and worthy reward for his instruction; it being certain that Epicurus for a long time called himself a Democritean, which as well others affirm, as Leonteus, a principal disciple of Epicurus, who in a letter which he writ to Lycophron says, that Epicurus honored Democritus, because he first attained, though a little at a distance, the right and sound understanding of the truth, and that in general all the treatise concerning natural things was called Democritean, because Democritus was the first who happened upon the principles and met with the primitive foundations of Nature. And Metrodorus says openly of philosophy, If Democritus had not gone before and taught the way, Epicurus had never attained to wisdom. Now if it be true, as Colotes holds, that to live according to the opinions of Democritus is not to live, Epicurus was then a fool in following Democritus, who led him to a doctrine which taught him not to live.

4. Now the first thing he lays to his charge is, that, by supposing every thing to be no more of one nature than another, he wholly confounds human life. But Democritus was so far from having been of this opinion, that he opposed Protagoras the philosopher who asserted it, and writ many excellent arguments concluding against him, which this fine fellow Colotes never saw nor read, nor yet so much as dreamed of; but deceived himself by misunderstanding a passage which is in his works, where he determines that τὸ δέν is no more than τὸ μηδέν, naming in that place the body by δέν, and the void by μηδέν, and meaning that the void has its own proper nature and subsistence, as well as the body.

But he who is of opinion that nothing is more of one nature than another makes use of a sentence of Epicurus, in which he says that all the apprehensions and imaginations given us by the senses are true. For if of two saying, the one, that the wine is sour, and the other, that it is sweet, neither of them shall be deceived by his sense, how shall the wine be more sour than sweet? And we may often see that some men using one and the same bath find it to be hot, and others find it to be cold; because those order cold water to be put into it, as these do hot. It is said that, a certain lady going to visit Berenice, wife to King Deiotarus, as soon as ever they approached each other, they both immediately turned their backs, the one, as it seemed, not being able to bear the smell of perfume, nor the other of butter. If then the sense of one is no truer than the sense of another, it is also probable, that water is no more cold than hot, nor sweet ointment or butter better or worse scented one than the other. For if any one shall say that it seems the one to one, and the other to another, he will, before he is aware, affirm that they are both the one and the other.

5. And as for these symmetries and proportions of the pores, or little passages in the organs of the senses, about which they talk so much, and those different mixtures of seeds, which, they say, being dispersed through all savors, odors, and colors, move the senses of different persons to perceive different qualities, do they not manifestly drive them to this, that things are no more of one quality than another? For to pacify those who think the sense is deceived and lies because they see contrary events and passions in such as use the same objects, and to solve this objection, they teach, — that all things being mixed and confounded together, and yet one nevertheless being more suitable and fitting to one, and another to another, it is not possible that there should in all cases be a contact and comprehension of one and the same quality, nor does the object equally affect all with all its parts, every one meeting only those to which it has its sense commensurate and

proportioned; so that they are to blame so obstinately to insist that a thing is either good or bad, white or not white, thinking to establish their own senses by destroying those of others; whereas they ought neither to combat the senses, — because they all touch some quality, each one drawing from this confused mixture, as from a living and large fountain, what is suitable and convenient, — nor to pronounce of the whole, by touching only the parts, nor to think that all ought to be affected after one and the same manner by the same thing, seeing that one is affected by one quality and faculty of it, and another by another. Let us then seek who those men are which bring in this opinion that things are not more of one quality than another, if they are not those who hold that every sensible thing is a mixture, composed of all sorts of qualities, like a mixture of new wine fermenting, and who confess that all their rules are lost and their faculty of judging quite gone, if they admit any sensible object that is pure and simple, and do not make each one thing to be many?

6. See now to this purpose, what discourse and debate Epicurus makes Polyaenus to have with him in his Banquet concerning the heat of wine. For when he asked, "Do you, Epicurus, say, that wine does not heat?" some one answered, "It is not universally to be affirmed that wine heats." And a little after: "For wine seems not to be universally a heater; but such a quantity may be said to heat such a person." And again subjoining the cause, to wit, the compressions and disseminations of the atoms, and having alleged their commixtures and conjunctions with others when the wine comes to be mingled in the body, he adds this conclusion: "It is not universally to be said that wine is endued with a faculty of heating; but that such a quantity may heat such a nature and one so disposed, while such a quantity to such a nature is cooling. For in such a mass there are such natures and complex-

ions of which cold might be composed, and which, joined with others in proper measure, would yield a refrigerative virtue. Wherefore some are deceived, who say that wine is universally a heater; and others, who say that it is universally a cooler." He then who says that most men are deceived and err, in holding that which is hot to be heating and that which is cold to be cooling, is himself in an error, unless he should believe that his assertion leads to the doctrine that one thing is not more of one nature than another. He farther adds afterwards, that oftentimes wine entering into a body brings with it thither neither a calefying nor refrigerating virtue, but, the mass of the body being agitated and disturbed, and a transposition made of the parts, the heat-effecting atoms being assembled together do by their multitude cause a heat and inflammation in the body, and sometimes on the contrary disassembling themselves cause a refrigeration.

7. But it is moreover wholly evident, that we may apply this argument to all those things which are called and esteemed bitter, sweet, purging, dormitive, and luminous, not any one of them having an entire and perfect quality to produce such effects, nor to do rather than to suffer when they are in the bodies, but being there susceptible of various temperatures and differences. For Epicurus himself, in his Second Book against Theophrastus, affirming that colors are not connatural to bodies, but are engendered there according to certain situations and positions with respect to the sight of man, says: "For this reason a body is no more colored than destitute of color." And a little above he writes thus, word for word: "But apart from this, I know not how a man may say that those bodies which are in the dark have color; although very often, an air equally dark being spread about them, some distinguish diversities of colors, others perceive them not through the weakness of their sight. And moreover, going into a

dark house or room, we at our first entrance see no color, but after we have stayed there awhile, we do. Wherefore we are to say that every body is not more colored than not colored. Now, if color is relative and has its being in regard to something else, so also then is white, and so likewise blue; and if colors are so, so also are sweet and bitter. So that it may truly be affirmed of every quality, that it cannot more properly be said to be than not to be. For to those who are in a certain manner disposed, they will be; but to those who are not so disposed, they will not be." Colotes therefore has bedashed and bespattered himself and his master with that dirt, in which he says those lie who maintain that things are not more of one quality than another.

8. But is it in this alone, that this excellent man shows himself

> To others a physician, whilst himself
> Is full of ulcers?[*]

No indeed; but yet much farther in his second reprehension, without any way minding it, he drives Epicurus and Democritus out of this life. For he affirms that the saying of Democritus — that the atoms are to the senses color by a certain law or ordinance, that they are by the same law sweetness, and by the same law concretion [†] — is at war with our senses, and that he who uses this reason and persists in this opinion cannot himself imagine whether he is living or dead. I know not how to contradict this discourse; but this I can boldly affirm, that this is as inseparable from the sentences and doctrines of Epicurus as they say figure and weight are from atoms. For what is it that Democritus says? "There are substances, in number infinite, called atoms (because they cannot be divided), without difference, without quality, and impassible, which move, being dispersed here and there, in the

---

[*] Euripides, Frag. 1071.   [†] The text is corrupt here. (G.)

infinite voidness; and that when they approach one
another, or meet and are conjoined, of such masses thus
heaped together, one appears water, another fire, another
a plant, another a man; and that all things are thus really
atoms (as he called them), and that there is nothing else;
for there can be no generation from what is not; and of
those things which are nothing can be generated, because
these atoms are so firm, that they can neither change, alter,
nor suffer; wherefore there cannot be made color of those
things which are without color, nor nature or soul of
those things which are without quality and impassible."
Democritus then is to be blamed, not for confessing those
things that happen upon his principles, but for supposing
principles upon which such things happen. For he should
not have supposed immutable principles; or having supposed them, he ought to have seen that the generation of
all quality is taken away; but having seen the absurdity,
to deny it is most impudent. But Epicurus says, that he
supposes the same principles with Democritus, but that he
says not that color, sweet, white, and other qualities, are
by law and ordinance. If therefore *not to say* is merely
not to confess, he does merely what he is wont to do. For
it is as when, taking away divine Providence, he nevertheless says that he leaves piety and devotion towards the
Gods; and when, choosing friendship for the sake of
pleasure, that he suffers most grievous pains for his friends;
and supposing the universe to be infinite, that he nevertheless takes not away high and low. . . . Indeed having
taken the cup, one may drink what he pleases, and return
the rest. But in reasoning one ought chiefly to remember
this wise apophthegm, that where the principles are not
necessary, the ends and consequences are necessary. It
was not then necessary for him to suppose or (to say better) to steal from Democritus, that atoms are the principles
of the universe; but having supposed this doctrine, and

having pleased and glorified himself in the first probable and specious appearances of it, he must afterwards also swallow that which is troublesome in it, or must show how bodies which have not any quality can bring all sorts of qualities to others only by their meetings and joining together. As — to take that which comes next to hand — whence does that which we call heat proceed, and how is it engendered in the atoms, if they neither had heat when they came, nor are become hot after their being joined together? For the one presupposes that they had some quality, and the other that they were fit to receive it. And you affirm, that neither the one nor the other must be said to belong to atoms, because they are incorruptible.

9. How then? Do not Plato, Aristotle, and Xenocrates produce gold from that which is not gold, and stone from that which is not stone, and many other things from the four simple first bodies? Yes indeed; but with those bodies immediately concur also the principles for the generation of every thing, bringing with them great contributions, that is, the first qualities which are in them; then, when they come to assemble and join in one the dry with the moist, the cold with the hot, and the solid with the soft, — that is active bodies with such as are fit to suffer and receive every alteration and change, — then is generation wrought by passing from one temperature to another. Whereas the atom, being alone, is deprived and destitute of all quality and generative faculty, and when it comes to meet with the others, it can make only a noise and sound because of its hardness and firmness, but nothing else. For they always strike and are stricken, not being able by this means to compose or make an animal, a soul, or a nature, nay, not so much as a mass or heap of themselves; for that as they beat upon one another, so they fly back again asunder.

10. But Colotes, as if he were speaking to some igno-

rant and unlettered king, again attacks Empedocles for breathing forth the same thought:

> I've one thing more to say. 'Mongst mortals there
> No Nature is; nor that grim thing men fear
> So much, called death. There only happens first
> A mixture, and mixt things asunder burst
> Again, when them disunion does befall.
> And this is that which men do Nature call.

For my part, I do not see how this is repugnant and contrary to life or living, especially amongst those who hold that there is no generation of that which is not, nor corruption of that which is, but that the assembling and union of the things which are is called generation, and their dissolution and disunion named corruption and death. For that he took Nature for generation, and that this is his meaning, he has himself declared, when he opposed Nature to death. And if they neither live nor can live who place generation in union and death in disunion, what else do these Epicureans? Yet Empedocles, gluing, (as it were) and conjoining the elements together by heats, softnesses, and humidities, gives them in some sort a mixtion and unitive composition; but these men who hunt and drive together the atoms, which they affirm to be immutable and impassible, compose nothing proceeding from them, but indeed make many and continual percussions of them.

For the interlacement, hindering the dissolution, more and more augments the collision and concussion; so that there is neither mixtion nor adhesion and conglutination, but only a confusion and combat, which according to them is called generation. And if the atoms do now recoil for a moment by reason of the shock they have given, and then return again after the blow is past, they are above double the time absent from one another, without either touching or approaching, so as nothing can be made of them, not even so much as a body without a soul. But as for sense, soul, understanding, and prudence, there is not any man who can in the least conceive or imagine how it is possible they should be made in a voidness, and of atoms which neither when separate and apart have any quality, nor any passion or alteration when they are assembled and joined together, especially seeing this their meeting together is not an incorporation or congress, making a mixture or coalition, but rather percussions and repercussions. So that, according to the doctrine of these people, life is taken away, and the being of an animal denied, since they suppose principles void, impassible, godless, and soulless, and such as cannot admit or receive any mixture or incorporation whatever.

11. How then is it, that they admit and allow Nature, soul, and living creature? Even in the same manner as they do an oath, prayer, and sacrifice, and the adoration of the Gods. Thus they adore by word and mouth, only naming and feigning that which by their principles they totally take away and abolish. If now they call that which is born Nature, and that which is engendered generation, — as those who ordinarily call the wood itself wood-work and the voices that accord and sound together symphony, — whence came it into his mind to object these words against Empedocles? "Why," says he, "do we tire ourselves in taking such care of ourselves, in desiring and longing after certain things, and shunning and avoiding others? For we neither are ourselves, nor do we live by making use of others." But be of good cheer, my dear little Colotes, may one perhaps say to him: there is none who hinders you from taking care of yourself by teaching that the nature of Colotes is nothing else but Colotes himself, or who forbids you to make use of things (now things with you are pleasures) by showing that there is no nature of tarts and marchpanes, of sweet odors, or of venereal delights, but that there are tarts, marchpanes, perfumes,

and women. For neither does the grammarian who says that "the strength of Hercules" is Hercules himself deny the being of Hercules; nor do those who say that symphonies and roofings are but bare derivations affirm that there are neither sounds nor timbers; since also there are some who, taking away the soul and prudence, do not yet seem to take away either living or being prudent.

And when Epicurus says that the nature of things consists in bodies and their place, do we so comprehend him as if he meant that Nature were something else than the things which are, or as if he insinuated that it is simply the things which are, and nothing else? — as, to wit, he is wont to call voidness itself the nature of voidness, and the universe, by Jupiter, the nature of the universe. And if any one should thus question him; What sayst thou, Epicurus, that this is voidness, and that the nature of voidness? No, by Jupiter, would he answer; but this community of names is in use by law and custom. I grant it is. Now what has Empedocles done else, but taught that Nature is nothing else save that which is born, and death no other thing but that which dies? But as the poets very often, forming as it were an image, say thus in figurative language,

> Strife, tumult, noise, placed by some angry God,
> Mischief, and malice there had their abode;*

so do most men attribute generation and corruption to things that are contracted together and dissolved. But so far has he been from stirring and taking away that which is, or contradicting that which evidently appears, that he casts not so much as one single word out of the accustomed use; but taking away all figurative fraud that might hurt or endamage things, he again restored the ordinary and useful signification to words in these verses:

* Il. XVIII. 535.

> When from mixed elements we sometimes see
> A man produced, sometimes a beast, a tree,
> Or bird, this birth and geniture we name;
> But death, when this so well compacted frame
> And juncture is dissolved. This use I do approve.

And yet I myself say that Colotes, though he alleged these verses, did not understand that Empedocles took not away men, beasts, trees, or birds, which he affirmed to be composed of the elements mixed together; and that, by teaching how much they are deceived who call this composition Nature and life, and this dissolution unhappy destruction and miserable death, he did not abrogate the using of the customary expressions in this respect.

12. And it seems to me, indeed, that Empedocles did not aim in this place at the disturbing the common form of expression, but that he really, as it has been said, had a controversy about generation from things that have no being, which some call Nature. Which he manifestly shows by these verses:

> Fools, and of little thought, we well may deem
> Those, who so silly are as to esteem
> That what ne'er was may now engendered be,
> And that what is may perish utterly.

For these are the words of one who cries loud enough to those which have ears, that he takes not away generation, but procreation from nothing; nor corruption, but total destruction, that is, reduction to nothing. For to him who would not so savagely and foolishly but more gently calumniate, the following verses might give a colorable occasion of charging Empedocles with the contrary, when he says:

> No prudent man can e'er into his mind
> Admit that, whilst men living here on earth
> (Which only life they call) both fortunes find,
> They being have, but that before the birth
> They nothing were, nor shall be when once dead.

For these are not the expressions of a man who denies those that are born to be, but rather of him who holds those to be that are not yet born or that are already dead. And Colotes also does not altogether accuse him of this, but says that according to his opinion we shall never be sick, never wounded. But how is it possible, that he who affirms men to have being both before their life and after their death, and during their life to find both fortunes (or to be accompanied both by good and evil), should not leave them the power to suffer? Who then are they, O Colotes, that are endued with this privilege never to be wounded, never to be sick? Even you yourselves, who are composed of atoms and voidness, neither of which, you say, has any sense. Now there is no great hurt in this; but the worst is, you have nothing left that can cause you pleasure, seeing an atom is not capable to receive those things which are to effect it, and voidness cannot be affected by them.

13. But because Colotes would, immediately after Democritus, seem to inter and bury Parmenides, and I have passed over and a little postponed his defence, to bring in between them that of Empedocles, as seeming to be more coherent and consequent to the first reprehensions, let us now return to Parmenides. Him then does Colotes accuse of having broached and set abroad certain shameful and villanous sophistries; and yet by these his sophisms he has neither rendered friendship less honorable, nor voluptuousness or the desire of pleasures more audacious and unbridled. He has not taken from honesty its attractive property or its being venerable or recommendable of itself, nor has he disturbed the opinions we ought to have of the Gods. And I do not see how, by saying that the All (or the universe) is one, he hinders or obstructs our living. For when Epicurus himself says that the All is infinite, that it is neither engendered nor perishable, that it can neither increase nor be diminished, he speaks of the universe as of one only thing. And having in the beginning of his treatise concerning this matter said, that the nature of those

things which have being consists of bodies and of voidness, he makes a division (as it were) of one thing into two parts, one of which has in reality no subsistence, being, as you yourselves term it, impalpable, void, and incorporeal; so that by this means, even with you also, all comes to be one; unless you desire, in speaking of voidness, to use words void of sense, and to combat the ancients, as if you were fighting against a shadow.

But these atomical bodies, you will say, are, according to the opinion of Epicurus, infinite in number, and every thing which appears to us is composed of them. See now, therefore, what principles of generation you suppose, infinity and voidness; one of which, to wit, voidness, is inactive, impassible, and incorporeal; the other, to wit, infinity, is disorderly, unreasonable, and incomprehensible, dissolving and confounding itself, because it cannot for its multitude be contained, circumscribed, or limited. But Parmenides has neither taken away fire, nor water, nor rocks and precipices, nor yet cities (as Colotes says) which are built and inhabited as well in Europe as in Asia; since he has both made an order of the world, and mixing the elements, to wit, light and dark, does of them and by them compose and finish all things that are to be seen in the world. For he has written very largely of the earth, heaven, sun, moon, and stars, and has spoken of the generation of man; and being, as he was, an ancient author in physiology, and one who in writing sought to deliver his own and not to destroy another's doctrine, he has passed over none of the principal things in Nature. Moreover, Plato, and before him Socrates himself, understood that in Nature there is one part subject to opinion, and another subject to intelligence. As for that which is subject to opinion, it is always unconstant, wandering, and carried away with several passions and changes, liable to diminution and increase, and to be variously disposed to various men, and not always appearing after one manner even to the same person. But as to the intelligible part, it is quite of another kind,

Constant, entire, and still engenerable,

as himself says, always like to itself, and perdurable in its being.

Here Colotes, sycophant-like, catching at his expressions and drawing the discourse from things to words, flatly affirms that Parmenides in one word takes away the existence of all things by supposing *ens* (or that which is) to be one. But, on the contrary, he takes away neither the one nor the other part of Nature; but rendering to each of them what belongs to it and is convenient for it, he places the intelligible in the idea of one and of "that which is," calling it *ens* because it is eternal and incorruptible, and one because it is always like itself and admits no diversity. And as for that part which is sensible, he places it in the rank of uncertain, disorderly, and always moving. Of which two parts, we may see the distinct judgment:

One certain truth and sincere knowledge is,

as regarding that which is intelligible, and always alike and of the same sort;

The other does on men's opinions rest,
Which breed no true belief within our breast,

because it is conversant in things which receive all sorts of changes, passions, and inequalities. Now how he could have left sense and opinion, if he had not also left any thing sensible and opinable, it is impossible for any man to say. But because to that which truly *is* it appertains to continue in its being, and because sensible things sometimes are, sometimes are not, continually passing from one being to another and perpetually changing their state, he thought they required some other name than that of *entia*, or things which always are. This speech therefore concerning *ens* (or that which is), that it should be but one, is not to take away the plurality of sensible things, but to show how they differ from that which is intelligible. Which difference Plato in his discourse of Ideas more fully declaring, has thereby afforded Colotes an opportunity of cavilling.

14. Therefore it seems not unreasonable to me to take next into our consideration, as it were all in a train, what he has also said against him. But first let us contemplate a little the diligence — together with the manifold and profound knowledge — of this our philosopher, who says, that Aristotle, Xenocrates, Theophrastus, and all the Peripatetics have followed these doctrines of Plato. For in what corner of the uninhabitable world have you, O Colotes, written your book, that, composing all these accusations against such personages, you never have lighted upon their works, nor have taken into your hands the books of Aristotle concerning Heaven and the Soul, nor those of Theophrastus against the Naturalists, nor the Zoroaster of Heraclides, nor his books of Hell, nor that of Natural Doubts and Difficulties, nor the book of Dicaearchus concerning the Soul; in all which books they are in the highest degree contradictory and repugnant to Plato about the principal and greatest points of natural philosophy? Nay, Strato himself, the very head and prince of the other Peripatetics, agrees not in many things with Aristotle, and holds opinions altogether contrary to Plato, concerning motion, the understanding, the soul, and generation. In fine, he says that the world is not an animal, and that what is according to Nature follows what is according to Fortune; for that Chance gave the beginning, and so every one of the natural effects was afterwards finished.

Now as to the ideas, — for which he quarrels with Plato, — Aristotle, by moving this matter at every turn, and alleging all manner of doubts concerning them, in his Ethics, in his Physics, and in his Exoterical Dialogues seems to some rather obstinately than philosophically to have disputed against these doctrines, as having proposed to himself the debasing and undervaluing of Plato's philosophy; so far he was from following it. What an impudent rashness then is this, that having neither seen nor understood what these persons have written and what were their opinions, he should go and devise such things as they never imagined; and persuading himself that he reprehends and refutes others, he should produce a proof, written with his own hand, arguing and convincing himself of ignorance, licentiousness, and shameful impudence, in saying that those who contradict Plato agree with him, and that those who oppose him follow him?

15. Plato, says he, writes that horses are in vain by us esteemed horses, and men men. And in which of Plato's commentaries has he found this hidden? For as to us, we read in all his books, that horses are horses, that men are men, and that fire is by him esteemed fire, because he holds that every one of these things is sensible and subject to opinion. But this fine fellow Colotes, as if he were not a hair's breadth removed from perfect wisdom, apprehends it to be one and the same thing to say, "Man is not" and "Man is a *non ens*."

Now to Plato there seems to be a wonderful great difference between not being at all and being a *non ens;* because the first imports an annihilation and abolishment of all substance, and the other shows the diversity there is between that which is participated and that which participates. Which diversity those who came after distinguished only into the difference of genus and species, and certain common and proper qualities or accidents, as they are called, but ascended no higher, falling into more logical doubts and difficulties. Now there is the same proportion between that which is participated and that which participates, as there is between the cause and the matter, the original and the image, the faculty and the effect. Wherein that which is by itself and always the same principally differs from that which is by another and never abides in one and the same manner; because the one never was nor ever shall be non-existent, and is therefore totally and essentially an *ens;* but to the other that very being, which it has not of itself but happens to take by participation from another, does not remain firm and constant, but it goes out of it by its imbecility, — the matter always gliding and sliding about the form, and receiving several affections and changes in the image of the substance, so that it is continually moving and shaking. As therefore he who says that the image of Plato is not Plato takes not away the sense and substance of the image, but shows the difference of that which exists of itself from that which exists only in regard to some other; so neither do they take away the nature, use, or sense of men, who affirm that every one of us, by participating in a certain common substance, that is, by the idea, is become the image of that which afforded the likeness for our generation. For neither does he who says that a red-hot iron is not fire, or that the moon is not the sun, but, as Parmenides has it,

>A torch which round the earth by night
>Does bear about a borrowed light,

take away therefore the use of iron, or the nature of the moon. But if he should deny it to be a body, or affirm that it is not illuminated, he would then contradict the senses, as one who admitted neither body, animal, generation, nor sense. But he who by his opinion imagines that these things subsist only by participation, and considers how far remote and distant they are from that which always is and which communicates to them their being, does not reject the sensible, but affirms that the intelligible is;

nor does he take away and abolish the effects which are wrought and appear in us; but he shows to those who follow him that there are other things, firmer and more stable than these in respect of their essence, because they are neither engendered, nor perish, nor suffer any thing; and he teaches them, more purely touching the difference, to express it by names, calling these ὄντα or *entia* (*things that have being*), and those γιγνόμενα or *fientia* (*things engendered*). And the same also usually befalls the moderns; for they deprive many — and those great things — of the appellation of *ens* or *being;* such as are voidness, time, place, and simply the entire genus of things spoken, in which are comprised all things true. For these things, they say, are not *entia* but *some things;* and they perpetually make use of them in their lives and in their philosophy, as of things having subsistence and existence.

16. But I would willingly ask this our fault-finder, whether themselves do not in their affairs perceive this difference, by which some things are permanent and immutable in their substances, — as they say of their atoms, that they are at all times and continually after one and the same manner, because of their impassibility and hardness, — but that all compounded things are fluxible, changeable, generated, and perishing; forasmuch as infinite images are always departing and going from them, and infinite others, as it is probable, repair to them from the ambient air, filling up what was diminished from the mass, which is much diversified and transvasated, as it were, by this change, since those atoms which are in the very bottom of the said mass can never cease stirring and reciprocally beating upon one another; as they themselves affirm. There is then in things such a diversity of substance But Epicurus is in this wiser and more learned than Plato, that he calls them all equally *entia*. — to wit, the impalpable voidness, the solid and resisting body, the principles,

and the things composed of them, — and thinks that the eternal participates of the common substance with that which is generated, the immortal with the corruptible, and the natures that are impassible, perdurable, unchangeable, and that can never fall from their being, with those which have their essence in suffering and changing, and can never continue in one and the same state. But though Plato had with all the justness imaginable deserved to be condemned for having offended in this, yet should he have been sentenced by these gentlemen, who speak Greek more elegantly and discourse more correctly than he, only as having confounded the terms, and not as having taken away the things and driven life from us, because he named them *fientia* (or things engendered), and not *entia* (things that have being), as these men do.

17. But because we have passed over Socrates, who should have come next after Parmenides, we must now turn back our discourse to him. Him therefore has Colotes begun at the very first to remove, as the common proverb has it, from the sacred line; and having mentioned how Chaerephon brought from Delphi an oracle, well known to us all, concerning Socrates, he says thus: " Now as to this narration of Chaerephon's, because it is odious and absolutely sophistical, we will overpass it." Plato then, that we may say nothing of others, is also odious, who has committed it to writing; and the Lacedaemonians are yet more odious, who reserve the oracle of Lycurgus amongst their most ancient and most authentic inscriptions. The oracle also of Themistocles, by which he persuaded the Athenians to quit their town, and in a naval fight defeated the barbarous Xerxes, was a sophistical fiction. Odious also were all the ancient legislators and founders of Greece, who established the most part of their temples, sacrifices, and solemn festivals by the answer of the Pythian Oracle. But if the oracle brought from Delphi concerning Socrates,

a man ravished with a divine zeal to virtue, by which he is styled and declared wise, is odious, fictitious, and sophistical, by what name shall we call your cries, noises, and shouts, your applauses, adorations and canonizations, with which you extol and celebrate him who incites and exhorts you to frequent and continual pleasures? For thus has he written in his epistle to Anaxarchus: "I for my part in cite and call you to continual pleasures, and not to vain and empty virtues, which have nothing but turbulent hopes of uncertain fruits." And yet Metrodorus, writing to Timarchus, says: "Let us do some extraordinarily excellent thing, not suffering ourselves to be plunged in reciprocal affections, but retiring from this low and terrestrial life, and elevating ourselves to the truly holy and divinely revealed ceremonies and mysteries of Epicurus." And even Colotes himself, hearing one day Epicurus discoursing of natural things, fell suddenly at his feet and embraced his knees, as Epicurus himself, glorying in it, thus writes: "For as if you had adored what we were then saying, you were suddenly taken with a desire, proceeding not from any natural cause, to come to us, prostrate yourself on the ground, embrace our knees, and use all those gestures to us which are ordinarily practised by those who adore and pray to the Gods. So that you made us also," says he, "reciprocally sanctify and adore you." Those, by Jupiter, well deserve to be pardoned, who say, they would willingly give any money for a picture in which should be presented to the life this fine story of one lying prostrate at the knees and embracing the legs of another, who mutually again adores him and makes his devout prayers to him. Nevertheless this devout service, how well soever it was ordered and composed by Colotes, received not the condign fruit he expected; for he was not declared wise; but it was only said to him: Go thy ways, and walk immortal; and understand that we also are in like manner immortal.

18. These men, knowing well in their consciences that they have used such foolish speeches, have had such motions, and such passions, dare nevertheless call others odious. And Colotes, having shown us these fine first-fruits and wise positions touching the natural senses, — that we eat meat, and not hay or forage; and that when rivers are deep and great, we pass them in boats, but when shallow and easily fordable, on foot, — cries out, "You use vain and arrogant speeches, O Socrates; you say one thing to those who come to discourse with you, and practise another." Now I would fain know what these vain and arrogant speeches of Socrates were, since he ordinarily said that he knew nothing, that he was always learning, and that he went enquiring and searching after the truth. But if, O Colotes, you had happened on such expressions of Socrates as are those which Epicurus writ to Idomeneus, "Send me then the first-fruits for the entertainment of our sacred body, for ourself and for our children: for so it comes upon me to speak:" what more arrogant and insolent words could you have used? And yet that Socrates spake otherwise than he lived, you have wonderful proofs in his gests at Delium, at Potidaea, in his behavior during the time of the Thirty Tyrants, towards Archelaus, towards the people of Athens, in his poverty, and in his death. For are not these things beseeming and answerable to the doctrine of Socrates? They would indeed, good sir, have been indubitable testimonies to show that he acted otherwise than he taught, if, having proposed pleasure for the end of life, he had led such a life as this.

19. Thus much for the calumnies he has uttered against Socrates. Colotes besides perceives not that he is himself found guilty of the same offences in regard to proofs which he objects against Socrates. For this is one of the sentences and propositions of Epicurus, that none but the wise man ought irrevocably and unchangeably to be persuaded

of any thing. Since then Colotes, even after those adorations he performed to Epicurus, became not one of the sages, let him first make these questions and interrogatories his own: How is it that being hungry he eats meat and not hay, and that he puts a robe about his body and not about a pillar, since he is not indubitably persuaded either that a robe is a robe or that meat is meat? But if he not only does these things, but also passes not over rivers, when they are great and high, on foot, and flies from wolves and serpents, not being irrevocably persuaded that any of these things is such as it appears, but yet doing every thing according to what appears to him; so likewise the opinion of Socrates concerning the senses was no obstacle to him, but that he might in like manner make use of things as they appeared to him. For it is not likely that bread appeared bread and hay hay to Colotes, because he had read those holy rules of Epicurus which came down from heaven, while Socrates through his vanity took a fancy that hay was bread and bread hay. For these wise men use better opinions and reasons than we; but to have sense, and to receive an impression from things as they appear, is common as well to the ignorant as to the wise, as proceeding from causes where there needs not the discourse of reason. And the proposition which affirms that the natural senses are not perfect, nor certain enough to cause an entire belief, hinders not that every thing may appear to us; but leaving us to make use of our senses in our actions according to that which appears, it permits us not so to give credit to them as if they were exactly true and without error. For it is sufficient that in what is necessary and commodious for use there is nothing better. But as for the science and knowledge which the soul of a philosopher desires to have concerning every thing, the senses have it not.

20. But as to this, Colotes will farther give us occasion

to speak of it hereafter, for he brings this objection against several others. Furthermore, whereas he profusely derides and despises Socrates for asking what man is, and in a youthful bravery (as he terms it) affirming that he was ignorant of it, it is manifest that he himself, who scoffs at it, never so much as thought of this matter; but Heraclitus on the contrary, as having done some great and worthy thing, said, I have been seeking myself. And of the sentences that were written in Apollo's temple at Delphi, the most excellent and most divine seems to have been this, Know thyself. And this it was which gave Socrates an occasion and beginning of doubting and enquiring into it, as Aristotle says in his Platonics. And yet this appears to Colotes ridiculous and fit to be scoffed at. And I wonder that he derides not also his master himself, who does as much whenever he writes concerning the substance of the soul and the origin of man. For if that which is compounded of both, as they themselves hold, — of the body, to wit, and the soul, — is man, he who searches into the nature of the soul consequently also searches into the nature of man, beginning from his chiefest principle. Now that the soul is very difficult to be comprehended by reason, and altogether incomprehensible by the exterior senses, let us not learn from Socrates, who is a vain-glorious and sophistical disputer, but let us take it from these wise men, who, having forged and framed the substance of the soul of somewhat hot, spiritual, and aerial, as far as to her faculties about the flesh, by which she gives heat, softness and strength to the body, proceed not to that which is the principal, but give over faint and tired by the way. For that by which she judges, remembers, loves, hates, — in a word, that which is prudent and rational, is, — say they, made afterwards of I know not what nameless quality. Now we well know, that this nameless thing is a confession of their shameful ignorance, whilst they pretend they cannot name what they are not able to understand or comprehend. But let this, as they say, be pardoned them. For it seems not to be a light and easy matter, which every one can at the first attempt find out and attain to, but has retired itself to the bottom of some very remote place, and there lies obscurely concealed. So that there is not, amongst so many words and terms as are in use, any one that can explain or show it. Socrates therefore was not a fool or blockhead for seeking and searching what himself was; but they are rather to be thought shallow coxcombs, who enquire after any other thing before this, the knowledge of which is so necessary and so hard to find. For how could he hope to gain the knowledge of other things, who has not been able to comprehend the principal part even of himself?

21. But granting a little to Colotes, that there is nothing so vain, useless, and odious as the seeking into one's self, let us ask him, what confusion of human life is in this, and how it is that a man cannot continue to live, when he comes once thus to reason and discourse in himself: "Go to now, what am I? Am I a composition, made up of soul and body; or rather a soul, serving itself and making use of the body, as an horseman using his horse is not a subject composed of horse and man? Or is every one of us the principal part of the soul, by which we understand, reason, and act; and are all the other parts, both of soul and body, only organs and utensils of this power? Or, to conclude, is there no proper substance of the soul at all apart, but is only the temperature and complexion of the body so disposed, that it has force and power to understand and live?" But Socrates does not by these questions overthrow human life, since all natural philosophers treat of the same matter. But those perhaps are the monstrous questions and enquiries that turn every thing upside down, which are in Phaedrus,* where he says, that every one

* Plato, Phaedrus, p. 230 A.

ought to examine and consider himself, whether he is a savage beast, more cautelous, outrageous, and furious than ever was the monster Typhon; or on the contrary, an animal more mild and gentle, partaking by Nature of a certain divine portion, and such as is free from pride. Now by these discourses and reasonings he overturns not the life of man, but drives from it presumption and arrogance, and those haughty and extravagant opinions and conceits he has of himself. For this is that monster Typhon, which your teacher and master has made to be so great in you by his warring against the Gods and divine men.

22. Having done with Socrates and Plato, he next attacks Stilpo. Now as for those his true doctrines and good discourses, by which he managed and governed himself, his country, his friends, and such kings and princes as loved him and esteemed him, he has not written a word; nor yet what prudence and magnanimity was in his heart, accompanied with meekness, moderation, and modesty. But having made mention of one of those little sentences he was wont in mirth and raillery to object against the sophisters, he does, without alleging any reason against it or solving the subtlety of the objection, stir up a terrible tragedy against Stilpo, saying that the life of man is subverted by him, inasmuch as he affirms that one thing cannot be predicated of another. "For how," says he, "shall we live, if we cannot style a man good, nor a man a captain, but must separately name a man a man, good good, and a captain a captain; nor can say ten thousand horsemen, or a fortified town, but only call horsemen horsemen, and ten thousand ten thousand, and so of the rest?" Now what man ever was there that lived the worse for this? Or who is there that, hearing this discourse, does not immediately perceive and understand it to be the speech of a man who rallies gallantly, and proposes to others this

logical question for the exercise of their wits? It is not, O Colotes, a great and dangerous scandal not to call man good, or not to say ten thousand horsemen; but not to call God God, and not to believe him to be God, — as you and the rest do, who will not confess that there is a Jupiter presiding over generation, or a Ceres giving laws, or a Neptune fostering the plants, — it is this separation of names that is pernicious, and fills our life with audaciousness and an atheistical contempt of the Gods. When you pluck from the Gods the names and appellations that are tied to them, you abolish also the sacrifices, mysteries, processions, and feasts. For to whom shall we offer the sacrifices preceding the tilling of the ground? To whom those for the obtaining of preservation? How shall we celebrate the Phosphoria, or torch-festivals, the Bacchanals, and the ceremonies that go before marriage, if we admit neither Bacchantes, Gods of light, Gods who protect the sown field, nor preservers of the state? For this it is that touches the principal and greatest points, being an error in things, — not in words, in the structure of propositions, or use of terms.

Now if these are the things that disturb and subvert human life, who are there that more offend and fail in language than you? For you take utterly away the whole class of namable things, which constitute the essence of language; and leave only words and their accidental objects, while you take away in the mean time the things particularly signified by them, by which are wrought disciplines, doctrines, preconceptions, intelligences, inclination, and assent, which you hold to be nothing at all.

23. But as for Stilpo, thus his argument stands. "If of a man we predicate good, and of an horse running, the predicate or thing predicated is not the same with the subject or that of which it is predicated, but the essential definition of man is one, and of good another. And again,

to be a horse differs from to be running. For being asked the definition of the one and of the other, we do not give the same for them both; and therefore those err who predicate the one of the other. For if good is the same with man, and to run the same with a horse, how is good affirmed also of food and medicine, and again (by Jupiter) to run of a lion and a dog? But if the predicate is different, then we do not rightly say that a man is good, and a horse runs." Now if Stilpo is in this exorbitant and grossly mistaken, not admitting any copulation of such things as are in the subject, or affirmed of the subject, with the subject itself; but holding that every one of them, if it is not absolutely one and the same thing with that to which it happens or of which it is spoken, ought not to be spoken or affirmed of it, — no, not even as an accident; it is nevertheless manifest, that he was only offended with some words, and opposed the usual and accustomed manner of speaking, and not that he overthrew man's life, and turned his affairs upside down.

24. Colotes then, having got rid of the old philosophers, turns to those of his own time, but without naming any of them; though he would have done better either to have reproved by name these moderns, as he did the ancients, or else to have named neither of them. But he who has so often employed his pen against Socrates, Plato, and Parmenides, evidently demonstrates that it is through cowardice he dares not attack the living, and not for any modesty or reverence, of which he showed not the least sign to those who were far more excellent than these. But his meaning is, as I suspect, to assault the Cyrenaics first, and afterwards the Academics, who are followers of Arcesilaus. For it was these who doubted of all things; but those, placing the passions and imaginations in themselves, were of opinion that the belief proceeding from them is not sufficient for the assuring and affirming of

things; but, as if it were in the siege of a town, abandoning what is without, they have shut themselves up in the passions, using only *it seems*, and not asserting *it is*, of things without. And therefore they cannot, as Colotes says of them, live or have the use of things. And then speaking comically of them, he adds: "These deny that there is a man, a horse, a wall; but say that they themselves (as it were) become walls, horses, men," or "are impressed with the images of walls, horses, or men." In which he first maliciously abuses the terms, as calumniators are usually wont to do. For though these things follow from the sayings of the Cyrenaics, yet he ought to have declared the fact as they themselves teach it. For they affirm that things then become sweet, bitter, lightsome, or dark, when each thing has in itself the natural unhindered efficacy of one of these impressions. But if honey is said to be sweet, an olive-branch bitter, hail cold, wine hot, and the nocturnal air dark, there are many beasts, things, and men that testify the contrary. For some have an aversion for honey, others feed on the branches of the olive-tree; some are scorched by hail, others cooled with wine; and there are some whose sight is dim in the sun but who see well by night. Wherefore opinion, containing itself within these impressions, remains safe and free from error; but when it goes forth and attempts to be curious in judging and pronouncing concerning exterior things, it often deceives itself, and opposes others, who from the same objects receive contrary impressions and different imaginations.

25. And Colotes seems properly to resemble those young children who are but beginning to learn their letters. For, being accustomed to learn them where they see them in their own horn-books and primers, when they see them written anywhere else, they doubt and are troubled; so those very discourses, which he praises and approves in the writ-

ings of Epicurus, he neither understands nor knows again, when they are spoken by others. For those who say that the sense is truly informed and moulded when there is presented one image round and another broken, but nevertheless permit us not to pronounce that the tower is round and the oar broken, confirm their own passions and imaginations, but they will not acknowledge and confess that the things without are so affected. But as the Cyrenaics must say that they are imprinted with the figure of a horse or of a wall, but do not speak of the horse or the wall; so also it is necessary to say that the sight is imprinted with a figure round or with three unequal sides, and not that the tower is in that manner triangular or round. For the image by which the sight is affected is broken; but the oar whence that image proceeds is not broken. Since then there is a difference between the impression and the external subject, the belief must either remain in the impression, or else — if it maintains the being in addition to the appearing — be reproved and convinced of untruth. And whereas they cry out and are offended in behalf of the sense, because the Cyrenaics say not that the thing without is hot, but that the impression made on the sense is such; is it not the same with what is said touching the taste, when they say that the thing without is not sweet, but that some impression and motion about the sense is such? And for him who says that he has received the apprehension of an human form, but perceives not whether it is a man, whence has he taken occasion so to say? Is it not from those who affirm that they receive an apprehension of a bowed figure and form, but that the sight pronounces not that the thing which was seen is bowed or round, but that a certain effigies of it is such? Yes, by Jupiter, will some one say; but I, going near the tower or touching the oar, will pronounce and affirm that the one is straight and the other has many angles and faces; but he, when he comes near it, will confess that it seems and appears so to him, and no more. Yes certainly, good sir, and more than this, when he sees and observes the consequence, that every imagination is equally worthy of belief for itself, and none for another; but that they are all in like condition. But this your opinion is quite lost, that all the imaginations are true and none false or to be disbelieved, if you think that these ought to pronounce positively of that which is without, but those you credit no farther than that they are so affected. For if they are in equal condition as to their being believed, when they are near or when they are far off, it is just that either upon all of them, or else not upon these, should follow the judgment pronouncing that a thing is. But if there is a difference in the being affected between those that are near and those that are far off, it is then false that one sense and imagination is not more express and evident than another. Therefore those which they call testimonies and counter-testimonies are nothing to the sense, but are concerned only with opinion. So, if they would have us following these to pronounce concerning exterior things, making being a judgment of opinion, and what appears an affection of sense, they transfer the judicature from that which is totally true to that which often fails.

26. But how full of trouble and contradiction in respect of one another these things are, what need is there to say at present? But the reputation of Arcesilaus, who was the best beloved and most esteemed of all the philosophers in his time, seems to have been no small eyesore to Epicurus; who says of him that, delivering nothing peculiar to himself or of his own invention, he imprinted in illiterate men an opinion and esteem of his being very knowing and learned. Now Arcesilaus was so far from desiring any glory by being a bringer-in of new opinions, and from arrogating to himself those of the ancients, that the so-

phisters of that time blamed him for attributing to Socrates, Plato, Parmenides, and Heraclitus the doctrines concerning the retention of assent, and the incomprehensibility of things; having no need so to do, but only that he might strengthen them and render them recommendable by ascribing them to such illustrious personages. For this therefore thanks to Colotes, and to every one who declares that the Academic doctrine was from higher times derived to Arcesilaus. Now as for the retention of assent and the doubting of all things, not even those who have much labored in the matter, and strained themselves to compose great books and large treatises concerning it, were ever able to stir it; but bringing at last out of the Stoa itself the cessation from all actions, as the Gorgon to frighten away the objections that came against them, they were at last quite tired and gave over. For they could not, what attempts and stirs soever they made, obtain so much from the instinct by which the appetite is moved to act, as to suffer itself to be called an assent, or to acknowledge sense for the origin and principle of its propension, but it appeared of its own accord to present itself to act, as having no need to be joined with any thing else. For against such adversaries the combat and dispute is lawful and just. And

> Such words as you have spoke, the like you may
> Expect to hear.[*]

For to speak to Colotes of instinct and consent is, I suppose, all one as to play on the harp before an ass. But to those who can give ear and conceive, it is said that there are in the soul three sorts of motions,— the imaginative, the appetitive, and the consenting. As to the imaginative or the apprehension, it cannot oe taken away, though one would. For one cannot, when things approach, avoid being informed and (as it were) moulded by them, and re-

[*] Il. XX. 250.

ceiving an impression from them. The appetite, being stirred up by the imaginative, effectually moves man to that which is proper and agreeable to his nature, just as when there is made a propension and inclination in the principal and reasonable part. Now those who withhold their assent and doubt of all things take not away this, but make use of the appetition or instinct naturally conducting every man to that which seems convenient for him. What then is the only thing that they shun? That in which is bred falsehood and deceit, — that is, opining, and precipitation in giving consent, — which is a yielding through weakness to that which appears, and has not any true utility. For action stands in need of two things, to wit, the apprehension or imagination of what is agreeable to Nature, and the instinct or appetition driving to that which is so imagined; of which, neither the one nor the other is repugnant to the retention of assent. For reason withdraws us from opinion, and not from appetition or imagination. When therefore that which is delectable seems to us to be proper for us, there is no need of opinion to move and carry us to it, but appetition immediately exerts itself, which is nothing else but the motion and inclination of the soul.

27. It is their own saying, that a man must only have sense and be flesh and blood, and pleasure will appear to be good. Wherefore also it will seem good to him who withholds his assent. For he also participates of sense, and is made of flesh and blood, and as soon as he has conceived an imagination of good, desires it and does all things that it may not escape from him; but as much as possibly he can, he will keep himself with that which is agreable to his nature, being drawn by natural and not by geometrical constraints. For these goodly, gentle, and tickling motions of the flesh are, without any teacher, attractive enough of themselves — even as these men for-

get not to say — to draw even him who will not in the least acknowledge and confess that he is softened and rendered pliable by them. "But how comes it to pass," perhaps you will say, "that he who is thus doubtful and withholds his assent hastens not away to the mountain, instead of going to the bath? Or that, rising up to go forth into the market-place, he runs not his head against the wall, but takes his way directly to the door?" Do you ask this, who hold all the senses to be infallible, and the apprehensions of the imagination certain and true? It is because the bath appears to him not a mountain, but a bath; and the door seems not a wall, but a door; and the same is to be said of every other thing. For the doctrine of retention does not pervert the sense, nor by absurd passions and motions work in it an alteration disturbing the imaginative faculty; but it only takes away opinions, and for the rest, makes use of other things according to their nature.

But it is impossible, you will say, not to consent to things that are evident; for to deny such things as are believed is more absurd than neither to deny nor affirm. Who then are they that call in question things believed, and contend against things that are evident? They who overthrow and take away divination, who say that there is not any government of Divine Providence, who deny the sun and the moon — to whom all men offer sacrifices and whom they honor and adore — to be animated. And do not you take away that which is apparent to all the world, that the young are contained in the nature of their parents? Do you not, contrary to the sense of all men, affirm that there is no medium between pleasure and pain, saying that not to be in pain is to be in the fruition of pleasure, that not to do is to suffer, and that not to rejoice is to be grieved?

28. But to let pass all the rest, what is more evident

and more generally believed by all men, than that those who are seized with melancholy distempers, and whose brain is troubled and whose wits are distracted, do, when the fit is on them and their understanding altered and transported, imagine that they see and hear things which they neither see nor hear? Whence they frequently cry out:

> Women in black arrayed bear in their hands,
> To burn mine eyes, torches and fiery brands.

And again:

> See, in her arms she holds my mother dear.*

These, and many other illusions more strange and tragical than these, — resembling those mormos and bugbears which they themselves laugh at and deride, as they are described by Empedocles to be, "with winding feet and undivided hands, bodied like ox and faced like man," — with certain other prodigious and unnatural phantoms, these men have gathered together out of dreams and the alienations of distracted minds, and affirm that none of them is a deception of the sight, a falsity, or inconsistence; but that all these imaginations are true, being bodies and figures that come from the ambient air. What thing then is there so impossible in Nature as to be doubted of, if it is possible to believe such reveries as these? For these men, supposing that such things as never any mask-maker, potter, carver of wonderful images, or skilful and all-daring painter durst join together, to deceive or make sport for the beholders, are seriously and in good earnest existent, — nay, which is more, affirming that, if they are not really so, all firmness of belief, all certainty of judgment and truth, is for ever gone, — do by these their suppositions and affirmations cast all things into obscurity, and bring fears into our judgments, and suspicions into our actions, — if the things which we apprehend, do, are familiarly

---

* Eurip. Iph. Taur. 289.

acquainted with, and have at hand are grounded on the same imagination and belief with these furious, absurd, and extravagant fancies. For the equality which they suppose to be in all apprehensions rather derogates from the credit of such as are usual and rational, than adds any belief to those that are unusual and repugnant to reason. Wherefore we know many philosophers who would rather and more willingly grant that no imagination is true than that all are so, and that would rather simply disbelieve all the men they never had conversed with, all the things they had not experimented, and all the speeches they had not heard with their own ears, than persuade themselves that any one of these imaginations, conceived by these frantic, fanatical, and dreaming persons, is true. Since then there are some imaginations which may, and others which may not be rejected, it is lawful for us to retain our assent concerning them, though there were no other cause but this discordance, which is sufficient to work in us a suspicion of things, as having nothing certain and assured, but being altogether full of obscurity and perturbation. For in the dissensions about the infinity of worlds and the nature of atoms and individuums and their inclinations, although they trouble and disturb very many, there is yet this comfort, that none of all these things that are in question is near us, but rather every one of them is far remote from sense. But as to this diffidence, perplexity, and ignorance concerning sensible things and imaginations (whether these be true or false), found even in our eyes, our ears, and our hands, what opinion does it not shock? What consent does it not turn upside down? For if men neither drunk, intoxicated, nor otherwise disturbed in their senses, but sober, sound in mind, and professedly writing of the truth and of the canons and rules by which to judge it, do in the most evident passions and motions of the senses set down either that which has no existence for true, or that which is existent for false, it is not to be wondered that a man should be silent about all things, but rather that he should give his assent to any thing; nor is it incredible that he should have no judgment about things which appear, but rather that he should have contrary judgments. For it is less to be wondered, that a man should neither affirm the one nor the other but keep himself in a mean between two opposite things, than that he should set down things repugnant and contrary to one another. For he that neither affirms nor denies, but keeps himself quiet, is less repugnant to him who affirms an opinion than he who denies it, and to him who denies an opinion than he who affirms it. Now if it is possible to withhold one's assent concerning these things, it is not impossible also concerning others, at least according to your opinion, who say that one sense does not exceed another, nor one imagination another.

29. The doctrine then of retaining the assent is not, as Colotes thinks, a fable or an invention of rash and light-headed young men who please themselves in babbling and prating; but a certain habit and disposition of men who desire to keep themselves from falling into error, not leaving the judgment at a venture to such suspected and inconstant senses, nor suffering themselves to be deceived by those who hold that in uncertain matters things which do not appear are credible and ought to be believed, when they see so great obscurity and uncertainty in things which appear. But the infinity you assert is a fable, and so indeed are the images you dream of; and he breeds in young men rashness and self-conceitedness, who writ of Pythocles, not yet eighteen years of age, that there was not in all Greece a better or more excellent nature, that he admirably well expressed his conceptions, and that he was in other respects like a woman, — praying that all these extraordinary endowments of the young man might not work him hatred

and envy. But these are sophisters and arrogant, who write so impudently and proudly against great and excellent personages. I confess indeed, that Plato, Aristotle, Theophrastus, and Democritus contradicted those who went before them; but never durst any man besides Colotes set forth with such an insolent title as this against all at once.

30. Whence it comes to pass that, like to such as have offended some Divinity, confessing his fault, he says thus towards the end of his book: " Those who have established laws and ordinances and instituted monarchies and other governments in towns and cities, have placed human life in great repose and security and delivered it from many troubles; and if any one should go about to take this away, we should lead the life of savage beasts, and should be every one ready to eat up one another as we meet." For these are the very words of Colotes, though neither justly nor truly spoken. For if any one, taking away the laws, should leave us nevertheless the doctrines of Parmenides, Socrates, Plato, and Heraclitus, we should be far from mutually devouring one another and leading the life of beasts. For we should fear dishonest things, and should for honesty alone venerate justice, the Gods, our superiors, and magistrates, believing that we have spirits and Daemons who are the guardians and superintendents of human life, esteeming all the gold that is upon and within the earth not to be equivalent to virtue; and doing that willingly by reason, as Xenocrates says, which we now do by force and through fear of the law. When then will our life become savage, unsocial, and bestial? When, the laws being taken away, there shall be left doctrines inciting men to pleasure; when the world shall be thought not to be ruled and governed by Divine Providence; when those men shall be esteemed wise who spit at honesty if it is not joined with pleasure; and when such

discourses and sentences as these shall be scoffed at and derided:

> For Justice has an eye which all things sees;

and again:

> God near us stands, and views whate'er we do;

and once more: "God, as antiquity has delivered to us, holding the beginning, middle, and end of the universe, makes a direct line, walking according to Nature. After him follows Justice, a punisher of those who have been deficient in their duties by transgressing the divine law."

For they who contemn these things as if they were fables, and think that the sovereign good of man consists about the belly, and in those other avenues by which pleasure is admitted, are such as stand in need of the law, and fear, and stripes, and some king, prince, or magistrate, having in his hand the sword of justice; to the end that they may not devour their neighbors through their gluttony, rendered confident by their atheistical impiety. For this is the life of brutes, because brute beasts know nothing better nor more honest than pleasure, understand not the justice of the Gods, nor revere the beauty of virtue; but if Nature has bestowed on them any point of courage, subtlety, or activity, they make use of it for the satisfaction of their fleshly pleasure and the accomplishment of their lusts. And the wise Metrodorus believes that this should be so, for he says: "All the fine, subtle, and ingenious inventions of the soul have been found out for the pleasure and delight of the flesh, or for the hopes of attaining to it and enjoying it, and every act which tends not to this end is vain and unprofitable." The laws being by such discourses and philosophical reasons as these taken away, there wants nothing to a beast-like life but lions' paws, wolves' teeth, oxen's paunches, and camels' necks; and these passions and doctrines do the beasts themselves, for want of speech and letters, express by their bellowings, neighings, and brayings, all their voice being for their belly and the pleasure of their flesh, which they embrace and rejoice in either present or future; unless it be perhaps some animal which naturally takes delight in chattering and garrulity.

31. No sufficient praise therefore or equivalent to their deserts can be given those who, for the restraining of such bestial passions, have set down laws, established policy and government of state, instituted magistrates and ordained good and wholesome laws. But who are they that utterly confound and abolish this? Are they not those who withdraw themselves and their followers from all part in the government? Are they not those who say that the garland of tranquillity and a reposed life are far more valuable than all the kingdoms and principalities in the world? Are they not those who declare that reigning and being a king is a mistaking the path and straying from the right way of felicity? And they write in express terms: " We are to treat how a man may best keep and preserve the end of Nature, and how he may from the very beginning avoid entering of his own free will and voluntarily upon offices of magistracy, and government over the people." And yet again, these other words are theirs: " There is no need at all that a man should tire out his mind and body to preserve the Greeks, and to obtain from them a crown of wisdom; but to eat and drink well, O Timocrates, without prejudicing, but rather pleasing the flesh." And yet in the constitution of laws and policy, which Colotes so much praises, the first and most important article is the belief and persuasion of the Gods. Wherefore also Lycurgus heretofore sanctified the Lacedaemonians, Numa the Romans, the ancient Ion the Athenians, and Deucalion universally all the Greeks, through prayers, oaths, oracles, and omens, rendering them devout and affectionate to the Gods by means of hopes and fears at once. And if you will take the

pains to travel through the world, you may find towns and cities without walls, without letters, without kings, without houses, without wealth, without money, without theatres and places of exercise; but there was never seen nor shall be seen by man any city without temples and Gods, or without making use of prayers, oaths, divinations, and sacrifices for the obtaining of blessings and benefits, and the averting of curses and calamities. Nay, I am of opinion, that a city might sooner be built without any ground to fix it on, than a commonweal be constituted altogether void of any religion and opinion of the Gods, — or being constituted, be preserved. But this, which is the foundation and ground of all laws, do these men, not going circularly about, nor secretly and by enigmatical speeches, but attacking it with the first of their most principal opinions, directly subvert and overthrow; and then afterwards, as if they were haunted by the Furies, they come and confess that they have grievously offended in thus taking away the laws, and confounding the ordinances of justice and policy, that they may not be capable of pardon. For to err in opinion, though it be not the part of wise men, is at least human; but to impute to others the errors and offences they commit themselves, how can any one declare what it is, if he forbears to give it the name it deserves?

32. For if, in writing against Antidorus or Bion the sophister, he had made mention of laws, policy, order, and justice, might not either of them have said to him, as Electra did to her mad brother Orestes:

<blockquote>Lie still at ease, poor wretch; keep in thy bed,*</blockquote>

and there cherish thy bit of flesh, leaving those to expostulate and find fault with me who have themselves lived a civil and domestic life? Now such are all those whom Colotes has reviled and railed at in his book. Amongst

---

* Eurip. Orest. 258.

whom, Democritus in his writings advises and exhorts to the learning of political science, as being the greatest of all, and to the accustoming one's self to bear fatigues, by which men attain to great wealth and honor. And as for Parmenides, he beautified and adorned his native country with most excellent laws which he there established, so that even to this day the officers every year, when they enter first on the exercise of their charges, are obliged to swear that they will observe the laws and ordinances of Parmenides. Empedocles brought to justice some of the principal of his city, and caused them to be condemned for their insolent behavior and embezzling of the public treasure, and also delivered his country from sterility and the plague — to which calamities it was before subject — by immuring and stopping up the holes of certain mountains, whence there issued an hot south wind, which overspread all the plain country and blasted it. And Socrates, after he was condemned, when his friends offered him, if he pleased, an opportunity of making his escape, absolutely refused to make use of it, that he might maintain the authority of the laws, choosing rather to die unjustly than to save himself by disobeying the laws of his country. Melissus, being captain general of his country, vanquished the Athenians in a battle at sea. Plato left in his writings excellent discourses concerning the laws, government, and policy of a commonweal; and yet he imprinted much better in the hearts and minds of his disciples and familiars, which caused Sicily to be delivered by Dion, and Thrace to be set at liberty by Pytho and Heraclides, who slew Cotys. Chabrias also and Phocion, those two great generals of the Athenians, came out of the Academy. As for Epicurus, he indeed sent certain persons into Asia to chide Timocrates, and had him removed out of the king's palace, because he had offended his brother Metrodorus; and this is written in their own books. But Plato sent of his disciples and friends, Aristonymus to the Arcadians, to set in order their commonweal, Phormio to the Eleans, and Menedemus to the Pyrrhaeans. Eudoxus gave laws to the Cnidians, and Aristotle to the Stagirites, who were both of them the intimates of Plato. And Alexander the Great demanded of Xenocrates rules and precepts for reigning well. And he who was sent to the same Alexander by the Grecians dwelling in Asia, and who most of all inflamed and stimulated him to embrace and undertake the war against the barbarian king of Persia, was Delius the Ephesian, one of Plato's familiars. Zeno, the disciple of Parmenides, having attempted to kill the tyrant Demylus, and failing in his design, maintained the doctrine of Parmenides, like pure and fine gold tried in the fire, that there is nothing which a magnanimous man ought to dread but dishonor, and that there are none but children and women, or effeminate and women-hearted men, who fear pain. For, having with his own teeth bitten off his tongue, he spit it in the tyrant's face.

33. But out of the school of Epicurus, and from among those who follow his doctrine, I will not ask what tyrant-killer has proceeded, nor yet what man valiant and victorious in feats of arms, what lawgiver, what prince, what counsellor, or what governor of the people; neither will I demand, who of them has been tormented or has died for supporting right and justice. But which of all these sages has for the benefit and service of his country undertaken so much as one voyage at sea, gone of an embassy, or expended a sum of money? What record is there extant of one civil action in matter of government, performed by any of you? And yet, because Metrodorus went down one day from the city as far as the haven of Piraeus, taking a journey of forty stadia to assist Mithres a Syrian, one of the king of Persia's court who had been arrested and taken prisoner, he writ of it to every one and in all his

letters, Epicurus also highly magnifying and extolling this wonderful voyage. What value then, think you, would they have put upon it, if they had done such an act as Aristotle did, who procured the restoration and rebuilding of Stagira, the town of his nativity, after it had been destroyed by King Philip? Or as Theophrastus, who twice delivered his city, when possessed and held by tyrants? Would not the river Nile sooner have given over to bear the paper-reed, than they have been weary of writing their brave exploits?

And it is not the greatest indignity, that, of so many sects of philosophers as have been extant, they alone should enjoy the benefits that are in cities, without having ever contributed to them any thing of their own; but far worse is it that, while there are not even any tragical or comical poets who do not always endeavor to do or say some good thing or other in defence of the laws and policy, these men, if peradventure they write, write of policy, that we may not concern ourselves in the government of the commonweal, — of rhetoric, that we may not perform an act of eloquence, — and of royalty, that we may shun the living and conversing with kings. Nor do they ever name any of those great personages who have intermeddled in civil affairs, but only to scoff at them and abolish their glory. Thus they say that Epaminondas had something of good, but that very little, or μικκόν, for that is the very word they use. They moreover call him iron-hearted, and ask what ailed him that he went marching his army through all Peloponnesus, and why he did not rather keep himself quiet at home with a night-cap on his head, employed only in cherishing and making much of his belly. But methinks I ought not in this place to omit what Metrodorus writ in his book of Philosophy, when, utterly abjuring all meddling in the management of the state, he said thus: "Some, through an abundance of vanity and arrogance, have so deep an insight into the business of it, that in treating about the precepts of good life and virtue, they suffer themselves to be carried away with the very same desires as were Lycurgus and Solon." What is this? Was it then vanity and abundance of vanity, to set free the city of Athens, to render Sparta well-policied and governed by wholesome laws, that young men might do nothing licentiously, nor get children upon common courtesans and whores, and that riches, delights, intemperance, and dissolution might no longer bear sway and have command in cities, but law and justice? For these were the desires of Solon. To this Metrodorus, by way of scorn and contumely, adds this conclusion: "It is then very well beseeming a free-born gentleman to laugh heartily, as at other men, so especially at these Solons and Lycurguses." But such a one, O Metrodorus, is not a gentleman, but a servile and dissolute person, and deserves to be scourged, not with that whip which is for free-born persons, but with that scourge strung with ankle-bones, with which those gelded sacrificers called Galli were wont to be chastised, when they failed of performing their duty in the ceremonies and sacrifices of the Goddess Cybele, the great Mother of the Gods.

34. But that they made war not against the lawgivers but against the laws themselves, one may hear and understand from Epicurus. For in his questions, he asks himself, whether a wise man, being assured that it will not be known, will do any thing that the laws forbid. To which he answers: "That is not so easy to determine simply," — that is, "I will do it indeed, but I am not willing to confess it." And again, I suppose, writing to Idomeneus, he exhorts him not to make his life a slave to the laws or to the opinions of men, unless it be to avoid the trouble they prepare, by the scourge and chastisement, so near at hand. If then those who abolish the laws, governments, and

policies of men subvert and destroy human life, and if Metrodorus and Epicurus do this, by dehorting and withdrawing their friends from concerning themselves in public affairs, by hating those who intermeddle in them, by reviling the first most wise lawgivers, and by advising contempt of the laws provided there is no fear and danger of the whip and punishment, I do not see that Colotes has brought so many false accusations against the other philosophers as he has alleged and advanced true ones against the writings and doctrines of Epicurus.

PLUTARCH'S CONSOLATORY LETTER TO HIS WIFE.

PLUTARCH TO HIS WIFE: ALL HEALTH.

1. As for the messenger you despatched to tell me of the death of my little daughter, it seems he missed his way as he was going to Athens. But when I came to Tanagra, I heard of it by my niece. I suppose by this time the funeral is over. I wish that whatever has been done may create you no dissatisfaction, as well now as hereafter. But if you have designedly let any thing alone, depending upon my judgment, thinking better to determine the point if I were with you, I pray let it be without ceremony and timorous superstition, which I know are far from you.

2. Only, dear wife, let you and me bear our affliction with patience. I know very well and do comprehend what loss we have had; but if I should find you grieve beyond measure, this would trouble me more than the thing itself. For I had my birth neither from a stock nor a stone;* and you know it full well, I having been assistant to you in the education of so many children, which we brought up at home under our own care. This daughter was born after four sons, when you were longing to bear a daughter; which made me call her by your own name. Therefore I know she was particularly dear to you. And grief must have a peculiar pungency in a mind tenderly affectionate to children, when you call to mind how naturally witty and

---

* See Il. XXII. 126.

innocent she was, void of anger, and not querulous. She was naturally mild, and compassionate to a miracle. And her gratitude and kindness not only gave us delight, but also manifested her generous nature; for she would pray her nurse to give suck, not only to other children, but to her very playthings, as it were courteously inviting them to her table, and making the best cheer for them she could.

3. Now, my dear wife, I see no reason why these and the like things, which delighted us so much when she was alive, should upon remembrance of them afflict us when she is dead. But I also fear lest, while we cease from sorrowing, we should forget her; as Clymene said,

> I hate the handy horned bow,
> And banish youthful pastimes now;

because she would not be put in mind of her son by the exercises he had been used to. For Nature always shuns such things as are troublesome. But since our little daughter afforded all our senses the sweetest and most charming pleasure; so ought we to cherish her memory, which will conduce many ways — or rather many fold — more to our joy than our grief. And it is but just, that the same arguments which we have oft-times used to others should prevail upon ourselves at this so seasonable a time, and that we should not supinely sit down and overwhelm the joys which we have tasted with a multiplicity of new griefs.

4. Moreover, they who were present at the funeral report this with admiration, that you neither put on mourning, nor disfigured yourself or any of your maids; neither were there any costly preparations nor magnificent pomp; but all things were managed with silence and moderation in the presence of our relatives alone. And it seemed not strange to me that you, who never used richly

to dress yourself for the theatre or other public solemnities, esteeming such magnificence vain and useless even in matters of delight, have now practised frugality on this sad occasion. For a virtuous woman ought not only to preserve her purity in riotous feasts, but also to think thus with herself, that the tempest of the mind in violent grief must be calmed by patience, which does not intrench on the natural love of parents towards their children, as many think, but only struggles against the disorderly and irregular passions of the mind. For we allow this love of children to discover itself in lamenting, wishing for, and longing after them when they are dead. But the excessive inclination to grief, which carries people on to unseemly exclamations and furious behavior, is no less culpable than luxurious intemperance. Yet reason seems to plead in its excuse; because, instead of pleasure, grief and sorrow are ingredients of the crime. What can be more irrational, I pray, than to check excessive laughter and joy, and yet to give a free course to rivers of tears and sighs, which flow from the same fountain? Or, as some do, quarrel with their wives for using artificial helps to beauty, and in the mean time suffer them to shave their heads, wear the mournful black, sit disconsolate, and lie in pain? And, which is worst of all, if their wives at any time chastise their servants or maids immoderately, they will interpose and hinder them, but at the same time suffering them to torment and punish themselves most cruelly, in a case which peculiarly requires their greatest tenderness and humanity?

5. But between us, dear wife, there never was any occasion for such contests, nor, I think, will there ever be. For there is no philosopher of our acquaintance who is not in love with your frugality, both in apparel and diet; nor a citizen, to whom the simplicity and plainness of your dress is not conspicuous, both at religious sacrifices

and public shows in the theatre. Formerly also you discovered on the like occasion a great constancy of mind, when you lost your eldest son; and again, when the lovely Chaeron left us. For I remember, when the news was brought me of my son's death, as I was returning home with some friends and guests who accompanied me to my house, when they beheld all things in order, and observed a profound silence everywhere, — as they afterwards declared to others, — they thought no such calamity had happened, but that the report was false. So discreetly had you settled the affairs of the house at that time, when no small confusion and disorder might have been expected. And yet you gave this son suck yourself, and endured the lancing of your breast, to prevent the ill effects of a contusion. These are things worthy of a generous woman, and one that loves her children.

6. Whereas, we see most other women receive their children in their hands as playthings with a feminine mirth and jollity; and afterwards, if they chance to die, they will drench themselves in the most vain and excessive sorrow. Not that this is any effect of their love, for that gentle passion acts regularly and discreetly; but it rather proceeds from a desire of vain-glory, mixed with a little natural affection, which renders their mourning barbarous, brutish, and extravagant. Which thing Aesop knew very well, when he told the story of Jupiter's giving honors to the Gods; for, it seems, Grief also made her demands, and it was granted that she should be honored, but only by those who were willing of their own accord to do it. And indeed, this is the beginning of sorrow. Everybody first gives her free access; and after she is once rooted and settled and become familiar, she will not be forced thence with their best endeavors. Therefore she must be resisted at her first approach; nor must we surrender the fort to her by any exterior signs, whether of apparel, or

shaving the hair, or any other such like symptoms of mournful weakness; which happening daily, and wounding us by degrees with a kind of foolish bashfulness, at length do so enervate the mind, and reduce her to such straits, that quite dejected and besieged with grief, the poor timorous wretch dare not be merry, or see the light, or eat and drink in company. This inconvenience is accompanied by a neglect of the body, carelessness of anointing and bathing, with whatsoever else relates to the elegancy of human life. Whereas, on the contrary, the soul, when it is disordered, ought to receive aid from the vigor of a healthful body. For the sharpest edge of the soul's grief is rebated and slacked, when the body is in tranquillity and ease, like the sea in a calm. But where, from an ill course of diet, the body becomes dry and hot, so that it cannot supply the soul with commodious and serene spirits, but only breathes forth melancholy vapors and exhalations, which perpetually annoy her with grief and sadness; there it is difficult for a man (though never so willing and desirous) to recover the tranquillity of his mind, after it has been disturbed with so many evil affections.

7. But that which is most to be dreaded in this case does not at all affrighten me, to wit, the visits of foolish women, and their accompanying you in your tears and lamentations; by which they sharpen your grief, not suffering it either of itself or by the help of others to fade and vanish away. For I am not ignorant how great a combat you lately entered, when you assisted the sister of Theon, and opposed the women who came running in with horrid cries and lamentations, bringing fuel as it were to her passion. Assuredly, when men see their neighbor's house on fire, every one contributes his utmost to quench it; but when they see the mind inflamed with furious passion, they bring fuel to nourish and increase the flame. When a man's

eye is in pain, he is not suffered to touch it, though the inflammation provoke him to it, nor will they that are near him meddle with it. But he who is galled with grief sits and exposes his distemper to every one, like waters that all may poach in; and so that which at first seemed a light itching or trivial smart, by much fretting and provoking, becomes a great and almost incurable disease. But I know very well that you will arm yourself against these inconveniences.

8. Moreover, I would have you endeavor to call often to mind that time when our daughter was not as yet born to us, and when we had no cause to complain of Fortune. Then, joining that time with this, argue thus with yourself, that we are now in the same condition as then. Otherwise, dear wife, we shall seem discontented at the birth of our little daughter, if we own that our circumstances were better before her birth. But the two years of her life are by no means to be forgotten by us, but to be numbered amongst our blessings, in that they afforded us an agreeable pleasure. Nor must we esteem a small good for a great evil; nor ungratefully complain against Fortune for what she has actually given us, because she has not added what we wished for. Certainly, to speak reverently of the Gods, and to bear our lot with an even mind without accusing Fortune, always brings with it a fair reward. But he who in such a case calls prosperous things to mind, and turning his thoughts from dark and melancholy objects, fixes them on bright and cheerful ones, will either quite extinguish his grief, or by allaying it with contrary sentiments, will render it weak and feeble. For, as perfumes bring delight to the nose, and arm it against ill scents, so the remembrance of happiness gives necessary assistance in adversity to those who avoid not the recollection of their past prosperity nor complain at all against Fortune. For certainly it would little become us to accuse

our life, if like a book it hath but one little blot in it, though all the rest be fair and clean.

9. For you have oftentimes heard, that true happiness consists in the right discourses and counsels of the mind, tending to its own constant establishment, and that the changes of Fortune are of no great importance to the felicity of our life. But even if we must also be governed by exterior things, and with the common sort of people have a regard to casualties, and suffer any kind of men to be judges of our happiness, however, do not you take notice of the tears and moans of such as visit you at present, condoling your misfortunes; for their tears and sighs are but of course. But rather, do you consider how happy every one of them esteems you for the children you have, the house you keep, and the life you lead. For it would be an ill thing, while others covet your fortune, though sullied with this affliction, that you should exclaim against what you enjoy, and not be sensible, from the taste of affliction, how grateful you ought to be for the happiness which remains untouched. Or, like some who, collecting all the defective verses of Homer, pass over at the same time so many excellent parts of his poems, so shall we peevishly complain of and reckon up the inconveniences of our life, neglecting at the same time promiscuously the benefits thereof? Or, shall we imitate covetous and sordid misers, who, having heaped together much riches, never enjoy what they have in possession, but bewail it if it chance to be lost?

But if you lament the poor girl because she died unmarried and without offspring, you have wherewithal to comfort yourself, in that you are defective in none of these things, having had your share. And these are not to be esteemed at once great evils where they are wanted, and small benefits where they are enjoyed. But so long as she is gone to a place where she feels no pain, what need is there of our grief? For what harm can befall us from her, when she is free from all hurt? And surely the loss of even great things abates the grief, when it is come to this, that we have no need or use of them. But thy Timoxena was deprived but of small matter; for she had no knowledge but of such, neither took she delight but in such small things. But for that which she never was sensible of, and which did not so much as once enter into her thoughts, how can you say it is taken from her?

10. As for what you hear others say, who persuade the vulgar that the soul, when once freed from the body, suffers no inconvenience or evil nor is sensible at all, I know that you are better grounded in the doctrines delivered down to us from our ancestors, as also in the sacred mysteries of Bacchus, than to believe such stories; for the religious symbols are well known to us who are of the fraternity. Therefore be assured, that the soul, being incapable of death, is affected in the same manner as birds that are kept in a cage. For if she has been a long time educated and cherished in the body, and by long custom has been made familiar with most things of this life, she will (though separable) return again, and at length enter the body; nor ceaseth it by new births now and then to be entangled in the chances and events of this life. For do not think that old age is therefore evil spoken of and blamed, because it is accompanied with wrinkles, gray hairs, and weakness of body. But this is the most troublesome thing in old age, that it maketh the soul weak in its remembrance of divine things, and too earnest for things relating to the body; thus it bendeth and boweth, retaining that form which it took of the body. But that which is taken away in youth, being more soft and tractable, soon returns to its native vigor and beauty. Just as fire that is quenched, if it be forthwith kindled again, sparkles and burns out immediately. . . . So most speedily

'Twere good to pass the gates of death,*

before too great a love of bodily and earthly things be engendered in the soul, and it become soft and tender by being used to the body, and (as it were) by charms and potions incorporated with it.

11. But the truth of this will appear in the laws and traditions received from our ancestors. For when children die, no libations nor sacrifices are made for them, nor any other of those ceremonies which are wont to be performed for the dead. For infants have no part of earth or earthly affections. Nor do we hover or tarry about their sepulchres or monuments, or sit by when their dead bodies are exposed. The laws of our country forbid this, and teach us that it is an impious thing to lament for those whose souls pass immediately into a better and more divine state. Wherefore, since it is safer to give credit to our traditions than to call them in question, let us comply with the custom in outward and public behavior, and let our interior be more unpolluted, pure, and holy. . . .

* See Il. V. 646; XXIII. 71.

OF THE THREE SORTS OF GOVERNMENT, MONARCHY, DEMOCRACY, AND OLIGARCHY.

1. As I was considering with myself to bring forth and propose to the judgment of this worthy company the discourse I held yesterday in your presence, methought I heard political virtue — not in the illusion of a dream, but in a true and real vision — say thus to me:

A golden ground is laid for sacred songs.

We have already laid the foundation of the discourse by persuading and exhorting persons to concern themselves in managing the affairs of the commonweal, and now we proceed to build upon it the doctrine which is due after such an exhortation. For after a man has received an admonition and exhortation to deal in the affairs of the state, there ought consequently to be given him the precepts of government, following and observing which, he may, as much as it is possible for a man to do, profit the public, and in the mean time honestly prosecute his own affairs with such safety and honor as shall be meet for him.

There is first then one point to be discoursed, which, as it is precedent to what we have hereafter to say, so depends on what we have said before. Now this is, what sort of policy and government is best? For as there are many sorts of lives in particular men, so also are there in people and states; and the life of a people or state is its policy and government. It is therefore necessary to declare which is the best, that a statesman may choose it from among the rest, or, if that is not possible for him to do, he may at least take that which has the nearest resemblance to the best.

2. Now there is one signification of this word policy (πολιτεία) which imports as much as *burgess-ship*, that is, a participation in the rights and privileges belonging to a town, city, or borough; as when we say that the Megarians, by an edict of their city, presented Alexander the Great with their *policy*, that is, their *burgess-ship*, and that, Alexander laughing at the offer they made him of it, they answered him, that they had never decreed that honor to any but Hercules and now to himself. This he wondering to hear accepted their present, thinking it honorable inasmuch as it was rare. The life also of a political person, who is concerned in the government of the commonweal, is called policy, as when we praise the policy of Pericles or Bias, that is, the manner of their government, and on the contrary, blame that of Hyperbolus and Cleon. Some moreover there are, who call a great and memorable action performed in the administration of a commonweal a policy, such as is the distribution of money, the suppressing of a war, the introduction of some notable decree worthy to be kept in perpetual memory. In which signification it is a common manner of speaking to say, This man to-day has done a policy, if he has peradventure effected some remarkable matter in the government of the state.

3. Besides all these significations there is yet another, that is, the order and state by which a commonweal is governed, and by which affairs are managed and administered. According to which we say that there are three sorts of policy or public government, — to wit, Monarchy, which is regality or kingship, Oligarchy, which is the government by peers and nobles, and Democracy, which is a popular or (as we term it) a free state. Now all these are

mentioned by Herodotus in his Third Book,* where he compares them one with another. And these seem to be the most general of all; for all other sorts are, as it were, the depravation and corruption of these, either by defect or excess; as it is in the first consonances of music, when the strings are either too straight or too slack.

Now these three sorts of government have been distributed amongst the nations that have had the mightiest and the greatest empire. Thus the Persians enjoyed regality or kingship, because their king had full absolute power in all things, without being liable to render an account to any one. The Spartans had a council consisting of a small number, and those the best and most considerable persons in the city, who despatched all affairs. The Athenians maintained popular government free and exempt from any other mixture. In which administration when there are any faults, their transgressions and exorbitances are styled tyrannies, oppressions of the stronger, unbridled licentiousness of the multitude. That is, when the prince who has the royalty permits himself to outrage whomever he pleases, and will not suffer any remonstrance to be made him concerning it, he becomes a tyrant; when a few lords or senators in whose hands the government is arrive at that arrogance as to contemn all others, they turn oppressors; and when a popular state breaks forth into disobedience and levelling, it runs into anarchy and unmeasurable liberty: and in a word, all of them together will be rashness and folly.

4. Even then as a skilful musician will make use of all sorts of instruments, and play on every one of them, accommodating himself in such manner as its quality can bear and as shall be fit to make it yield the sweetest sound, but yet, if he will follow Plato's counsel, will lay aside fiddles, many-stringed virginals, psalteries, and harps, pre-

* Herod. III. 82.

ferring before all other the lute and bandore; in like manner, an able statesman will dexterously manage the Laconic and Lycurgian seignory or oligarchy, fitting and accommodating his companions who are of equal authority with him, and by little and little drawing and reducing them to be managed by himself. He will also carry himself discreetly in a popular state, as if he had to deal with an instrument of many and differently sounding strings, one while letting down and remitting some things, and again extending others, as he shall see his opportunity and find it most convenient for the government, to which he will vigorously apply himself, well knowing when and how he ought to resist and contradict; but yet, if he might be permitted to make his choice from amongst all sorts of government, as from so many musical instruments, he would not, if Plato's advice might be taken, choose any other but monarchy or regal authority, as being that which is indeed alone able to support that most perfect and most lofty note of virtue, without suffering him either by force or by grace and favor, to frame himself for advantage and gain. For all other sorts of governments do in a manner as much rule a statesman as he does them, no less carrying him than they are carried by him; forasmuch as he has no certain power over those from whom he has his authority, but is very often constrained to cry out in these words of the poet Aeschylus, which King Demetrius, surnamed the Town-taker, often alleged against Fortune, after he had lost his kingdom:

> Thou mad'st me first, and now undoest me quite.

WHETHER THE ATHENIANS WERE MORE RENOWNED FOR THEIR WARLIKE ACHIEVEMENTS OR FOR THEIR LEARNING.

1. . . . . THESE things he rightly spoke to the commanders that accompanied him, to whom he opened the way for future performances, while he expelled the barbarians and restored Greece to her ancient liberty. And the same thing may be said to those that magnify themselves for their writings. For if there were none to act, there would be none to write. Take away the political government of Pericles, and the naval trophies of Phormio at Rhium, and the brave achievements of Nicias at Cythera, Megara, and Corinth, Demosthenes's Pylos, and the four hundred captives taken by Cleon, Tolmides sailing round the Peloponnesus, and Myronidas vanquishing the Boeotians at Oenophyta: and you murder Thucydides. Take away the daring braveries of Alcibiades in the Hellespont, and of Thrasyllus near Lesbos; the dissolution of the oligarchy by Theramenes; Thrasybulus, Archippus, and the seventy that from Phylae ventured to attack the Lacedaemonian tyranny; and Conon again enforcing Athens to take the sea: and then there is an end of Cratippus. For as for Xenophon, he was his own historian, relating the exploits of the army under his command, but saying that Themistogenes the Syracusan had written the history of them; dedicating the honor of his writing to another, that writing of himself as of another, he might gain the more credit. But all the other historians, as the Clinodemi,

Diyli, Philochorus, Philarchus, were but the actors of other men's deeds, as of so many plays, while they compiled the acts of kings and great generals, and thrusting themselves into the memory of their fame, partake of a kind of lustre and light from them. For there is a certain shadow of glory which reflects from those that act to those that write, while the actions of another appear in the discourse as in a mirror.

2. But this city was the mother and charitable nurse of many other arts and sciences; some of which she first invented and illustrated, to others she gave both efficacy, honor, and increase. More especially to her is painting beholden for its first invention, and the perfection to which it has attained. For Apollodorus the painter, who first invented the mixing of colors and the softening of shadows, was an Athenian. Over whose works there is this inscription:

> 'Tis no hard thing to reprehend me;
> But let the men that blame me mend me.

Then for Euphranor, Nicias, Asclepiodorus, and Plistaenetus the brother of Phidias, some of them painted the victories, others the battles of great generals, and some of them heroes themselves. Thus Euphranor, comparing his own Theseus with another drawn by Parrhasius, said, that Parrhasius's Theseus ate roses, but his fed upon beef. For Parrhasius's piece was daintily painted, and perhaps it might be something like the original. But he that beheld Euphranor's Theseus might well exclaim,

> Race of Erechtheus bold and stout,
> Whom Pallas bred.*

Euphranor also painted with great spirit the battle of Mantinea, fought by the cavalry between the Athenians and Epaminondas. The story was thus. The Theban

---

* Il. II. 547.

Epaminondas, puffed up with his victory at Leuctra, and designing to insult and trample over fallen Sparta and the glory of that city, with an army of seventy thousand men invaded and laid waste the Lacedaemonian territory, stirred up the subject people to revolt, and not far from Mantinea provoked the Spartans to battle; but they neither being willing nor indeed daring to encounter him, being in expectation of a reinforcement from Athens, Epaminondas dislodged in the night-time, and with all the secrecy imaginable fell into the Lacedaemonian territory; and missed but little of taking Sparta itself, being destitute of men to defend it. But the allies of the Lacedaemonians made haste to its relief; whereupon Epaminondas made a show as if he would again return to spoiling and laying waste the country; and by this means deceiving and amusing his enemies, he retreats out of Laconia by night, and with swift marches coming upon the Mantineans unexpectedly, at what time they were deliberating to send relief to Sparta, presently commanded the Thebans to prepare to storm the town. Immediately the Thebans, who had a great conceit of their warlike courage, took their several posts, and began to surround the city. This put the Mantineans into a dismal consternation, and filled the whole city with dreadful outcries and hurly-burly, as being neither able to withstand such a torrent of armed men ready to rush in upon them, nor having any hopes of succor.

But at the same time, and by good fortune, the Athenians came down from the hills into the plains of Mantinea, not knowing any thing of the critical moment that required more speedy haste, but marching leisurely along. However, so soon as they were informed of the danger of their allies, by one that scouted out from the rest, though but few in respect of the number of their enemies, single of themselves, and tired with their march, yet they presently drew up into order of battle; and the cavalry charging up to the very gates of Mantinea, there happened a terrible battle between the horse on both sides; wherein the Athenians got the better, and so saved Mantinea out of Epaminondas's hands. This conflict was painted by Euphranor, and you see in the picture with what strength, what fury and vigor they fought. And yet I do not believe that any one will compare the skill of the painter with that of the general; or would endure that any one should prefer the picture before the trophy, or the imitation before the truth itself.

3. Though indeed Simonides calls painting silent poetry, and poetry speaking painting. For those actions which painters set forth as they were doing, those history relates when they were done. And what the one sets forth in colors and figures, the other relates in words and sentences; only they differ in the materials and manner of imitation. However, both aim at the same end, and he is accounted the best historian, who can make the most lively descriptions both of persons and passions. Therefore Thucydides always drives at this perspicuity, to make the hearer (as it were) a spectator, and to inculcate the same passions and perturbations of mind into his readers as they were in who beheld the causes of those effects. For Demosthenes embattling the Athenians near the rocky shore of Pylos; Brasidas hastening the pilot to run the ship aground, then going to the rowers' seats, then wounded and fainting, sinking down in that part of the vessel where the oars could not trouble him; the land fight of the Spartans from the sea, and the sea engagement of the Athenians from the land; then again in the Sicilian war, both a land fight and sea engagement, so fought that neither had the better,*
. . . So that if we may not compare painters with generals, neither must we equal historians to them.

---

* The text of several lines which follow here is hopelessly corrupt, but it is evident that Plutarch refers to the description in Thucyd. VII. 71. (G.)

Thersippus of Eroeadae brought the first news of the victory at Marathon, as Heraclides of Pontus relates. But most report that Eucles, running armed with his wounds recking from the fight, and falling through the door into the first house he met, expired with only these words in his mouth, "God save ye, we are well." Now this man brought the news himself of the success of a fight wherein he was present in person. But suppose that any of the goat-keepers or herd-men had beheld the combat from some high hill at a distance, and seeing the success of that great achievement, greater than by words can be expressed, should have come to the city without any wound or blood about him, and should have claimed the honors done to Cynaegirus, Callimachus, and Polyzelus, for giving an account of their wounds, their bravery and deaths, wouldst thou not have thought him impudent above impudence itself; seeing that the Lacedaemonians gave the messenger that brought the news of the victory at Mantinea* no other reward than a quantity of victuals from the public mess? But historians are (as it were) well-voiced relators of the actions of great men, who add grace and beauty and dint of wit to their relations, and to whom they that first light upon them and read them are indebted for their pleasing tidings. And being read, they are applauded for transmitting to posterity the actions of those that do bravely. For words do not make actions, though we give them the hearing.

4. But there is a certain grace and glory of the poetic art, when it resembles the grandeur of the actions themselves; according to that of Homer,

> And many falsities he did unfold,
> That looked like truth, so smoothly were they told. †

It is reported also, that when one of his familiar friends said to Menander, The feasts of Bacchus are at hand, and

---

* Thucyd. V. 73.   † Odyss. XIX. 203.

thou hast made ne'er a comedy; he made him this answer: By all the Gods, I have made a comedy, for I have laid my plot; and there remains only to make the verses and measures to it. So that the poets themselves believe the actions to be more necessary than the words, and the first things to be considered. Corinna likewise, when Pindar was but a young man and made too daring a use of his eloquence, gave him this admonition, that he was no poet, for that he never composed any fables, which was the chiefest office of poetry; in regard that strange words, figures, metaphors, songs, and measures were invented to give a sweetness to things. Which admonition Pindar laying up in his mind, wrote a certain ode which thus begins:

> Shall I Ismenus sing,
> Or Melia, that from spindles all of gold
> Her twisted yarn unwinds,
> Or Cadmus, that most ancient king,
> Or else the sacred race of Sparti bold,
> Or Hercules, that far in strength transcends.

Which when he showed to Corinna, she with a smile replied: When you sow, you must scatter the seed with your hand, not empty the whole sack at once. And indeed we find that Pindar intermixes in his poetic numbers a collection of all sorts of fables. Now that poetry employs itself in mythology is agreed by Plato likewise. For a fable is the relation of a false story resembling truth, and therefore very remote from real actions; for relation is the image of action, as fable is the image of relation. And therefore they that feign actions fall as far behind historians as they that speak differ from those that act.

5. Athens therefore never bred up any true artist in epic or lyric verse. For Cinesias was a troublesome writer of dithyrambics, a person of mean parentage and of no repute; and being jeered and derided by the comedians, proved very unfortunate in the pursuit of fame.

Now for the dramatic poets, the Athenians looked upon comedy to be so ignoble and troublesome, that they published a law that no Areopagite should make any comedies. But tragedy flourished and was cried up, and with wonder and admiration heard and beheld by all people in those days, deceiving them with fables and the display of various passions; whereby, as Gorgias says, he that deceived was more just than he that deceived not, and he that was deceived was wiser than he who was not deceived. He that deceived was more just, because it was no more than what he pretended to do; and he that was deceived was wiser, for that he must be a man of no sense that is not taken with the sweetness of words. And yet what benefit did those fine tragedies procure the Athenians? But the shrewdness and cunning of Themistocles walled the city, the industry of Pericles adorned their citadel, and Cimon advanced them to command their neighbors. But as for the wisdom of Euripides, the eloquence of Sophocles, the lofty style of Aeschylus, what calamity did they avert from the city; or what renown or fame did they bring to the Athenians? Is it fitting then that dramatic poems should be compared with trophies, the stage with the generals' office, or lists of dramas with noble achievements?

6. Would ye that we should introduce the men themselves carrying before them the marks and signals of their own actions, permitting them to enter in order, like the actors upon the stage? But then poets must go before them, with flutes and lyres, saying and singing:

> Far from our choirs who in this lore's unskilled,
> Or does not cherish pure and holy thoughts,
> Nor views nor joins the Muses' generous rites,
> Nor is perfected in the Bacchic tongue,
> With which Cratinus bull-devourer sang.*

And then there must be scenes, and vizards, and altars, and versatile machines. There must be also the tragedy-

---

* Aristophanes, Frogs, 354.

actors, the Nicostrati, Callippidae, Menisci, Theodori, Poli, the dressers, and sedan-men of tragedy, — like those of some sumptuously apparelled lady, or rather like the painters, gilders, and colorers of statues, — together with a costly preparation of vessels, vizards, purple coats, and machines, attended by an unruly rabble of dancers and guards; and let all the preparation be exceeding costly and magnificent. A Lacedaemonian once, beholding all this, not improperly said: How strangely are the Athenians mistaken, consuming so much cost and labor upon ridiculous trifles; that is to say, wasting the expenses of navies and of victualling whole armies upon the stage. For if you compute the cost of those dramatic preparations, you will find that the Athenians spent more upon their Bacchae, Oedipuses, and Antigone, and the woes of Medea and Electra, than in their wars against the barbarians for liberty and extending their empire. For their general oft-times led forth the soldiers to battle, commanding them to make provisions only of such food as needed not the tedious preparation of fire. And indeed their admirals and captains of their ships went aboard without any other provision than meal, onions, and cheese. Whereas the masters of the choruses, feeding their dancers with eels, lettuce, the kernels of garlic, and marrow, feasted them for a long time, exercising their voices and pleasing their palates by turns. And as for these captains, if they were overcome, it was their misfortune to be contemned and hissed at; and if they were victors, there was neither tripod, nor consecrated ornament of victory, as Demetrius says, but a life prolonged among cables, and an empty house for a tomb. For this is the tribute of poetry, and there is nothing more splendid to be expected from it.

7. Now then let us consider the great generals as they approach, to whom, as they pass by, all those must rise up and pay their salutations who have never been famous for

any great action, military or civil, and were never furnished with daring boldness nor purity of wisdom for such enterprises, nor initiated by the hand of Miltiades that overthrew the Medes, or of Themistocles that vanquished the Persians. This is the martial gang, at once combating with phalanxes by land, and engaging with navies by sea, and laden with the spoils of both. Give ear, Alala, daughter of War, to this same prologue of swords and spears.

Hasten to death, when for your country vowed,

as Epaminondas said, — for your country, your sepulchres, and your altars, throwing yourselves into most noble and illustrious combats. Their victories methinks I see approaching toward me, not dragging after them a goat or ox for a reward, nor crowned with ivy and smelling of the dregs of wine. But whole cities, islands, continents, and colonies well peopled are their rewards, being surrounded with trophies and spoils of all sorts. Whose statues and symbols of honor are Parthenons, a hundred feet in length, South-walls, houses for ships, the Propylaea, the Chersonesus, and Amphipolis. Marathon displays the victory of Miltiades, and Salamis the glory of Themistocles, triumphing over the ruins of a thousand vessels. The victory of Cimon brings away a hundred Phoenician galleys from the Eurymedon. And the victory of Cleon and Demosthenes brings away the shield of Brasidas, and the captive soldiers in chains from Sphacteria. The victory of Conon and Thrasybulus walls the city, and brings the people back at liberty from Phylae. The victory of Alcibiades near Sicily restores the languishing condition of the city; and Greece beheld Ionia raised again by the victories of Neleus and Androclus in Lydia and Caria.

If you ask what benefit every one of the rest procured to the city; one will answer Lesbos, another Samos, another Cyprus, another the Pontus Euxinus, another five hundred galleys with three banks of oars, and another ten thousand talents, the rewards of fame and trophies won. For these victories the city observes public anniversary festivals, for these victories she sacrifices to the Gods; not for the victories of Aeschylus and Sophocles, not because Carcinus was victorious * with his Aerope, or Astydamas with his Hector. But upon the sixth of September, even to this day, the Athenians celebrate a festival in memory of the fight at Marathon. Upon the sixteenth of the same month libations are poured in remembrance of the naval victory won by Chabrias near Naxos. Upon the twelfth they offer thanksgiving sacrifices for the recovery of their liberty. For upon that day they returned back from Phylae. The third of the same month they won the battle of Plataea. The sixteenth of April was consecrated to Diana, when the moon appeared in the full to the Greeks victorious at Salamis. The twelfth of June was made sacred by the battle of Mantinea, wherein the Athenians, when their confederates were routed and fled, alone by themselves obtained the victory and triumph over their victorious enemies. Such actions as these procured honor and veneration and grandeur to the city; for these acts it was that Pindar called Athens the support of Greece; not because she had set the fortune of the Greeks upright by the tragedies of Phrynichus and Thespis, but because (as he says) "near Artemisium the Athenian youth laid the first glorious foundation of freedom;" and afterwards fixing it upon the adamantine pillars of Salamis, Mycale, and Plataea, they multiplied their felicity to others.

8. But as for the writings of the poets, they are mere bubbles. But rhetoricians and orators indeed have something in them that renders them in some measure fit to be compared with great captains. For which reason, Aes-

---

* I follow Baehr's emendation (or rather substitution) ἐνίκα for συνῆν, which is demanded by the obvious sense of the whole passage. (G.)

chines in derision reports of Demosthenes, that he said he
was bringing a suit in behalf of the orator's stand against
the generals' office.* But for all that, do you think it
proper to prefer the Plataic oration of Hyperides to the
Plataic victory of Aristides? Or the oration of Lysias
against the Thirty Tyrants, to the acts of Thrasybulus and
Archias that put them to death? Or that of Aeschines
against Timarchus for unchastity, to the relieving of Byzantium by Phocion, by which he prevented the sons of the
confederates from being the scorn and derision of the Macedonians? Or shall we set before the public crowns
which Demosthenes received for setting Greece at liberty,
his oration on the Crown, wherein the rhetorician has
behaved himself most splendidly and learnedly, swearing
by their progenitors that ventured their lives at Marathon
for the liberty of Greece,† rather than by those that instructed youth in the schools? And therefore the city buried
these heroes at the expense of the public, honoring the
sacred relics of their bodies, not men like Isocrates, Antiphon, and Isaeus, and the orator has translated them into
the number of the Gods; and by these it was that he
chose to swear, though he did not follow their example.
Isocrates also was wont to say, that they who ventured
their lives at Marathon fought as if they had been inspired
with other souls than their own; and extolling their daring
boldness and contempt of life, to one that asked him
(being at that time very aged) how he did, — As well, said
he, as one who, being now above fourscore and ten years
old, esteems death to be the worst of evils. For neither
did he spend his years to old age in whetting his sword, in
grinding and sharpening his spear, in scouring and polishing his helmet, in commanding navies and armies, but in
knitting and joining together antithetical and equally bal-

* See Aeschines against Ctesiphon, § 146.
† Demosthenes on the Crown, p. 297, 11.

anced clauses, and words of similar endings, all but smoothing and adapting his periods and sentences with files, planes, or chisels. How would that man have been affrighted at the clattering of weapons or the routing of a phalanx, who was so afraid of suffering one vowel to clash with another, or to pronounce a sentence where but one syllable was wanting!

Miltiades, the very next day after the battle of Marathon, returned a victor to the city with his army. And Pericles, having subdued the Samians in nine months, derided Agamemnon that was ten years taking of Troy. But Isocrates was nearly three Olympiads (or twelve years) in writing his Panegyric; in all which time he had neither been a general nor an ambassador, neither built a city, nor been an admiral, notwithstanding the many wars that harassed Greece within that time. But while Timotheus freed Euboea from slavery, while Chabrias vanquished the enemy near Naxos, while Iphicrates defeated and cut to pieces a whole battalion of the Lacedaemonians near Lechaeum, while the Athenians, having shaken off the Spartan yoke, set the rest of Greece at liberty, with as ample privileges as they had themselves; he sits poring at home in his study, seeking out proper phrases and choice words for his oration, as long a time as Pericles spent in erecting the Propylaea and the Parthenon. Though the comic poet Cratinus seems to deride even Pericles himself as one that was none of the quickest, where he says of the middle wall:

> In words the mighty Pericles
> Has rais'd us up a wall;
> But 'tis a wall in only words,
> For we see none at all.

Consider now the poor spirit of this great orator, who spent the ninth part of his life in compiling one single oration. But to say no more of him, is it rational to compare the harangues of Demosthenes the orator with the martial exploits of Demosthenes the great leader? For example, the oration against Conon for an assault, with the trophies which the other erected before Pylos? Or the declamation against Amathusius concerning slaves, with the noble service which the other performed in bringing home the Spartan captives? Neither can it be said, that Demosthenes for his oration in regard to foreigners . . . deserved as much honor as Alcibiades, who joined the Mantineans and Eleans as confederates with the Athenians against the Lacedaemonians. And yet we must acknowledge that the public orations of Demosthenes deserve this praise, that in his Philippics he bravely encourages the Athenians to take arms, and he extols the enterprise of Leptines. . . .

AGAINST RUNNING IN DEBT, OR TAKING UP MONEY UPON USURY.

1. PLATO in his Laws * permits not any one to go and draw water from his neighbor's well, who has not first digged and sunk a pit in his own ground till he is come to a vein of clay, and has by his sounding experimented that the place will not yield a spring. For the clay or potter's earth, being of its own nature fatty, solid, and strong, retains the moisture it receives, and will not let it soak or pierce through. But it must be lawful for them to take water from another's ground, when there is no way or means for them to find any in their own; for the law ought to provide for men's necessity, but not favor their laziness. Should there not be the like ordinance also concerning money; that none should be allowed to borrow upon usury, nor to go and dive into other men's purses, — as it were into their wells and fountains, — before they have first searched at home and sounded every means for the obtaining it; having collected (as it were) and gathered together all the gutters and springs, to try if they can draw from them what may suffice to supply their most necessary occasions? But on the contrary, many there are who, to defray their idle expenses and to satisfy their extravagant and superfluous delights, make not use of their own, but have recourse to others, running themselves deeply into debt without any necessity. Now this may

---

* Plato, Laws, VIII. p. 844 B.

easily be judged, if one does but consider that usurers do not ordinarily lend to those which are in distress, but only to such as desire to obtain somewhat that is superfluous and of which they stand not in need. So that the credit given by the lender is a testimony sufficiently proving that the borrower has of his own; whereas on the contrary, since he has of his own, he ought to keep himself from borrowing.

2. Why shouldst thou go and make thy court to a banker or a merchant? Borrow from thine own table. Thou hast tankards, dishes, and basins of silver. Make use of them for thy necessity, and when they are gone to supply thy wants, the pleasant town of Aulis or isle of Tenedos will again refurnish thy board with fair vessels of earth, far more cleanly and neat than those of silver. For they are not scented with the strong and unpleasant smell of usury, which, like rust, daily more and more sullies and tarnishes the lustre of thy sumptuous magnificence. They will not be every day putting thee in mind of the Kalends and new moons, which, being of themselves the most holy and sacred days of the months, are by reason of usuries rendered the most odious and accursed. For as to those who choose rather to carry their goods to the brokers and there lay them in pawn for money taken upon usury than to sell them outright, I do not believe that Jupiter Ctesius himself can preserve them from beggary. They are ashamed forsooth to receive the full price and value of their goods; but they are not ashamed to pay use for the money they have borrowed on them. And yet the great and wise Pericles caused that costly ornament of fine gold, weighing about forty talents, with which Minerva's statue was adorned, to be made in such a manner that he could take it off and on at his pleasure; to the end (said he) that when we shall stand in need of money to support the charges of war, we may take it and make

use of it, putting afterwards in its place another of no less value. Thus we ought in our affairs, as in a besieged town, never to admit or receive the hostile garrison of a usurer, nor to endure before our eyes the delivering up of our goods into perpetual servitude; but rather to cut off from our table what is neither necessary nor profitable, and in like manner from our beds, our couches, and our ordinary expenses, and so to keep ourselves free and at liberty, in hopes to restore again what we shall have retrenched, if Fortune shall hereafter smile upon us.

3. The Roman ladies heretofore willingly parted with their jewels and ornaments of gold, for the making a cup to be sent as an offering to the temple of Apollo Pythius in the city of Delphi. And the Carthaginian matrons did with their own hands cut the hair from their heads, to make cords for the managing of their warlike engines and instruments, in defence of their besieged city. But we, as if we were ashamed of being able to stand on our own legs without being supported by the assistance of others, go and enslave ourselves by engagements and obligations; whereas it were much better that, restraining our ambition and confining it to what is profitable for us, we should of our useless and superfluous plate, which we should either melt or sell, build a temple of Liberty for ourselves, our wives, and our children. The Goddess Diana in the city of Ephesus gives to such debtors as can fly into her temple freedom and protection against their creditors; but the sanctuary of parsimony and moderation in expenses, into which no usurer can enter to pluck thence and carry away any debtor prisoner, is always open for the prudent, and affords them a long and large space of joyful and honorable repose. For as the prophetess which gave oracles in the temple of the Pythian Apollo, about the time of the Persian wars, answered the Athenians, that God had for their safety given them a wall of wood, upon

which, forsaking their lands, their city, their houses, and all their goods, they had recourse to their ships for the preservation of their liberty ; so God gives us a table of wood, vessels of earth, and garments of coarse cloth, if we desire to live and continue in freedom.

Aim not at gilded coaches, steeds of price,
And harness, richly wrought with quaint device ;

for how swiftly soever they may run, yet will usuries overtake them and outrun them.

Take rather the first ass thou shalt meet or the first packhorse that shall come in thy way, and fly from that cruel and tyrannical enemy the usurer, who asks thee not earth and water, as heretofore did the barbarous king of Persia, but — which is worse — touches thy liberty, and wounds thy honor by proscriptions. If thou payest him not, he troubles thee ; if thou hast wherewithal to satisfy him, he will not receive it, unless it be his pleasure. If thou sellest, he will have thy goods for nothing, or at a very under rate ; and if thou wilt not sell, he will force thee to it ; if thou suest him, he speaks to thee of an accommodation ; if thou swearest to give him content, he will domineer over thee ; if thou goest to his house to discourse with him, he shuts his door against thee ; if thou stayest at home, he is always knocking at thy door and will never stir from thee.

4. Of what use to the Athenians was the decree of Solon, by which he ordained that the body should not be obliged for any public debt? For they who owe are in bondage to all bankers, and not to them alone (for then there would be no great hurt), but to their very slaves, who are proud, insolent, barbarous, and outrageous, and in a word exactly such as Plato describes the devils and fiery executioners to be, who in hell torment the souls of the wicked. For thus do these wretched usurers make the court where justice is administered a hell to the poor

debtors, preying on some and gnawing them, vulture-like, to the very bones, and

> Piercing into their entrails with sharp beaks;*

and standing over others, who are, like so many Tantaluses, prohibited by them from tasting the corn and fruits of their own ground and drinking the wine of their own vintage. And as King Darius sent to the city of Athens his lieutenants Datis and Artaphernes with chains and cords, to bind the prisoners they should take; so these usurers, bringing into Greece boxes full of schedules, bills, and obligatory contracts, as so many irons and fetters for the shackling of poor criminals, go through the cities, sowing in them, as they pass, not good and profitable seed, — as did heretofore Triptolemus, when he went through all places teaching the people to sow corn, — but roots and grains of debts, that produce infinite labors and intolerable usuries, of which the end can never be found, and which, eating their way and spreading their sprouts round about, do in fine make cities bend under the burden, till they come to be suffocated. They say that hares at the same time suckle one young leveret, are ready to kindle and bring forth another, and conceive a third; but the usuries of these barbarous and wicked usurers bring forth before they conceive. For at the very delivery of their money, they immediately ask it back, taking it up at the same moment they lay it down; and they let out that again to interest which they take for the use of what they have before lent.

5. It is a saying among the Messenians,

> Pylos before Pylos, and Pylos still you'll find;

but it may much better be said against the usurers,

> Use before use, and use still more you'll find.

So that they laugh at those natural philosophers who hold

---

* Odyss. XI. 578.

that nothing can be made of nothing and of that which has no existence; but with them usury is made, and engendered of that which neither is nor ever was. They think the taking to farm the customs and other public tributes, which the laws nevertheless permit, to be a shame and reproach; and yet themselves on the contrary, in opposition to all the laws in the world, make men pay tribute for what they lend upon interest; or rather, if truth may be spoken, do in the very letting out their money to use, basely deceive their debtor. For the poor debtor, who receives less than he acknowledges in his obligation, is falsely and dishonestly cheated. And the Persians indeed repute lying to be a sin only in a second degree, but to be in debt they repute to be in the first; forasmuch as lying frequently attends those that owe. Now there are not in the whole world any people who are oftener guilty of lying than usurers, nor that practise more unfaithfulness in their day-books, in which they set down that they have delivered such a sum of money to such a person, to whom they have not given nigh so much. And the moving cause of their lying is pure avarice, not want or poverty, but an insatiable desire of always having more, the end of which is neither pleasurable nor profitable to themselves, but ruinous and destructive to those whom they injure. For they neither cultivate the lands of which they deprive their debtors, nor inhabit the houses out of which they eject them, nor eat at the tables which they take away from them, nor wear the clothes of which they strip them. But first one is destroyed, and then a second soon follows, being drawn on and allured by the former. For the mischief spreads like wildfire, still consuming, and yet still increasing by the destruction and ruin of those that fall into it, whom it devours one after another. And the usurer who maintains this fire, blowing and kindling it to the undoing of so many people, reaps no other advantage from it but only that he now and then takes his book of accounts, and reads in it how many poor debtors he has caused to sell what they had, how many he has dispossessed of their lands and livings, whence his money came which he is always turning, winding, and increasing.

6. Think not that I speak this for any ill-will or enmity that I have borne against usurers;

> For never did they drive away
> My horses or my kine.*

But my only aim is to show those who are so ready to take up money upon use, how much shame and slavery there is in it, and how it proceeds only from extreme folly, sloth, and effeminacy of heart. For if thou hast of thy own, borrow not, since thou hast no need of it; and if thou hast nothing, borrow not, because thou wilt not have any means to pay. But let us consider the one and the other apart. The elder Cato said to a certain old man, who behaved himself ill: My friend, seeing old age has of itself so many evils, why dost thou go about to add to them the reproach and shame of wickedness? In like manner may we say to a man oppressed with poverty: Since poverty has of itself so many and so great miseries, do not heap upon them the anguishes of borrowing and being in debt. Take not from poverty the only good thing in which it is superior to riches, to wit, freedom from pensive care. Otherwise thou wilt subject thyself to the derision of the common proverb, which says,

> A goat I cannot bear away,
> Therefore an ox upon me lay.

Thou canst not bear poverty, and yet thou art going to load on thyself a usurer, which is a burden even to a rich man insupportable.

But you will say perhaps, how then would you have me to live? Is this a question fit for thee to ask, who hast

---

* Il. I. 154.

hands, feet, and a voice, who in brief art a man, whose property it is to love and be beloved, to do and receive a courtesy? Canst thou not teach, bring up young children, be a porter or doorkeeper, travel by sea, serve in a ship? There is in all these nothing more shameful or odious, than to be dunned with the importunate clamors of such as are always saying, Pay me, give me my money.

7. Rutilius that rich Roman, coming one day to Musonius the philosopher, whispered him thus in his ear: Musonius, Jupiter the Savior, whom you philosophers profess to imitate and follow, takes not up money at interest. Musonius smiling presently answered him: Nor yet does he lend for use. For this Rutilius, who was himself an usurer, upbraided the other with borrowing upon use. Now what a foolish stoical arrogance was this. For what need was there of bringing here Jupiter the Savior, when he might have given him the same admonition by things that were familiar and before his eyes? Swallows run not themselves into debt, ants borrow not upon interest; and yet Nature has given them neither reason, hands, nor art. But she has endued men with such abundance of understanding, that they maintain not only themselves, but also horses, dogs, partridges, hares, and jays. Why then dost thou condemn thyself, as if thou wert less able to persuade than a jay, more dumb than a partridge, and more ungenerous than a dog, in that thou couldst not oblige any man to be assistant to thee, either by serving him, charming him, guarding him, or fighting in his defence? Dost thou not see how many occasions the land, and how many the sea affords thee for thy maintenance? Hear also what Crates says:

> Here I saw Miccylus the wool to card,
> Whilst his wife spun, that they by labor hard
> In these hard times might 'scape the hungry jaws
> Of famine.

King Antigonus, when he had not for a long time seen

Cleanthes the philosopher, said to him, Dost thou yet, O Cleanthes, continue to grind? Yes, sir, replied Cleanthes, I still grind, and that I do to gain my living and not to depart from philosophy. How great and generous was the courage of this man, who, coming from the mill and the kneading-trough, did with the same hand which had been employed in turning the stone and moulding the dough, write of the nature of the Gods, moon, stars, and sun! And yet we think these to be servile works.

Therefore, forsooth, that we may be free, we take up money at interest, and to this purpose flatter base and servile persons, wait on them, treat them, make them presents, and pay them pensions; and this we do, not being compelled by poverty (for no usurer will lend a poor man money) but to gratify our prodigality. For if we would be content with such things as are necessary for human life, usurers would be no less rare in the world than Centaurs and Gorgons. But luxury and excess, as it produced goldsmiths, silversmiths, perfumers, and dyers of curious colors, so has it also brought forth usurers. For we run not into debt for bread and wine, but for the purchasing of stately seats, numerous slaves, fine mules, costly banqueting halls, rich tables, and for all those foolish and superfluous expenses to which we frequently put ourselves for the exhibiting of plays to the people, or some such vain ambition, from which we frequently reap no other fruit but ingratitude. Now he that is once entangled in usury remains a debtor all his life, not unlike in this to the horse, who, having once taken the bridle into his mouth and the saddle on his back, receives one rider after another. Nor is there any means for these debtors to make their escape into those fair pastures and meadows which once they enjoyed, but they wander about, like those Daemons mentioned by Empedocles to have been driven out of heaven by the offended Gods:

> By the sky's force they're thrust into the main,
> Which to the earth soon spews them back again.
> Thence to bright Titan's orb they're forced to fly,
> And Titan soon remits them to the sky.

In like manner do such men fall from the hand of one usurer or banker to another, sometimes of a Corinthian, sometimes of a Patrian, sometimes of an Athenian, till, having been deceived and cheated by all, they finally find themselves dissipated and torn in pieces by usury. For as he who is fallen into the dirt must either rise up and get out of it, or else lie still in the place into which he first fell, for that by tumbling, turning, and rolling about, he does but still more and more bemire himself; so also those who do but change their creditor, and cause their names to be transcribed from one usurer's book to another's, do by loading and embroiling themselves with new usuries become more and more oppressed. Now in this they properly resemble persons distempered with cholera, who cannot receive any medicine sufficient to work a perfect cure, but continually vomit up all that is given them, and so make way for the choleric humor to gather more and more. For in the same manner these men are not willing to be cleansed at once, but do with grievous anguish and sorrow pay their use at every season of the year, and no sooner have they discharged one, but another drops and stills immediately after, which causes them both aching hearts and heads; whereas they should have taken care to get wholly clear, that they might remain free and at liberty.

8. For I now turn my speech to those who are more wealthy, and withal more nice and effeminate, and whose discourse is commonly in this manner: How shall I remain then without servants, without fire, and without a house or place to which I may repair? Now this is the same thing as if one who is sick of a dropsy and puffed up as a barrel should say to a physician: How? Would you have me become slender, lean, and

empty? And why not, provided you thereby get your health? Thus it is better you should be without servants, than that you should yourself become a slave; and that you should remain without possessions, than that you should be made the possession of another. Give ear a little to the discourse of the two vultures, as it is reported in the fable. One of them was taken with so strong a fit of vomiting, that he said: I believe I shall cast up my very bowels. Now to this his companion answered: What hurt will there be in it? For thou wilt not indeed throw up thine own entrails, but those of the dead man which we devoured the other day. So he who is indebted sells not his own inheritance nor his own house, but that of the usurer who lent him the money, to whom by the law he has given the right and possession of them. Nay, by Jupiter (will he say to me); but my father left me this estate. I believe it well, but he left thee also liberty and a good repute, of which thou oughtest to make more account and be more careful. He who begat thee made thy foot and thy hand, and nevertheless, if they happen to be mortified, thou wilt give money to the chirurgeon to cut them off. Calypso presented Ulysses with a robe breathing forth the sweet-scented odor of an immortal body, which she put on him, as a token and memorial of the love she had borne him. But when his ship was cast away and himself ready to sink to the bottom, not being able to keep above the water by reason of his wet robe, which weighed him downwards, he put it off and threw it away, and having girt his naked breast with a broad swaddling band,

Swam, gazing on the distant shore.*

And afterwards, when the danger was over and he seen to be landed, he wanted neither food nor raiment. And is it not a true tempest, when the usurer after some time

* Odyss. V. 439.

comes to assault the miserable debtors with this word Pay?

> This having said, the clouds grow thick, the sea
> Is troubled, and its raging waves beat high,
> Whilst east, south, west winds through the welkin fly.*

These winds are use, and use upon use, which roll one after another; and he that is overwhelmed by them and kept down by their weight cannot serve himself nor make his escape by swimming, but at last sinks down to the bottom, where he perishes, carrying with him his friends who were pledges and sureties for him.

Crates, the Theban philosopher, acted far otherwise; for owing nothing, and consequently not being pressed for payment by any creditor, but only tired with the cares and troubles of housekeeping and the solicitude requisite to the management of his estate, he left a patrimony of eight talents' value, and taking only his cloak and wallet, retired to philosophy and poverty. Anaxagoras also forsook his plentiful and well-stocked pastures. But what need is there of alleging these examples, seeing that the lyric poet Philoxenus, being one of those who were sent to people a new city and new land in Sicily, where there fell to his share a good house and great wealth with which he might have lived well at his ease, yet seeing that delights, pleasure, and idleness, without any exercise of good letters, reigned in those quarters, said: These goods, by all the Gods, shall not destroy me, but I will rather lose them. And immediately leaving to others the portion that was allotted to himself, he again took shipping, and returned to Athens. Whereas those who are in debt bear and suffer themselves to be sued, taxed, made slaves of, and cheated with false money, feeding like King Phineus certain winged harpies. For these usurers fly to them, and ravish out of their hands their very food. Neither yet have they patience to stay and expect the season; for they buy their

---

* Odyss. V. 291, 295.

debtors' corn before it is ready for harvest, bargain for the oil before the olives are ripe, and in like manner for their wines. I will have it, says the usurer, at such a price; and immediately he gets the writing signed; and yet the grapes are still hanging on the vine, expecting the rising of Arcturus.

PLUTARCH'S PLATONIC QUESTIONS.

QUESTION I.

WHAT IS THE REASON THAT GOD BADE SOCRATES TO ACT THE MID-WIFE'S PART TO OTHERS, BUT CHARGED HIMSELF NOT TO GENERATE; AS HE SAYS IN THEAETETUS?*

1. FOR he would never have used the name of God in such a merry, jesting manner, though Plato in that book makes Socrates several times to talk with great boasting and arrogance, as he does now. "There are many, dear friend, so affected towards me, that they are ready even to bite me, when I offer to cure them of the least madness. For they will not be persuaded that I do it out of good-will, because they are ignorant that no God bears ill-will to man, and that therefore I wish ill to no man; but I cannot allow myself either to stand in a lie or to stifle the truth." † Whether therefore did he style his own nature, which was of a very strong and pregnant wit, by the name of God, — as Menander says, "For our mind is God," and as Heraclitus, "Man's genius is a Deity"? Or did some divine cause or some Daemon or other impart this way of philosophizing to Socrates, whereby always interrogating others, he cleared them of pride, error, and ignorance, and of being troublesome both to themselves and to others? For about that time there happened to be in Greece several sophisters; to these some young men paid great sums of money, for which they purchased a strong

* See Plato, Theaet. p. 149 B. † Theaet. p. 151 C.

opinion of learning and wisdom, and of being stout disputants; but this sort of disputation spent much time in trifling squabblings, which were of no credit or profit. Now Socrates, using an argumentative discourse by way of a purgative remedy, procured belief and authority to what he said, because in refuting others he himself affirmed nothing; and he the sooner gained upon people, because he seemed rather to be inquisitive after the truth as well as they, than to maintain his own opinion.

2. Now, however useful a thing judgment is, it is mightily impeached by the begetting of a man's own fancies. For the lover is blinded with the thing loved; and nothing of a man's own is so beloved as is the opinion and discourse which he has begotten. And the distribution of children, said to be the justest, in respect of discourses is the unjustest; for there a man must take his own, but here a man must choose the best, though it be another man's. Therefore he that has children of his own, is a worse judge of other men's; it being true, as the sophister said well, "The Eleans would be the most proper judges of the Olympic games, were no Eleans gamesters." So he that would judge of disputations cannot be just, if he either seeks the bays for himself, or is himself antagonist to either of the antagonists. For as the Grecian captains, when they were to decide by their suffrages who had behaved himself the best, every man of them voted for himself; so there is not a philosopher of them all but would do the like, besides those that acknowledge, like Socrates, that they can say nothing that is their own; and these only are the pure uncorrupt judges of the truth. For as the air in the ears, unless it be still and void of noise in itself, without any sound or buzzing, does not exactly take sounds; so the philosophical judgment in disputations, if it be disturbed and obstreperous within, is hardly comprehensive of what is said without. For our familiar and inbred

opinion will not admit that which is at variance with itself, as the number of sects and parties proves, of which philosophy — if she deals with them in the best manner — must hold one to be right, and all the others to be at war with the truth in their opinions.

3. Furthermore, if men can comprehend and know nothing, God did justly interdict Socrates the procreation of false and unstable discourses, which are like wind-eggs, and bid him convince others who were of any other opinion. And reasoning, which rids us of the greatest of evils, error and vanity of mind, is none of the least benefit to us; "For God has not granted this to the Esculapians."* Nor did Socrates give physic to the body; indeed he purged the mind of secret corruption. But if there be any knowledge of the truth, and if the truth be one, he has as much that learns it of him that invented it, as the inventor himself. Now he the most easily attains the truth, that is persuaded he has it not; and he chooses best, just as he that has no children of his own adopts the best. Mark this well, that poetry, mathematics, oratory, and sophistry, which are the things the Deity forbade Socrates to generate, are of no value; and that of the sole wisdom about what is divine and intelligible (which Socrates called amiable and eligible for itself), there is neither generation nor invention by man, but reminiscence. Wherefore Socrates taught nothing, but suggesting principles of doubt, as birth-pains, to young men, he excited and at the same time confirmed the innate notions. This he called his Art of Midwifery, which did not (as others professed) extrinsically confer intelligence upon his auditors; but demonstrated it to be innate, yet imperfect and confused, and in want of a nurse to feed and strengthen it.

* Theognis, vs. 432.

QUESTION II.

WHY DOES HE CALL THE SUPREME GOD FATHER AND MAKER OF ALL THINGS?*

1. Is it because he is (as Homer calls him) of created Gods and men the Father, and of brutes and things that have no soul the maker? If Chrysippus may be credited, he is not properly styled the father of the afterbirth who supplied the seed, although it springs from the seed. Or has he figuratively called the maker of the world the father of it? In his Convivium he calls Phaedrus the father of the amatorious discourse which he had introduced; and so in his Phaedrus† he calls him "father of noble children," when he had been the occasion of many excellent discourses about philosophical matters. Or is there any difference between a father and a maker? Or between procreation and making? For as what is procreated is also made, but not the contrary; so he that procreated did also make, for the procreation of an animal is the making of it. Now the work of a maker — as of a builder, a weaver, a musical-instrument maker, or a statuary — is altogether distinct and separate from its author; but the principle and power of the procreator is implanted in the progeny, and contains his nature, the progeny being a piece pulled off the procreator. Since therefore the world is neither like a piece of potter's work nor joiner's work, but there is a great share of life and divinity in it, which God from himself communicated to and mixed with matter, God may properly be called Father of the world — since it has life in it — and also the maker of it.

2. And since these things come very near to Plato's opinion, consider, I pray, whether there may not be some

* Plato, Timaeus, p. 28 C.   † Phaedrus, p. 261 A.

probability in them. Whereas the world consists of two parts, body and soul, God indeed made not the body; but matter being provided, he formed and fitted it, binding up and confining what was infinite within proper limits and figures. But the soul, partaking of mind, reason, and harmony, was not only the work of God, but part of him: not only made by him, but begot by him.

QUESTION III.

In the Republic,* he supposes the universe, as one line, to be cut into two unequal sections; again he cuts each of these sections in two after the same proportion, and supposes the two sections first made to constitute the two genera of things sensible and things intelligible in the universe. The first represents the genus of intelligibles, comprehending in the first subdivision the primitive forms or ideas, in the second the mathematics. Of sensibles, the first subdivision comprehends solid bodies, the second comprehends the images and representations of them. Moreover, to every one of these four he has assigned its proper judicatory faculty; — to the first, reason; to the mathematics, the understanding; to sensibles, belief; to images and likenesses, conjecture.

BUT WHAT DOES HE MEAN BY DIVIDING THE UNIVERSE INTO UNEQUAL PARTS? AND WHICH OF THE SECTIONS, THE INTELLIGIBLE OR THE SENSIBLE, IS THE GREATER? FOR IN THIS HE HAS NOT EXPLAINED HIMSELF.

1. At first sight it will appear that the sensible is the greater portion. For the essence of intelligibles being indivisible, and in the same respect ever the same, is contracted into a little, and pure; but an essence divisible and pervading bodies constitutes the sensible part. Now what

* Republic, VI. pp. 509 D — 511 E.

is immaterial is limited; but body in respect of matter is infinite and unlimited, and it becomes sensible only when it is defined by partaking of the intelligible. Besides, as every sensible has many images, shadows, and representations, and from one and the same original several copies may be taken both by nature and art; so the latter must needs exceed the former in number, according to Plato, who makes things intelligible to be patterns or ideas of things sensible, like the originals of images and reflections. Further, Plato derives the knowledge of ideas from body by abstraction and cutting away, leading us by various steps in mathematical discipline from arithmetic to geometry, thence to astronomy, and setting harmony above them all. For things become geometrical by the accession of magnitude to quantity; solid, by the accession of profundity to magnitude; astronomical, by the accession of motion to solidity; harmonical, by the accession of sound to motion. Abstract then sound from moving bodies, motion from solids, profundity from superficies, magnitude from quantity, we are then come to pure intelligible ideas, which have no distinction among themselves in respect of the one single intelligible essence. For unity makes no number, unless joined by the infinite binary; then it makes a number. And thence we proceed to points, thence to lines, from them to superficies, and profundities, and bodies, and to the qualities of the bodies so and so qualified. Now the reason is the only judicatory faculty of intelligibles; and the understanding is the reason in the mathematics, where intelligibles appear as by reflection in mirrors. But as to the knowledge of bodies, because of their multitude, Nature has given us five powers or distinctions of senses; nor are all bodies discerned by them, many escaping sense by reason of their smallness. And though every one of us consists of a body and soul, yet the hegemonic and intellectual faculty is small, being hid in the huge mass of flesh. And the case is the same in the universe, as to sensible and intelligible. For intelligibles are the principles of bodily things, but every thing is greater than the principle whence it came.

2. Yet, on the contrary, some will say that, by comparing sensibles with intelligibles, we match things mortal with divine, in some measure; for God is in intelligibles. Besides, the thing contained is ever less than the containing, and the nature of the universe contains the sensible in the intelligible. For God, having placed the soul in the middle, hath extended it through all, and hath covered it all round with bodies. The soul is invisible, and cannot be perceived by any of the senses, as Plato says in his Book of Laws; therefore every man must die, but the world shall never die. For mortality and dissolution surround every one of our vital faculties. The case is quite otherwise in the world; for the corporeal part, contained in the middle by the more noble and unalterable principle, is ever preserved. And a body is said to be without parts and indivisible for its minuteness; but what is incorporeal and intelligible is so, as being simple and sincere, and void of all firmness and difference. Besides, it were folly to think to judge of incorporeal things by corporeal. The present, or *now*, is said to be without parts and indivisible, since it is everywhere and no part of the world is void of it. But all affections and actions, and all corruptions and generations in the world, are contained by this *now*. But the mind is judge only of what is intelligible, as the sight is of light, by reason of its simplicity and similitude. But bodies, having several differences and diversities, are comprehended, some by one judicatory faculty, others by another, as by several organs. Yet they do not well who despise the intelligible and intelligent faculty in us; for being great, it comprehends all sensibles, and attains to things divine. The most important thing he himself

teaches in his Banquet, where he shows us how we should use amatorious matters, turning our minds from sensible goods to things discernible only by the reason, that we ought not to be enslaved by the beauty of any body, study, or learning, but laying aside such pusillanimity, should turn to the vast ocean of beauty.*

QUESTION IV.

WHAT IS THE REASON THAT, THOUGH PLATO ALWAYS SAYS THAT THE SOUL IS ANCIENTER THAN THE BODY, AND THAT IT IS THE CAUSE AND PRINCIPLE OF ITS RISE, YET HE LIKEWISE SAYS, THAT NEITHER COULD THE SOUL EXIST WITHOUT THE BODY, NOR THE REASON WITHOUT THE SOUL, BUT THE SOUL IN THE BODY AND THE REASON IN THE SOUL? FOR SO THE BODY WILL SEEM TO BE AND NOT TO BE, BECAUSE IT BOTH EXISTS WITH THE SOUL, AND IS BEGOT BY THE SOUL.

Perhaps what we have often said is true; viz., that the soul without reason and the body without form did mutually ever coexist, and neither of them had generation or beginning. But after the soul did partake of reason and harmony, and being through consent made wise, it wrought a change in matter, and being stronger than the other's motions, it drew and converted these motions to itself. So the body of the world drew its original from the soul, and became conformable and like to it. For the soul did not make the Nature of the body out of itself, or out of nothing; but it wrought an orderly and pliable body out of one disorderly and formless. Just as if a man should say that the virtue of the seed is with the body, and yet that the body of the fig-tree or olive-tree was made of the seed, he would not be much out; for the body, its innate motion and mutation proceeding from the seed, grew up and became what it is. So, when formless and indefinite matter was once formed by the inbeing soul, it received such a form and disposition.

* See Plato's Symposium, p. 210 D.

QUESTION V.

WHY, SINCE BODIES AND FIGURES ARE CONTAINED PARTLY BY RECTILINEARS AND PARTLY BY CIRCLES, DOES HE MAKE ISOSCELES TRIANGLES AND TRIANGLES OF UNEQUAL SIDES THE PRINCIPLES OF RECTILINEARS; OF WHICH THE ISOSCELES TRIANGLE FORMS THE CUBE, THE ELEMENT OF THE EARTH; AND A SCALENE TRIANGLE FORMS THE PYRAMID WHICH IS THE SEED OF FIRE, THE OCTAHEDRON WHICH IS THE SEED OF AIR, AND THE ICOSAHEDRON WHICH IS THE SEED OF WATER;—WHILE HE DOES NOT MEDDLE WITH CIRCULARS, THOUGH HE DOES MENTION THE GLOBE, WHERE HE SAYS THAT EACH OF THE AFORE-RECKONED FIGURES DIVIDES A ROUND BODY THAT ENCLOSES IT INTO EQUAL PARTS.*

1. Is their opinion true who think that he ascribed a dodecahedron to the globe, when he says that God made use of it in delineating the universe? For upon account of the multitude of its bases and the obtuseness of its angles, avoiding all rectitude, it is flexible, and by circumtension, like globes made of twelve skins, it becomes circular and comprehensive. For it has twenty solid angles, each of which is contained by three obtuse planes, and each of these contains one and the fifth part of a right angle. Now it is made up of twelve equilateral and equangular quinquangles (or pentagons), each of which consists of thirty of the first scalene triangles. Therefore it seems to resemble both the Zodiac and the year, it being divided into the same number of parts as these.

2. Or is a right line in Nature prior to circumference; or is circumference but an accident of rectilinear? For a right line is said to bend; and a circle is described by a centre and distance, which is the place of a right line by which a circumference is measured, this being everywhere equally distant from the middle. And a cone and a cylinder are made by rectilinears; a cone by keeping one side of a triangle fixed and carrying another round with the

---

* See Timaeus, pp. 53-56.

base, — a cylinder, by doing the like with a parallelogram. Further, that is nearest to principle which is less; but a right is the least of all lines, as it is simple; whereas in a circumference one part is convex without, another concave within. Besides, numbers are before figures, as unity is before a point, which is unity in position. But indeed unity is triangular; for every triangular number* taken eight times, by adding unity, becomes quadrate; and this happens to unity. Therefore a triangle is before a circle, whence a right line is before a circumference. Besides, no element is divided into things compounded of itself; indeed there is a dissolution of all other things into the elements. Now a triangle is divided into no circumference, but two diameters cut a circle into four triangles; therefore a rectilinear figure is before a circular, and has more of the nature of an element. And Plato himself shows that a rectilinear is in the first place, and a circular is only consequential and accidental. For when he says the earth consists of cubes, each of which is contained with rectilinear superficies, he says the earth is spherical and round. Therefore there was no need of making a peculiar element for round things, since rectilinears, fitted after a certain manner among themselves, do make up this figure.

3. Besides, a right line, whether great or little, preserves the same rectitude; but as to the circumference of a circle, the less it is, the crookeder it is; the larger, the straighter. Therefore if a convex superficies stands on a plane, it sometimes touches the subject plane in a point, sometimes in a line. So that a man may imagine that a circumference is made up of little right lines.

4. But observe whether this be not true, that no circle

---

* Triangular numbers are those of which equilateral triangles can be formed in this way: — Such are 3, 6, 10, 15, 21, 28, 36, 45, &c.; that is, numbers formed by adding the digits in regular order. (G.)

or sphere in this world is exact; but since by the tension and circumtension of the right lines, or by the minuteness of the parts, the difference disappears, the figure seems circular and round. Therefore no corruptible body moves circularly, but altogether in a right line. To be truly spherical is not in a sensible body, but is the element of the soul and mind, to which he has given circular motion, as being agreeable to their nature.

QUESTION VI.

How comes it to pass that in Phaedrus it is said, that the Nature of a Wing, by which any thing that is Heavy is carried upwards, participates most of the Body of God?*

Is it because the discourse is of love, and love is of beauty inherent in a body? Now beauty, by similitude to things divine, moves and reminds the soul. Or it may be (without too much curiosity) he may be understood in plain meaning, to wit, that the several faculties of the soul being employed about bodies, the power of reasoning and understanding partakes most about divine and heavenly things; which he did not impertinently call a wing, it raising the soul from mean and mortal things to things above.

QUESTION VII.

In what Sense does Plato say, that the Antiperistasis (or Reaction) of Motion — by Reason there is no Vacuum — is the Cause of the Effects in Physicians' Cupping-Glasses, in Swallowing, in Throwing of Weights, in the Running of Water, in Thunder, in the Attraction of the Loadstone, and in the Harmony of Sounds?†

1. For it seems unreasonable to ascribe the reason of such different effects to the selfsame cause.

2. How respiration is made by the reaction of the air,

* See Phaedrus, p. 246 D. † See Timaeus, pp. 79–81.

he has sufficiently shown. But the rest, he says, seem to be done miraculously, but really the bodies thrust each other aside and change places with one another; while he has left for us to determine how each is particularly done.

3. As to cupping-glasses, the case is thus: the air next to the flesh being comprehended and inflamed by the heat, and being made more rare than the pores of the brass, does not go into a vacuum (for there is no such thing), but into the air that is without the cupping-glass, and has an impulse upon it. This air drives that before it; and each, as it gives way, strives to succeed into the place which was vacuated by the cession of the first. And so the air approaching the flesh comprehended by the cupping-glass, and exciting it, draws the humors into the cupping-glass.

4. Swallowing takes place in the same way. For the cavities about the mouth and stomach are full of air; when therefore the meat is squeezed down by the tongue and tonsils, the elided air follows what gives way, and also forces down the meat.

5. Weights also thrown cleave the air and dissipate it, as they fall with force; the air recoiling back, according to its natural tendency to rush in and fill the vacuity, follows the impulse, and accelerates the motion.

6. The fall also of thunderbolts is like to darting any thing. For by the blow in the cloud, the fiery matter exploded breaks into the air; and it being broken gives way, and again being contracted above, by main force it presses the thunderbolt downwards contrary to Nature.

7. And neither amber nor the loadstone draws any thing to it which is near, nor does any thing spontaneously approach them. But this stone emits strong exhalations, by which the adjoining air being impelled forceth that which is before it; and this being carried round in the circle, and returning into the vacuated place, forcibly draws the iron in the same direction. In amber there is a flammeous and

spirituous nature, and this by rubbing on the surface is emitted by recluse passages, and does the same that the loadstone does. It also draws the lightest and driest of adjacent bodies, by reason of their tenuity and weakness; for it is not so strong nor so endued with weight and strength as to force much air and to act with violence and to have power over great bodies, as the magnet has. But what is the reason the air never draws a stone, nor wood, but iron only, to the loadstone? This is a common question both by them who think the coition of these bodies is made by the attraction of the loadstone, and by such as think it done by the incitement of the iron. Iron is neither so rare as wood, nor altogether so solid as gold or a stone; but has certain pores and asperities, which in regard of the inequality are proportionable to the air; and the air being received in certain seats, and having (as it were) certain stays to cling to, does not slip away; but when it is carried up to the stone and strikes against it, it draws the iron by force along with it to the stone. Such then may be the reason of this.

8. But the manner of the waters running over the earth is not so evident. But it is observable that the waters of lakes and ponds stand immovable, because the air about them stagnates immovable and admits of no vacuity. For the water on the surface of lakes and seas is troubled and fluctuates as the air is moved, it following the motion of the air, and moving as it is moved. For the force from below causes the hollowness of the wave, and from above the swelling thereof; until the air ambient and containing the water is still. Therefore the flux of such waters as follow the motion of the retreating air, and are impelled by that which presses behind, is continued without end. And this is the reason that the stream increases with the waters, and is slow where the water is weak, the air not giving way, and therefore suffering less reaction. So the

water of fountains must needs flow upwards, the extrinsic air succeeding into the vacuity and throwing the water out. In a close house, that keeps in the air and wind, the floor sprinkled with water causes an air or wind, because, as the sprinkled water falls, the air gives way. For it is so provided by Nature that air and water force one another and give way to one another; because there is no vacuity in which one can be settled without feeling the change and alteration in the other.

9. Concerning symphony, he shows how sounds harmonize. A quick sound is acute, a slow is grave. Therefore acute sounds move the senses the quicker; and these dying and grave sounds supervening, what arises from the contemperation of one with the other causes pleasure to the ear, which we call harmony. And by what has been said, it may easily be understood that air is the instrument of these things. For sound is the stroke upon the sense of the hearer, caused by the air; and the air strikes as it is struck by the thing moving, — if violent, acutely, — if languid, softly. The violent stroke comes quick to the ear; then the circumambient air receiving a slower, it affects and carries the sense along with it.

QUESTION VIII.

WHAT MEANS TIMAEUS,[*] WHEN HE SAYS THAT SOULS ARE DISPERSED INTO THE EARTH, THE MOON, AND INTO OTHER INSTRUMENTS OF TIME?

1. Does the earth move like the sun, moon, and five planets, which for their motions he calls organs or instruments of time? Or is the earth fixed to the axis of the universe; yet not so built as to remain immovable, but to turn and wheel about, as Aristarchus and Seleucus have

[*] See Timaeus, p. 42 D.

shown since; Aristarchus only supposing it, Seleucus positively asserting it? Theophrastus writes how that Plato, when he grew old, repented him that he had placed the earth in the middle of the universe, which was not its place.

2. Or is this contradictory to Plato's opinion elsewhere, and in the Greek instead of χρόνου should it be written χρόνῳ, taking the dative case instead of the genitive, so that the stars will not be said to be instruments, but the bodies of animals? So Aristotle has defined the soul to be " the actual being of a natural organic body, having the power of life."* The sense then must be this, that souls are dispersed into meet organical bodies in time. But this is far besides his opinion. For it is not once, but several times, that he calls the stars instruments of time; as when he says, the sun was made, as well as other planets, for the distinction and conservation of the numbers of time.

3. It is therefore most proper to understand the earth to be here an instrument of time; not that the earth is moved, as the stars are; but that, they being carried about it, it standing still makes sunset and sunrising, by which the first measures of time, nights and days, are circumscribed. Wherefore he called it the infallible guard and artificer of night and day. For the gnomons of dials are instruments and measures of time, not in being moved with the shadows, but in standing still; they being like the earth in intercepting the light of the sun when it is down, — as Empedocles says that the earth makes night by intercepting light. This therefore may be Plato's meaning.

4. And so much the rather might we consider whether the sun is not absurdly and without probability said to be made for the distinction of time, with the moon and the rest of the planets. For as in other respects the dignity

---

* See Aristotle on the Soul, II. 1, with Trendelenburg's note. (G.)

of the sun is great; so by Plato in his Republic* the sun is called the king and lord of the whole sensible nature, as the Chief Good is of the intelligible. For it is said to be the offspring of Good, it giving both generation and appearance to things visible; as it is from Good that things intelligible both are and are understood. But that this God, having such a nature and so great power, should be only an instrument of time, and a sure measure of the difference that happens among the eight orbs, as they are slow or swift in motion, seems neither decent nor highly rational. It must therefore be said to such as are startled at these things, that it is their ignorance to think that time is the measure of motion in respect of sooner or later, as Aristotle calls it; or quantity in motion, as Speusippus; or an interval of motion and nothing more, as some of the Stoics define it, by an accident, not comprehending its essence and power, which Pindar has not ineptly expressed in these words: Time, who surpasses all in the seats of the blest. Pythagoras also, when he was asked what time was, answered, it was the soul of this world. For time is no affection or accident of motion, but the cause, power, and principle of that symmetry and order that confines all created beings, by which the animated nature of the universe is moved. Or rather, this order and symmetry itself — so far as it is motion — is called time. For this,

> Walking by still and silent ways,
> Mortal affairs with justice guides.†

According to the ancients, the essence of the soul is a number moving itself. Therefore Plato says that time and heaven were coexistent, but that motion was before heaven had being. But time was not. For then there neither was order, nor measure, nor determination; but indefinite motion, as it were, the formless and rude matter of time.

---

* Plato, Republic, VI. pp. 508, 509.   † Euripides, Troad. 887.

... But when matter was informed with figures, and motion with circuitions, from that came the world, from this time. Both are representations of God; the world, of his essence; time, of his eternity in the form of motion, as the world is God in creation. Therefore they say heaven and motion, being bred together, will perish together, if ever they do perish. For nothing is generated without time, nor is any thing intelligible without eternity; if this is to endure for ever, and that never to die when once bred. Time therefore, having a necessary connection and affinity with heaven, cannot be called simple motion, but (as it were) motion in order having terms and periods; whereof since the sun is prefect and overseer, to determine, moderate, produce, and observe changes and seasons, which (according to Heraclitus) produce all things, he is coadjutor to the governing and chief God, not in trivial things, but in the greatest and most momentous affairs.

QUESTION IX.

Since Plato in his Commonwealth, discoursing of the faculties of the soul, has very well compared the symphony of reason and of the irascible and the concupiscent faculties to the harmony of the middle, lowest, and highest chord,* some men may properly ask this question : —

DID PLATO PLACE THE RATIONAL OR THE IRASCIBLE FACULTY IN THE MIDDLE? FOR HE IS NOT CLEAR IN THE POINT.

1. Indeed, according to the natural order of the parts, the place of the irascible faculty must be in the middle, and of the rational in the highest, which the Greeks call hypate. For they of old called the chief and supreme ὕπατος. So Xenocrates calls Jove, in respect of immutable things, ὕπατος (or *highest*), in respect of sublunary things

* See Republic, IV. p. 443 D.

νέατος (or *lowest.*) And long before him, Homer calls the chief God ὕπατος κρειόντων, *Highest of Rulers.* And Nature has of due given the highest place to what is most excellent, having placed reason as a steersman in the head, and the concupiscent faculty at a distance, last of all and lowest. And the lowest place they call νεάτη, as the names of the dead, νέρτεροι and ἔνεροι, do show. And some say, that the south wind, inasmuch as it blows from a low and obscure place, is called νότος. Now since the concupiscent faculty stands in the same opposition to reason in which the lowest stands to the highest and the last to the first, it is not possible for the reason to be uppermost and first, and yet for any other part to be the one called ὕπατος (or *highest*). For they that ascribe the power of the middle to it, as the ruling power, are ignorant how they deprive it of a higher power, namely, of the highest, which is competible neither to the irascible nor to the concupiscent faculty; since it is the nature of them both to be governed by and obsequious to reason, and the nature of neither of them to govern and lead it. And the most natural place of the irascible faculty seems to be in the middle of the other two. For it is the nature of reason to govern, and of the irascible faculty both to govern and be governed, since it is obsequious to reason, and commands the concupiscent faculty when this is disobedient to reason. And as in letters the semi-vowels are middling between mutes and vowels, having something more than those and less than these; so in the soul of man, the irascible faculty is not purely passive, but hath often an imagination of good mixed with the irrational appetite of revenge. Plato himself, after he had compared the soul to a pair of horses and a charioteer, likened (as every one knows) the rational faculty to the charioteer, and the concupiscent to one of the horses, which was resty and unmanageable altogether, bristly about the ears, deaf and disobedient both to whip

and spur; and the irascible he makes for the most part
very obsequious to the bridle of reason, and assistant to it.
As therefore in a chariot, the middling one in virtue and
power is not the charioteer, but that one of the horses which
is worse than his guider and yet better than his fellow;
so in the soul, Plato gives the middle place not to the
principal part, but to that faculty which has less of reason
than the principal part and more than the third. This
order also observes the analogy of the symphonies, i.e. the
relation of the irascible to the rational (which is placed
as hypate) forming the diatessaron (or fourth), that of the
irascible to the concupiscent (or nete) forming the dia-
pente (or fifth), and that of the rational to the concupiscent (as hypate to nete) forming an octave or diapason.
But should you place the rational in the middle, you would
make the irascible farther from the concupiscent; though
some of the philosophers have taken the irascible and
the concupiscent faculty for the selfsame, by reason of
their likeness.

2. But it may be ridiculous to describe the first, middle,
and last by their place; since we see hypate highest in
the harp, lowest in the pipe; and wheresoever you place
the mese in the harp, provided it is tunable, it sounds more
acute than hypate, and more grave than nete. Nor does
the eye possess the same place in all animals; but where-
ever it is placed, it is natural for it to see. So a pedagogue,
though he goes not foremost but follows behind, is said to
lead (ἄγειν), as the general of the Trojan army,

> Now in the front, now in the rear was seen,
> And kept command;*

but wherever he was, he was first and chief in power.
So the faculties of the soul are not to be ranged by mere
force in order of place or name, but according to their

* Il. XI. 64.

power and analogy. For that in the body of man reason is in the highest place, is accidental. But it holds the chief and highest power, as mese to hypate, in respect of the concupiscent; as mese to nete, in respect of the irascible; insomuch as it depresses and heightens, — and in fine makes a harmony, — by abating what is too much and by not suffering them to flatten and grow dull. For what is moderate and symmetrous is defined by mediocrity. Still more is it the object of the rational faculty to reduce the passions to moderation, which is called sacred, as effecting a harmony of the extremes with reason, and through reason with each other. For in chariots the best of the beasts is not in the middle; nor is the skill of driving to be placed as an extreme, but it is a mediocrity between the inequality of the swiftness and the slowness of the horses. So the force of reason takes up the passions irrationally moved, and reducing them to measure, constitutes a **mediocrity betwixt too much and too little.**

QUESTION X.

WHY SAID PLATO, THAT SPEECH WAS COMPOSED OF NOUNS AND VERBS?[*]

1. For he seems to make no other parts of speech but them. But Homer in a sportive humor has comprehended them all in one verse:

Αὐτὸς ἰὼν κλισίηνδε τὸ σὸν γέρας, ὄφρ' εὖ εἰδῇς.[†]

For in it there is pronoun, participle, noun, preposition, article, conjunction, adverb, and verb, the particle -δε being put instead of the preposition εἰς; for κλισίηνδε, *to the tent*, is said in the same sense as Ἀθήναζε, *to Athens*. What then shall we say for Plato?

[*] Plato's Sophist, p. 262 A.   [†] Il. I. 185.

Is it that at first the ancients called that λόγος, or speech, which once was called protasis and now is called axiom or proposition, — which as soon as a man speaks, he speaks either true or false? This consists of a noun and verb, which logicians call the subject and predicate. For when we hear this said, "Socrates philosophizeth" or "Socrates is changed," requiring nothing more, we say the one is true, the other false. For very likely in the beginning men wanted speech and articulate voice, to enable them to express clearly at once the passions and the patients, the actions and the agents. Now, since actions and affections are sufficiently expressed by verbs, and they that act and are affected by nouns, as he says, these seem to signify. And one may say, the rest signify not. For instance, the groans and shrieks of stage-players, and even their smiles and reticence, make their discourse more emphatic. But they have no necessary power to signify any thing, as a noun and verb have, but only an ascititious power to vary speech; just as they vary letters who mark spirits and quantities upon letters, these being the accidents and differences of letters. This the ancients have made manifest, whom sixteen letters sufficed to speak and write any thing.

2. Besides, we must not neglect to observe, that Plato says that speech is composed *of* these, not *by* these; nor must we blame Plato for leaving out conjunctions, prepositions, and the like, any more than we should cavil at a man who should say such a medicine is composed of wax and galbanum, because fire and utensils are omitted, without which it cannot be made. For speech is not composed of these; yet by their means, and not without them, speech must be composed. As, if a man pronounce *beats* or *is beaten*, and put Socrates and Pythagoras to the same, he offers us something to conceive and understand. But if a man pronounce *indeed* or *for* or *about*, and no more,

none can conceive any notion of a body or matter; and unless such words as these be uttered with verbs and nouns, they are but empty noise and chattering. For neither alone nor joined one with another do they signify any thing. And join and confound together conjunctions, articles, and prepositions, supposing you would make something of them; yet you will be taken to babble, and not to speak sense. But when there is a verb in construction with a noun, the result is speech and sense. Therefore some do with good reason make only these two parts of speech; and perhaps Homer is willing to declare himself of this mind, when he says so often,

Ἔπος τ' ἔφατ' ἔκ τ' ὀνόμαζεν.

For by ἔπος he usually means a verb, as in these verses.

Ὦ γύναι, ἦ μάλα τοῦτο ἔπος θυμαλγὲς ἔειπες,

and,

*Χαῖρε, πάτερ, ὦ ξεῖνε, ἔπος δ' εἴπερ τι λέλεκται
Δεινὸν, ἄφαρ τὸ φέροιεν ἀναρπάξασαι ἄελλαι.**

For neither conjunction, article, nor preposition could be called δεινόν (*terrible*) or θυμαλγές (*soul-grieving*), but only a verb expressing a base action or a foolish passion of the mind. Therefore, when we would praise or dispraise poets or writers, we are wont to say, such a man uses Attic nouns and good verbs, or else common nouns and verbs; but none can say that Thucydides or Euripides used Attic or good or common articles.

3. What then? may some say, do the rest of the parts conduce nothing to speech? I answer, They conduce, as salt does to victuals, or water to barley cakes. And Euenus calls fire the best sauce. Though sometimes there is neither occasion for fire to boil, nor for salt to season our food, which we have always occasion for. Nor has speech always occasion for articles. I think I may say

* Odyss. XXIII. 183; VIII. 408.

this of the Latin tongue, which is now the universal language; for it has taken away all prepositions, saving a few, nor does it use any articles, but leaves its nouns (as it were) without skirts and borders. Nor is it any wonder, since Homer, who in fineness of epic surpasses all men, has put articles only to a few nouns, like handles to cans, or crests to helmets. Therefore these verses are remarkable wherein the articles are expressed:

> Αἴαντι δὲ μάλιστα δαΐφρονι θυμὸν ὄρινε
> Τῷ Τελαμωνιάδῃ· *

and,

> Ποίεον ὄφρα τὸ κῆτος ὑπεκπροφυγὼν ἀλέαιτο· †

and some few besides. But in a thousand others, the omission of the articles hinders neither perspicuity nor elegance of phrase.

4. Now neither an animal nor an instrument nor arms nor any thing else is more fine, efficacious, or graceful, for the loss of a part. Yet speech, by taking away conjunctions, often becomes more persuasive, as here:

> One rear'd a dagger at a captive's breast;
> One held a living foe, that freshly bled
> With new-made wounds; another dragg'd a dead. ‡

And this of Demosthenes:

"A bully in an assault may do much which his victim cannot even describe to another person, — by his mien, his look, his voice, — when he stings by insult, when he attacks as an avowed enemy, when he smites with his fist, when he gives a blow on the face. These rouse a man; these make a man beside himself who is unused to such foul abuse."

And again:

"Not so with Midias; but from the very day, he talks, he abuses, he shouts. Is there an election of magistrates?

---

* Il. XIV. 459.   † Il. XX. 147.   ‡ Il. XVIII. 536.

Midias the Anagyrrasian is nominated. He is the advocate of Plutarchus; he knows state secrets; the city cannot contain him."*

Therefore the figure asyndeton, whereby conjunctions are omitted, is highly commended by writers of rhetoric. But such as keep overstrict to the law, and (according to custom) omit not a conjunction, rhetoricians blame for using a dull, flat, tedious style, without any variety in it. And inasmuch as logicians mightily want conjunctions for the joining together their axioms, as much as charioteers want yokes, and Ulysses wanted withs to tie Cyclop's sheep; this shows they are not parts of speech, but a conjunctive instrument thereof, as the word conjunction imports. Nor do conjunctions join all, but only such as are not spoken simply; unless you will make a cord part of the burthen, glue a part of a book, or distribution of money part of the government. For Demades says, that money which is given to the people out of the exchequer for public shows is the glue of a democracy. Now what conjunction does so of several propositions make one, by knitting and joining them together, as marble joins iron that is melted with it in the fire? Yet the marble neither is nor is said to be part of the iron; although in this case the substances enter into the mixture and are melted together, so as to form a common substance from many and to be mutually affected. But there be some who think that conjunctions do not make any thing one, but that this kind of discourse is merely an enumeration, as when magistrates or days are reckoned in order.

5. Moreover, as to the other parts of speech, a pronoun is manifestly a sort of noun; not only because it has cases like the noun, but because some pronouns, when they are applied to objects heretofore defined, by their mere utterance give the most distinct and proper designation of them.

* Demosthenes against Midias, p. 537, 25, and p. 578, 29.

Nor do I know whether he that says *Socrates* or he that says *this one* does more by name declare the person.

6. The thing we call a participle, being a mixture of a verb and noun, is nothing of itself, as are not the common names of male and female qualities (i.e. adjectives), but in construction it is put with others, in regard of tenses belonging to verbs, in regard of cases to nouns. Logicians call them ἀνάκλιστοι, (i.e. *reflected*), — as φρονῶν comes from φρόνιμος, and σωφρονῶν from σώφρονος, — having the force both of nouns and appellatives.

7. And prepositions are like to the crests of a helmet, or footstools and pedestals, which (one may rather say) do belong to words than are words themselves. See whether they rather be not pieces and scraps of words, as they that are in haste write but dashes and pricks for letters. For it is plain that ἐμβῆναι and ἐκβῆναι are abbreviations of the whole words ἐντὸς βῆναι and ἐκτὸς βῆναι, προγενέσθαι for πρότερον γενέσθαι, and καθίζειν for κάτω ἵζειν. As undoubtedly for haste and brevity's sake, instead of λίθους βάλλειν and τοίχους ὀρύττειν men first said λιθοβολεῖν and τοιχωρυχεῖν.

8. Therefore every one of these is of some use in speech; but nothing is a part or element of speech (as has been said) except a noun and a verb, which make the first juncture admitting of truth or falsehood, which some call a proposition or protasis, others an axiom, and which Plato called speech.

PARALLELS, OR A COMPARISON BETWEEN THE GREEK AND ROMAN HISTORIES.*

Most people are apt to take the histories of former times for mere forgeries and fables, because of many passages in those relations that seem to be very extravagant. But yet, according to my observation, we have had as strange occurrences of a later date in the Roman times as any we have received from antiquity; for proof whereof, I have here matched several stories of the ancients with modern instances, and cited my authorities.

1. Datis, an eminent Persian commander, drew out three hundred thousand men to Marathon, a plain of Attica, where he encamped and declared war against the inhabitants. The Athenians made no reckoning at all of so barbarous a rabble, but sent out nine thousand men against him, under the command of Cynaegirus, Polyzelus, Callimachus, and Miltiades. Upon the joining of battle, Polyzelus was struck blind at the sight of a wonderful ap-

---

* It seems impossible to believe this treatise to be the work of Plutarch, and equally impossible to believe it to be the work of any full-grown man of sound mind. In this case, and in that of the next treatise, no satisfaction is gained by merely supposing the work spurious. One of these Parallel Histories is usually a well-known story, and the other is an absurd imitation of it. An instance may be seen in section 12, where the common story of Manlius Torquatus and his son is matched by an absurd one of Epaminondas and his son; on which Wyttenbach remarks: "Romanum constat: Graecum non modo ementitum, sed stulte ementitum." We might almost suspect that many of them are some school-boy's compositions, half historical, and half imitations of well-known stories fortified by imaginary authorities. Is it possible that this school-boy can have been Plutarch himself? (G.)

parition; Callimachus's body was struck through with a great many lances, continuing in an upright posture even when he was dead; Cynaegirus had both his hands cut off upon laying hold of a Persian ship that was endeavoring to get away.

King Asdrubal, having possessed himself of Sicily, proclaimed war against the Romans. Metellus, who was appointed by the Senate to command in chief, overcame him. L. Glauco, a patrician, laid hold of the vessel that Asdrubal was in, and lost both his hands upon it. — *Aristides Milesius gives this account in his First Book of the Affairs of Sicily, and Dionysius Siculus had it from him.*

2. Xerxes came with an army of five millions of men to Artemisium, and declared war against the country. The Athenians, in a very great surprise, sent Agesilaus, the brother of Themistocles, to discover the motions of the enemy, notwithstanding a dream of his father Neocles, that his son had lost both his hands. This Agesilaus put himself into a Persian habit, and entered the barbarians' camp; where, taking Mardonius (an officer of the king's guards) for Xerxes himself, he killed him. Whereupon he was immediately seized, bound, and carried to Xerxes, who was just then about to sacrifice an ox to the Sun. The fire was kindled upon the altar, and Agesilaus put his right hand into it, without so much as shrinking at the pain. He was ordered upon this to be untied; and told the king that the Athenians were all of the same resolution, and that, if he pleased, he should see him burn his left hand too. This gave Xerxes an apprehension of him, so that he caused him to be still kept in custody. — *This I find in Agatharchides the Samian, in the Second Book of his Persian History.*

Porsena, a king of Tuscany, encamped himself beyond the Tiber, and made war upon the Romans, cutting off the supplies, till they were brought to great want of provi sions. The Senate were at their wits' end what to do, till Mucius, a nobleman, got leave of the consuls to take four hundred of his own quality to advise with upon the matter. Mucius, upon this, put himself into the habit of a private man, and crossed the river; where finding one of the king's officers giving orders for the distribution of necessaries to the soldiers, and taking him for the king himself, he slew him. He was taken immediately and carried to the king, where he put his right hand into a fire that was in the room, and with a smile in the middle of his torments, — Barbarian, says he, I can set myself at liberty without asking you leave; and be it known to you, that I have left four hundred men in the camp as daring as myself, that have sworn your death. This struck Porsena with such a terror, that he made peace with the Romans upon it. — *Aristides Milesius is my author for this, in the Third Book of his History.*

3. There happened a dispute betwixt the Argives and Lacedaemonians about a claim to the possession of Thyreatis. The Amphictyons gave their opinion for a trial of it by battle, so many and so many of a side, and the possession to go to the victor. The Lacedaemonians made choice of Othryades for their captain, and the Argives of Thersander. The battle was fought, and the only two survivors that appeared were Agenor and Chromius, both Argives, who carried their city the news of the victory. In this interim, Othryades, who was not as yet quite dead, made a shift to raise himself by the help of broken lances, gathered the shields of the dead together, and erected a trophy with this inscription upon it in his own blood. " To Jupiter the Guardian of Trophies." The controversy still depended, till the Amphictyons, upon an ocular examination of the matter, gave it for the Lacedaemonians. — *This is according to Chrysermus, in his Third Book of the Peloponnesian History.*

In a war that the Romans had with the Samnites, they made Posthumius Albinus their general. He was surprised in the difficult pass called the Caudine Forks, where he was hemmed in and lost three legions, he himself likewise falling upon the place grievously wounded. In the dead of the night, finding himself near his end, he gathered together the targets of his dead enemies, and raised a trophy with them, which he inscribed with his hand dipped in blood, " Erected by the Romans to Jupiter, Guardian of the Trophies, for a victory over the Samnites." But Fabius Gurges, that was despatched away with troops under his command, so soon as he came to the place and saw the trophy, took up an auspicious omen upon it, fought the enemy, and overcame them, took their king prisoner, and sent him to Rome. — *This is in the Third Book of Aristides Milesius's Italian History.*

4. Upon the Persians falling into Greece with a body of five millions of men, the Spartans sent out Leonidas with a party of three hundred soldiers to secure the Pass of Thermopylae. As they were at dinner, the barbarians fell in upon them ; upon which, Leonidas bade them eat as if they were to sup in another world. Leonidas charged at the head of his men into the body of the barbarians ; and after many wounds received, got up to Xerxes himself, and took his crown from his head. He lost his life in the attempt, and Xerxes causing him to be cut up when he was dead, found his heart all hairy. — *Aristides, in the First Book of his Persian History.*

In the Punic war the Romans sent out three hundred men under the command of Fabius Maximus, where they were all lost; and he himself, after he had received a mortal wound, assaulting Hannibal, took his diadem from his head, and died in the action. *According to Aristides Milesius.*

5. There was a terrible earthquake, with a wonderful eruption of water, at Celaenae, a city of Phrygia, that swallowed up a great many houses, people and all. Midas upon this consults the oracle, which gave him for answer, that if he would cast into that gulf the most precious thing that he had in the world, the earth should close again. Whereupon he threw in a mass of gold and silver; but never the better. This put it in the head of Anchurus, the son of Midas, to consider, that the most precious thing in Nature is the life and soul of a man ; so that he went presently and embraced his father and his wife Timothea, mounted his horse, and leaped into the abyss. The earth closed upon it, and Midas raised a golden altar in the place, laid his hand upon it, and dedicated it TO JUPITER IDAEUS. This altar becomes stone at that time of the year when it was usual to have these eruptions ; and after that season was over, it is turned to gold again. — *My author is Callisthenes, in his Second Book of Transformations.*

The River Tiber, in its course over the Forum, opened a huge cavity in the ground, so that a great many houses were buried in it. This was looked upon as a judgment upon the place, from Jupiter Tarsius ; who, as the oracle told them, was not to be appeased without throwing into it what they held most valuable. So they threw a quantity of gold and silver into it. But Curtius, one of the bravest young men they had, gave a better guess at the mind of the oracle ; and reflecting upon it, that the life of a man was much more excellent than treasure, took his horse and plunged himself into the gulf, and so redeemed his country.— *Aristides, in the Fortieth Book of his Italian History.*

6. As several great captains were making merry with Polynices, an eagle passing by made a stoop, and carried

up into the air the lance of Amphiaraus, who was one of the company; and then falling down, it stuck in the ground, and was turned into a laurel. The next day, when the armies were in action, the earth opened and swallowed up Amphiaraus with his chariot, in that very place where at present the city Harma stands, so called from that chariot. — *This is in Trisimachus's Third Book of the Foundations of Cities.*

When the Romans made war upon Pyrrhus, the king of the Epirots, the oracle promised Aemilius Paulus the victory in case he should erect an altar in that place where he should see an eminent man with his chariot swallowed up into the ground. Some three days after, Valerius Conatus, a man skilled in divining, was commanded in a dream to take the pontifical habit upon him. He did so, and led his men into the battle, where, after a prodigious slaughter of the enemy, the earth opened and swallowed him up. Aemilius built an altar here, obtained a great victory, and sent a hundred and sixty castle-bearing elephants to Rome. This altar delivers oracles about that season of the year in which Pyrrhus was overcome. — *Critolaus has this in his Third Book of the History of the Epirots.*

7. Pyraechmes, king of the Euboeans, made war upon the Boeotians. Hercules, when he was yet a youth, overcame this king, had him drawn to pieces with horses, and threw away the carcass unburied. The place where this was done is called Pyraechmes's horses. It lies upon the River Heraclius, and there is heard a neighing whensoever any horse drinks of that river. — *This is in the Third Book of Rivers.*

Tullus Hostilius, a king of the Romans, waged war against the Albans, whose king's name was Metius Fufetius; and he many times kept off from fighting. He had the ill luck to be once worsted, upon which the Albans gave themselves up to drinking and making good cheer, till Tullus fell in upon them when they were in their cups, and tore their king to pieces betwixt two horses. — *Alexarchus, in the Fourth Book of his Italian History.*

8. Philip had a design to sack Olynthus and Methone, and in trying to pass the River Sandanus, was shot in the eye with an arrow by one Aster, an Olynthian, with these words: It is Aster that sends Philip this mortal shaft. Philip upon this swam back again to his own people, and with the loss of an eye saved his life. — *Callisthenes, in his Third Book of the Macedonics.*

Porsena made war upon the Romans, and pitched his camp on the further side of the Tiber, where he intercepted all relief, till they were pinched with famine. Horatius Cocles, being chosen general, took possession of the wooden bridge, where he opposed himself to the enemy that were pressing to come over; but finding himself overpowered with numbers, he commanded his people to cut down the bridge behind him, by which means he hindered them from coming over. But in the mean time receiving a wound in his eye, he threw himself into the river, and swam over to his own party. — *So Theotimus in the Second Book of his Italian History.*

9. Eratosthenes in Erigone tells a story of Icarius, that entertained Bacchus under his roof; and it runs thus. Saturn, having taken up his lodging with an husbandman who had a very beautiful daughter named Entoria, took her to his bed, and had several sons by her, Janus, Hymnus, Faustus, and Felix. He taught his host Icarius the use of wine and the way of dressing his vines, with a charge that he should likewise instruct his neighbors in the mystery. His acquaintance, hereupon finding that this strange drink had cast them into a deeper sleep than ordi-

nary, took a fancy that they were poisoned, and stoned Icarius in revenge; whereupon his grandchildren hanged themselves for grief.

Upon a time, when the plague was very hot in Rome, the Pythian oracle being consulted gave this answer, that upon the appeasing the wrath of Saturn, and the Manes of those that were unjustly killed, the pestilence would cease. Lutatius Catulus, a man of the first quality, caused a temple upon this occasion to be erected near the Tarpeian Mount, which he dedicated to Saturn, placing an altar in it with four faces; possibly with a respect to Saturn's four children, or to the four seasons of the year. He also instituted the month of January. But Saturn translated them all to heaven among the stars, some of which are called Protrygeteres, as forerunners of the vintage; only Janus rises first, and has his place at the feet of the Virgin. — *Critolaus, in his Fourth Book of Celestial Appearances.*

10. In the time of the devastation of Greece by the Persians, Pausanias, the Lacedaemonian commander, took a bribe of 500 talents of Xerxes, to betray Sparta. The treason being discovered, his father Agesilaus pressed him so hard, that he was fain to take sanctuary in the temple of Minerva, called Chalcioecos, where he caused the doors to be bricked up, and his son to be immured till he died of hunger; and his mother after this would not suffer the body to be buried. — *Chrysermus, in his Second Book of Histories.*

The Romans, being in war with the Latins, made choice of P. Decius for their general. Now there was a certain patrician, a young man and poor (Cassius Brutus by name), who proposed for a certain reward to open the gates to the enemy; but being detected, he fled to the temple of Minerva Auxiliaria. But his father Cassius, an ensign-bearer, shut him up there till he died of famine, and his dead body was not allowed burial. — *Clitonymus, in his Italian History.*

11. Darius, the Persian, had a battle with Alexander near the River Granicus, where he lost seven satraps, and five hundred and two chariots armed with scythes. And yet he would have tried the fortune of another battle the day following; but his son Ariobarzanes, in favor of Alexander, undertook to betray his father into his hands. The father was so transported with passion at the indignity of the thing, that he cut off his son's head for it. — *Aretades Cnidius, in the Third of his Macedonian History.*

Brutus, that was created consul by the unanimous vote of the citizens, forced away Tarquinius Superbus into banishment for his abominable tyranny. He fled to the Tuscans, and by their assistance made war upon the Romans. The sons were treating to betray the father; the business was discovered, and they lost their heads for it. — *Aristides Milesius, in his Italian History.*

12. Epaminondas, a Theban general, managed a war against the Spartans. He went from the army to Thebes, to be present there at a public election of magistrates; but first enjoined his son Stesimbrotus that he should not fight the enemy in his absence upon any terms. The Spartans being informed that Epaminondas was not with the army, reproached the young man with want of courage, and so far provoked him, that without any regard to his father's command he gave the Spartans battle, and overcame them. His father was so incensed against him for this action, that though he crowned him for the victory, he cut off his head for his disobedience. — *Ctesiphon, in his Third Book of the Boeotian History.*

In a war that the Romans had against the Samnites,

they gave the command to Manlius, surnamed Imperiosus. He had occasion to go to Rome, to be present there at the choice of consuls, and gave his son in charge not to engage the enemy in the mean time. The Samnites, understanding this, irritated the young man with opprobrious words, as if he declined fighting out of cowardice, and in the end provoked him to a battle; upon which action he carried the day; but his father caused his head to be struck off for breaking his order. — *This is in Aristides Milesius.*

13. Hercules made love to Iole, but she gave him the repulse, and so he went and assaulted Oechalia. Iole threw herself headlong down from the wall, but the whiffling of the wind under her garments broke the fall, and she had no hurt. — *This story is in Nicias Maleotes.*

Valerius Torquatus was the Romans' general in the war they had with the Tuscans; who, upon the sight of Clusia, the daughter of the Tuscan king, fell in love with her, and when he found he could do no good on't, laid siege to the city. Clusia, upon this, threw herself headlong from a tower; but Venus was so careful of her, that by the playing of the wind in the folds of her garments, she was wafted safe to the ground. Torquatus, however, offered her violence, and for so doing he was banished by a public decree into the isle of Corsica. — *Theophilus, in the Third Book of his Italian History.*

14. While the Carthaginians were treating an alliance with the Sicilians against the Romans, the Roman general Metellus was observed to omit sacrificing only to Vesta, who revenged herself upon him by sending a cross wind to the navy. But Caius Julius, a soothsayer, being consulted in the matter, gave answer, that this obstacle would

be removed upon the general's sacrificing his daughter, so that he was forced to produce his daughter Metella for a sacrifice. But Vesta had compassion for her, and so sent her away to Lamusium, substituting a heifer in her stead, and made a priestess of her to the dragon that is worshipped in that place. — *So Pythocles, in the Third Book of his Italian History.*

Something like this happened to Iphigenia in Aulis, a city of Boeotia. — *See Meryllus, in the First Book of his Boeotic History.*

15. Brennus, a king of the Gauls, after the wasting of Asia, came to Ephesus, and there fell in love with a country girl, who promised him that for such a certain reward in bracelets and other curiosities of value he should have the use of her body, and that she would further undertake to deliver up Ephesus into his hands. Brennus ordered his soldiers to throw all the gold they had into the lap of this avaricious wretch, which they did, till she perished under the weight of it. — *Clitophon in the First Book of his Gallican History.*

Tarpeia, a virgin that was well born, and had the keeping of the Capitol in the war betwixt the Sabines and the Romans, passed a promise unto Tatius, that she would open him a passage into the Tarpeian Mount, provided that he would give her all the jewels that the Sabines wore, for a reward. The Sabines hearing this crushed her to death — *Aristides's Milesius, in his Italic History.*

16. After a long war betwixt two cities, Tegea and Phenea, they came to an agreement to refer the decision of the controversy, by combat, to three twin-brothers on each side, the sons of Reximachus for Tegea, and the sons of Damostratus for Phenea. Upon the encounter, two of the sons of Reximachus were slain; but Critolaus, the third, had a

fetch beyond his two brothers; for, under a pretence of running away, he divided his enemies that pursued him, and so taking them one by one, he killed them all. The Tegeans upon his return went all overjoyed to gratulate the victor. Only his sister Demodice was not so well pleased; for she was betrothed, it seems, to Demodicus, one of the brothers, that was now slain. Which Critolaus took so ill that he killed his sister, and being afterwards indicted for murder at the instigation of his mother, he was acquitted. — *Demaratus, in his Second Book of the Arcadian History.*

In the heat of the war betwixt the Romans and Albans, they came to this agreement, that the cause should be determined by a trial at arms betwixt three and three twins on each side, the Curiatii for the Albans, and the Horatii for the Romans. Upon the encounter, the Curiatii killed two of the others; the third survivor, under the color of flying, destroyed his enemies one by one, as they followed him. All his friends came to joy him of his victory, save only his sister Horatia; for one of the Curiatii, that her brother killed, was her sweetheart. Horatius for this killed his sister. — *Aristides Milesius, in his Italian Commentaries.*

17. The temple of Minerva in Ilium happened to be on fire. Ilus ran presently to save the Palladium (an image dropped from heaven); but upon the taking of it up, he was struck blind, it being a thing unlawful for any man to look upon. But upon appeasing the Deity, he was afterwards restored to his sight. — *Dercyllus, in his First Book of Foundations.*

Metellus, an eminent man, as he was walking out of the city, was interrupted by ravens, that laid hold of him and kept a flapping of him with their wings. This omen surprised him, and back he went into the city again, where he found the temple of Vesta all in a flame. He went and took away the Palladium, and fell blind upon't. But some time after, the Goddess being pacified gave him the use of his eyes again. — *Aristides Milesius, in his Italian History.*

18. Upon a time when the Thracians were engaged in a war against the Athenians, the oracle promised them victory if they would but save the life of Codrus. Codrus upon this puts himself in a coarse disguise, and away he goes into the enemies' camp with a scythe in his hand, where he killed one, and another killed him, so that the Athenians got the better on't. — *Socrates, in his Second Book of his Thracian History.*

Publius Decius, a Roman, at a time when they were in war with the Albans, had a dream that his death would bring a great advantage to the Romans; upon which consideration he charged into the middle of his enemies, where he killed many, and was slain himself: his son Decius did the like in the Gallic war, for the conservation of the Roman State. — *Aristides Milesius is my author.*

19. There was one Cyanippus a Syracusan, that sacrificed to all the Gods but Bacchus; who took the contempt so heinously that he made him drunk, in which fit he got his daughter Cyane into a corner and lay with her. She in the mean time slipped his ring off his finger, and gave it to her nurse to keep, as a circumstance that some time or other might come to be brought in evidence. There brake out a pestilence, and the Pythian oracle advised the sacrificing of an incestuous person to the Gods that are the averters of such calamities, as the only remedy. Cyane, that understood the meaning of the oracle better than other people, took her father by the hair of the head and dragged him forth, first stabbing him and then her-

self. — *Dositheus, in the Third Book of his Sicilian History.*

In the time of celebrating the Bacchanalia at Rome, Aruntius, that had never drunk any wine since he was born, did not show such reverence for the power of the God as he ought to have done, so that Bacchus intoxicated him; and in that freak, Aruntius ravished his daughter Medullina. She came to know the ravisher by his ring, and an exploit came into her head, above what from her age could have been expected. She made her father drunk and set a garland upon his head, carrying him to the altar of Thunder, where with tears she killed him for robbing her so treacherously of her virginity. — *Aristides, in the Third Book of his Italian History.*

20. Erechtheus was told in a war he had with Eumolpus, that he should have the better of his enemy if he would but sacrifice his daughter. He advised upon the matter with his wife Praxithea, and delivered up his daughter after the manner of a common sacrifice. — *Euripides, in his Erechtheus.*

Marius, finding himself hard put to it in the Cimbrian war, had it revealed to him in a dream, that he should overcome his enemies if he would but sacrifice his daughter Calpurnia. He did it, preferring the common safety before any private bond of Nature, and he got the victory. There are two altars in Germany, where about that time of the year may be heard the sound of trumpets. — *Dorotheus, in the Fourth Book of his Italian History.*

21. There was one Cyanippus, a Thessalian, who was a great lover of the chase and was often abroad a hunting. This same Cyanippus was newly married, and his staying out so long and so often in the woods gave his wife a jealousy of an intrigue there with some other woman; in-

somuch that she followed him one time, and got into a
thicket to watch him. The rustling of the boughs in the
place where she lay brought the dogs thither in expectation
of some game, where they tore this tender-hearted woman
to pieces, as if she had been a brute beast. Cyanippus
was so surprised with so dismal and unthought-of a spectacle, that he killed himself. — *Parthenias the Poet.*

Sybaris is a city of Italy, where there was one Aemilius,
a very handsome young man, and a lover of hunting. His
wife (whom he had lately married) took up a suspicion
that, under color of the chase, he carried on an assignation
with some other woman. She traced him to the wood, and
upon the noise of the boughs in her passage, the dogs ran
presently to her and tore her to pieces; and her husband
stabbed himself immediately upon this miserable accident. — *Clitonymus, in the Second Book of his Sybaritics.*

22. One Smyrna (to whom Venus owed a shame, it
seems) fell passionately in love with her father Cinyras, and
made the nurse her confidant. She goes craftily to work
with her master, and tells him of a maid there in the
neighborhood that loved him above all things in the world,
but she could not in modesty appear publicly to him. So
the father lay ignorantly with his own daughter. But
some time after, having a great mind to see his mistress,
he called for a light, and when he saw who it was, he
pursued the incestuous wretch with his drawn sword; but
by the providence of Venus, she was rescued from that
danger, and turned into a myrrh-tree. — *Theodorus, in
his Transformations.*

One Valeria Tusculanaria (for whom Venus had no
kindness) fell downright in love with her father Valerius.
She told the nurse the secret, who ordered it so that she
brought the father and the daughter together, telling him,
that a maid there hard by was fallen desperately in love

with him, but that she durst not lie with him for fear of being known. The father was got into his cups, and as he was in bed with his daughter, called for a candle. The nurse waked Valeria, and away she goes wandering up and down the country with her great belly. She had at last a fall from a precipice, but escaped without so much as any miscarriage; for she was delivered at her time, and the child's name was Sylvanus (or goat-footed Pan). Valerius, in the anxiety of his mind, threw himself from the same precipice. — *Aristides Milesius, in the Third Book of his Italian History.*

23. Diomedes, after the destruction of Troy, was cast by stress of weather upon the coast of Libya, where Lycus the son of Mars was king, whose custom it was to sacrifice all strangers to his father; but his daughter Callirrhoe falling in love with Diomede, betrayed her father and set Diomede at liberty; who presently went his way without any regard to his benefactress, and Callirrhoe hanged herself upon it. — *Juba, Book the Third of his Libyan History.*

Calpurnius Crassus, a famous man bearing arms with Regulus, was sent to the Massyllians to attack the castle of Garaetius, being a very strong place. He was taken in the enterprise, and designed for a sacrifice to Saturn; but Bisaltia, the king's daughter, out of a passionate kindness to Calpurnius, betrayed her father. Calpurnius left her, and after his departure Bisaltia cut her own throat. — *Hesianax's Third Book of African History.*

24. When Priam found that Troy was given for lost, he sent his young son Polydore into Thrace with a vast sum of gold, and put all into the hands of Polymestor his kinsman. So soon as Troy was taken, Polymestor killed the child, and took the gold to himself. Hecuba, being

driven upon that quarter, overreached Polymestor by craft, under pretence of giving him a great treasure, at which time she, with the assistance of her fellow-prisoners, tore out his eyes with her nails. — *Euripides the Tragedian.*

When Hannibal was ravaging the country of Campania, Lucius Thymbris deposited his son Rustius, with a vast sum of money, in the hands of Valerius Gestius his kinsman; who upon intelligence that the enemy carried all before him, out of pure avarice and without any regard to humanity or justice, killed the child. It so fell out that Thymbris, as he was walking about the fields, found the dead body of his son; whereupon he called his kinsman under pretence of a treasure that he would show him. He took his opportunity, put out his eyes, and crucified him. — *Aristides's Third Book of his Italic History.*

25. Aeacus had two sons by Psamathe, Phocus and Telamon, the former better beloved than the other. Telamon one day took out his brother a hunting; and a boar presenting himself, he threw his lance in pretence at the boar, but in truth at his brother, whom he hated, and so killed him; for which his father banished him. — *Dorotheus's First Book of Transformations.*

Caius Maximus had two sons, Rhesus the one, by Ameria, . . . and the other Similius. The brothers were a hunting together, and Rhesus having killed the other, put it off — when he came home — that it was by chance, and far from any design of doing it. But his father, when he came in time to know the truth of it, banished the son. — *Aristocles, in the Third Book of his Italian History.*

26. Mars is said to have begotten Meleager upon Althaea. — *Euripides, in his Meleager.*

Septimius Marcellus took to wife one Sylvia, and a great lover of hunting he was. Mars put himself in the habit of a shepherd, whored the new wife and got her with child; which being done, he told her who he was, and gave her a spear, telling her that the fate of the child she went withal was wrapped up in the fate of that spear. . . .

Septimius slew Tuscinus; but Mamercus, in his sacrificing to the Gods for a fruitful season, omitted only Ceres, who in revenge sent a wild boar into his grounds. Whereupon getting a knot of huntsmen together, he killed him, and delivered the head and skin to his sweetheart; but Scymbrates and Muthias, the maid's uncles, took them away from her. Mamercus in a rage killed them upon it, and the mother burned the spear.—*Menyllus, in the Third Book of his Italian History.*

27. When Telamon, the son of Aeacus and Endeis, came to Euboea, he debauched Periboea the daughter of Alcathous, and fled away by night. The father understanding this, and suspecting the villany to be done by some of the citizens, he delivered his daughter to one of the guards to be thrown into the sea. But the soldier, in compassion to the woman, rather sold her, and she was carried away by sea to the island of Salamis, where Telamon bought her, and had by her Ajax.—*Aretades Cnidius, in his Second Book of Islands.*

Lucius Troscius had by Patris a daughter called Florentia, who, being corrupted by Calpurnius a Roman, was delivered by her father to a soldier, with a charge to throw her in the sea and drown her. The man had compassion of her, and rather sold her. And when good fortune brought the ship to Italy, Calpurnius bought her, and had Contruscus by her. . . .

28. Aeolus, a great king of Etruria, had by Amphithea six daughters, and as many sons. Macareus, the youngest

of them, had the carnal knowledge of one of his sisters, who was delivered of a boy. Her father sent her a sword to kill the child with; but that was so impious, that she chose rather to kill herself. And Macareus laid violent hands upon himself too. — *Sostratus, in his Second Book of Tuscan History.*

Papirius Tolucer married Julia Pulchra, by whom he had six sons and six daughters. Papirius Romanus, the eldest of the six, got Canulia his sister with child. When the father came to the knowledge of it, he sent his daughter a sword, with which she killed herself; and Romanus did the same. — *Chrysippus, in his First Book of Italian History.*

29. Aristonymus, an Ephesian and the son of Demostratus, was a woman-hater; but he had to do with an ass, which brought him forth in the ordinary course of time a most beautiful daughter. which he called Onoscelis. — *Aristotle's Second Book of Paradoxes.*

Fulvius Stellus had an aversion to women too; but entertained himself to his satisfaction with a mare, by which he had a very handsome daughter, that he called Hippona; and this is the goddess that has the care of the breed of horses. — *According to Agesilaus, in the Third Book of his Italian History.*

30. The Sardians, being engaged in war with the Smyrnaeans, besieged Smyrna, and sent them word by their ambassadors, that they would never raise the siege till the Smyrnaeans should deliver up their wives to their embraces. The men of Smyrna would have been hard put to it upon this pinching necessity, if it had not been for the advice of a pretty wench that was a maid-servant to Phylarchus. Her counsel to her master was this; that instead of sending free women, they should rather dress up the servants

and send them. The Smyrnaeans followed their advice; and when the Sardians had wearied themselves with their mistresses, the Smyrnaeans easily overcame them. From whence there is a festival day observed under the name of Eleutheria, which is celebrated among the Smyrnaeans with great solemnity; the servants being dressed up with all the ornaments of the free women. — *Dositheus, in the Third Book of his Lydian History.*

Atepomarus, a king of the Gauls, being in war with the Romans, made a public declaration, that he would never agree to a peace till the Romans should prostitute their wives to them. The Romans advised with the maid-servants, and sent them in the place of the free women; the barbarians plied the work so hard, that they were soon tired and fell asleep. Retana (who was the authoress of the counsel) climbed a fig-tree, and so got on the wall; and finding how it was, gave notice of it to the consuls. The Romans upon this made a sally and routed the enemy; in memory whereof was instituted the Servants' Holiday, and this was the rise of it. — *Aristides Milesius, in the First Book of his Italian History.*

31. In the war betwixt the Athenians and Eumolpus, provisions falling short, the commissary Pyrandrus, upon a point of prudence and good husbandry, made some small abatement in the soldiers' proportions. The citizens suspected treachery in the case, and stoned him to death. — *Callisthenes, Third Book of his History of Thrace.*

The Romans being in war with the Gauls, and provisions for the belly being very scarce, Cinna contracted the soldiers' allowance to a less proportion than they had formerly. The citizens interpreted this abatement to an ambitious design he had upon the government, and so stoned him for it. — *Aristides, Book Third of his Italian History.*

32. In the time of the Peloponnesian war, Pisistratus an Orchomenian had a spite at the nobility, and to make himself popular, favored the common people. The Senate conspired against him, and treacherously killed him, cutting him into small gobbets which they carried away with them in their bosoms, and paring off the surface of the ground that no signs of the murder might appear. The common people, however, upon a jealousy of the matter, went tumultuously to the senate house; but the king's younger son Telesimachus that was dipped in the conspiracy, diverted them with a sham story, telling them that he himself had seen his father in a form more than human, walking as lively as was possible up the Pisaean mountain. And so he imposed upon the people. — *Theophilus's Second Book of Peloponnesian Histories.*

The Senate of Rome, being hard put to it for the maintaining of a war with so many of their neighbors, thought it good husbandry to shorten the people's allowance of corn, which Romulus the king took very ill; and not only did he restore it to the people, but several great men were punished for it. Upon this he was murdered in the Senate by a conspiracy of the nobles, who cut him all to pieces, and carried them severally away in the lappets of their garments. The Romans came to the senate house in a hurry, and brought fire with them to set all in a flame; but Julius Proculus, one that was in the plot, told them that he saw Romulus upon a mountain, of a size larger than any man, and that he was translated into the number of the Gods. The Romans believed him, and quietly withdrew. — *Aristobulus, in the Third Book of his History of Italy.*

33. Pelops the son of Tantalus and Euryanassa, had two children, Atreus and Thyestes, by his wife Hippodamia; and by the Nymph Danais he had Chrysippus,

whom he loved better than his lawful children. But Laius
the Theban in the heat of his lust forcibly abused his
body; and being taken by Atreus and Thyestes, obtained
his pardon from Pelops, in regard that love had provoked
him to it. Hippodamia's advice to Atreus and Thyestes
was, that they should kill Chrysippus, as one that would
interpose between them and the crown. Upon their refusal to do so base a thing, she herself put her own hands to
the work, and in the dead of the night took Laius's sword
when he was asleep, wounded Chrysippus with it, and left
the weapon in his body. This circumstance of Laius's
sword brought him into suspicion of the murder, till he
was cleared by Chrysippus himself, who, being as yet but
half dead, gave his testimony to the truth. Pelops buried
his son. and then banished his wife. — *Dositheus, in his
Pelopidae.*

Ebius Toliex had two sons by his wife Nuceria, and a
third called Firmus by an enfranchised woman, who was
very handsome and better beloved by the father than those
that were legitimate. Nuceria that hated this by-blow,
advised her sons to despatch Firmus; but upon their refusal, she did it herself; and in the dead of the night got
the sword of him that guarded the body of Firmus, gave
him a mortal wound, and left the weapon sticking in his
body. The boy cleared his keeper by a particular account
of the matter of fact; the father buried his son, and sent
away his wife into banishment. — *Dositheus, Book Third
of his Italian History.*

34. Theseus, the true son of Neptune, had Hippolytus
by the Amazon Hippolyta, and afterward married Phaedra
the daughter of Minos, who fell deep in love with Hippolytus, and made use of the nurse's mediation to help
forward the incest. But Hippolytus upon this left Athens
and went away to Troezen, where he diverted himself with

hunting. Now this lascivious woman, finding her design disappointed, forged several scandalous letters to the prejudice of the chaste young man, and ended her days with a halter. Theseus gave credit to the slander, and Neptune having promised him a grant of any three things he would ask, he made it his request that he would destroy Hippolytus. So Neptune sent a bull to the coast where Hippolytus was driving his chariot, which put his horses into such a fright, that they ran away with them, and overturning the chariot killed the master.

Comminius Super, a Laurentine, had a son by the nymph Egeria, whom he called Comminius; after which he married one Gidica, who fell passionately in love with her son-in-law. And receiving a repulse, she framed slanderous letters against him, which she left behind her, and so hanged herself. Comminius, reflecting upon the crime and believing the calumny, applied himself to Neptune, who with a terrible bull frighted the horses so, while the youth was in the chariot, that they overturned all, and killed him with the fall. — *Dositheus, Book Third of Italian Histories.*

35. In the time of a great plague in Lacedaemon, they were told by the oracle, that the pestilence would cease upon the sacrificing of a noble virgin every year. It fell one time by lot to Helena, who was brought out and dressed up ready for the sacrifice. An eagle at that time flying by took away the sword, and carrying it into a herd of cattle laid it down upon a heifer; whereupon they spared the virgin. — *Aristodemus, in his Third Collection of Fables.*

There was a dreadful plague in Falerii, which the oracle said would be removed upon the sacrificing of a virgin to Juno every year. While this superstition was in course, it fell to Valeria Luperca's lot to be the sacrifice. An eagle flew away with the drawn sword, but laid a stick upon the fuel prepared for the fire, with a little mallet fixed to it. The sword he threw upon a heifer feeding near the temple. The virgin perceiving this sacrificed the heifer; and taking up the mallet, went about from house to house, and with a gentle knock called to those that were sick, bidding them be of good health. And this was the rise of the ceremony which continues to this day. — *Aristides, in his Nineteenth Book of Italian Histories.*

36. Philonome, the daughter of Nyctimus and Arcadia, went many times to the chase with Diana. Mars lay with her in the shape of a shepherd, and fetched up her belly. She was delivered in time of twins, which for fear of her father she threw into the river Erymanthus. By a strange fatality of providence they were driven safe into a hollow oak, which happening to be the kennel of a wolf, this wolf threw her whelps into the river, and suckled the children. Tyliphus a shepherd, that had seen this with his own eyes, took these children and brought them up as his own, calling one of them Lycastus, and the other Parrasius, which reigned successively in Arcadia. — *This is reported by Zopyrus Byzantius, in the Third Book of his Histories.*

Amulius dealing very tyrannically with his brother Numitor, killed his son Aenitus as they were a hunting, and made his daughter Sylvia . . . a priestess of Juno. Mars got her with child, and when she had laid her belly of twins, she confessed the truth to the tyrant; which put him in such an apprehension, that he exposed them both on the side of the river Tiber, where they were carried by the stream to a place where a she-wolf had her whelps. The wolf cast away her own, and gave suck to these children. Faustus a shepherd, observing this, took the children to himself, and called them by the names of Romus and Romulus, which came afterwards to be the founders of Rome. — *Aristides's Italian Histories.*

37. After the destruction of Troy, Agamemnon and Cassandra were killed; but Orestes, that was brought up with Strophius, revenged the death of his father. — *Pyrander's Fourth Book of Peloponnesian Histories.*

Fabius Fabricianus, a kinsman of Fabius Maximus, having taken Tuxium, the chief city of the Samnites, sent to Rome the image of Venus Victrix, which among them was held in great veneration. His wife Fabia was debauched by Petronius Valentinus, a handsome young man, and afterwards she treacherously murdered her husband; but for her son Fabricianus who was yet in his infancy, she shifted him away to be privately brought up, and so provided for his security. When he was grown up, he destroyed both his mother and the adulterer, and was formally acquitted for it by a decree of the Senate. — *Dositheus's Third Book of Italian History.*

38. Busiris, the son of Neptune and Anippe the daughter of Nilus, was used to invite strangers in to him under a pretence of hospitality, and then to murder them; but divine vengeance met with him at last, for Hercules found out the villany, and killed him with his club. — *Agatho the Samian.*

Hercules, as he was driving Geryon's oxen through Italy, took up his lodging with King Faunus there, the son of Mercury, whose custom it was to sacrifice strangers to his father. He set upon Hercules, and had his brains beaten out for his pains. — *Dercyllus's Third Book of Italian History.*

39. Phalaris of Agrigentum, a cruel tyrant, was wont to put strangers and travellers to the most exquisite torment.

Perillus, a brass-founder, made a cow of brass, and presented it to the king for a new invention, that he might burn strangers alive in it. Phalaris for this once was just, in making the first proof of it upon Perillus himself; and the invention was so artificial, that upon putting it in execution, the engine itself seemed to bellow. — *Second Book of Questions or Causes.*

In Egesta, a city of Sicily, there was a certain tyrant called Aemilius Censorinus, who was so inhuman that he proposed rewards to the inventors of new tortures. There was one Aruntius Paterculus that had framed a brazen horse, and made a present of it to the tyrant to practise with it upon whom he pleased. It was the first piece of justice that ever the tyrant did, to make trial of the torment upon the author of it, that he might first feel himself the torments he had provided for others. He was afterwards thrown down from the Tarpeian Rock. It may be thought that unmerciful rulers are from this tyrant called Aemilii. — *Aristides's Fourth Book of Italian History.*

40. Evenus, the son of Mars and Sterope, had a daughter Marpessa by his wife Alcippe, the daughter of Oenomaus; and this girl he had a mind to keep a virgin. But Idas, the son of Aphareus, ran away with her from a choir. Evenus pursued him, and finding he could not overtake him, he threw himself into the river Lycormas, and became immortal. — *Dositheus's First Book of Italian History.*

Anius, a king of the Tuscans, had a delicate, handsome daughter, whose name was Salia, and he took great care to keep her a virgin. But Cathetus, a man of quality, seeing her sporting herself, fell passionately in love with her, and carried her away to Rome. The father made after her, and when he saw there was no catching of her, he threw himself into a river that from him took the name of Anio. Cathetus begot Latinus and Salius upon the body of Salia, the root of a noble race. — *Aristides Milesius, and Alexander Polyhistor's Third Book of Italian History.*

41. Hegesistratus an Ephesian committed a murder in his family, and fled to Delphi; on consulting the oracle what place to settle in, the answer was, that when he should come to a place where he should see the country people dancing with garlands of olive-leaves, he should settle there. He travelled into a certain country of Asia, where he found as the oracle told him, and there built a city which he called Elacus. — *Pythocles the Samian, in the Third Book of his Georgics.*

Telegonus, the son of Ulysses by Circe, was sent to find out his father, and commanded by an oracle to erect a city where he should see the country people dancing with garlands. He came into a certain place of Italy, where he found the countrymen dancing with wreaths of ilex about their heads; so that there he built a city, and called it Prinistum, for an ilex in Greek is πρῖνος. The Romans corruptly call this city Praeneste. — *Aristocles, in the Third Book of his Italian History.*

OF THE NAMES OF RIVERS AND MOUNTAINS, AND OF SUCH THINGS AS ARE TO BE FOUND THEREIN.*

I. HYDASPES.

THIS is a river of India, which falls with an extraordinary swift stream into the Saronitic Syrtis. Chrysippe, by the impulse of Venus, whom she had offended, fell in love with her father Hydaspes, and not being able to curb her preternatural desires, by the help of her nurse, in the dead of the night got to his bed and received his caresses; after which, the king proving unfortunate in his affairs, he buried alive the old bawd that had betrayed him, and crucified his daughter. Nevertheless such was the excess of his grief for the loss of Chrysippe, that he threw himself into the river Indus, which was afterwards called by his name Hydaspes.

Moreover in this river there grows a stone, which is called lychnis, which resembles the color of oil, and is very bright in appearance. And when they are searching after it, which they do when the moon increases, the pipers play all the while. Nor is it to be worn by any but the richer sort. Also near that part of the river which is called Pylae, there grows an herb which is very like a heliotrope, with the juice of which the people anoint their skins to prevent sunburning, and to secure them against the scorching of the excessive heat.

* A very slight inspection of this strange treatise will convince the reader that it is justly placed among the Pseudoplutarchea. It is reprinted here merely because it was included in the original translation. (G.)

The natives whenever they take their virgins tardy, nail them to a wooden cross, and fling them into this river, singing at the same time in their own language a hymn to Venus. Every year also they bury a condemned old woman near the top of the hill called Therogonos; at which time an infinite multitude of creeping creatures come down from the top of the hill, and devour the insects that hover about the buried carcass. This Chrysermus relates in his History of India, though Archelaus gives a more exact account of these things in his Treatise of Rivers.

Near to this river lies the mountain Elephas, so called upon this occasion. When Alexander the Macedonian advanced with his army into India, and the natives were resolved to withstand him with all their force, the elephant upon which Porus, king of that region, was wont to ride, being of a sudden stung with a gad-bee, ran up to the top of the mountain of the sun, and there uttered these words distinctly in human speech: "O king, my lord, descended from the race of Gegasius, forbear to attempt any thing against Alexander, for he is descended from Jupiter." And having so said, he presently died. Which when Porus understood, afraid of Alexander, he fell at his feet and sued for peace. Which when he had obtained, he called the mountain Elephas;—as Dercyllus testifies in his Third Book of Mountains.

II. Ismenus.

ISMENUS is a river of Boeotia, that washes the walls of Thebes. It was formerly called the foot of Cadmus, upon this occasion. When Cadmus had slain the dragon which kept the fountain of Mars, he was afraid to taste of the water, believing it was poisoned; which forced him to wander about in search of another fountain to allay his thirst. At length, by the help of Minerva, he came to the Corycian den, where his right leg stuck deep in the mire. And from that hole it was that, after he had pulled his leg out again, sprung a fair river, which the hero, after the solemnity of his sacrifices performed, called by the name of Cadmus's foot.

Some time after, Ismenus, the son of Amphion and Niobe, being wounded by Apollo and in great pain, threw himself into the said river, which was then from his name called Ismenus; — as Sostratus relates in his Second Book of Rivers.

Near to this river lies the mountain Cithaeron, formerly called Asterion for this reason. Boeotus the son of Neptune was desirous, of two noble ladies, to marry her that should be most beneficial to him; and while he tarried for both in the night-time upon the top of a certain nameless mountain, of a sudden a star fell from heaven upon the shoulders of Eurythemiste, and immediately vanished. Upon which Boeotus, understanding the meaning of the prodigy, married the virgin, and called the mountain Asterion from the accident that befell him. Afterwards it was called Cithaeron upon this occasion. Tisiphone, one of the Furies, falling in love with a most beautiful youth whose name was Cithaeron, and not being able to curb the impatience of her desires, declared her affection to him in a letter, to which he would not return any answer. Whereupon the Fury, missing her design, pulled one of the serpents from her locks, and flung it upon the young lad as he was keeping his sheep on the top of the mountain Asterion; where the serpent twining about his neck choked him to death. And thereupon by the will of the Gods the mountain was called Cithaeron; — as Leo of Byzantium writes in his History of Boeotia.

But Hermesianax of Cyprus tells the story quite otherwise. For he says, that Helicon and Cithaeron were two brothers, quite different in their dispositions. For Helicon was affable and mild, and cherished his aged parents. But Cithaeron, being covetous and greedily gaping after the estate, first killed his father, and then treacherously threw his brother down from a steep precipice, but in striving together, fell himself along with him. Whence, by the providence of the Gods, the names of both the mountains were changed. Cithaeron, by reason of his impiety, became the haunt of the Furies. Helicon, for the young man's love to his parents, became the habitation of the Muses.

III. Hebrus.

Hebrus is a river of Thrace, deriving its former name of Rhombus from the many gulfs and whirlpools in the water.

Cassander, king of that region, having married Crotonice, had by her a son whom he named Hebrus. But then being divorced from his first wife, he married Damasippe, the daughter of Atrax, and brought her home over his son's head; with whom the mother-in-law falling in love, invited him by letters to her embraces. But he, avoiding his mother-in-law as a Fury, gave himself over to the sport of hunting. On the other side the impious woman, missing her purpose, belied the chaste youth, and accused him of attempting to ravish her. Upon this Cassander, raging with jealousy, flew to the wood in a wild fury, and with his sword drawn pursued his son, as one that treacherously sought to defile his father's bed. Upon which the son, finding he could no way escape his father's wrath, threw himself into the river Rhombus, which was afterwards called Hebrus from the name of the young man; — as Timotheus testifies in his Eleventh Book of Rivers.

Near to this river lies the mountain Pangaeus, so called upon this occasion. Pangaeus, the son of Mars and Critobule, by a mistake lay with his own daughter; which perplexed him to that degree that he fled to the Carmanian mountain, where, overwhelmed with a sorrow that he could not master, he drew his sword and slew himself. Whence, by the providence of the Gods, the place was called Pangaeus.

In the river before mentioned, grows an herb not much unlike to origanum; the tops of which the Thracians cropping off burn upon a fire, and after they are filled with the fruits of Ceres, they hold their heads over the smoke, and snuff it up into their nostrils, letting it go down their throats, till at last they fall into a profound sleep.

Also upon the mountain Pangaeus grows an herb, which is called the harp upon this occasion. The women that tore Orpheus in pieces cast his limbs into the river Hebrus; and his head being changed, the whole body was turned into the shape of a dragon. But as for his harp, such was the will of Apollo, it remained in the same form. And from the streaming blood grew up the herb which was called the harp; which, during the solemnity of the sacrifices to Bacchus, sends forth a sound like that of an harp when played upon. At which time the natives, being covered with the skins of young hinds and waving their thyrsuses in their hands, sing a hymn, of which these are part of the words,

> When wisdom all in vain must be,
> Then be not wise at all; —

as Clitonymus reports, in his Third Book of Thracian Relations.

IV. Ganges.

Ganges is a river in India, so called for this reason. A certain Calaurian nymph had by Indus a son called Ganges, conspicuous for his beauty. Who growing up to manhood, being once desperately overcome with wine, in the heat of his intoxication lay with his mother. The next day he was informed by the nurse of what he had done; and such was the excess of his sorrow, that he threw himself into a river called Chliarus, afterwards called Ganges from his own name.

In this river grows an herb resembling bugloss, which the natives bruise, and keep the juice very charily. With this juice in the dead of the night they go and besprinkle the tigers' dens; the virtue of which is such, that the tigers, not being able to stir forth by reason of the strong scent of the juice, are starved to death; — as Callisthenes reports in his Third Book of Hunting.

Upon the banks of this river lies the mountain called the Anatole for this reason. The Sun, beholding the nymph Anaxibia innocently spending her time in dancing, fell passionately in love with her, and not able to curb his loose amours, pursued her with a purpose to ravish her. She therefore, finding no other way to escape him, fled to the temple of Orthian Diana, which was seated upon the mountain called Coryphe, and there immediately vanished away. Upon which the Sun, that followed her close at the heels, not knowing what was become of his beloved, overwhelmed with grief, rose in that very place. And from this accident it was that the natives called the top of that mountain Anatole, or the rising of the Sun; — as Caemaron reports in his Tenth Book of the Affairs of India.

V. Phasis.

Phasis is a river of Scythia, running by a city of the same name. It was formerly called Arcturus, deriving its name from the situation of the cold regions through which it runs. But the name of it was altered upon this occasion.

Phasis, the child of the Sun and Ocyrrhoe daughter of Oceanus, slew his mother, whom he took in the very act of adultery. For which being tormented by the Furies appearing to him, he threw himself into the river Arcturus, which was afterwards called by his own name Phasis.

In this river grows a reed, which is called leucophyllus, or the reed with the white leaf. This reed is found at the dawning of the morning light, at what time the sacrifices are offered to Hecate, at the time when the divinely inspired paean is chanted, at the beginning of the spring; when they who are troubled with jealous heads gather this reed, and strew it in their wives' chambers to keep them chaste. And the nature of the reed is such, that if any wild extravagant person happens to come rashly in drink into the room where it lies, he presently becomes deprived of his rational thoughts, and immediately confesses whatever he has wickedly done and intended to do. At what time they that are present to hear him lay hold of him, sew him up in a sack, and throw him into a hole called the Mouth of the Wicked, which is round like the mouth of a well. This after thirty days empties the body into the Lake Maeotis, that is full of worms; where of a sudden the body is seized and torn to pieces by several vultures unseen before, nor is it known from whence they come; — as Ctesippus relates in his Second Book of Scythian Relations.

Near to this river lies the mountain Caucasus, which was before called Boreas's Bed, upon this occasion. Boreas in the heat of his amorous passion ravished away by force Chione, the daughter of Arcturus, and carried her to a certain hill which was called Niphantes, and upon her begot a son whom he called Hyrpax, who succeeded Heniochus in his kingdom. For which reason the mountain was first called Boreas's Bed; but afterwards Caucasus upon this occasion. After the fight of the Giants, Saturn, to avoid the menaces of Jupiter, fled to the top of Boreas's Bed, and there being turned into a crocodile [lay concealed. But Prometheus] slew Caucasus one of the shepherds inhabiting that place; and cutting him up and observing the disposition of his entrails, he foresaw that his enemies were not far off. Presently Jupiter appearing, and binding his father with a woollen list, threw him down to hell. Then changing the name of the mountain in honor of the shepherd Caucasus, he chained Prometheus to it, and caused him to be tormented by an eagle that fed upon his entrails, because he was the first that found out the inspection of bowels, which Jupiter deemed a great cruelty;— as Cleanthes relates in his Third Book of the Wars of the Gods.

Upon this mountain grows an herb which is called Prometheus, which Medea gathering and bruising made use of to protect Jason against her father's obstinacy.

VI. Arar.

Arar is a river in Gallia Celtica, deriving the name from its being mixed with the river Rhone. For it falls into the Rhone within the country of the Allobroges. It was formerly called Brigulus, but afterwards changed its name upon this occasion. Arar, as he was a hunting, entering into the wood, and there finding his brother Celtiber torn in pieces by the wild beasts, mortally wounded himself for grief, and fell into the river Brigulus; which from that accident was afterwards called by his own name Arar.

In this river there breeds a certain large fish, which by the natives is called Clupaea. This fish during the increase of the moon is white; but all the while the moon is in the wane, it is altogether black; and when it grows over bulky, it is (as it were) stabbed by its own fins. In the head of it is found a stone like a corn of salt, which, being applied to the left parts of the body when the moon is in the wane, cures quartan agues; — as Callisthenes the Sybarite tells us in the Thirteenth Book of Gallic Relations, from whom Timagenes the Syrian borrowed his argument.

Near to this river stands a mountain called Lugdunum, which changed its name upon this occasion. When Momorus and Atepomarus were dethroned by Seseroneus, in pursuance of the oracle's command they designed to build a city upon the top of the hill. But when they had laid the foundations, great numbers of crows with their wings expanded covered all the neighboring trees. Upon which Momorus, being a person well skilled in augury, called the city Lugdunum. For *lugdon* in their language signifies a crow, and *dunum* * any spacious hill. — This Clitophon reports, in his Thirteenth Book of the Building of Cities.

VII. PACTOLUS.

PACTOLUS is a river of Lydia, that washes the walls of Sardis, formerly called Chrysorrhoas. For Chrysorrhoas, the son of Apollo and Agathippe, being a mechanic artist, and one that only lived from hand to mouth upon his trade, one time in the middle of the night made bold to break open the treasury of Croesus; and conveying thence a good quantity of gold, he made a distribution of it to his family. But being pursued by the king's officers, when he saw he must be taken, he threw himself into the river which was afterwards from his name called Chrysorrhoas, and afterwards changed into that of Pactolus upon this occasion.

Pactolus, the son of . . . and Leucothea, during the performance of the mysteries sacred to Venus, ravished Demodice his own sister, not knowing who she was; for

---

* Whence probably our English word *down*.

which being overwhelmed with grief, he threw himself into the river Chrysorrhoas, which from that time forward was called Pactolus, from his own name. In this river is found a most pure gold sand, which the force of the stream carries into the bosom of the Happy Gulf.

Also in this river is to be found a stone which is called the preserver of the fields, resembling the color of silver, very hard to be found, in regard of its being mixed with the gold sand. The virtue of which is such, that the more wealthy Lydians buy it and lay it at the doors of their treasuries, by which means they preserve their treasure, whatever it be, safe from the seizure of pilfering hands. For upon the approach of thieves or robbers, the stone sends forth a sound like that of a trumpet. Upon which the thieves surprised, and believing themselves apprehended by officers, throw themselves headlong and break their necks; insomuch that the place where the thieves thus frighted come by their violent deaths is called Pactolus's prison.

In this river also there grows an herb that bears a purple flower, and is called chrysopolis; by which the inhabitants of the neighboring cities try their purest gold. For just before they put their gold into the melting-pot, they touch it with this herb; at what time, if it be pure and unmixed, the leaves of the herb will be tinctured with the gold and preserve the substance of the matter; but if it be adulterated, they will not admit the discoloring moisture; — as Chrysermus relates in his Third Book of Rivers.

Near to this river lies the mountain Tmolus, full of all manner of wild beasts, formerly called Carmanorion, from Carmanor the son of Bacchus and Alexirrhoea, who was killed by a wild boar as he was hunting; but afterward Tmolus upon this occasion.

Tmolus, the son of Mars and Theogone, king of Lydia,

while he was a hunting upon Carmanorion, chanced to see the fair virgin Arrhippe that attended upon Diana, and fell passionately in love with her. And such was the heat of his love, that not being able to gain her by fair means, he resolved to vitiate her by force. She, seeing she could by no means escape his fury otherwise, fled to the temple of Diana, where the tyrant, contemning all religion, ravished her, — an infamy which the nymph not being able to survive immediately hanged herself. But Diana would not pass by so great a crime; and therefore, to be revenged upon the king for his irreligious insolence, she set a mad bull upon him, by which the king being tossed up in the air, and falling down upon stakes and stones, ended his days in torment. But Theoclymenus his son, so soon as he had buried his father, altered the name of the mountain, and called it Tmolus after his father's name.

Upon this mountain grows a stone not unlike a pumice-stone, which is very rare to be found. This stone changes its color four times a day; and is to be seen only by virgins that are not arrived at the years of understanding. But if marriageable virgins happen to see it, they can never receive any injury from those that attempt their chastity; — as Clitophon reports.

VIII. Lycormas.

Lycormas is a river of Aetolia, formerly called Evenus for this reason. Idas the son of Aphareus, after he had ravished away by violence Marpessa, with whom he was passionately in love, carried her away to Pleuron, a city of Aetolia. This rape of his daughter Evenus could by no means endure, and therefore pursued after the treacherous ravisher, till he came to the river Lycormas But then despairing to overtake the fugitive, he threw himself for madness into the river, which from his own name was called Evenus.

In this river grows an herb which is called sarissa, because it resembles a spear, of excellent use for those that are troubled with dim sight; — as Archelaus relates in his First Book of Rivers.

Near to this river lies Myenus, from Myenus the son of Telestor and Alphesiboea; who, being beloved by his mother-in-law and unwilling to defile his father's bed, retired himself to the mountain Alphius. But Telestor, being made jealous of his wife, pursued his son into the wilderness; and followed him so close, that Myenus, not being able to escape, flung himself headlong from the top of the mountain, which for that reason was afterwards called Myenus.

Upon this mountain grows a flower called the white violet, which, if you do but name the word step-dame, presently dies away; — as Dercyllus reports in his Third Book of Mountains.

IX. MAEANDER.

MAEANDER is a river of Asia, formerly called the Returner. For of all rivers in the world it is the only stream which, taking its rise from its own fountain, seems to run back to its own head.

It is called Maeander from Maeander, the son of Cercaphus and Anaxibia, who, waging war with the Pessinuntines, made a vow to the Mother of the Gods, that if he obtained the victory, he would sacrifice the first that came to congratulate him for his good success. Now it happened that the first that met him were his son Archelaus, his mother, and his sister. All which, though so nearly related to him, he offered in sacrifice to the satisfaction of his vow. But then no less grieved for what he had done, he cast himself into the river, which from this accident was afterwards called by his own name Maeander; — as Timolaus tells us in his First Book of Phrygian Relations.

Agathocles the Samian also makes mention of this story, in his Commonwealth of Pessinus.

But Demostratus of Apamea relates the story thus: Maeander being a second time elected general against the Pessinuntines, and obtaining the victory quite contrary to his expectation, gave to his soldiers the offerings due to the Mother of the Gods. At which the Goddess being offended, she deprived him of his reason to that degree, that in the height of his madness he slew both his wife and his son. But coming somewhat to himself and repenting of what he had done, he threw himself into the river, which by his name was called Maeander.

In this river there is a certain stone, which by Antiphrasis is called sophron, or the sober-stone; which if you drop into the bosom of any man, it presently makes him mad to that degree as to murder his nearest relations, but having once atoned the Mother of the Gods, he is presently restored to his wits; — as Damaratus testifies in his Third Book of Rivers. And Archelaus makes mention of the same in his First Book of Stones.

Near to this river lies the mountain Sipylus, so called from Sipylus the son of Agenor and Dioxippe. For he having killed his mother by mistake, and being haunted by the Furies, retired to the Ceraunian mountain, and there hanged himself for grief. After which, by the providence of the Gods, the mountain was called Sipylus.

In this mountain grows a stone that resembles a cylinder, which when children that are obedient to their parents find, they lay it up in the temple of the Mother of the Gods. Nor do they ever transgress out of impiety; but reverence their parents, and are obedient to their superior relations; — as Agatharchides the Samian relates in his Fourth Book of Stones, and Demaratus in his Fourth Book of Phrygia.

X. MARSYAS.

MARSYAS is a river of Phrygia, flowing by the city Celaenae, and formerly called the fountain of Midas for this reason. Midas, king of Phrygia, travelling in the remoter parts of the country, and wanting water, stamped upon the ground; and there presently appeared a golden fountain. But the water proving gold, and both he and his soldiers being ready to perish for thirst, he invoked the compassion of Bacchus, who listening to his prayers supplied him with water. The Phrygians having by this means quenched their thirst, Midas named the river that issued from the spring the Fountain of Midas. Afterwards it was called Marsyas, upon this occasion.

Marsyas being overcome and flayed by Apollo, certain Satyrs are said to have sprung from the stream of his blood; as also a river bearing the name of Marsyas; — as Alexander Cornelius recites in his Third Book of Phrygian Relations.

But Euemeridas the Cnidian tells the story after this manner. It happened that the wine-bag which was made of Marsyas's skin, being corroded by time and carried away negligently by the wind, fell at last from the land into Midas's well; and driving along with the stream, was taken up by a fisherman. At what time Pisistratus the Lacedaemonian, being commanded by the oracle to build near the place where the relics of the Satyr were found, reflected upon the accident, and in obedience to the oracle having built a fair city, called it Noricum, which in the Phrygian language signifies a wine-bag.

In this river grows an herb called the pipe, which being moved in the wind yields a melodious sound; — as Dercyllus reports in his First Book of Satyrics.

Near to this river also lies the mountain Berecyntus, deriving its name from Berecyntus, the first priest to the

Mother of the Gods. Upon this mountain is found a stone which is called machaera, very much resembling iron; which if any one happens to light upon while the solemnities of the Mother of the Gods are performing, he presently runs mad; — as Agatharchides reports in his Phrygian Relations.

XI. STRYMON.

STRYMON is a river of Thrace, that flows along by the city Edonis. It was formerly called Palaestinus, from Palaestinus the son of Neptune. For he being at war with his neighbors, and seized with a violent sickness, sent his son Haliacmon to be general of his army; who, rashly giving battle to his enemies, was slain in the fight. The tidings of which misfortune being brought to Palaestinus, he privately withdrew himself from his guards, and in the desperation of his grief flung himself into the River Conozus, which from that accident was afterwards called Palaestinus. But as for Strymon, he was the son of Mars and Helice; and hearing that his son Rhesus was slain, he flung himself into the river Palaestinus, which was after that called Strymon, by his own name.

In this river grows a stone which is called pausilypus, or the grief-easing stone. This stone if any one find who is oppressed with grief, he shall presently be eased of his sorrow; — as Jason of Byzantium relates in his Thracian Histories.

Near to this river lie the mountains Rhodope and Haemus. These being brother and sister, and both falling in love with each other, the one was so presumptuous as to call his sister his Juno, the other to call her brother her Jupiter; which so offended the Deities, that they changed them into mountains bearing their own names.

In these two mountains grow certain stones, which are

called philadelphi, or the loving brethren. These stones are of a crow-color, and resembling human shape, and if they chance to be named when they are separated one from another, they presently and separately, as they lie, dissolve and waste away; — as Thrasyllus the Mendesian testifies in his Third Book of Stones, but more accurately in his Thracian Histories.

XII. SAGARIS.

SAGARIS is a river of Phrygia, formerly called Xerobates because in the summer time it was generally dry. But it was called Sagaris for this reason: Sagaris, the son of Myndon and Alexirrhoe, contemning and slighting the mysteries of the Mother of the Gods, frequently affronted and derided her priests the Galli. At which the Goddess heinously offended, struck him with madness to that degree, that in one of his raging fits he flung himself into the river Xerobates, which from that time forward was called Sagaris.

In this river grows a stone, which is called autoglyphus, that is, naturally engraved; for it is found with the Mother of the Gods by nature engraved upon it. This stone, which is rarely to be found, if any of the Galli or gelded priests happen to light upon, he makes no wonder at it, but undauntedly brooks the sight of a preternatural action; — as Aretazes reports in his Phrygian Relations.

Near to this river lies the mountain Ballenaeus, which in the Phrygian language signifies *royal;* so called from Ballenacus, the son of Ganymede and Medesigiste, who perceiving his father almost wasted with a consumption, instituted the Ballenaean festival, observed among the natives to this day.

In this river is to be found a stone called aster, which from the latter end of autumn shines at midnight like fire.

It is called in the language of the natives *ballen*, which being interpreted signifies a king ; — as Hermesianax the Cyprian affirms in his Second Book of his Phrygian Relations.

XIII. SCAMANDER.

SCAMANDER is a river of Troas, which was formerly called Xanthus, but changed its name upon this occasion. Scamander, the son of Corybas and Demodice, having suddenly beheld the ceremonies while the mysteries of Rhea were solemnizing, immediately ran mad, and being hurried away by his own fury to the River Xanthus, flung himself into the stream, which from thence was called Scamander.

In this river grows an herb like a vetch, that bears a cod with berries rattling in it when they are ripe ; whence it derived the name of *sistrum*, or the *rattle* ; whoever has this herb in possession fears no apparition nor the sight of any God ; — as Demostratus writes in his Second Book of Rivers.

Near to this river lies the mountain Ida, formerly Gargarus ; on the top of which stand the altars of Jupiter and of the Mother of the Gods. But it was called Ida upon this occasion. Aegesthius, who descended from Jupiter, falling passionately in love with the nymph Ida, obtained her good-will, and begat the Idaean Dactyli, or priests of the Mother of the Gods. After which, Ida running mad in the temple of Rhea, Aegesthius, in remembrance of the love which he bare her, called the mountain by her name.

In this mountain grows a stone called cryphius, as being never to be found but when the mysteries of the Gods are solemnizing ; — as Heraclitus the Sicyonian writes in his Second Book of Stones.

XIV. TANAIS.

TANAIS is a river of Scythia, formerly called the Amazonian river, because the Amazons bathed themselves therein; but it altered its name upon this occasion. Tanais, the son of Berossus and Lysippe, one of the Amazons, became a vehement hater of the female sex, and looking upon marriage as ignominious and dishonorable, applied himself wholly to martial affairs. This so offended Venus, that she caused him to fall passionately in love with his own mother. True it is, at first he withstood the force of his passion; but finding he could not vanquish the fatal necessity of yielding to divine impulse, and yet desirous to preserve his respect and piety towards his mother, he flung himself into the Amazonian river, which was afterwards called Tanais, from the name of the young man.

In this river grows a plant which is called halinda, resembling a colewort; which the inhabitants bruising, and anointing their bodies with the juice of it, find themselves in a condition better able to endure the extremity of the cold; and for that reason, in their own language they call it Berossus's oil.

In this river grows a stone not unlike to crystal, resembling the shape of a man with a crown upon his head. Whoever finds the stone when the king dies, and has it ready against the time that the people meet upon the banks of the river to choose a new sovereign, is presently elected king, and receives the sceptre of the deceased prince; — as Ctesiphon relates in his Third Book of Plants; and Aristobulus gives us the same account in his First Book of Stones.

Near to this river also lies a mountain, in the language of the natives called Brixaba, which signifies the *forehead of a ram*. And it was so called upon this occasion. Phryxus having lost his sister Helle near the Euxine Sea, and, as Nature in justice required, being extremely troubled for his loss, retired to the top of a certain hill to disburden himself of his sorrow. At which time certain barbarians espying him, and mounting up the hill with their arms in their hands, a gold-fleeced ram leaping out of a thicket, and seeing the multitude coming, with articulate language and the voice of a man, awakened Phryxus, who was fast asleep, and taking him upon his back, carried him to Colchis. From this accident it was that the mountainous promontory was called the ram's forehead.

In this mountain grows an herb, by the barbarians called phryxa (which being interpreted signifies *hating the wicked*), not unlike our common rue. If the son of a former mother have it in his possession, he can never be injured by his step-dame. It chiefly grows near the place which is called Boreas's Den, and being gathered, is colder than snow. But if any step-dame be forming a design against her son-in-law, it sets itself on fire and sends forth a bright flame. By which means they who are thus warned avoid the danger they are in; — as Agatho the Samian testifies in his Second Book of Scythian Relations.

XV. Thermodon.

Thermodon is a river of Scythia, deriving its name from this accident. It was formerly called Crystallus, as being often frozen in the summer, the situation of the place producing this effect. But that name was altered upon this occasion. . . .

XVI. Nile.

The Nile is a river in Egypt, that runs by the city of Alexandria. It was formerly called Melas, from Melas the son of Neptune; but afterwards it was called Aegyptus upon this occasion. Aegyptus, the son of Vulcan and

Leucippe, was formerly king of the country, between whom and his own subjects happened a civil war; on which account the river Nile not increasing, the Egyptians were oppressed with famine. Upon which the oracle made answer, that the land should be again blessed with plenty, if the king would sacrifice his daughter to atone the anger of the Gods. Upon which the king, though greatly afflicted in his mind, gave way to the public good, and suffered his daughter to be led to the altar. But so soon as she was sacrificed, the king, not able to support the burden of his grief, threw himself into the river Melas, which after that was called Aegyptus. But then it was called Nilus upon this occasion.

Garmathone, queen of Egypt, having lost her son Chrysochoas while he was yet very young, with all her servants and friends most bitterly bemoaned her loss. At what time Isis appearing to her, she surceased her sorrow for a while, and putting on the countenance of a feigned gratitude, kindly entertained the goddess. She, willing to make a suitable return to the queen for the piety which she expressed in her reception, persuaded Osiris to bring back her son from the subterranean regions. When Osiris undertook to do this, at the importunity of his wife, Cerberus — whom some call the Terrible — barked so loud, that Nilus, Garmathone's husband, struck with a sudden frenzy, threw himself into the river Aegyptus, which from thence was afterwards called Nilus.

In this river grows a stone, not unlike to a bean, which so soon as any dog happens to see, he ceases to bark. It also expels the evil spirit out of those that are possessed, if held to the nostrils of the party afflicted.

There are other stones which are found in this river, called kollotes, which the swallows picking up against the time that Nilus overflows, build up the wall which is called the Chelidonian wall, which restrains the inundation of the water and will not suffer the country to be injured by the fury of the flood; — as Thrasyllus tells us in his Relation of Egypt.

Upon this river lies the mountain Argyllus, so called for this reason.

Jupiter in the heat of his amorous desires ravished away the Nymph Arge from Lyctus, a city of Crete, and then carried her to a mountain of Egypt called Argillus, and there begat a son, whom he named Dionysus (or Bacchus); who, growing up to years of manhood, in honor of his mother called the hill Argillus; and then mustering together an army of Pans and Satyrs, first conquered the Indians, and then subduing Spain, left Pan behind him there, the chief commander and governor of those places. Pan by his own name called that country Pania, which was afterward by his posterity called Spania; — as Sosthenes relates in the Thirteenth Book of Iberian Relations.

XVII. EUROTAS.

HIMERUS, the son of the Nymph Taygete and Lacedaemon, through the anger of offended Venus, at a revelling that lasted all night, deflowered his sister Cleodice, not knowing what he did. But the next day being informed of the truth of the matter, he laid it so to heart, that through excess of grief he flung himself into the river Marathon, which from thence was called Himeros; but after that Eurotas, upon this occasion.

The Lacedaemonians being at war with the Athenians, and staying for the full moon, Eurotas their captain-general, despising all religion, would needs fight his enemies, though at the same time he was warned by thunder and lightning. However, having lost his army, the ignominy of his loss so incessantly perplexed him, that he flung himself into the river Himerus, which from that accident was afterwards called Eurotas.

In this river grows a stone which is shaped like a helmet, called thrasydeilos, or *rash and timorous*. For if it hears a trumpet sound, it leaps toward the bank of the river; but if you do but name the Athenians, it presently sinks to the bottom of the water. Of these stones there are not a few which are consecrated and laid up in the temple of Minerva of the Brazen House; — as Nicanor the Samian relates in his Second Book of Rivers.

Near to this river lies the mountain Taygetus, deriving its name from the nymph Taygete, who, after Jupiter had deflowered her, being overcome by grief, ended her days by hanging at the summit of the mountain Amyclaeus, which from thence was called Taygetus.

Upon this mountain grows a plant called Charisia, which the women at the beginning of the spring tied about their necks, to make themselves more passionately beloved by men; — as Cleanthes reports in his First Book of Mountains. But Sosthenes the Cnidian is more accurate in the relation of these things, from whom Hermogenes borrowed the subject of his writing.

XVIII. Inachus.

Inachus is a river in the territories of Argos, formerly called Carmanor. Afterwards Haliacmon, for this reason.

Haliacmon, a Tirynthian by birth, while he kept sheep upon the mountain Coccygium, happened against his will to see Jupiter and Rhea sporting together; for which being struck mad, and hurried by the violence of the frenzy, he flung himself into the river Carmanor, which after that was called Haliacmon. Afterwards it was called Inachus upon this occasion.

Inachus, the son of Oceanus, after that Jupiter had deflowered his daughter Io, pursued the Deity close at the heels, abusing and cursing him all the way as he went.

Which so offended Jupiter, that he sent Tisiphone, one of the Furies, who haunted and plagued him to that degree, that he flung himself into the river Haliacmon, afterwards called by his own name Inachus.

In this river grows an herb called cynura, not unlike our common rue, which the women that desire to miscarry without any danger lay upon their navels, being first steeped in wine.

There is also found in this river a certain stone, not unlike a beryl, which in the hands of those who intend to bear false witness will grow black. Of these stones there are many laid up in the temple of Juno Prosymnaea; — as Timotheus relates in his Argolica, and Agatho the Samian in his Second Book of Rivers.

Agathocles the Milesian, in his History of Rivers, also adds, that Inachus for his impiety was thunderstruck by Jupiter, and so the river dried up.

Near to this river lie the mountains Mycenae, Apesantus, Coccygium, and Athenaeum; so called for these reasons. Apesantus was first called Selenaeus. For Juno, resolving to be revenged upon Hercules, called the moon (Selene) to her assistance, who by the help of her magical charms filled a large chest full of foam and froth, out of which sprang an immense lion; which Iris binding with her own girdle carried to the mountain Opheltium, where the lion killed and tore in pieces Apesantus, one of the shepherds belonging to that place. And from that accident, by the will of the Gods, the hill was called Apesantus; — as Demodocus writes in his First Book of the History of Hercules.

In this river grows an herb called selene, with the froth of which, being gathered in the spring, the shepherds anoint their feet, and keep them from being bit or stung by any creeping vermin.

Mycenae was formerly called Argion, from the many-eyed

Argos; but afterwards the name was changed upon this occasion.

When Perseus had slain Medusa, Stheno and Euryale, sisters to her that was killed, pursued him as a murderer. But coming to this hill and despairing to overtake him, out of that extreme love which they had for their sister they made such a bellowing (μυκηθμός), that the natives from thence called the top of the mountain Mycenae;—as Ctesias the Ephesian relates in his First Book of the Acts of Perseus. But Chrysermus the Corinthian relates the story thus in the First Book of his Peloponnesiacs. For he says that, when Perseus was carried aloft in the air and lit upon this mountain, he lost the chape of his scabbard. At what time this same Gorgophonos (or Gorgon-slayer), king of the Epidaurians, being expelled his kingdom, received this answer upon his consulting the oracle, that he should visit all the cities of the Argolic territory, and that where he found the chape of a scabbard (called in Greek μυκής), he should build a city. Thereupon coming to the mountain Argium, and finding there an ivory scabbard, he built a city, and from the accident called it Mycenae.

In this mountain there is found a stone, which is called corybas, of a crow-color, which he that finds and wears about him shall never be afraid of any monstrous apparitions. As for the mountain Apesantus, this may be added, that Apesantus, the son of Acrisius, as he was a hunting in that place, chanced to tread upon a venomous serpent, which occasioned his death. Whom when his father had buried, in memory of his son he named the hill Apesantus, which before was called Selinuntius.

The mountain Coccygium derived its name from this accident. Jupiter falling desperately in love with his sister Juno, and having vanquished her by his importunity, begat a male child. From whence the mountain, before called Lyrceum, was named Coccygium;—as Agathonymus relates in his Persis.

In this mountain grows a tree, which is called paliurus; upon the boughs of which whatever fowl happens to perch, it is presently entangled as it were with bird-lime, and cannot stir; only the cuckoo it lets go free, without any harm; — as Ctesiphon testifies in his First Book of Trees.

As for the mountain Athenaeum, it derives its name from Minerva. For after the destruction of Troy, Diomede returning to Argos, ascended the mountain Ceraunius, and there erecting a temple to Minerva, called the mountain Athenaeum from her name Athena.

Upon the top of this mountain grows a root like to that of rue, which if any woman unwarily taste of, she presently runs mad. This root is called Adrastea; — as Plesimachus writes in his Second Book of the Returns of the Heroes.

XIX. ALPHEUS.

ALPHEUS is a river of Arcadia, running by the walls of Pisa, a city of Olympia. It was formerly called Stymphelus, from Stymphelus the son of Mars and Dormothea; who, having lost his brother Alcmaeon, threw himself for grief into the river Nyctimus, for that reason called Stymphelus. Afterwards it was called Alpheus upon this occasion.

Alpheus, one of those that derive their descent from the Sun, contending with his brother Cercaphus about the kingdom, slew him. For which being chased away and pursued by the Furies, he flung himself into the river Nyctimus, which after that was called Alpheus.

In this river grows a plant which is called cenchritis, resembling a honey-comb, the decoction of which, being given by the physicians to those that are mad, cures them of their frenzy; — as Ctesias relates in his First Book of Rivers.

Near to this river lies the mountain Cronium, so called upon this occasion. After the Giants' war, Saturn, to avoid the threats of Jupiter, fled to the mountain Cturus, and called it Cronium from his own name. Where after he had absconded for some time, he took his opportunity, and retired to Caucasus in Scythia.

In this mountain is found a stone, which is called the cylinder, upon this occasion. For as oft as Jupiter either thunders or lightens, so often this stone through fear rolls down from the top of the mountain; — as Dercyllus writes in his First Book of Stones.

XX. Euphrates.

Euphrates is a river of Parthia, washing the walls of Babylon, formerly called Medus from Medus the son of Artaxerxes. He, in the heat of his lust, having ravished away and deflowered Roxane, and finding he was sought after by the king, in order to be brought to punishment, threw himself into the river Xaranda, which from thenceforward was called by his name Medus. Afterwards it was called Euphrates upon this occasion.

Euphrates the son of Arandacus, finding his son Axurta abed with his mother, and thinking him to be some one of the citizens, provoked by his jealousy, drew his sword and nailed him to the bed. But perceiving himself the author of what could not be recalled, he flung himself for grief into the river Medus, which from that time forward was called by his name Euphrates.

In this river grows a stone called actites, which midwives applying to the navels of women that are in hard labor, it causes them to bring forth with little pain.

In the same river also there grows an herb which is called axalla, which signifies heat. This herb they that are troubled with quartan-agues apply to their breasts, and are presently delivered from the fit; — as Chrysermus writes in his Thirteenth Book of Rivers.

Near this river lies the mountain Drimylus, where grows a stone not unlike a sardonyx, worn by kings and princes upon their diadems, and greatly available against dimness of sight; — as Nicias Mallotes writes in his Book of Stones.

XXI. CAICUS.

CAICUS is a river of Mysia, formerly called Astraeus, from Astraeus the son of Neptune. For he, in the height of Minerva's nocturnal solemnities having deflowered his sister by a mistake, took a ring at the same time from her finger; by which when he understood the next day the error which he had committed, for grief he threw himself headlong into the river Adurus, which from thence was called Astraeus. Afterwards it came to be called Caicus upon this occasion.

Caicus, the son of Hermes and Ocyrrhoe the Nymph, having slain Timander one of the noblemen of the country, and fearing the revenge of his relations, flung himself into the river Astraeus, which from that accident was called Caicus.

In this river grows a sort of poppy, which instead of fruit bears stones. Of these there are some which are black and shaped like harps, which the Mysians throw upon their ploughed lands; and if the stones lie still in the place where they are thrown, it is a sign of a barren year; but if they fly away like so many locusts, they prognosticate a plentiful harvest.

In the same river also grows an herb which is called elipharmacus, which the physicians apply to such as are troubled with immoderate fluxes of blood, as having a peculiar virtue to stop the orifices of the veins; — according to the relation of Timagoras in his First Book of Rivers.

Adjoining to the banks of this river lies the mountain

Teuthras, so called from Teuthras king of the Mysians; who in pursuance of his sport, as he was a hunting, ascending the hill Thrasyllus and seeing a monstrous wild boar, followed him close with the rest of his train. On the other side, the boar, to prevent the hunters, like a suppliant fled to the temple of Orthosian Diana, into which when the hunters were about to force their entrance, the boar in articulate words cried out, Spare, O king. the nursling of the Goddess. However, Teuthras, exalted with his good success, killed the poor boar. At which Diana was so highly offended, that she restored the boar to life, but struck the offender with scurf and madness. Which affliction the king not enduring betook himself to the tops of the mountains. But his mother Leucippe, understanding what had befallen her son, ran to the forest, taking along with her the soothsayer Polyidus, the son of Coeranus; by whom being informed of all the several circumstances of the matter, by many sacrifices she at last atoned the anger of the Goddess, and having quite recovered and cured her son, erected an altar to Orthosian Diana, and caused a golden boar to be made with a man's face. Which to this day, if pursued by the hunters, enters the temple, and speaks with the voice of a man the word "spare." Thus Teuthras, being restored to his former health, called the mountain by his own name Teuthras.

In this mountain grows a stone called antipathes (or the resister), which is of excellent virtue to cure scabs and leprosies, being powdered and mixed with wine; — as Ctesias the Cnidian tells us in his Second Book of Mountains.

XXII. Achelous.

Achelous is a river of Aetolia, formerly called Thestius. This Thestius was the son of Mars and Pisidice, who upon some domestic discontent travelled as far as Sicyon, where after he had resided for some time, he returned to his native home. But finding there his son Calydon and his mother both upon the bed together, believing him to be an adulterer, he slew his own child by a mistake. But when he beheld the unfortunate and unexpected fact he had committed, he threw himself into the river Axenos, which from thence was afterwards called Thestius. And after that, it was called Achelous upon this occasion.

Achelous, the son of Oceanus and the Nymph Nais, having deflowered his daughter Cletoria by mistake, flung himself for grief into the river Thestius, which then by his own name was called Achelous.

In this river grows an herb, which they call zaclon, very much resembling wool; this if you bruise and cast into wine, it becomes water, and preserves the smell but not the virtues of the wine.

In the same river also is found a certain stone of a mixed black and lead color, called linurgus from the effect; for if you throw it upon a linen cloth, by a certain affectionate union it assumes the form of the linen, and turns white; — as Antisthenes relates in the Third Book of his Meleagris, though Diocles the Rhodian more accurately tells us the same thing in his Aetolics.

Near to this river lies the mountain Calydon, so called from Calydon, the son of Mars and Astynome; for that he, by an accident having seen Diana bathing herself, was transformed into a rock; and the mountain which before was named Gyrus was afterwards by the providence of the Gods called Calydon.

Upon this mountain grows an herb called myops. This if any one steep in water and wash his face with it, he shall lose his sight, but upon his atoning Diana, he shall recover it again; — as Dercyllus writes in his Third Book of Aetolics.

XXIII. ARAXES.

ARAXES is a river in Armenia, so called from Araxus the son of Pylus. For he, contending with his grandfather Arbelus for the empire, shot him with an arrow. For which being haunted by the Furies, he threw himself into the river Bactros, for that reason called Araxes; — as Ctesiphon testifies in his First Book of the Persian Affairs. Araxes, king of the Armenians, being at war with his neighbors the Persians, before they came to a battle, was told by the oracle that he should win the victory if he sacrificed to the Gods two of the most noble virgins in his kingdom. Now he, out of his paternal affection to his children, spared his own daughters, and caused two lovely virgins, the daughters of one of his nobility, to be laid upon the altar. Which Mnesalces, the father of the victims, laying to heart, for a time concealed his indignation; but afterwards, observing his opportunity, he killed both the king's daughters, and then leaving his native soil fled into Scythia. Which when Araxes understood, for grief he threw himself into the river Halmus, which then was altered and called Araxes.

In this river grows a plant which is called araxa, which in the language of the natives signifies a virgin-hater. For that if it happen to be found by any virgin, it falls a bleeding and dies away.

In the same river there is also found a stone of a black color, called sicyonus. This stone, when the oracle advises the sacrificing of a human victim, is laid upon the altar of the mischief-diverting Gods. And then, no sooner does the priest touch it with his knife, but it sends forth a stream of blood; at what time the superstitious sacrificers retire, and with howlings and loud ohoning carry the stone to the temple; — as Dorotheus the Chaldaean relates in his Second Book of Stones.

Near to this river lies the mountain Diorphus, so called from Diorphus the son of the Earth, of whom this story is reported. Mithras desirous to have a son, yet hating woman-kind, lay with a stone, till he had heated it to that degree that the stone grew big, and at the prefixed time was delivered of a son, called Diorphus; who, growing up and contending with Mars for courage and stoutness, was by him slain, and by the providence of the Gods was transformed into the mountain which was called Diorphus by his name.

In this mountain grows a tree, not unlike a pomegranate-tree, which yields plenty of apples, in taste like grapes. Now if any one gather the ripest of this fruit, and do but name Mars while he holds it in his hand, it will presently grow green again; — as Ctesiphon witnesses in his Thirteenth Book of Trees.

XXIV. TIGRIS.

TIGRIS is a river of Armenia flowing into Araxes and the lake of Arsacis, formerly called Sollax, which signifies running and carried downward. It was called Tigris upon this occasion.

Bacchus, through the design of Juno running mad, wandered over sea and land, desirous to be quit of his distemper. At length coming into Armenia, and not being able to pass the river before-mentioned, he called upon Jupiter; who, listening to his prayers, sent him a tiger that carried him safely over the water. In remembrance of which accident, he called the river Tigris; — as Theophilus relates in his First Book of Stones. But Hermesianax the Cyprian tells the story thus: —

Bacchus falling in love with the Nymph Alphesiboea, and being able to vanquish her neither with presents nor entreaties, turned himself into the shape of the river Tigris, and overcoming his beloved by fear, took her away, and carrying her over the river, begat a son whom he called Medus; who growing up in years, in remembrance of the accident he called the river by the name of Tigris; — as Aristonymus relates in his Third Book . . .

In this river a stone is to be found, called myndan, very white; which whoever possesses shall never be hurt by wild beasts; — as Leo of Byzantium relates in his Third Book of Rivers.

Near to this river lies the mountain Gauran; so called from Gauran the son of the satrap Roxanes; who, being extremely religious and devout towards the Gods, received this reward of his piety, that of all the Persians he only lived three hundred years; and dying at last without being ever afflicted with any disease, was buried upon the top of the mountain Gauran, where he had a sumptuous monument erected to his memory. Afterwards, by the providence of the Gods, the name of the mountain was changed to that of Mausorus.

In this mountain grows an herb, which is like to wild barley. This herb the natives heat over the fire, and anointing themselves with the oil of it, are never sick, till the necessity of dying overtakes them; — as Sostratus writes in his First Collection of Fabulous History.

XXV. Indus.

Indus is a river in India, flowing with a rapid violence into the country of the fish-devourers. It was first called Mausolus, from Mausolus the son of the Sun, but changed its name for this reason.

At the time when the mysteries of Bacchus were solemnized and the people were earnest at their devotion, Indus, one of the chief of the young nobility, by force deflowered Damasalcidas, the daughter of Oxyalcus the king of the country, as she was carrying the sacred basket; for which being sought for by the tyrant, in order to bring him to condign punishment, for fear he threw himself into the river Mausolus, which from that accident was afterwards called Indus.

In this river grows a certain stone called . . . which if a virgin carry about her, she need never be afraid of being deflowered.

In the same river also grows an herb, not unlike to bugloss. Which is an excellent remedy against the king's-evil, being administered to the patient in warm water ; — as Clitophon the Rhodian reports in his First Book of Indian Relations.

Near to this mountain lies the mountain Lilacus, so called from Lilaeus a shepherd; who, being very superstitious and a worshipper of the Moon alone, always performed her mysteries in the dead time of the night. Which the rest of the Gods taking for a great dishonor, sent two monstrous lions that tore him in pieces. Upon which the Moon turned her adorer into a mountain of the same name.

In this mountain a stone is found which is called clitoris, of a very black color, which the natives wear for ornament's sake in their ears ; — as Aristotle witnesses in his Fourth Book of Rivers.

INDEX.

A.

"A BIRD in the hand is worth two in the bush," a proverb among the Greeks, iv. 229.
"Abstain from beans," meaning of the aphorism, i. 29.
Achelous, a river in Aetolia, v. 504.
Acrotatus, apothegm of, i. 400.
Actaeon, a beautiful youth of Corinth, murdered, iv. 313-315.
Ada, queen of Caria, sends delicacies to Alexander, i. 199.
Adimantus, admiral of the Corinthian fleet at the battle of Salamis; his courage vindicated, iv. 361.
Adrastus, anecdote of, i. 238.
Advice to a new-married couple, ii. 486-507.
Aeacus, his two sons, v. 466.
Aemilius Censorinus, v. 475.
Aemilius of Sybaris, v. 464.
Aemilius Paulus, sayings of, i. 232; iv. 201.
Aeolus King of Etruria, v. 467.
Aeschines, quoted, Prom. i. 40; anecdote of, 55; Eumen. 59; Frag. 163; Prom. 299; Ctesiphon, 334; his early life, and concern in public affairs, v. 34; incurs the hostility of Demosthenes, *ib.*; accused by Demosthenes and acquitted, 34, 35; impeaches Ctesiphon, is fined and exiled, 35; his school at Rhodes, *ib.*; his death, *ib.*; his orations, *ib.*; his public employments, 36.
Aeschylus, quoted, Septem, i. 210, 286; 315, 329, 493; quoted, ii. 47; anecdote of, 77, 160; Frag. 48, 83, 127, 165, 374, 413, 458, 463, 474, 477; quoted, iii. Frag. 24, 222; quoted, iv. 20, 54, 385; Frag. 276, 279; quoted, v. Frag. 170 Prom. 241, 320, 398.
Aesop murdered by the citizens of Delphi, iv. 160; their punishment, 161. *See Esop.*
Agamedes and Trophonius built the temple at Delphi, i. 313.
Agasicles, apothegms of, i. 385.
Agatharcides the Samian, his Persian History, v. 451.
Agatho the Samian, v. 474.
Agathocles, anecdote of, i. 46; ii. 317.
Aged Men, shall they meddle in State Affairs? v. 64-96.
Agesianax, quoted, v. 235, 236.
Agesilaus, reply of, i. 73, 219, 220; his sayings and great actions, 385-397; his upright character, ii. 109; 115, 319, 455; iii. his punishment, 47; 79; anecdote of, v. 67; his faults, 118; 457; his Italian History, 468.
Agesipolis, two of the name, apothegms of, i. 397, 398.
Agis, king of Sparta, his sayings, i. 218, 221; anecdote of, v. 95.
Agis, son of Archidamus, apothegm of i. 398.
Agis the Argive, ii. 125.
Agis the Last, apothegm of, i. 400.
Agis the Younger, apothegms of, i. 400.
Ajax's soul, her place in Hell, iii. 442.
Alba, king of, torn in pieces by horses, v. 455.
Albinus, a Roman general, v. 453.
Alcaeus, quoted ii. 296; iii. 264.
Alcamenes, apothegm of, i. 400.
Alcibiades, i. 143; his sayings, 211; his lustful conduct, 489; the prince of flatterers, ii. 108, 471; failure of, 460; spoke with hesitation, v. 110, 112.
Alcippus, a Lacedaemonian, banished for his virtue; his wife slays herself and her daughters, iv. 320-322.
Alcmaeon, saying of, i. 288; philosophical opinions; of the planets iii. 140; of hearing, 170; of smelling, 170; of taste, 170; of the barrenness of mules, 182; of embryos, 184; of the formation of the body, 184; of the cause of sleep, 188; of health, sickness, and old age, 192.
Alcman, quoted; Frag. i. 494; iii. 16; v. 279.
Alcmaeonidae, unfairly represented by Herodotus, iv. 338, 347.
Alenas the Thessalian, iii. 67.
Alexander of Macedon and Porus i. 46; lament of, 140; and Criso the runner, 152; his sayings, 198-202; the Fortune or Virtue of, 475-516; anecdotes of, ii.

128, 138, 473; his moderation, 475; was he a great drinker, iii. 29, 219; his purpose to attack the Romans, iv. 219; v. 140.
Alexander, tyrant of Pherae, his cruel temper softened by a play, i. 492.
Alexandridas, apothegm of, i. 401.
Alexarchus, his Italian History, v. 456.
Alexidemas, at the Banquet of the Seven Wise Men, ii. 3-41.
Alexinus, the sophist, i. 76.
Alexis, quoted, ii. 58.
Alpha, why placed first in the Alphabet, iii. 438.
Alpheus, a river in Arcadia, v. 501.
Amasis, king of Egypt, required to drink the ocean dry, ii. 13; questions of, 16.
Ammonius, teacher of Plutarch, anecdote of, ii. 147.
Amphiaraus, quoted, i. 317; his lance turned into a laurel, v. 455.
Amphidamas, poets meet at his grave in Chalcis, ii. 19.
Amphion, first invented playing on the harp and lyric poesy, i. 105.
Anarcharsis, and Eumetis, ii. 8; his utterances at the Banquet of the Seven Wise Men, 12, 15, 20, 21, 27, 39.
Anatole, a mountain, v. 482.
Anaxagoras, saying of, i. 159; said the sun was red-hot metal, 179; anecdote of, 332, 357, iii. 35, 37; philosophical opinions; Homœomeries, 108; of the origin of bodies, 119; how bodies are mixed, 126; of fortune, 131; of the world's inclination, 136; of the stars, 138, 140; of the sun, 142, 143; of the moon, 145, 147; of the milky way, 149; of shooting stars, 150; of thunder, lightning and hurricanes, 151; of the rainbow, 153; of earthquakes, 157; of the sea, 158; of the overflow of the Nile, 160; of the voice, 172; of generation, 178; of the generation of animals, 186; of reason in animals, 187; of sleep, 190; v. 145, 255.
Anaxander, apothegm of, i. 401.
Anaxilas, apothegm of, i. 402.
Anaximander, philosophical opinions; of principles, iii. 107; the stars were heavenly deities, 121; of the stars, 140; of the essence and magnitude of the sun, 141, 142; of eclipses of the sun, 144; of the moon, 145; of fire from clouds, 150; of winds, 154; of the earth, 155; of the sea, 158; of the generation of animals, 186.
Anaximenes, philosophical opinions; air is the principle of all beings, iii. 107; of heaven, 137; of the stars, 139, 140; cause of summer and winter, 141; of the shape of the sun and summer and winter soltice, 143; of the moon, 146; of clouds 151; of the rainbow, 153; of the earth, 155; of earthquakes, 157; v. 313.
Ancients, suppers of the, iii. 255-259.
Andocides, one of the ten Attic orators, v. 21-23; of a noble family, 21; accused of impious acts, 22; his adventures in Cyprus, 22, 23; his exile, 23; his orations, ib.
Androclidas, apothegm of, i. 402.
Anecdotes of
Aeschylus, ii. 458.
Agathocles, i. 46.
Agesilaus, i. 73, 219, 220; v. 67, 118.
Agis, king of Sparta, v. 95.
Alcibiades, ii. 108, 109.
Alexander the Great, i. 45; ii. 473.
Ammonius, ii. 147.
Anaxagoras, i. 332.
Antigonus, i. 44, 47, 67, 202, 205, 334; iv. 231.
Antimachus, i. 308.
Antiochus Hierax, iii. 60.
Antipater, i. 64, 197, 205, 215.
Antony and Cleopatra, ii. 127.
Apelles the painter, i. 16, 153; ii. 122, 133.
Appius Claudius, v. 89.
Arcesilaus and Apelles, ii. 133.
Archelaus of Macedon, i. 67, 193.
Archidamus, i. 74.
Archimedes, ii. 174; v. 71.
Archytas of Tarentum, i. 18, 24.
Aristippus, i. 11, 55, 147, 459; ii. 55.
Athenian barber, iv. 238.
Attalus and Eumenes, iii. 61.
Augustus Caesar and Fulvius, iv. 235, 236.
Bocchoris, i. 63.
Brasidas, ii. 458.
Caesar, i. 293; iv. 204, 205; v. 67.
Cato, i. 295; ii. 490.
Cato and Catulus, i. 73.
Cleon, v. 100, 116.
Corinna, v. 404.
Crassus, i. 288, 290.
Croesus and Solon, ii. 122.
Demades and Phocion, ii. 298.
Demaratus and Philip, ii. 146.
Demetrius Phalereus, ii. 145; iii. 21.
Demosthenes, i. 15, 65, 334; ii. 460; v. 44, 49, 50-53.
Diogenes, i. 51, 67, 141, 142, 166, 283, 285, 311, 487; ii. 455, 458; iii. 21, 29.
Diogenes and Philip, ii. 147.
Diogenes and the mouse, ii. 453.
Dion, i. 64, 333.
Dionysius of Syracuse, i. 83, 152, 493; ii. 108, 140; iv. 238.
Epaminondas, v. 72, 95, 101, 120, 121, 125, 401.
Euclid, i. 55.
Eudoxus, ii. 174.
Eumenes; iii. 61; iv. 232.
Fulvius and Augustus, iv. 235, 236.
Hiero, i. 291.

Hyperides, v. 55, 56
Isocrates, v. 31.
Leaena, iv. 229, 230.
Lucretia, i. 355.
Lycurgus, the lawgiver, i. 7.
Lycurgus, the orator, v. 30.
Lysander, i. 72; ii. 495.
Lysias, iv. 226.
Magas, i. 45.
Menander, v. 403.
Nasica, i. 285.
Nero, v. 123.
Nicias, the Athenian general, i. 177.
Nicias, the painter, ii. 173; v. 71.
Nicostratus and Archidamus, i. 74.
Olympias, ii. 494, 495.
Pericles, i. 15, 18, 66, 211, 332; ii. 309, 315; v. 67, 106.
Philip of Macedon, i. 305; ii. 146, 147, 494.
Phocion, ii. 298; v. 118.
Pindar, v. 404.
Pisistratus, iii. 41.
Plato, i. 71.
Plato and Socrates, ii. 148.
Polemon, i. 55.
Pompey, v. 70.
Postumia, i. 290.
Priest of Hercules, iii. 90.
Prometheus, i. 289.
Ptolemy Lagus, i. 45.
Pythagoras, ii. 174.
Roman Senator and his wife, iv. 233–235.
Scaurus, i. 295.
Scilurus, a Scythian king, iv. 244.
Seleucus Callinicus, iv 237.
Seneca, i. 53.
Simonides, v. 68.
Socrates, i. 11, 13, 23, 26, 38, 53, 141, 150.
Socrates and Plato, ii. 148.
Solon, v. 89.
Solon and Croesus, ii. 122.
Sophocles, v. 68.
Stasicrates, i. 495.
Stilpo the philosopher, ii. 468.
Stratonicus, iii. 21.
Sylla, v. 72.
Terpander, i. 91, 92.
Themistocles, i. 73, 200, 236; iii. 21; v. 120
Theramenes, i. 306.
Timotheus the musician, i 92.
Valeria, i. 356.
Xanthippe, wife of Socrates, i. 53, 292.
Xenocrates, i. 71.
Xenophon, i. 333.
Xerxes and Ariamenes, iii. 59, 60
Zeno, i. 72, 142, 283; ii. 455; iii. 25; iv. 225.
Anger, concerning the cure of, i. 33–59.
Animal Food, shall it be eaten? Of Eating of Flesh, v. 3–16.
Animals, generation of, iii. 186; how many species of, 187; appetites and pleasures

of, 191; ails and cures of, 510; their intelligence, v. 157–217.
Anius, king of the Tuscans, v. 475.
Antalcidas, his sayings, i. 222, 402; his reply to a railing Athenian, v. 125.
Anthes, the first author of hymns, i. 105.
Anthias, the sacred fish, v. 208.
Anthipphus, Lydian harmony first used by, i. 114.
Antichthon, the, iii. 155.
Antigonus, anecdote of, i. 25; saying of, 44, 47, 67, 202, 205, 334, 484; iv. 231.
Antigonus the Second, his sayings, i. 205; ii. 319.
Antimachus, anecdote of, i. 308.
Antiochus and Charicles, iii. 49.
Antiochus and Seleucus, iii. 60.
Antiochus, apothegm of, i. 403.
Antiochus Hierax, anecdotes of, i, 206; iii. 60.
Antiochus Sidetes, anecdotes of, i. 207.
Antiochus the Spartan, his saying, i. 221.
Antiochus the Third, anecdotes of, i. 206.
Antipater, anecdotes of, i. 64, 197, 205, 215; ii. 135, 208; v. 249, 517.
Antiperistasis of motion, v 435.
Antiphanes, witty saying of his, ii. 456.
Antiphon, one of the ten Attic orators, ii. 142; v. 17–21; his birth, education, &c., 17; wrote speeches for others, *ib.*; a man of great talent and learning, 18; concerned in the revolution which subverted the popular government, *ib.*; on the overthrow of the oligarchical party he was involved in their ruin, *ib.*; number of his orations, 19; decree of the senate against him, 20; his condemnation and punishment, 21; opinion concerning the moon, iii. 146; of the sea, 158.
Antisthenes, quoted, i. 77, 289, 496; v. 125.
Antony and Cleopatra, ii. 127.
Apelles, the painter, anecdotes of, i. 16, 153; his picture of Alexander, 494; and Megabyzus, ii. 122; and Arcesilaus, 133.
Aphareus, adopted son of Isocrates, wrote orations and tragedies, v. 32.
Apis, the sacred bull of the Egyptians, iv. 68; slain by Ochus, king of Persia, 74, 92.
Apollo and the dragon Python, iv. 20.
Apollo, inventor of the flute and harp, i. 113.
Apollo, temple of, iv. 478–498; the inscription ει over its gate, 479.
Apollodorus first invented the mixing of colors and the softening of shadows, v. 400.
Apollonides, of shadow, v. 265; of spots in the moon, 269.
Apollonis of Cyzicum, iii. 41.
Apollonius, consolation to, i. 299–399.
Apollonius, the Peripatetic, iii. 57

514 INDEX.

Apothegms of Kings and Great Commanders, i. 185-250.
Agathocles, sayings of, i. 193.
Agesilaus, 219.
Agis, 218-221.
Alcibiades, 211.
Alexander the Great, 198-202.
Antalcidas, 222.
Antigonus, 202.
Antigonus the Second, 205.
Antiochus Sidetes, 207.
Antiochus the Spartan, 221.
Antiochus the Third, 206.
Antipater, 205.
Archelaus, 193.
Archidamus, 218.
Aristides, 210.
Artaxerxes Longimanus, 187.
Artaxerxes Mnemon, 188.
Ateas, 189.
Augustus Caesar, 248-250.
Brasidas, 218.
Caecilius Metellus, 239.
Caius Fabricius, 227.
Caius Marius, 239.
Caius Popilius, 240.
Cato the Elder, 233-235.
Chabrias, 213.
Charillus, 217.
Cicero, 244.
Cneus Domitius, 231.
Cneus Pompeius, 241-244.
Cotys, 189.
Cyrus the Elder, 186.
Cyrus the Younger, 188.
Darius, 186.
Demetrius, 204.
Demetrius Phalereus, 217.
Dion, 193.
Dionysius the Elder, 191.
Dionysius the Younger, 192.
Epaminondas, 222-226.
Eudaemonidas, 221.
Eumenes of Pergamus, 206.
Fabius Maximus, 227-228.
Gelo, 190.
Hegesippus, 213.
Hiero, 190.
Idathyrsus, 189.
Iphicrates, 212.
Lucullus, 241.
Lycurgus, 217.
Lysander, 219.
Lysimachus, 205.
Manius Curius, 226.
Memnon, 189.
Nicostratus, 221.
Orontes, 188.
Parysatis, 188.
Paulus Aemilius, 232.
Pelopidas, 225.
Pericles, 211.
Philip of Macedon, 194-198.
Phocion, 213, 216.
Pisistratus, 216.
Poltys, 189.
Ptolemy Lagus, 202.
Pyrrhus the Epirot, 207.
Pythens, 213.
Scilurus, 190.
Scipio Junior, 235-239.
Scipio the Elder, 229.
Semiramis, 187.
Teres, 189.
Themistocles, 208.
Theopompus, 217.
Timotheus, 212.
Titus Quinctius, 230.
Xerxes, 187.
Apple tree, of the, iii. 333.
Appius Claudius, anecdote of, v. 89.
Arar, a river in Gaul, v. 484.
Aratus, quoted, ii. 98; iii. 116; of the stars, 141; quoted, 334, 497; quoted, v. 112; 177.
Araxes, a river in Armenia, v. 506.
Arcadian prophet in Herodotus, iii. 38.
Arcadio the Archaean, saying of, i. 44.
Arcesilaus, i. 53, 148; quoted, 258, 315; and Battus, ii. 115; his kindness to Apelles, 133; v. 371, 391.
Archelaus, king of Macedon, anecdote of, i. 67, 193.
Archelaus, his opinions concerning principles, iii. 109.
Archias, ii. 379 et seq.; iv. 313-315.
Archidamidas, apothegms of, i. 404.
Archidamus, i. 4, 74, 218, 404; ii, 379 et seq.
Archilochus the poet, banished from Sparta, i. 96; quoted, 97; his improvements in music, 122, 123, 177; phrase of, ii. 17; 61, 84; iii. 26; v. 108, 216, 320.
Archimedes, of the sun's diameter, v. 71; ii. anecdote of, 173, 174.
Archytas of Tarentum, anecdotes of, i. 18, 24.
Ardalus, a minstrel at the Banquet of the Seven Wise Men, ii. 11, 12.
Aregeus, apothegm of, i. 403.
Aretades Cnidus, his Macedonian History, v. 458; his Second Book of Islands, 467
Aretaphila, her fortitude and virtue, i. 367
Argive women, their repulse of the Spartan army, i 346.
Argives, wrestling matches of, i. 121; imposed a fine for playing with more than seven strings, 130; combat of the, v. 45; combat with the Lacedaemonians, 452.
Ariamenes yields the throne of Persia to his younger brother Xerxes, iii. 59.
Arion and the dolphins, ii. 33-36.
Aristarchus, iii. 36; concerning the eclipse of the sun, 144; v. 246.
Aristides, his Persian History, v. 453.
Aristides, his sayings, i. 210; ii. 495.
Aristides Milesius, his Italian History, v. 451, 452, 453, 458, 459, 460, 462, 463, 465, 466; Italian Commentaries, 461,

INDEX. 515

quoted, 462; Italian History, 469, 473, 474, 475, 476.
Aristippus, anecdotes of, i. 11, 55, 79, 147, 459, ii. 55, 205, 459.
Aristo of Chios, ii. 369.
Aristobolus, his Third Book of Italian History, v. 470.
Aristocles, Third Book of his Italian History, v. 466, 476.
Aristoclia, a beautiful maiden, iv. 312, 313.
Aristodemus, his Third Collection of Fables, v. 274.
Aristodemus, king of Messenia, i. 177.
Aristodemus, the Epicurean, ii. 158, 159, 180.
Aristomenes, preceptor of Ptolemy, ii. 149.
Ariston, apothegm of, i. 403; iii. 18; his opinion of moral virtue, 462; v. 111.
Aristonicus the musician, i. 494.
Aristonymus, a woman hater, v. 468.
Aristophanes, his comedy of "The Clouds," i. 23; quoted, 79, 125, 500; quoted, ii. 78, 149, 429; his coarseness and buffoonery, iii. 11; compared with Menander, 11-14; quoted, iv. 196, 273; quoted, v. 42, 405.
Aristotinus, tyranny of, i. 357-363; v 172.
Aristotle quoted, i. 37; 50; on harmony, 119; 155, 272, 326; the teacher of Alexander, 478, ii. 302, 319; letter of, 455; quoted, iii. 11, 79; his philosophical opinions ; of nature, 105; of principles and elements, 106; of God, 121; of matter, 123; of ideas, 123; of causes, 124; of a vacuum, 127; of motion, 128; of fortune, 131; of the world, 133, 134, 135; of vacuum, 137; of the world, 137; of heaven, 137; of the stars, 140; of the sun, 142; of the summer and winter solstices, 143 ; of the moon, 146 ; of the milky way, 148; of comets, 149; of thunder and lightning, 151; of earthquakes, 157; of tides, 159; of the motion of the soul, 164; of the senses, 166 ; of the voice, 172; of generative seed, 177; of the sperm, 177; of emission of women, 177; of conception, 178; of generation, 179; of the first form in the womb, 184; of seven months' children, 185; of the species of animals, 187; of sleep, 189; of plants, 190; quoted, 225, 226; opinions concerning the soul, 465; opinion concerning a plurality of worlds, iv. 33; concerning prophetic inspiration, 54, v. 189, 258, 262, 313, 316, 355 ; quoted, 439; his Second Book of Paradoxes, 468.
Aristoxenus, of music, i. 114, 115, 125, 134.
Arsione Queen, i. 319.
Artaxerxes Longimanus, his sayings, i. 187.
Artaxerxes Mnemon, his sayings, i. 188.
Aruntius and Medullina, v. 463.
Asclepiades, opinions : of the soul, iii. 161;
of respiration, 174; of two or three children at one birth, 180; animals in the womb, 188; of health, sickness, and old age, 192.
Aster the archer, v. 456.
Astycratidas, apothegm of, i. 405.
Ateas, saying of, i. 189 ; ii. 177.
Atephomarus, king of the Gauls, v. 469.
Atheism and superstition compared, i. 168, et seq.
Athenian barber, iv. 238.
Athenian citizens, their number, v. 42 ; their temper and disposition, 100.
Athenians, whether they were more renowned for their warlike achievements, or for their learning, v. 399-411.
Athenodorus, memorable action of, iii. 50.
Athens, not renowned for epic or lyric verse, i. 404; was a democracy, v. 397; the nurse of history, of painting, and poetry, 400, 401.
Atoms, doctrine of, v. 346-348.
Atreus and Thyestes, v. 470. 471.
Attalus and Eumenes, their kindness and fidelity to each other, iii. 61, 62.
Attica, invasion of, by Datis, v. 450, 451.
Augustus Caesar, his sayings, i. 248-250 ; the favored son of Fortune, iv. 205 ; v. 67.
Augustus Caesar and Fulvius, anecdote of, iv. 235, 236.
Autobulus, v. 156, et seq.
Autumn, dreams in, iii. 432.

B.

Bacchus, ii. 12, 29; iv. 256, 264, 269.
Ballenaeus, mount, v. 492.
Banishment, or flying one's country, iii. 15-35.
Banquet of the Seven Wise Men ; Solon, Bias, Thales, Anacharsis, Cleobulus, Pittacus, Chilo, ii. 3-41.
Barley, sow, in dust, iii. 505.
Barrenness in women, iii. 181.
Barrenness of mules, iii. 182.
Bashfulness, i. 60-77.
Basilocles, iii 69, 70.
Baths, hot and cold, iii. 512.
Battus, ii 115.
Bear, cunning of the, v. 186.
Bears, flesh of, iii. 509.
Beasts, flesh of sacrificial, iii. 36.
Bees cannot abide smoke, iii. 515 ; stinging of, 516.
Bellerophon, fable of, i. 351
Berecyntus, mount, v. 490.
Berosus concerning the eclipse of the moon, iii. 146.
Bewitching, power of, iii. 327.
Bias, quoted, 1. 17, 406 ; at the Banquet of the Seven Wise Men, ii. 4, 14, 128.
Bion, saying of, i. 76; his opinion concerning the punishment of children for

INDEX.

the sins of their fathers, iv. 171; saying of, v. 170.
Bird or the egg, which was first, iii. 242–246.
Birds, prophetic nature of, v. 193.
Birth, two or three at one, iii. 180.
Birthdays of famous men, iii. 400.
Biton and Cleobis, their filial piety, i. 313.
Boar and the toil, iii 152.
Bocchoris, anecdote of, i. 63.
Bodies, of, iii. 124; division of, 126; how mixed with one another, 126.
Body, passions of the, iii. 175; what part is first formed, 184; diseases of the, iv. 504–508.
Book of Rivers, v. 455.
Boedromion, month of, iii. 444.
Boethus, his opinion concerning comets, iii. 150.
Brasidas, apothegm of, i. 218; ii. 458.
Brennus, king of the Gauls, v. 460.
Britain, longevity in, iii. 193.
Brixaba, mount, v. 494.
Brotherly love, iii. 36–68.
Brute animals, ails and cures of, iii. 510; their intelligence; which are the most crafty, water or land animals? v. 157–217.
Brute beasts make use of reason, v. 218–233.
Bucephalus, the horse, v. 183.
Bulimy or the greedy disease, iii. 355.
Busiris, king of Egypt, strangers murdered by, v. 474.

C.

Caecilius Metellus, apothegm of, i. 239.
Caesar, Augustus, his sayings, i. 248–250; anecdotes of, 293; iv. 205; and Fulvius, 235, 236; v. 67, 132.
Caesar, C. Julius, his sayings, i. 246–248; his magnanimity, 293; his reliance on fortune, iv. 205.
Caesar, Tiberius, sayings of, i. 277; ii. 126; iii. 23; v. 288.
Caicus, a river, v. 503.
Caius Fabricius, apothegm of, i. 227.
Caius Gracchus, i. 40; v. 99.
Caius Marius, apothegm of, i. 239.
Caius Maximus, and his two sons, v. 466.
Caius Popilius, apothegm of, i. 240.
Callicratidas, apothegms of, i. 412; saying of, ii. 187.
Callimachus, saying of, i. 323; ii. 118; iii. 23, 321.
Callisthenes, saying of, i. 37; his Book of Transformations, v. 454; Third Book of the Macedonics, 456; Third Book of History of Thrace, v. 469.
Calpurnius Crassus, liberated from captivity, v. 465.
Calpurius and Florentia, v. 467.
Calydon, mount, v. 505.

Camillus, anecdote of, iv. 204.
Canima, the Galatian, her revenge, i. 372.
Canus, the piper, v. 71.
Caphene and Nymphaeus, i 348.
Caphisias, ii. 379, et seq.
Carneades, i. 160; a striking observation of his, ii. 123.
Cassius, a Roman traitor, v. 457.
Castor and Pollux, iii. 48.
Cato and Catulus, anecdotes of, i. 73.
Cato, saying of, i. 61, and Catulus, 78; his integrity, 295; his sayings, ii. 42, 72, 76, 261, 318, 490; v. 10, 66, 67; anecdotes of, 83, 112, 120, 123, 144, 155, 418.
Cato the Elder, apothegms of, i. 233–235.
Catoptrics, doctrine of the, v. 257.
Cattle, salt given to, v. 497.
Catulus, v. 457.
Caucasus, mount, v. 483.
Caudine Forks, defeat of the Romans at the, v. 452, 453.
Cause of a fever, iii. 192.
Causes, of, iii. 123.
Causes of sleep and death, iii. 188.
Celtic women, virtue of the, i. 347.
Cephisocrates, ii. 133.
Cephisophan, a rhetorician, i. 98.
Ceres, mistress of earthly things, v. 285, 286.
Chabrias, his sayings, i. 213.
Chaeremon, quoted; Frag. ii. 475.
Chamelon, the, v. 202.
Chaplet of flowers at table, iii. 260–265.
Charicles and Antrochus, iii. 49.
Charillus, his sayings, i. 217, 432; ii. 97, 116.
Charon, the Theban, ii. 381.
Chasms in the earth closed by men leaping into them, v. 454.
Chersias at the Banquet of the Seven Wise Men, ii. 3–41.
Children, training of, i. 3–32; similitude to their parents, iii. 180; similitude to strangers, 181.
Chilo, i. 280; at the Banquet of the Seven Wise Men, ii. 8–41.
Chilon, saying of, i. 471.
Chiomara of Galatia, i. 374.
Chios women, virtue of the, i. 344.
Chorus of the Aeantis, iii. 226–228.
Chorus of the Leontis, iii. 227.
Chromatic scale, in music, i. 117.
Chrysermus, his Peloponnesian History, v. 452; Second Book of Histories, 457; First Book of Italian History, 468.
Chrysippus, ii. 87; his opinion concerning fate, iii. 130; of moral virtue, 462; his doctrines refuted, 488; iv. 372, et seq., 428–477; v. 205; his opinion concerning the cause of cold combated, 324, 471.
Cicero, apothegm of, i. 244; 310, 311; v 96.
Cilician geese, v. 175.
Cinesias, the lyric poet, i. 180.

INDEX. 517

Cinna stoned to death, v. 469.
Cios, maids of, i. 354.
Circe, her supposed conversation with Ulysses, v. 218-219.
Cithæron, mount, v. 479.
Cleanthes, his opinion concerning the stars, iii. 139, 140; v. 176, 420.
Cleobis and Biton, i. 313.
Cleobulus at the Banquet of the Seven Wise Men, ii. 3-41.
Cleodemus at the Banquet of the Seven Wise Men, ii. 3-41; first brought the cupping-glass into request, 20.
Cleodorus, the physician, ii. 16.
Cleombrotus, i. 413; iv. 3, 4, 26.
Cleomenes, v. 161.
Cleon, anecdotes of, v. 100, 116.
Cleonienes, apothegms of, i. 413, 416, 346.
Clisthenes, vindicated from the aspersions of Herodotus, iv. 343.
Clitonymus, his Italian History, v. 458; Second Book of his Sybaritics, v. 464.
Clitophon, his First Book of Gallican History, v. 460.
Cloelia and Valeria, i. 356.
Clonas, a musical composer, i. 107, 109.
Clouds, eruption of fire out of the, iii. 150; rain, hail, and snow, 151.
Cneus Domitius, apothegm of, i. 231
Cneus Pompeius, apothegms of, i. 241-244.
Cocles, the Roman, v. 145.
Codrus, king of Athens, v. 462.
Coeranus and the dolphins, v. 215.
Cold, First Principle of, v. 309-330.
Color, does it exist in the dark, v. 344, 345.
Colors, of, iii. 125.
Colotes the Epicurean, ii. 187; misrepresents Democritus; v. 341; his doctrines, 349; misrepresents Plato, 355, 356; falls at the feet of Epicurus, 360; disparagement of Socrates 361; against Stilpo, 367; assaults the Philosophers, 367; condemns the opinion of Epicurus, 368; Cyrenaic philosophers ridiculed, 369; treats Arcesilaus unfairly, 371; absurdity of Epicurianism, 373; opinions of Epicurus, 274; danger of his doctrines, 377, 378, 338-385; book written by, v. 388.
Comets and shooting fires, iii. 149.
Comminius Super, a Laurentine, v. 472.
Common conceptions against the Stoics, iv. 372-427.
Comparison betwixt Aristophanes and Menander, iii. 11-14.
Comparison between the actions of the Greeks and Romans, v. 450-476.
Conception, how it is made, iii. 178.
Concerning Music, i. 102-135.
Concerning such whom God is slow to punish, iv. 140-188.
Concerning the fortune of the Romans, iv. 198-219
Concerning the virtue of Homer, i. 340-384.

Concerning the virtue of women, i. 340-384.
Conciseness of speech recommended, iv. 243; examples given, 243, 244.
Conjugal Precepts, ii. 486-507; Advice to a New-married Couple.
Consolation to Apollonius, i. 299-339.
Consolatory Letter from Plutarch to his Wife, Timoxena, on Occasion of the Death of their Daughter, two years old, v. 386-394.
Contingent and possible defined, v. 299.
Contradictions of the Stoics, iv. 428-477.
Cora and Proserpine, v. 285.
Corinna, anecdote of, v. 404.
Corinthian Hall at Delphi, iii. 80-82.
Cornelius Scipio, consul, v. 96, 112, 114, 136.
Cotys, his sayings, i. 189.
Crabs charmed by fifes, v. 163.
Cranes, flight of, v. 175, 203.
Crantor, quoted, i. 300, 304, 324, 326; his opinion of the soul, ii. 327, 328, 345, 349, 360.
Crassus, anecdotes of, i. 288, 290; v. 125.
Crassus Calpurnius, v. 465.
Crassus's mullet, v. 196.
Crates, i. 141; saying of, 495; ii. 145; opinion of the stars, iii. 140; 321, v. 419, 423.
Cratinus the comic poet, v. 410.
Crato, iii. 198.
Creon's daughter, i. 472.
Cretinus, the Magnesian, v. 121.
Criticism on passages in Homer, ii 69-72, 74-84, 89, 90.
Criticism on Sophocles, ii. 72.
Critolaus, his History of the Epirots, v. 455; Fourth Book of Celestial Appearances, 457.
Crocodile, story of a, v. 196, 206, 210.
Croesus, ii. 85, 122; iv. 3, 39.
Cronium, mount, v. 501.
Ctesiphon, his Third Book of the Boeotian History, v. 458.
Ctesiphon the Pancratiast, i. 42.
Curatii and Horatii, v. 461.
Cure of anger, i. 33-59.
Curiosity, of, ii. 424-445; mischiefs of vain, iv. 236.
Cuttle-fish, wariness of the, v. 200; sign of a storm, 505.
Cyanippus, a Syracusan, v. 462.
Cyanippus, a Thessalian, v. 463.
Cyclades islands, iii. 24.
Cyclobonis, a brook near Athens, v. 110.
Cynaegirus, an Athenian commander, story of, v. 450.
Cyprus, female parasites of, called Steps, ii. 103.
Cyrus the Elder, his sayings, i. 186; ii. 319; enlarges the Persian empire, iv. 85.
Cyrus the Younger, his sayings, i. 188.

518   INDEX.

D.

Daemon of Socrates, Discourse concerning the, ii. 378–423.
Daemons, their nature, attributes, and actions, iv. 14, *et seq.*; some of them are malignant and cruel, 19; they are mortal, 15, 23, 24; vain-glorious, 28; have the care of oracles, 21, 27; sometimes have quarrels and combats with one another, 27; our souls are by nature endued with similar powers, 50, *et seq.*; in the Moon, v. 289; will of the, 304; providence of the, 307, 308.
Damindas, apothegm of, i 407.
Damis, apothegm of, i. 406.
Damonidas, apothegm of. i. 406.
Darius, his sayings, i. 186, 502; v. 458.
Darkness, whether visible, iii. 169.
Datis, a Persian commander, his invasion of Attica, v. 450.
Daughters who had carnal knowledge of their fathers, v. 464.
Death appertains to soul or body, iii. 189.
Death a reward for distinguished piety; illustrated by the cases of Bion and Cleobis, of Agamedes and Trophonius, of Pindar and Euthynous, i. 313, 314.
Death of fire is the generation of air, v. 316.
Death the brother of sleep, i. 311.
Debates at entertainments, iii. 394.
Debt, Evils of. Against running in Debt, or Taking up Money upon Usury, v. 412–424.
Debt of nature, i. 309.
Decrees proposed to the Athenians, v. 58.
Decius of Rome, v. 462.
Deity, knowledge of a, whence derived, iii. 115.
Delay of Providence in Punishing the Wicked. De sera Numinis Vindicta, iv. 140–188.
Delight in hearing the passions of men represented, iii. 314.
Delphi, a walk in, iii. 69; the statues there, 70; atmosphere of, 72; ancient oracles of, 73; Corinthian Hall at, 80–82; statue of Phyrne, 83.
Delphic Oracle, inscription on the, Know thyself, and Nothing too much, i. 328.
Demades and Phocion, anecdotes of, ii. 298; v. 141, 148.
Demaratus and Philip, anecdote of, ii. 146.
Demaratus, apothegm of, i. 407, 482; his Second Book of Arcadian History, v. 461.
Demetrius Phalereus, his saying, i. 217; anecdotes of, ii. 145; iii. 21; v. 145.
Demetrius, his sayings, i. 204.
Demetrius of Tarsus, comes to Delphi, iv. 3.
Demochares, a nephew of Demosthenes, procures a statue to be set up for his uncle, v. 58–60; a decree for a statue for himself, 60, 61.
Democracy and Oligarchy, v. 395–398.
Democrates, saying of, v. 109.
Democritus, saying of, i. 22, 263, 275; ii. 440; iii. 7; his philosophical opinions, 121, 123, 126, 127, 128, 129, 132, 133, 135, 139, 140, 142, 145, 149, 155, 156, 157, 160, 162, 163, 164, 166, 168, 169, 171, 176, 177, 179, 183, 187, 227; his opinions misrepresented, v. 341; his doctrine concerning atoms, 345, 346, 381.
Demodocus, i. 105.
Demonides, the cripple, ii. 51.
Demosthenes, the orator, anecdotes of, i. 15, 65; quoted 67, 145, 286, 313, 315, 325; anecdote of, 334, 481; quoted, ii. 300; anecdote of, 460; quoted, iv. 212; quoted, v. 34, 35; sketch of his life, 43–53; his birth, education, and early years, 43; calls his guardians to account, *ib.*; is chosen choregus, 44; his methods to obtain excellence in speaking, *ib.*; opposes the designs of Philip, 45; describes "action" as of supreme importance in oratory, *ib.*; his early failures as an orator, *ib.*; defends the Olynthians, 46; is admired by Philip, though an enemy, *ib.*; his magnanimity, 47; his conduct at Chaeronea, *ib.*; his patriotism, *ib.*; the oration for the Crown, *ib.*; accused of receiving a bribe, 48; his exile, *ib.*; recalled, *ib.*; returns to the administration of public affairs, 49; leaves Athens to avoid being delivered up to Antipater, *ib.*; his death, 50; his family, *ib.*; honors paid to his memory, 51; anecdotes of him, 49, 50–53; his great temperance, 53; his public services recounted in a decree, 58–60; quoted. 69, 109, 110, 124, 138, 146, 409, 411, 448.
Dercyllidas, apothegm of, i. 407.
Dercyllus, his First Book of Foundations, v. 461; Third Book of Italian History, 474.
Destiny, or fate, iii. 130.
Deucalion [like Noah] sent forth a dove from the ark, and with like purpose, v. 179.
Diagoras the Melian, iii. 118.
Diana Orthia, rites of, i. 98.
Dicaearchus, opinion concerning the soul, iii. 161; of divination, 176; v. 93.
Dignity of places at table, iii. 210, 212.
Dinarchus, an Athenian orator, v. 57, 58; becomes rich, 57; his exile in Chalcis, 58; restored, *ib.*; his orations, *ib.*
Diocles at the Banquet of the Seven Wise Men, ii. 3–41; his philosophical opinions, iii. 179, 182, 192, 185, 182.
Diogenes Laertes, quoted, i. 77.
Diogenes quoted, i. 4, 12; anecdotes of 51, 67, 141, 142, 166, 283, 285, 311, 487

INDEX. 519

quoted, ii. 58, 155, 193; story of the mouse, 453; iv. 311, 455, 458, 465, 466, iii. 21, 27, 29, 31; his philosophical opinions, 132, 136, 138, 143, 148, 163, 183, 187, 189; 494; v. 8, 65.
Diogenes and Philip, ii. 147.
Diogenianus, iii. 71, 73, *et seq.*
Diomedes, ii. 41; liberated from captivity, v. 465.
Dion, example of, i. 64, 193, 333.
Dionysius, tyrant of Sicily, does not relish the Lacedaemonian broth, i. 83; his unreasonable anger, 152; his sayings, 449, 484, 491; his ungenerous behavior, 493; parasites of, ii. 166; 314; anecdote of, iv. 238.
Dionysius and Plato, ii. 108, 140.
Dionysius the Elder, his sayings, i. 191; v. 84.
Dionysius the Younger, his sayings, i. 192, 501.
Diophantus, saying of, i. 4.
Diorphus, mount, v. 507.
Discourse to an Unlearned Prince, iv. 323-330.
Diseases of the body, iv. 504-508.
Divination, of, iii. 176; iv. 59.
Dog, habit of biting of stones, iii. 516; affection for his master, v. 180, 182, 184; docility of the, 191.
Dolphin, sagacity of the, v. 200; nature of the, 204; story of a, 213; its love of music, 214; stories of affectionate, 215, 216.
Dolphin and Arion, ii. 33-36; and the lad of Jasus, v. 215.
Domitian is mentioned [which fixes the era of Plutarch] ii. 443.
Domitius, anecdote of, i. 288, 295; v. 125.
Dorian Mood, of music, i. 109, 115.
Doriaus pray for bad making of their hay, iii. 504.
Dorotheus, his First Book of Transformations, v. 466; his Fourth Book of Italian History, v. 463.
Dositheus, his Third Book of Sicilian History, v. 463, 471, 472, 474; Third Book of Lydian History, 469; his Pelopidal, 471; First Book of Sicilian History, 475.
Dream, a romantic, ii. 407-411.
Dreams and Omens, ii. 401, 402.
Dreams in Autumn, iii. 432.
Dreams, whence do they arise, iii. 176.
Drink either five or three, iii. 282-284.
Drink passeth through the lungs, iii. 363.

E.

Earth, its nature and magnitude, iii. 154; figure of the, 155; site and position of the, 155; inclination of the, 155; motion of the, 156; zones of the, 156; exhalations from the, iv. 53; its form and its place, v. 247; an instrument of time, 439.
Earthquakes, of, iii. 157.
Echo, what gives the, iii. 172.
Eclipse of the moon, iii. 146.
Eclipses of the sun, iii. 144.
Ecphantus, his opinion concerning the motion of the earth, iii. 156.
Egg or the bird, which was first, iii. 242-246.
Egypt, its Religion and Philosophy; of Isis and Osiris, or of the Ancient Religion and Philosophy of Egypt, iv. 65-139.
Egyptian skeleton at feasts, ii. 6.
Egyptians in Ethiopia, iii. 20.
Ei at Apollo's temple at Delphi, iv. 479-498.
Eleans, the, v. 426.
Elements, mixture of the, iii. 126.
Elephant, understanding of the, v. 178; stories of, 178; of king Porus, 183; most beloved by the Gods, 187; amour of the, 188; chirurgery of the, 192.
Elephas, mount, v. 478.
Elysian fields in the moon, v. 289.
Elysius the Terinean, vision of, i. 314.
Embryo, how nourished, iii. 183; is an animal, *ib.*
Empedocles, i. 59; saying of, 158, 183, 195, 357, 469; quoted, ii. 49; quoted, iii. 34, 81; his philosophical opinions, 112, 114, 125-129, 131, 132, 136-138, 143, 145, 147, 154, 158, 163, 165, 163-170, 174, 178-184, 188-191; quoted, 209, 262, 293, 333, 497, 518; quoted, iv. 21, 52, 85, 87, 108, 273; quoted, v. 169, 232, 246, 249, 252, 255, 318, 348, 350, 351; misunderstood by Colotes, 35; quoted, 381, 420, 421, 439, 497.
Emprepes, apothegm of, i. 408.
Enemies, how a man may profit by his, i. 280-298.
Entertainment, late to an, iii. 417.
Envy and Hatred, ii. 95-99.
Epaminondas, his sayings, i. 222-226, 277; his great actions, 225; his consistency of character, ii. 109; 182, 185, 309, 313, 319, 381, 396, 399, 414; iii. 6; v. 72, 75, 95, 101, 121, 125; his invasion of Laconia, 401, 407, 458.
Epaminondas, son of, beheaded, v. 458.
Epimenides, long sleep of, v. 66; 279.
Ephorus, his opinion concerning the overflowing of the Nile, iii. 161.
Epicharmus, quoted, i. 315, 496; ii. 141; quoted, 496; iv. 242.
Epicureans, misrepresentations of the, v. 352-354.
Epicurus, quoted, i. 138, 189, 159; famous sentence of, ii. 92; his doctrine; refutation of it; pleasure is not attainable, 157-203; reverence of his brothers, iii. 57; his philosophical opinions, 111, 122, 124, 127, 128, 131, 134, 135, 139, 142,

143, 151, 163, 164, 165, 169, 177, 183; opinions of, v. 350, 374; danger of his doctrines, 377, 378; disciples of, 383, 385.
Epigenes, opinion concerning comets, iii. 150.
Erasistratus, his opinion of the soul, iii. 163; of superfetation, 180; his definition of a fever, 192.
Eratosthenes, his philosophical opinions; of time, iii. 128; of the sun, 147; v. 456.
Erectheus, sacrifice of his daughter, v. 463.
Eryxo of Cyrene, i. 378.
Esop, fable of, ii. 11, 12, 16, 19-22, 23; dog of, 25; at the Banquet of the Seven Wise Men, 3-41; iii. 63, 202.
Eteocles the Theban, i. 257.
Euboea, king of, drawn in pieces by horses, v. 455.
Euboidas, apothegm of, i. 408.
Euclid, anecdote of, i. 55; ii. 173.
Euclides, his brotherly love, iii. 61.
Euctus and Eulaeus, ii. 146.
Eudaemonidas, his sayings, i. 221.
Eudamidas, apothegm of, i. 408.
Eudemus, of matter, ii. 334.
Eudorus, system of numbers, ii. 343, 345.
Eudoxus, anecdotes of, ii. 174; his opinion of the cause of winter and summer, iii. 141; of the overflow of the Nile, 161.
Euemerus, his opinion of God, iii. 118.
Eumenes of Pergamus, his sayings, i. 206; anecdotes of, iii. 61, iv. 232
Eumetis at the Banquet of the Seven Wise Men, ii. 3-41; her riddle, 20.
Euphorion, quoted v. 321.
Euphrates, the river, v. 302
Euphranor, the painter, v. 400.
Eupolis, saying of, ii. 112.
Euphorion, quoted, iii. 321.
Euripides quoted, i. 3, 158, 201, 300, 301, 302, 308, 320, 329, 330, 335, 458; Hippol, 4, 14, 471; Protesilaus, 23; Dictys, 26, 58; Bellerophon, 63, 141; Frag. 287, 472; Pirithous, 70; Orestes 37, 137, 140, 165, 170, 286; Medea, 64, 71, 255; Iph. Aul. 153. 302; Bacchae, 163; Troad, 170; Phoeniss, 257, 303, 327; Danae, 307; Adrastus, 288; Stheneboea, 301; Ino, 303, 304; Alcestis, 310; Phaed. 312; Suppliants, 316; Cresphontes, 316; Erectheus, 500; Hypsipyle, 317, 465; ii. 51, 56, 62, 87, 92, 121, 148, 150, 251, 300, 306, 357, 363, 391, 472; Cresphontes, 93; Hippol. 73, 108, 173, 198, 373, 374; Frag. 86, 181, 318, 437, 501; Orestes, 143, 443; Medea, 66; Iph. Aul. 49, 85; Phoeniss, 51, 61, 66, 130, 151; Ion, 102, 131, 144; Erectheus, 132; Electra, 85; Aeolus, 85, 88, 175; Herc. Furens, 151; Hecuba, 197; Iph. Taur. 447; iii. 27, 90, 116, 194; Frag. 3, 19, 33, 41, 42, 94, 230, 458, 475, 512; Hippol. 483; Orestes, 168, 437; Phoeniss, 16, 32, 43, 49, 257; Stheneboea, 217; Iph, Taur. 21; Androm., 232; Hipsipyle, 291, iv. 17, 128, 142, 270, 308, 450, 478, 497; Frag. 47, 220, 233, 251, 272, 273, 292, 301, 325, 392, 461, 475; Bacchae, 223, 272, 422, 506; Hippol. 294, 298; Cyclops, 56; Aeolus, 105; Troad, 132; Orestes, 141, 507; Ino, 158, 231, 415; Alcestis, 197; Danae, 274, 283; Stheneboea, 288; Androm. 401; Herc. Furens, 459, 467; v. 126, 128, 157, 172; Frag. 15, 79, 105, 108, 118, 345; Aeolus, 71; Hippol. 158; Iph. Taur. 374; Orestes, 77, 380; Troad, 440; Erectheus, 463; Meleager, 466.
Eurotas, a river in Laconia, v. 497.
Eurycratidas, apothegm, i. 410.
Eurydice of Hierapolis, her epigram, i. 32.
Euthrymenes, his opinion of the overflow of the Nile, iii. 160.
Euthynous and Pindar, i. 313.
Eutropion, anecdote of, i. 25.
Evenus quoted, ii. 102, 192.
Evenus, son of Mars, v. 475.
Exercises, different kinds of, iii. 248-250.
Exile, consolations of, iii. 15-35.
Eyes, images of the, iii. 169.

F.

Fabius Maximus, his sayings, i. 227, 228; in the Punic war, v. 453.
Fable of Minerva, i. 41.
Fable of the defeat of Neptune, iii. 444.
Fable of the Fox and Leopard, ii. 72.
Fable of the Lydian mule, ii, 11.
Fabricianus, v. 474.
Fabricius, iv. 201.
Face appearing in the moon, v. 234-292.
Fasting creates more thirst than hunger, iii. 339.
Fate or destiny, iii. 130; nature of, 130; v. 293-308.
Faunus King of Italy; strangers murdered by, v. 474.
Fever, cause of a, iii. 192.
Fig-trees, of, iii. 250, 335.
Figures, of, iii. 125.
Filial treachery in Persian and Roman history, v. 458.
Fire or water, which is most useful, v. 331-337.
Firmus and Nucerica, v. 471.
Fish called the fisherman, v. 201.
Fish, eating of, iii. 472.
Fisherman's nets, rotting of, iii. 503.
Fishes, of; the labrax, mullet, scate, anthias, dolphin, cuttlefish, starfish, torpedo, the fisherman, tunny, amiae, pionetras, sponge, porphyrae, hegemon, whale, pinoterus, gilthead, phycides, galeus, tortoise, v. 195, 208.

Fittest time for a man to know his wife, iii. 274-279.
Fives, we reckon by, iv. 42-47.
Five tragical histories of Love, iv. 312-322.
Flattery: How to know a Flatterer from a Friend, ii. 100-156.
Flattery fatal to whole kingdoms, ii. 118
Flesh exposed to the moon, iii. 284-287.
Flute girls, whether they are to be admitted to a feast, iii. 388.
Folly of Seeking Many Friends, i. 464-474.
Food, digesting of, iii. 280-295.
Fortune, of, ii. 475-481; iii. 131; is a cause by accident, v. 302; not the same as chance, 303; relates to men only, 303.
Fortune of the Romans, iv. 193-219.
Fox, cunning of the, v. 179.
Fresh water washes clothes better than salt, iii. 224-226.
Friends, folly of seeking many, i. 464-474.
Frogs, croaking of, v. 210.
Frost makes hunting difficult, iii. 510.
Fruit, salt not found in, iii. 498.
Fulvius and Augustus, anecdotes of, iv. 235, 236.
Fulvius Stellus, v. 468.
Fundanus, i. 34, 35.

G.

Galaxy or milky way, iii. 148.
Galeus, affection of for their young, v. 209.
Ganges, the river, v. 481.
Garlands at sacred games, iii. 411.
Garrulity, or Talkativeness, iv. 220-253.
Gauran, mount, v. 508.
Gelo, his saying, i. 190.
Generation and corruption, iii. 128.
Generation of males and females, iii. 178; of animals, 186; of the Gods, 400.
Generative seed, iii. 177.
Geniuses and heroes, opinions concerning, iii. 122.
Geometer, God always plays the, iii. 402.
Germanicus, ii. 96.
Gnatho, the Sicilian, iii. 3.
Gobryas, a Persian noble, ii. 104.
God always plays the Geometer, iii. 402.
God bade Socrates act the Midwife's part, v. 425.
God, Father and Maker of all things, v. 428.
God, what is, iii. 118.
Gods, generation of the, iii. 400.
Gorgias, i. 340; at the Banquet of the Seven Wise Men, ii. 3-41; 44, 134; ii. 502, v. 405.
Government. Of the Three Sorts of Government, Monarchy, Democracy, and Oligarchy, v. 395-398.
Gracchus, Caius, example of, i 40.
Greek music, principles of, i. 102, 103
Greek Questions, ii. 265-293.

Groom, saying of the king's, i. 21.
Gryllus, v. 218, *et seq.*
Guests, should the entertainer seat the, iii. 203-210; to a wedding supper, 300; that are called shadows, iii. 381.
Gylippus, his dishonesty, i. 23.

II.

Habits of animals, v. 173-177.
Halo, of the, iii. 160.
Halyeon, of the, v. 211.
Hannibal and Fabius, i. 228.
Hares, cunning of the, v. 185.
Harp, an invention of Apollo, i. 113.
Hart, tears of the, iii. 507.
Health, preservation of, i. 251-279.
Health, sickness, and old age, iii. 192.
Hearing, of, i. 441-463; iii. 170.
Heaven, its nature and essence, iii. 137; division of, 137.
Hebrus, a river of Thrace, v. 480.
Hedgehog, ingenuity of the, v. 186.
Hedgehog of the sea, v. 203.
Hegemon, of the fish, v. 206.
Hegesippus, sayings of, &c., i. 213.
Hegesistratus, an Ephesian, v. 476.
Helicon the mathematician, i. 57.
Hephaestion, the friend of Alexander, i. 489, 505.
Heracleo, v. 194.
Heraclides, his compendium of music, i. 105; ii. 158; his philosophical opinions, iii. 139, 149, 150, 165.
Heraclides the wrestler, iii. 220.
Heraclitus, i. 44, 79, 276, 308, 448, 453; ii. 74, 165, 330, 358, 477; iii. 26, 74; his philosophical opinions, 122, 125, 127, 128, 130, 131, 143, 144, 145, 146; apothegm, v. 9; quoted, 78, 169, 425.
Hercules and Iole, v. 459.
Hercules in Antisthenes, precept of, i. 77.
Hercules, ridiculous representation of, v. 70; and King Faunus, 474.
Hercules, the woman-hater; his temple in Phocis, iii. 90; singular anecdote, *ib*
Hermes, iv. 74.
Hermias, v. 121.
Hermogenes, ii. 194; iii. 161.
Herodotus, quoted, i. 80, 441; saying of, ii. 202, 489; Arcadian prophet, iii. 38; quoted, iv. 248, 335 *et seq.*; malice of, iv. 331-371; v. 397.
Herondas, apothegm of, i. 410.
Herons, artificies of the, v. 176.
Herophilus, opinion of, iii. 128, 163.
Hesianax, his Third Book of African History, v. 465.
Hesiod, quoted, Works and Days, i. 22, 65, 70, 138, 156, 178, 261, 296, 307, 325, 327; ii. Works and Days, 24; spare diet recommended by, 27; and the dolphin 36; Works and Days, 63, 64, 65, 73, 87, 92, 302, 303, 449, 452, 480,

483; Theogony, 102; iii. Works and Days, 64, 210, 382, 416, 436, 438; iv. 15; Works and Days, 48, 49, 68, 87, 154, 173, 264, 385, 442, 457; Theogony, 53, 118, 324, 458; iv. 86; v. Works and Days, 153, 168, 172, 279.
Hicetes, his opinion of the earth, iii. 154.
Hiero, his sayings, i. 190; anecdote of, 291.
Hiero the Spartan, statue of, iii. 76.
Hiero the Tyrant, statue of, iii. 75.
Hieronymus, saying of, i. 38, 50; 462.
Himerius, an Athenian parasite, ii. 126.
Hippasus, opinions of, iii. 111.
Hippocrates, saying of, i. 4; quoted, 261, 292; ii. 165, 185; his magnanimity, ii. 466.
Hippocratidas, apothegm of, i. 412.
Hippodamus, apothegm of, i. 411.
Hippolytus, son of Theseus, v. 471, 472
Hippomacus, ii. 294.
Hipponax, i. 108.
History of music, i. 104 *et seq.*
History of wind instruments, i. 108.
Homer, passages in, criticised, ii. 69–72, 74–84, 89, 90.
Homer, virtue of, i. 340–384; quoted; Iliad, i. 34, 38, 39, 51, 55, 62, 104, 132, 138, 141, 151, 153, 154, 156, 161, 165, 178, 180, 181, 200, 251, 292, 303, 305, 300, 310, 324, 325, 329, 330, 331, 385, 466, 469, 475, 486, 490, 507, 508, 510, 511; ii. 28, 32, 41, 44, 47, 48, 49, 52, 53, 55, 56, 59, 62, 63, 65, 67, 68, 74, 75, 77, 79, 81, 82, 84, 88, 89, 90, 91, 108, 114, 115, 120, 123, 131, 140, 142, 145, 150, 151, 152, 154, 185, 197, 198, 200, 237, 295, 305, 310, 311, 314, 317, 319, 413, 501, 505; iii 25, 26, 47, 53, 54, 107, 120, 152, 206, 207, 221, 231, 248, 255, 301, 313, 317, 321, 323, 325, 336, 354, 364, 381, 394, 401, 413, 418, 437, 442, 447, 448, 449, 450, 480, 486, 492, 493, 515; iv. 16, 65, 108, 111, 152, 191, 194, 195, 216, 237, 238, 280, 285, 291, 327, 329, 383, 386, 401, 405, 434, 462, 488, 490, 499, 504; v. 78, 79, 85, 88, 90, 92, 96, 104, 119, 122, 123, 134, 135, 138, 146, 147, 171, 182, 200, 208, 214, 266, 276, 281, 315, 339, 350, 371, 386, 394, 400, 418, 443, 444, 447; Odyss. i. 52, 134, 138, 154, 236, 252, 305, 310, 318, 325, 452, 469; ii. 41, 43, 47, 48, 52, 53, 54, 56, 59, 63, 65, 67, 70, 71, 82, 83, 108, 110, 114, 115, 127, 140, 149, 158, 159, 162, 184, 195, 304, 316, 317, 320, 371, 427, 463, 467, 478; iii. 10, 42, 45, 72, 81, 101, 196, 201, 207, 226, 232, 233, 249, 259, 280, 285, 321, 333, 336, 359, 365, 395, 419, 425, 437, 438, 451, 466, 477, 499; iv. 5, 80, 86, 97, 191, 200, 219, 224, 226, 230, 231, 280, 307, 325, 401, 405; v. 3, 11, 105, 106, 143, 171, 184, 281, 285, 290, 315, 328, 403, 416, 422, 423, 446.

Honey, the bottom of, iii. 870.
Horatii and Curatii, v. 460, 461.
Horatius Cocles, v. 456.
Horsehair, for fishing lines, iii. 505.
Horses, called λυχοσπάδες, iii. 253.
Horus, son of Osiris, iv. 80, 114 *et seq.*
Hounds that hunt hares, v. 184.
How animals are begotten, iii. 186.
How a man may receive advantage and profit from his enemies, i. 280–298.
How a man may praise himself without being envied, ii. 306.
How a young man ought to hear poems, ii. 43.
How plants grow, and whether they are animals, iii. 190.
How to know a flatterer, ii. 100–156.
Hunger, cause of, iii. 841; allayed by drinking, 345.
Hurricanes, of, iii. 150.
Hyagnis, first that sung to the pipe, i. 107.
Hydraspes, a river in India, v. 477.
Hyperides, the Athenian orator, ii. 140; v. 53–57; his part in public affairs, 53; his friendship for Demosthenes, 54; this friendship broken, *ib.*; demanded by Antipater, he escapes to Aegina, *ib.*; is apprehended, tortured, and put to death, 55; an excellent orator, *ib.*; his amorous propensities, 55, 56; his patriotism, 56; sent as ambassador, 56, 57.
Hypsipyle, foster-child of, i. 465.

I.

Ibis, habits of, imitated by the Egyptians, v. 192.
Ibycus, the poet, iv. 240.
Ichneumon, of the, v. 174.
Ida, mount, v. 493.
Idathyrsus, his sayings, i. 189.
Ideas, of, iii. 123.
Images presented to our eyes in mirrors, iii. 169.
Imagination, imaginable and phantom, difference between, iii. 167.
Immortality of the soul, argument for it, iv. 169, 170.
Impotency in men, iii. 181.
Improbabilities of the Stoics, iii. 194–196.
Inachus, a river in Argolis, v. 498
Incest, case of, v. 467.
Indus, the river, v. 508.
Infants, seven months', iii. 184.
Inquisitiveness, or vain curiosity; of curiosity, or an over-busy inquisitiveness into things impertinent, ii. 424–445.
Iole, the beloved of Hercules, v. 459.
Ion the tragedian, i. 322, 328; v. 186, 254.
Iphicrates, his saying, i. 80, 212; v. 105.
Iphigenia at Aulis, v. 459, 460.
Irascible faculty, v. 441.
Isaeus, an Athenian orator, v. 33; considered by some equal to Lysias, *ib.*; the

teacher of Demosthenes, *ib.*; number of his orations, *ib.*
Isis and Osiris, iv. 66-135.
Ismenodora, iv. 256, 264, 269, 311.
Ismenus, a river of Boeotia, v. 478.
Isocrates, an Athenian orator, iii. 198; v. 27-33; his parentage, birth, and education, 27; composed orations for others, 28; his school at Chios, *ib.*; his great success as a teacher of rhetoric, *ib.*; lived to a great age, 29; his death and burial, 30; number of his orations, 31; his timidity, 27, 31; his description of the use of rhetoric, 31; the two suits against him, 32, 409; his Panegyric, 410.
Isthmian games, iii. 318.
Ivy, nature of, iii. 265-268.

J.

Jason, saying of, v. 140.
Jewish religion, statements and conjectures respecting it, iii. 307-312.
Jews, their fatal inaction in war because it was their Sabbath day, i. 178.
Juba, his third Book of Lybian History, v. 465.

L.

Lacedaemonians, their laws and customs, i. 82-101; their currency, 99; influx of gold and silver, 100; refuse to assist Philip and Alexander in their designs against Persia, 101; lose all their ancient glory, 101; combat with the Argives, v. 452.
Lachares, tyranny of, ii. 166.
Laconic answers, iv. 243.
Laconic Apothegms, of, i. 385-440.
 Acrotatus, 400.
 Agasicles, 385.
 Agesilaus, 385-397.
 Agesipolis, 397, 398.
 Agis, son of Archidamus, 398.
 Agis the Last, 400.
 Agis the Younger, 400.
 Alcamenes, the son of Teleclus, 400.
 Alexandridas, 401.
 Anaxander, 401.
 Anaxilas, 402.
 Androclidas, 402.
 Antalcidas, 402.
 Antiochus, 403.
 Archidamidas, 404.
 Archidamus, two of the name, 404.
 Aregeus, 403.
 Ariston, 403.
 Astycratidas, 405.
 Bias, 406.
 Callicratidas, 412.
 Charillus, 432.
 Cleombrotus, 413.
 Cleomenes, son of Cleombrotus, 418, 416.
 Damindas, 407.
 Damis, 406.
 Damonidas, 406.
 Demaratus, 407.
 Dercyllidas, 407.
 Emprepes, 408.
 Euboidas, 408.
 Eudamidas, son of Archidamas, 408.
 Eurycratidas, 410.
 Herondas, 410.
 Hippocratidas, 412.
 Hippodamus, 411.
 Lampsace, 366.
 Lasus, 123.
 Leonidas, the son of Anaxandrias, 417.
 Leo, the son of Eucratidas, 417.
 Leotychidas, 416.
 Linus, i. 105.
 Lycurgus, the Lawgiver, 419-425.
 Lysander, 425.
 Namertes, 427.
 Nicander, 427.
 Paedaretus, 429.
 Panthoidas, 427.
 Pausanias, son of Cleombrotus, 428.
 Pausanias, son of Plistoanax, 428.
 Phoebidas, 431.
 Plistoanax, 430.
 Polycratidas, 431.
 Polydorus, 430.
 Soos, 431.
 Telecrus, 431.
 Thectamenes, 411.
 Themistens, 410.
 Theopompus, 410.
 Thorycion, 411.
 Zeuxidamus, 410.
Lacydes, King of the Argives, i. 290.
Lais, murder of, iv. 302.
Lampis, a sea commander, v. 73.
Lampsace, apothegm of, i. 366.
Lamps and tables of the ancients, iii. 372.
Land, food of the, iii. 302-306.
Lasus, apothegm of, i. 123.
Leaena, anecdote of, iv. 229, 230.
Least things in nature, iii. 125.
Leo, apothegm of, i. 417.
Leo Byzantinus, saying of, i. 288; and his wife, v. 110.
Leonidas, apothegm of, i. 417; vindicated from the statements of Herodotus, iv. 354; v. 156; at thermopylæ, 453.
Leotychidas, apothegm of, i. 427.
Leprosy caused by dewy trees, iii. 500.
Leptis, custom in, ii. 498.
Leucippius, his opinions of the world, iii. 135; of the earth, 155; of the senses, 165.
Light and darkness, of, v. 325.
Lightning, of, iii. 150.
Light, of reflected, iii. 168, 169; v. 236, *et seq.*
Lilæus, mount, v. 508, 509.

Linus, elegies of, i. 105.
Lions, of, v. 187.
Liquids, of, iii. 359.
Live concealed, whether 'twere rightly said, iii. 3–10.
Lives of the ten Attic orators, v. 17–63.
Love: Five tragical histories of, iv. 312–322.
Love, of, iv. 254–311; makes a man a poet, iii. 217–219.
Love of wealth, ii. 294–305.
Lucretia, the Roman matron, i. 355.
Lucullus, apothegm of, i. 241; quoted, iii. 51; v. 84.
Lugudumum, mount, v. 485.
Lyaeus and choraeus, i. 54.
Lybian crows, v. 175.
Lycastus and Parasius, v. 472.
Lycian women, virtue of the, i. 351.
Lycoronas, a river in Aetolia, v. 487.
Lycurgus, an Athenian orator, v. 36–42; treasurer of the commonwealth, 36; his great public services, 37; his fidelity in office and great reputation, 37; his justice and integrity, 37, 38; useful laws procured by his influence, 38; his diligence in the study and practice of oratory, 39; his incorruptible honesty, 39; his death, ib.; honors paid to his memory, ib.; his family, 40, 41; his orations and success as an orator, 41; his benevolence, 42; a decree for honors to be paid to his memory, 61–63.
Lycurgus, the Spartan lawgiver, anecdote of, i. 7; his institutions, 82, et seq.; their final overthrow, 101, 217, 419–425; his sayings, ii. 22, 312; v. 12, 92.
Lydian mood, of music, i. 109, 114.
Lyric nomes, i. 106.
Lysander, i. 72, his great victory over the Athenians, 99; introduces gold and silver into Lacedaemon, 100; the results, ib.; his sayings, 219, 425; saying of, ii. 149; anecdote of, 495; iii. 100; v. 92.
Lysias, the Athenian orator, his remarks on music, i. 104; anecdote of, iv. 226; v. 24–26; his birth, early residence in Athens, residence in Thurii, and return to Athens, 24; banished by the Thirty Tyrants, 25; return after their overthrow, ib.; death, ib.; number of his orations, ib.; his other works, 26; his eloquence, ib.; v. 33.
Lysimache, the priestess, i. 73.
Lysimachus, his sayings, i. 205, 259.
Lysippus, his statue of Alexander, i. 494.

M.

Madness of animals v. 167.
Macandar, a river in Asia, v. 488.
Magas, anecdote of, i. 45.
Magpie, story of a, v. 189.
Maimactes, king of the gods, i. 45.
Man, perfection of a, iii. 189; most unhappy of all creatures, iv. 504; compounded of three parts, v. 286.
Maneros, the foster-son of Isis, iv. 79.
Mnnius Curius, apothegm of, i. 226.
Manlius, son of, beheaded, v. 458.
Man's progress in virtue, ii. 446–474.
Mantinea, battle of, v. 401.
Marius, sacrifice of his daughter, v. 463.
Mars, some bad actions of his, v. 466, 467.
Marsyas, a river in Phrygia, v. 490.
Marsyas, the musician, i. 41, 108.
Massinissa, his vigorous old age, v. 83.
Mathematics applied to Music, i. 118–121; affords unspeakable delight, ii. 173, 174.
Matter, of, iii. 122.
Medius, the parasite, ii. 137.
Megasthenes, saying of, v. 275.
Megisto and Micca, and other women of Elis, i. 357–363.
Meilichius, king of the gods, i. 45.
Melannippedes, quoted, iv. 279.
Melanthius, quoted, i. 35, 449; ii. 108; iv. 147.
Melian women, virtue of the, i. 348.
Melisponda, and Nephalia, i. 59.
Melissus; his opinion of generation, iii. 128.
Mimnermus, quoted, iii. 475.
Memnon, his saying, i. 189.
Menalippides, i. 114, 123.
Menander quoted, i. 70, 138, 158, 161, 164, 335; quoted, ii. 52, 57, 65, 86, 87, 124, 192, 297, 334, 335, 470; his superiority to Aristophanes, iii. 11–14; quoted, 38, 65, 196, 488; iv. 290; anecdote of, v. 403; saying of, 425.
Mendesian goat, v. 225.
Menedemus, i. 77; ii. 115, 464; his opinion of the nature of moral virtue, iii. 461.
Menelaus, the mathematician, v. 257.
Men, impotency in, iii. 181; elements of, 188; have better stomachs in autumn, 240; temper of, 270–272; when asleep are never thunderstruck, 295–300; leaping into chasms, v. 464; having carnal knowledge of brutes, 468.
Menon, his definition of virtue, i. 464.
Menyllus, his First Book of Boeotic History, v. 460; Third Book of Italian History, 467.
Messenians, saying among the, v. 416.
Metellus, quoted, iii. 53; iv. 201; v. 459, 461.
Meteors, of, which resemble rods, iii. 153.
Metiochus, ins misuse of power, v. 127.
Metius Fufetius, king of Alba, torn in pieces, v. 455.
Metrocles, i. 144.
Metrodorus, ii. 158, 160, 161, 167, 169, 175, 180, 183, 496; his philosophical opinions, iii. 115, 127, 132, 149, 150, 151, 153, 154, 155, 157, 158; v. 378, 383, 384.
Micca and Megisto, and other women of Elis, i. 357–363.

INDEX.   525

Midas, i. 326; v. 454.
Miletus, maidens of, i. 354.
Mills of the gods grind slowly, but they grind fine, iv. 143.
Miltiades, v. 408–411.
Mind, tranquillity of the, i. 136–167.
Minerva admonished by a satyr, i. 41; iii. 195; temple of, v. 461.
Mirrors, causes and reasons of, iii. 169; v. 236, et seq.
Mithridates, i. 204; ii. 121; story of, iii. 219.
Mixture of the elements, iii. 126.
Mnemosyne, the mother of the Muses, i. 22.
Mnesarete, statue of, iii. 83.
Mnesiphilus, at the Banquet of the Seven Wise Men, ii 3–41.
Mnesitheus, the physician, iii. 511.
Monarchy, Democracy, and Oligarchy, v. 395–398.
Money upon usury, v. 412–424.
Monstrous births, of, iii. 179.
Moon: essence of the, iii. 145; magnitude of the, 145; figure of the, 145; whence her light, 145; eclipses of the, 146; phases of the, 147; distance from the sun, 147; of the face appearing within the orb of the moon, v. 234–292; its distance from the earth, 246; its nature, 253–260; its size, 261; why called Glaucopis, 267; is it inhabited, 274, 275.
Moot point in Homer's Iliad, iii. 446.
Moral virtue, essay on, iii. 461–494.
Moschio, dialogue on health, i. 251, 252.
Motherland a Cretan expression, v. 85.
Motion, of, iii. 128.
Mount Athos' shade, v. 270.
Mule and the salt, v. 184.
Mule, superannuated, v. 182.
Mules, barrenness of, iii. 182.
Mullet, of the, v. 213.
Muses, number of the, iii. 450.
Mushrooms produced by thunder, iii. 295–300.
Music, treatise concerning, i. 102–185; pleasures from bad, iii. 876; for entertainments, 389.
Musonius, his rule of health, i. 35.
Must, sweet, iii. 511.
Mycende, mount, 501.

N.

Namertes, apothegm of, i. 427.
Names of rivers and mountains, and of such things as are to be found therein, and the fables connected therewith, v. 477–509.
Nasica, his saying, i. 285.
Natural affection towards one's offspring, iv. 180–197.
Natural philosophy, iii. 105.
Natural Questions, Plutarch's, iii. 495–518.

Nature, of, iii 131; what is, 105; things that are least in, 125; animated, v. 160.
Necessity, of, iii. 129; nature of, 129; defined, v. 200.
Nephalia and Melisponda, i. 59.
Neptune, ii. 38, 39, 41; iii. 44.
Nero, i. 53; iv. 228, 229; anecdote of, v 123.
New diseases and how caused, iii. 42.
New-married couple, advice to, ii. 486-507.
New wine, of, iii. 279.
Nicander, apothegm of, i. 427, 441.
Nicias Maleotes, quoted, v. 459.
Nicias, the Athenian general, superstition of, i. 177; v. 107.
Nicias, the painter, anecdote of, ii. 173; v. 71.
Nicostratus and Archidamus, i. 74; apothegm of, 221.
Niger, anecdote of, i. 267.
Nightingale, of the, v. 189.
Nile, the river, v. 495; overflow of the, iii. 160; water of the, 415.
Niloxenus, at the Banquet of the Seven Wise Men, ii. 3–41.
Niobe, i. 328.
Noises in the night and day, iii. 406.
Numa, of the reign of, iv. 208–210.

O.

Oenopides, his discovery of the obliquity of the Zodiac, iii. 138.
Ogyia, an island west from Britain and its neighbor islands, described, v. 281–283.
Oil, top of the, iii. 370; on the sea, 503; is transparent, v. 318; does not easily freeze, 319.
Old age, health, and sickness, iii. 192.
Old men love pure wine, iii. 221; read best at a distance, 221–224; easily foxed, 268–270; in state affairs, v. 64–96.
Oligarchy, Monarchy, and Democracy, v. 395–398.
Olympias, anecdotes of, ii. 494, 495.
Olympus, a Phrygian player, i. 107, 108 110, 112, 115, 116, 128.
Omens and dreams, ii. 401, 402.
Onesicrates, banquet of, i. 108; 133.
Onomademus, wisdom of, i. 295; v. 129.
Opinions of philosophers, iii. 104–193.
Optatus, v. 171.
Oracle in Cilicia, iv. 55.
Oracles of Delphi, iii. 73.
Oracles, why they cease to give answers, iv. 3–64.
Orestes, slays his mother, v. 474.
Origin of things, opinions concerning the, iii. 107–113.
Orontes, his saying, i. 188.
Orpheus, never imitated any one, i. 107.
Orphic Fragments, iv. 59, 404.
Oryx, fables of the, v. 193.

Osiris, iv. 75–135; story about his birth, 74; great actions of, 75; his death, 76; his body torn in pieces by Typhon, 80; is identical with Serapis and Bacchus, 89; with the bull Apis, 90; sacred vestments of, 185.
Othryadas, ii. 338.
Otus, the bird, v. 163.
Oxen, teaching of, v. 193.

P.

Paeans, makers of, i. 110.
Paedaretus, apothegm of, i. 429.
Painter, neat saying of a, ii. 379.
Painting is silent poetry, v. 402.
Palladium in Ilium and in Rome, v. 461.
Palm tree, of the, iii. 514.
Panaetius, sayings of, i. 57.
Pancrates, i. 117.
Pandora's box, i. 306.
Pangaeus, mount, v. 480.
Panthoidas, apothegm of, i. 427.
Papirius Tolucer, v. 468.
Parallels, or a comparison between the actions of Greeks and Romans, v. 450–476.
Parmenides, ii. 357; his philosophical opinions: of generation and corruption, iii. 128; of necessity, 129; of the world, 135; of the moon, 145; of the galaxy, 149; of the earth, 155; of earthquakes, 157; of the soul, 163; defended from the misrepresentations of the Epicurean, v. 352–354; quoted, 357; 359, 381.
Partridge, cunning of the, v. 185.
Parysatis, her saying, i. 188.
Passions of the body, iii. 175.
Passions of the soul, or diseases of the body, which are worse, iv. 504, 508.
Paulus Aemilius, apothegm of, i. 232.
Pausanias, i. 305; apothegm of, 428.
Pausanias, the Spartan traitor, v. 457.
Pauson the Painter, iii. 73.
Pederasty, or the love of boys, iv. 259; defended, 259, 260; instances of its power, 284–286; severely condemned, 304; the connection is uncertain and short-lived, 307; it ceases on the sprouting of the beard, 307.
Pelopidas, his saying, i. 225.
Pelops and his two sons, v. 470, 471.
Pemplides, iv. 272, 275, 279.
Pergamus, woman of, i. 374.
Periander, at the Banquet of the Seven Wise Men, ii. 3–41; tyrant of Corinth sends three hundred boys to be castrated, vi. 341; the crime prevented, 342.
Pericles, anecdotes of, i. 15, 18, 66, 211, 332; ii. 309, 315; v. 67, 102; his absolute sway over the Athenians, 106; his soliloquy when about to address the people, 130, 131; 410, 413.

Periclitus, a Lesbian harper, i. 108.
Persaeus, anecdote of, i. 70.
Perseus, king of Macedonia, his sorrow on losing his kingdom, i. 160.
Persian Magi, killers of mice, ii. 96.
Persian women, virtue of the, i. 347.
Persians had a monarchy, v. 397.
Pestilence, relief from, a virgin sacrificed for, v. 472.
Petron, doctrine of, i. 30.
Phaedimus, v. 171, 194.
Phaeton, i. 141.
Phalaris, brazen cow of, v. 474.
Pharmaces, of the moon, v. 265.
Phasisa, a river of Thrace, v. 482.
Phayllus, iv. 282.
Phemius, the poet, i. 105.
Pherecrates, fragment of, i. 124.
Phidias, statue of Venus, ii. 498; iv. 133.
Philammon, verses in honor of Latona, Diana, and Apollo, i. 105.
Philemon and Magas, i. 45.
Philinus, iii. 69, 70.
Philip of Macedonia, examples from, i. 44, 45; sayings of. 194–198, 305; anecdotes of, ii. 141, 146, 147, 494; iii. 22; v. 115.
Philippides, the comedian, ii. 430.
Philippus, his demonstration of the figure of the moon, ii. 173.
Philolaus, his philosophical opinions: of the nutriment of the world, iii. 134; of the essence of the sun, 142; of the position of the earth, 155; of the motion of the earth, 156.
Philosophers ought chiefly to converse with great men, ii. 368–377.
Philosophers, their various opinions. Of those sentiments concerning nature with which philosophers were delighted, iii. 104–193.
Philosophical discourses at merry meetings, iii. 198–203.
Philosophy, threefold division of, iii. 104.
Philotas and Antigona, i. 504.
Philotas, son of Parmenio, i. 504.
Philotimus, the physician, i. 452; ii. 153.
Philoxenus, i. 125; sayings of, ii. 42; iii. 3; iv. 289, 423.
Phocian women, virtue of the, i. 343; 355.
Phocion, his saying, on the death of Alexander, i. 49; his sayings, 70; wife of, 102; 216; ii. 135, 298, 311, 321, 328; v. 83, 109, 118; his magnanimity, 122; his reply to Demades, 125; 142, 149.
Phocus, a story of love respecting him, iv 319.
Phocylides the poet, quoted i. 9, 462.
Phoebidas, apothegm of, i. 431; v. 48.
Phoenix, tutor to Achilles, i. 9; ii. 150.
Phrygian mood of music, i. 109.
Phryne, the statue of, iii. 83.
Phrynis, the musician, ii. 470.

INDEX. 527

Pieria and other women of Myus, i. 363, 364.
Pierus, the first that wrote in praise of the Muses, i. 105.
Pindar and Euthynous, i. 314.
Pindar, his sayings, i. 10, 15, 77, 114; quoted, 143, 173, 174, 286, 293, 308, 304, 310, 313, 328; his description of the state of the blessed, 336; quoted, ii. 57, 143, 177, 193, 306; quoted, iii. 9, 23, 74, 93, 95, 96, 194, 207, 218, 377, 455, 458, 491, 516; quoted, iv. 96, 150, 163, 260, 289, 405, 497; quoted, v 64, 111, 117, 141, 144, 148, 194, 197, 202, 214, 249, 252, 255, 256, 316, 330, 404; anecdote of, 404, 440.
Pine, sacred to Neptune and Bacchus, iii. 318.
Pine trees, of, iii. 250.
Pinoteras, the fish, v. 204.
Pisias, of love, iv. 270, *et seq.*
Pisistratus, i. 216; anecdote of, iii. 41; 200
Pittacus, sayings of, i. 31, 150; his reply to Myrsilus, ii. 5; at the Banquet of the Seven Wise Men, 3–41; iii. 50; iv. 231; v. 145.
Pitwater, of, iii. 514.
Place, of, iii. 127; v. 470.
Place at table called Consular, iii. 210–212.
Plague in Falerie and in Lacedaemon, v. 472.
Plain of truth, i. 29.
Planetiades, i. 9, 11.
Plants grow, how, iii. 190; nourishment and growth of, 191.
Plato, quoted, i. 9, 19, 24, 26; saying of, 27; quoted, 30, 41, 57, 71, 74, 79; on harmony, 115, 118; quoted, 141, 173, 256, 264, 279, 287; laws, 292; quoted, 297, 311, 314, 321, 337, 339, 456; quoted, ii. 49, 92, 100, 104, 106; at the court of Dionysius, 108, 141; 109, 146; and Socrates, 148; 150, 168, 174, 261, 326; concerning the soul, 328 *et seq.*, 334; quoted, 344, 352, 353, 355, 356, 359, 364, 455, 456, 457, 492, 496, 504; quoted, iii. 19, 81; his philosophical opinions: of the universe, 112, 114, 115; of the understanding, 116; what is God, 119; of God, 121; of matter and ideas, 123; of causes and of bodies, 124; of colors, 125; of bodies, 126; of place and time, 127, 128; of motion, 128; of necessity, 129; of fate, 130; of fortune, 131; of the world, 134, 135, 137; of the stars, 137–141; of the sun, 142, 143; of the moon, 145, 146; of the rainbow, 152; of earthquakes, 158; of the sea, 159; of the soul, 161–165; of sight, 168; of hearing, 170; of the voice, 171; of the echo, 172; of divination, 176; of generative seed, 177; of the embryo, 183; of reason in animals, 187; of sleep, 189; that plants are animals, 190; quoted,

200, 201, 213, 221, 223, 243, 368–370, 401, 406, 462, 464, 499; iv. 18, 28, 30, 41. 45; his opinion about daemons, 86, 87; 109, 115–117, 119, 146, 254, 261, 292, 305; quoted, v. 10, 82, 103, 116, 120, 172, 257, 276, 288, 293, 295, 297, 302, 305, 306, 328, 355, 364, 377, 381, 413, 425–433, 435, 440, 441, 444.
Pleasure not attainable according to Epicurus, ii. 157-203.
Pleasures from bad music, iii. 376.
Plistoanax, apothegm of, i. 430.
Plurality of worlds, iv. 29–39.
Plutarch, his rules for the preservation of health, i. 251–279; his Symposiacs, 197–460; his natural questions, iii. 495–518; on the immortality of the soul, iv. 169; v. 137, 339; consolatory letter to his wife, 386, 394; his Platonic questions, 425–449; his spurious remains, 450–500.
Poet, love makes a man a, iii. 217–219.
Poetry, essay on. How a young man ought to hear poems, ii. 92–94.
Polemon, his kind reply, i. 55.
Policy or government defined, v. 396.
Political precepts, v. 47–156.
Poltys, saying of, i. 189.
Polus, the tragedian, v. 69.
Polybus, of seven-months' infants, iii. 185; v. 83.
Polycephalus, the nome, i. 108.
Polycratidas, apothegm of, i. 431.
Polycrita, a woman of Naxos, i. 364, 366.
Polydorus, apothegm of, i. 430.
Polyhistor, his Third Book of Italian History, 476.
Polymnestus, his improvements in music, i. 107, 110, 112, 123.
Polypus, why it changes color, iii. 506; many-colored, v. 202.
Polysperchon's treachery, i. 64; 71.
Pompey, his great actions and sayings, 1 241; 290, statutes of, 293, v. 70, 102, 112, 114; owed his success to Sylla, 115.
Porsena of Clusium, war with the Romans, v. 451, 456.
Porus, an Indian king, i. 202.
Posidonius, his opinion of fate, iii. 130; of a vacuum, 137; of eclipses, v. 262.
Possible and contingent defined, v. 299.
Postumia, chastity of, i. 290.
Power, necessity, &c., defined, v. 300.
Praise, inordinate, a sign of a flatterer, ii. 116, 117, 120; young people are often spoiled by it, 123.
Preservation of health, rules for, i. 251–279.
Priam and Polydore, v. 465
Price of peace, women given as the, v. 468.
Priest of Hercules, iii. 90.
Principle and element, difference between iii. 106.

Principle of cold, v. 309-330.
Principles, what they are, iii. 106.
Prize for poets at the games, iii. 316.
Procles, tyrant of Epidaurus, puts Timarchus to death, iii. 89; his own unhappy end, *ib.*
Procreation of the soul as discussed in the Timaeus of Plato, ii. 326-367.
Progress in virtue, how it may be ascertained, ii. 446-474.
Prometheus, anecdote of, i. 289.
Prosodia, songs called, 1, 106.
Proserpine, the same as Isis, iv. 88; and Cora, v. 285, 286.
Protagoras quoted, i. 332.
Protogenes, iv. 257, 258, 260-265.
Providence of God, iv. 140-188; v. 305; of the inferior gods, 306; of the Daemons, 307, 308.
Ptolemaeus Philadelphus, i. 25.
Ptolemaeus Soter, i. 88.
Ptolemy Lagus, anecdote of, i. 45; his saying, 202; ii. 177.
Publius Decius, his dream, v. 462.
Publius Nigidius, v. 96.
Punishment of the wicked, why so long delayed, iv. 140-188.
Pupius Piso, the rhetorician, iv. 245.
Purple shell fish, v. 205.
Pylades and Orestes, their friendship, i. 465.
Pyraechmes's horses, v. 455.
Pyrander, his Fourth Book of Peloponnesian Histories, v. 474.
Pyrandus, the commissary, v. 469.
Pyrrhon the Stoic philosopher, anecdote of, ii. 467.
Pyrrhus, the Epirot, his saying, i. 207.
Pythagoras, his aphorisms, i. 28, 29; of music, 130; quoted, 175; aphorism, 179, 294; symbols of, 419, 454, 471; his unseasonable reproof, ii. 118; his joy on discovering the relation to each other of the three sides of a right-angled triangle, 174; his philosophical opinions; of the principles of things, iii. 109; of the unity of God, 121; of geniuses and heroes, 122; of matter, 123; of causes, 124; of bodies, 126; of time, 127; of motion, 128; of generation and corruption, 129; of the world, 132-137; of the zodiac, 138; of the summer and winter solstice, 143; of the moon, 145; of the zones, 156; of the soul, 161-164; of the voice, 172; of divination, 176; of generative seed, 177; of reason in animals, 187; precepts of, derived his philosophy from Egyptian priests, iv. 72.
Pythagorean philosophy of dreams, daemons, ii. 412, 413.
Pythagoreans, why they do not eat fish, i. 422-426; iii. 22.
Pytheas, his saying, i. 213; iii. 159; apothegm of 107, 110.

Pythian games, iii. 316.
Pythian priestess, i. 8, 9, 62, 63; why she now ceases to deliver her oracles in verse, iii. 69-103.
Pythes, the Lydian, i. 382.
Pythocles, his Third Book of Italian History, v. 460; Third Book of the Georgics, 476.
Pythoclides the flute player, i. 114.
Python of Aenos, ii. 314.

Q.

Quarry of Carystus, i. 54.
Questions or Causes, Second Book of, v. 475.

R.

Raillery, of, iii. 229-240.
Rain, snow and hail, of, iii. 151.
Rainbow, of the, iii. 151.
Rational faculty, of the, v. 441.
Reason, beasts make use of, v. 218-233.
Reason, habit of our, iii. 166.
Remarkable speeches of some obscure men amongst the Spartans, i. 432-440.
Remora or Echeues, iii. 252.
Reproof, how to be administered, ii. 138-156.
Respiration or breathing, iii. 173.
Rhesus and Similius, v. 466.
Rhohope and Haemus, mountains, v. 491.
Riddles and their solutions, ii. 19, 20.
Roman questions, ii. 204-264.
Roman senator and his wife, iv. 283-285.
Rome saved by the cackling of geese, iv. 211; favored by fortune, 215.
Romans, fortune of the, iv. 198-219.
Romulus, his birth and education, iv. 206-208; murdered in the senate, v. 470; and Remus, suckled by a she-wolf, 473.
Rules for the preservation of health, i. 251-279.
Rutilius the usurer, v. 419.

S.

Sabinus of Galatia, iv. 308.
Sacadas, a flute player, i. 109, 110, 112.
Sacred games, garlands of, iii. 411.
Sacrificed beasts, iii. 361.
Sagaris, a river in Phrygia, v. 492.
Salmantica, women of, i. 352.
Salt and cummin, why does Homer call it divine, iii. 336.
Salt given to cattle, iii. 497; not found in fruit, 498.
Sappho, i. 42, 114; ii. 506; quoted, iii. 97, 263, 506; quoted, iv. 260.
Sappho's measures, grace in, iii. 74.
Sardanapalus, his luxury and lust, i. 497.
Sardians and Smyrnaeans, v. 468.

INDEX.

Saturn and his four children, v. 456, 457.
Satyrus the orator, i. 47.
Scamander, a river in Troas, v. 493.
Scaurus, his magnanimity, i. 295.
Scilurus, his saying, i. 199; anecdote of, iv. 244.
Scipio the Elder, apothegm of, i. 229; ii. 475; iv. 201; v. 96, 112, 114, 136.
Scipio the Younger, his sayings and great actions, i. 235-239.
Scopas, saying of, ii. 303.
Scythinus, verses of, iii. 86.
Sea calves, of, v. 210.
Sea, of the, iii. 158; ebbing and flowing of the, 159; food of the, 302-306; made hot by wind, 501.
Sea-sickness, iii. 502.
Sea water nourishes not trees, iii. 495; upon wine, 502; oil on the, 503.
Seed, nature of generative, iii. 177; that fall on the oxen's horns, 368; watering of, 496; watered by thunder showers, 498;
Seleucus, the mathematician, iii. 159.
Seleucus Callinicus, anecdote of, iv. 237.
Self-praise. How a man may inoffensively praise himself without being liable to envy, ii. 306-325.
Semiramis, her saying, i. 187; 497; iv. 85
Seneca, anecdote of, i. 53.
Senses, of the, iii. 164; represent what is true, 165; number of the, 165; actions of the, 166.
Sentiments concerning Nature with which Philosophers were delighted, iii. 104-193.
Serapio, iii. 74, 79, 81, 82.
Serapis is Pluto, iv. 88, 89.
Serpent and the Aetolian woman, v. 188.
Seven months' infants, of, iii. 184.
Seven Wise Men, Banquet of the, ii. 3-41.
Servius Tullius, his birth, elevation, and prosperous reign, iv. 212, 213.
Shadows, guests called, iii. 381.
Sheep bitten by wolves, iii. 254.
She-wolves, of, iii. 517.
Ships in winter, sailing of, iii. 500.
Sibyl with her frantic grimaces, iii. 74.
Sight, of our, iii. 168.
Silence commended, iv. 230, 243.
Simonides quoted, i. 149, 257, 295, 305, 309, 318; quoted, ii. 44, 101, 136, 436, 457, 471; quoted, iii. 22, 87, 259, 409, 451, 459, 478; quoted, iv. 158; saying of, v. 66, 68, 71; 121.
Sipylus mount, v. 489.
Siramnes, saying of, i 185.
Sleep or death, causes of, iii. 188; whether it appertains to the soul or body, 189.
Smelling, of, iii. 170.
Smyrna and Cinyras, v. 464.
Snow, preservation of, iii. 350.
Soclarus, iv. 202; v. 156, 158, 160, 166, 168, 170, 171, 216.
Socrates, anecdotes of, i. 11, 13, 23, 26, 38, 53, 141, 150, 162; rules of health, 255; quoted, 307, 310, 312, 326, 336; ii. 46, 148, 150, 338, 441; his Daemon, 378-423, 441, 495; iii. 19. 35, 112, 121, 123; iv. 249; v. 98, 359, 361, 362, — 364, 377, 381.
Socrates, his Second Book of Thracian History, v. 462.
Soil, deep, for wheat, iii. 504; lean soil for barley, 504.
Solon and Croesus, anecdote of, ii. 122.
Solon quoted, i. 155, 297; at the Banquet of the Seven Wise Men, ii. 3-41; quoted, 297, 454, 487; quoted, iii. 50; anecdote of, iv. 260, 304; v. 89, 113, 118, 68, 72, 131.
Sophocles quoted, i. 13, 46, 57, 244, 288; Thamyras, 39; Frag. 58, 63; Tyro, 206, 467; Antig 51, 462; Oed Tyr. 179, 470; quoted, ii. 45, 57. 61, 72; criticisms on, ii. 72; Frag. 173, 241, 244, 298, 481, 452, 456, 470, 495; Oed. Tyr. 60, 170, 442, 476, 495; Antig. 110; Trachin. 311; Electra, 440; quoted iii. 97, 210, 222; Frag. 7 Antig. 45, 227, Oed. Tyr. 4, 235, 474; Oed. Col. 232; Electra, 437; quoted, iv. 87, 246, 287, 304; Oed. Tyr. 197, 202; Trachin. 281; Antig. 239, 283, 404; Frag. 221, 226, 274, 284, 301; quoted, v. 69, 76, 158, 216; Oed. Col. 68; Frag. 75, 84, 110, 116; anecdote of, 68, 72.
Sostratus, his Second Book of Tuscan History, v. 468.
Sotades, jest of, i. 25.
Soterichus, the musician, i. 103, 112.
Soul of Ajax, her place in hell, iii. 442.
Soul or body, death appertains to, iii. 189.
Soul, procreation of the, ii. 326-367; its nature and essence, iii. 161, 163; parts of the, 162; principal part of the, 173; in what part of the body it resides, 163; motion of the, 163; immortality of the, 164; state of, after death, v. 371; three sorts of motion in the, 393; state of after death, 393, 394; ancienter than the body, 432.
Souls dispersed into the earth, moon, &c., v. 438.
Sounds in the night and day, iii. 406.
Sows, tame and wild, iii. 508.
Space, of, iii. 127.
Sparta had an oligarchy, v. 397.
Speech composed of nouns and verbs, v 444.
Speech of a statesman, what it should be, v. 107.
Sperm, whether it be a body, iii. 177.
Spermatic emission of women, iii. 177
Sphodrias, v. 118.
Spiders, labor of the, v. 174.
Sponge, of the, v. 205.
Spurious remains of Plutarch, v. 450-509
Star-fish, subtlety of the, v. 201.
Stark drunk, those that are, iii. 281.

Stars, essence of the, iii. 138; what figure they are, 139; order and place of, 139; motion and circulation of, 140; whence do they receive their light, 140; which are called the Dioscuri, the twins or Castor and Pollux, 141; how they prognosticate, 141; number of the, whether odd or even, 446.
Stasicrates proposes to turn Mount Athos into a statue of Alexander, i. 495.
Stesichorus, i. 109, 112; iv. 497.
Steward of a feast, iii. 212-216.
Stilpo, the philosopher, i. 13, 76, 144, 161; anecdote of, ii. 468; defended, v. 365-367.
Stoics speak greater improbabilities than the poets, iii. 194-460; their opinions concerning dæmons, iv. 24; common conceptions against the, 372-427; contradictions of the, 428-477.
Strabo, quoted, i. 27.
Strato, i. 155; iii. 163; v. 161.
Stratonica of Galatia, i. 373.
Stratonicus, anecdote of, ii. 298; iii. 21.
Strymon, a river in Thrace, v. 491.
Subtlety and cunning, instances of.
Summer and winter, cause of, iii. 141.
Summer and winter solstice, iii. 143.
Sun, essence of the, iii. 141; magnitude of the, 142; figure or shape of the, 143; turning and returning of the, 143; eclipses of the, 144.
Superstition of the Gauls, Scythians, and Carthagenians, i. 182, 183.
Superstition, or indiscreet devotion, i. 168-184; folly of, ii. 387.
Supper, many guests at, iii. 323.
Supper-room, why too narrow at first for guests, iii. 326.
Suppers of the ancients, iii. 255-259.
Swallows in the house, iii. 419; intelligence of the, v. 174.
Sylla, i. 32-35; anecdote of, v. 72, 115, 135.
Symposiacs, or table discourses, iii. 197-460.
Synonix and Camma, iv. 302.

T.

Table, dignity of places at, iii. 210-212.
Tables and lamps of the ancients, iii. 372
Talkativeness, or garrulity, iv. 220-253.
Talk, deliberate or tumultuous, iii. 395.
Tarpeia, a virgin, the story of, v. 460.
Tarrais, a river in Scythia, v. 494.
Taste, of, iii. 170.
Taxiles of India, i. 201.
Taygetus, mount, v. 498.
Tears of the hart, iii. 507.
Tears of wild boars, iii. 507
Telamon and Periboea, v. 467.
Telamon and Phocus, v. 466.
Telecrus, apothegm of, i. 431.

Telegonus, son of Ulysses, v. 476.
Telephanes of Megara, i. 117.
Telephus, i. 289.
Telesias the Theban, an eminent flute-player, i. 125.
Telesphorus, in an iron cage, iii. 31.
Temple of Apollo, iv. 478-498.
Teres, his saying, i. 189.
Teribazus, anecdote of, i. 176.
Terpander, the musician, fined by the Ephori, and why? i. 91, 92; an inventor of ancient music, 102, 105, 109; an excellent composer to the harp, 106, 112; added the octave to the heptachord, 102, 122.
Teuthras, mount, v. 503, 504.
Thales, at the Banquet of the Seven Wise Men, ii. 3-41; first of philosopers; the Ionic sect took its denomination from him, iii. 107; his philosophical opinions; difference between a principle and an element, 106; that the intelligence of the world was God, 121; of geniuses and heroes, 122; of division of bodies, 126; of necessity, 129; of the division of heaven, 137; of the eclipses of the sun, 144; that the moon borrows her light from the sun, 146; that the earth is globular, and the centre of the universe, 155; of earthquakes, 157; of the overflow of the Nile, 160; of the soul, 161; iv. 337, 480.
Thaletas, a composer, i. 110, 112; power of his music, 133.
Thamyras, the singer, i. 105.
Theanor, ii. 395, 396.
Thebes, liberation of, ii. 414-523.
Thectamenes, apothegm of, i. 411.
Themisteas, apothegm of, i. 410.
Themistocles quoted, i. 73; his saying, 208; suspected of treason, 290; 296, 480; quoted, ii. 97, 311, 471; his kind reception by the Persian king, iii. 21, 30; iv. 208, 361, 364; v. 101, 116, 120, 121, 127.
Theo, iii. 70, 71, 74, 88.
Theocritus, his remark and death, i. 25, 73; ii. 380; iii. 516.
Theodorus, saying of, i. 142; ii. 321; 349; iii. 31; his Book of Transformations, v. 464.
Theognis, i. 473; ii. 59, 473; iii. 506.
Theon, ii. 157, *et seq.*; v. 273-275.
Theophilus, his Third Book of Italian History, v. 459; Second Book of Peloponnesian Histories, 470.
Theophrastus, sayings of, i. 276, 304, 442, ii. 303; iii. 45, 64; v. 202, 218, 219, 331, 427.
Theopompus, his sayings, i. 217, 410; v. 137.
Theotinus, his Italian History, v. 456.
Theramenes, anecdote of, i. 306.
Thermodon, a river in Scythia, v. 495
Thero, anecdote of, iv. 286.

INDEX. 531

Theseus and his son Hippolytus, v. 471.
Thespecius, iv. 177, 182, *et seq.* 188.
Thirst, cause of. iii. 341.
Thorycion, apothegm of, i. 411.
Thrasonides, quoted, ii. 297.
Thucydides, quoted, i. 70, 76, 472, 490; quoted, ii. 98, 117, 149, 152, 458; quoted, iii. 88; quoted, iv. 141; quoted, v. 65, 100, 403.
Thunder, of, iii. 150.
Thymbris, and his son Rustius, v. 466.
Tides, of, iii. 159.
Tigris, the river, v. 507.
Timaeus, his opinion of tides, iii. 159.
Timesias, the oracle and, i. 471; anecdote of, v. 127.
Time, essence and nature of, iii. 127, 128.
Timoclea, at the taking of Thebes, i. 376.
Timoleon, ii. 314.
Timotheus, the musician, anecdote of, i. 92, 106; ii. 83, 179, 212, 260; v. 76.
Titus Quinctius, apothegm of, i. 230.
Tmolus, mount, v. 486.
Torpedo or crampfish, v. 201.
Torquatus and Clusia, v. 459.
Tortoise, their care for their young, v. 209.
Training of children, i. 3–32.
Tranquillity of the mind, the, i. 136–167.
Transmutation of bodies, i. 14.
Trees and seeds, watering of, iii. 496.
Trees not nourished by sea-water, iii. 495.
Triangles, of, v. 433.
Trisimachus, his book of Foundations of Cities, v. 455.
Trochilus and crocodile, v. 206.
Troilus wept less than Priam, i. 323.
Trojan women, virtue of the, i. 342.
Trophonius and Agamedes, i. 313.
True friendship, of, i. 464–474; ii. 100–134.
True happiness, of, v. 392.
Tullus Hostilius, v. 455.
Tunnies, dim sight of the, v. 204.
Typhon, in Egyptian mythology, iv. 80, 81, 86, 88, 91, 92, 99, 101, 105, 109, 114, 118, 122.
Tyrrhene women, virtue of the, i. 349.

U.

Ulysses, i 160; in the island of Circe, v. 218, *et seq.*
Unity of God. Of the word εἰ engraven over the gate of the temple of Apollo at Delphi, iv. 478–498.
Universe, whether it is one, iii. 114; division of the, v. 429.
Unlearned Prince, discourse to an, ii. 323–330.
Usurers, what sort of men they are, 471.
Usury, evils of, v. 412–424.

V.

Vacuum, of a, iii. 126; there can be none in nature, iv. 33; suppose there were, it would have no beginning, middle, or end, 34.
Valeria and Cloelia, i. 356.
Valerius Conatus swallowed up alive, v. 455.
Valeria Tusculanaria, v. 464.
Venus's hands wounded by Diomedes, iii. 141.
Verses seasonably and unseasonably applied, iii. 436.
Vice and virtue, ii. 480, 485.
Vice, whether it is sufficient to render a man unhappy, iv. 499–503.
Vines irrigated with wine, iii. 513; rank of leaves, iii. 513.
Virtue and vice, ii. 482–485.
Virtue may be taught, i. 78–80.
Virtue of Homer, i. 340–384.
Virtue or fortune, to which of these was due the greatness and glory of Rome? iv. 198–219.
Virtue, progress in, ii. 446–474.
Virtues of women, i. 340–384.
Vision, doctrine of, iii. 168; v. 236, *et seq.*
Voice is incorporeal, iii. 172.
Voice, of the, iii. 171.
Vowels and semi-vowels, iii. 438.

W.

Water made colder by stones and lead, iii. 348.
Water or fire, which is more useful? v. 331–337.
Water, white and black, iii. 518.
Wealth, the love of, ii. 294–305.
Well water, change of the temperature in, iii. 347.
West wind the swiftest, iii. 515.
Whale, of the, v. 207.
Wheat, sow, in clay, iii. 505.
Whether an aged man ought to meddle in state affairs, v. 64–96.
Whether vice is sufficient to render a man unhappy, iv. 499–503.
Whether the passions of the soul, or diseases of the body, are worse, iv. 504–508.
Whether 'twere rightly said, "Live concealed," iii. 3–10.
Whirlwinds, of, iii. 150.
Why the oracles cease to give answers, iv. 3–64.
Wicked, delay of Providence in punishing the, iv. 140–188.
Widows in India, iv. 502.
Wild beasts, steps of, iii. 509; their tracks, 509.
Wild boars, tears of the, iii. 507.

Winds, of, iii. 154.
Wine, whether it is potentially cold, iii. 272-274; straining of, 351; middle of, 370; sea water upon, 502; irrigation with, 513.
Winter and summer, cause of, iii. 141, 154.
Winter, ships in, iii. 500; sea least hot in, 501.
Wise Men, the Seven, Banquet of, ii 3-41; their names, iv. 480.
Woman, of Pergamus, i. 374.
Woman of Thessaly torn in pieces by dogs, v. 463.
Women, the virtues of, i. 340-384; barrenness in, iii. 181; are hardly foxed, 268-270; temper of, 270-272; given as the price of peace, v. 468.
Word *ei* at Apollo's temple at Delphi, iv. 479-498.
World, how it was brought into its present order, iii. 113.
World, of the, iii. 132; figure of the, 133; whether it be an animal, 133; whether it is eternal and incorruptible, 133; its nutriment, 134; from what element was it raised, 134; in what form and order was it composed, 135; cause of its inclination, 136; thing which is beyond the, 136; what parts on the right and left hand, 137.
Worlds, plurality of, iv. 29-38.
Wrestling, of, iii. 246.

X.

Xanthippe, wife of Socrates, anecdotes of, i. 53, 292.
Xenœntus, v. 109.
Xenocrates, anecdote of, i. 71; 442; his opinions concerning the soul, ii. 327; 439; of triangles, iii. 17; 24, 139; his opinion about daemons, iv. 87; saying of, v. 10, 494.
Xenocrita, a composer, i. 110; 380.
Xenodamus, a composer, i. 110.
Xenophanes, his reply, i. 66, 183; his philosophical opinions, iii. 134, 138, 141, 144, 145, 150, 155; quoted, ii. 49; iv. 291.
Xenophon quoted, i. 137; maxim of, 281, 333, 447; ii. 115, 144, 178, 301, 307; the scene of his old age, iii. 24; v. 67, 72, 121, 113. 139.
Xerxes, his saying, i. 30, 187; and Arimanes, iii. 59, 60; invasion of Greece, v. 451, 452.

Y.

Year, length of, in different planets, iii 147.

Z.

Zaleucus, laws of, ii. 315.
Zaratas, ii. 327.
Zeno, saying of, i. 56; anecdotes of, 72, 142, 283; ii. 321, 365, 455; quoted, 467; 481; iii. 25, 113, 125, 128, 132-135, 139; his definition of virtue, 462; anecdote of, iv. 225; v. 382.
Zenocrates, v. 288, 377, 441.
Zeuxidamus, apothegm of, i. 410.
Zeuxippus, dialogue on health, i. 251-277 ii. 157 *et seq.*; iv. 270, 278, 288.
Zeuxis, reply of, i. 468.
Zopyrus Byzantius, his Third Book of Histories, v. 473.
Zoroaster, ii. 357; iv. 106.

www.ingramcontent.com/pod-product-compliance
Lightning Source LLC
Chambersburg PA
CBHW031943290426
44108CB00011B/653